China's New Urbanization Strategy

Urbanization is one of the major challenges facing China. Of China's 1.3 billion people, around half still live in rural areas. There has been huge migration from rural areas to cities in recent years, a trend that is likely to continue strongly for some time. The strains that this vast migration puts on China's cities are enormous. This book makes available for the English-speaking reader the results of a large group of research projects undertaken by CDRF, one of China's leading think tanks, into the details of rural–urban migration, the resulting urban growth and the associated problems. The book goes on to put forward a new strategy, which aims to ensure that China's urbanization proceeds in an orderly manner and that people and their needs are put at the centre of the strategy. Key parts of the strategy include that 'city clusters' should become the main form of urbanization; that these should be arranged geographically in a pattern of 'two horizontal lines and three vertical lines'; that industrial and employment structures should highlight regional features and diversity; that urban public services should be more equitably distributed; that there should be new forms of urbanization management and city governance to accelerate urbanization and ensure harmonious social development; and that the whole process should be conducted in an ecological, 'green' way.

China Development Research Foundation is one of the leading economic think tanks in China, where many of the details of China's economic reform have been formulated. Its work and publications therefore provide great insights into what the Chinese themselves think about economic reform and how it should develop.

Routledge studies on the Chinese economy

Series Editor Peter Nolan
Sinyi Professor, Judge Business School,
Chair, Development Studies, University of Cambridge

Founding Series Editors
Peter Nolan
University of Cambridge and
Dong Fureng
Beijing University

The aim of this series is to publish original, high-quality, research-level work by both new and established scholars in the West and the East, on all aspects of the Chinese economy, including studies of business and economic history.

Routledge Studies on the Chinese Economy – Chinese Economists on Economic Reform

China's New Urbanization Strategy

China Development Research Foundation

Routledge
Taylor & Francis Group

LONDON AND NEW YORK

中国发展研究基金会
China Development Research
Foundation

First published 2013
by Routledge
2 Park Square, Milton Park, Abingdon, Oxon OX14 4RN

Simultaneously published in the USA and Canada
by Routledge
711 Third Avenue, New York, NY 10017

Routledge is an imprint of the Taylor & Francis Group, an informa business

British Library Cataloguing in Publication Data
A catalogue record for this book is available from the British Library

Library of Congress Cataloging in Publication Data
China's new urbanization strategy/China Development Research
Foundation.
    p. cm. – (Routledge studies on the Chinese economy; 49)
Includes bibliographical references and index.
1. Urbanization–China. 2. City planning–China. 3. Rural-urban
migration–China. I. China Development Research Foundation.
HT384.C6C537 2013
307.760951–dc23   2012029317

ISBN: 978-0-415-62590-6 (hbk)
ISBN: 978-0-203-07493-0 (ebk)

Typeset in Times New Roman
by Cenveo Publisher Services

Contents

Illustrations

Tables

Figures

Project team

Advisors

Wang Mengkui	Former President of the Development Research Center of the State Council and Chairman of the Executive Board of the China Development Research Foundation
Chen Yuan	Chairman of the Board of Directors of the China Development Bank

Project Coordinator

Lu Mai	Secretary-General and Research Fellow of the China Development Research Foundation

Project Leader

Tang Min	Deputy Secretary-General of the China Development Research Foundation

Authors of Main Report

Yang Weimin	Secretary-General of the National Development and Reform Commission
Cai Fang	President of the Institute of Population and Labor Economics of the Chinese Academy of Social Sciences

Authors of Background Reports

Han Jun	Head of the Rural Economic Research Department of the Development Research Center of the State Council
Gu Chaolin	Professor in the School of Urban Planning and Design of Tsinghua University
Liu Jingsheng	Managing Director of the China International Capital Corporation Limited

Li Shantong	Research Fellow of the Development Research Center of the State Council
Zhang Zengxiang	Deputy Director of the Center for Resource and Environmental Remote Sensing Applications of the Institute of Remote Sensing Applications of the Chinese Academy of Social Sciences
Liu Shouying	Research Fellow of the Rural Economic Research Department of the Development Research Center of the State Council
Liu Minquan	Professor in the School of Economics of Peking University
Chen Huai	Director of Policy Research Center of the Ministry of Housing and Urban–Rural Development
Wang Yanzhong	President of the Institute of Labor and Social Security of the Chinese Academy of Social Sciences
Pan Jiahua	Director of the Center for Urban Development and Environment of the Chinese Academy of Social Sciences
Li Shi	Professor in the College of Economic and Business Administration of Beijing Normal University
Qiu Xiuhu	Section Chief of the Development Planning Department of the National Development and Reform Commission
Du Yang	Research Fellow of the Institute of Population and Labor Economics of the Chinese Academy of Social Sciences
Ye Xiafei	Professor at Tongji University
Pu Zhan	Associate Research Fellow of the Policy Research Center of the Ministry of Housing and Urban–Rural Development
Wang Meiyan	Associate Research Fellow of the Institute of Population and Labor Economics of the Chinese Academy of Social Sciences
Li Ming	Senior Manager of the Strategic Research Department of the China International Capital Corporation Limited
Ji Xi	Research Fellow of the Center for Economic and Human Development Research of the School of Economics of Peking University
Yang Hao	Manager of the Strategic Research Department of the China International Capital Corporation Limited
Du Zhixin	Project Director of the China Development Research Foundation
Yu Jiantuo	Project Director of the China Development Research Foundation

Project Officer

Du Zhixin	Project Director of the China Development Research Foundation

Preface I

Urbanization has been a major force behind economic growth in China in recent years and will continue to be a driving force for the foreseeable future. For the next decade or two, and even beyond, urbanization will be providing enormous room for economic development. Understanding China therefore means understanding how the country is urbanizing: how that occurred in the past, how it is happening now, and what the country's policy options and tasks are as it moves forward.

[Note: The term used here for 'urbanization' is *cheng shi hua*, as distinguished from the 'old form of urbanization', which was *cheng zhen hua*. See Appendix 18.]

China has 1.3 billion people, more than half of whom still live in rural areas. Although the country has made great progress, it is still 'developing' and indeed faces pronounced problems of uneven, uncoordinated, and unsustainable development. China's urbanization faces challenges that are unprecedented in the world when one takes into account the size of the population and the complexities involved. Just one facet of China's reality should suffice to describe the challenge: within the next 10–20 years, the size of the rural population that China must 'shift' to urban areas in the course of urbanization and industrialization exceeds the population of any single country in the world, with the exception of India, and possibly the USA.

Pursuing a sound process of urbanization will necessarily involve the conscientious study of the experience of other countries. At the same time, it must be based on the actual situation in China at this stage in the country's development. It must be based on policies and development strategies that are feasible and that employ creative approaches to China's specific conditions. For that reason, our task now is to sum up our actual experience of urbanization to date, and to research and discuss both theoretical and policy issues relating to urbanization in the future.

This comprehensive Report incorporates the latest findings and information on the process of China's urbanization. It is the culmination of a major research effort organized by the China Development Research Foundation. It presents both theoretical analysis and policy recommendations, and is intended to serve as an aid in both policy formulation and academic discourse. We hope it will be useful to all those who seek to understand the 'modernization' of contemporary China.

Wang Mengkui
Chairman of the Executive Board of the China
Development Research Foundation
and
Former President of the State Council's
Development Research Centre
3 September 2010

Preface II

Advancing the process of urbanization is a necessary part of furthering China's social and economic development. 'Urbanization' symbolizes how civilizations progress in general, but it also serves as the concentrated expression of a country's overall strength and international competitiveness. In modern societies, urbanization lies at the heart of social and economic development. All national governments now find that a key part of their mission is to nurture and improve the competitiveness of their cities. China, at this specific stage in building up the country, recognizes the way in which urbanization has a unique and substantive role to play in development. Urbanization is an important engine of socioeconomic growth within the country itself, but is also highly significant in terms of global economic development.

It is a great honor for the China Development Bank to be participating as a leading partner in the publication of this *China Development Report 2010*. Organized and prepared by the China Development Research Foundation, the Report presents in vivid fashion the importance and the orientation of China's future urbanization. It calls for a 'strategy for a new form of urbanization that enhances the overall development of human beings'. As such, the Report is thought-provoking and forward-thinking in its approach. The approach is built on a solid foundation of research that has been conducted by highly regarded authorities, organized into teams by subject areas. While also drawing on international experience, their research has explored the applicability of all aspects, features, and objectives of 'urbanization' to China's specific circumstances.

The result is a tool that is both highly readable and very powerful in helping formulate policy. It consolidates the latest research results from many spheres, including urban economics, planning, environmental study, sociology, and public administration and governance.

The China Development Bank is the primary financial institution involved in financing China's medium- and long-term development. We regard as key responsibilities the policy goals of '*establishing a moderately prosperous society in an all-round way*' and '*promoting urban development in a scientific way*'. Since the Bank was founded, it has played a major role in advancing the building of the country's infrastructure and supporting its 'foundation industries' and 'pillar industries', as well as attending to the 'people's livelihood' and to international cooperation. At the same time, the Bank is proud of its remarkable market performance.

An important component of the work of the Bank involves cooperating in research on major issues to do with national development. As a wholly state-owned bank, we also regard such cooperation as an expression of the Bank's sense of social responsibility. In 2007 and 2010, the Bank engaged in very fruitful cooperation with the China Development Research Foundation on issues of 'anti-poverty' and 'urbanization'. In addition to providing useful research results to relevant government departments within China, the process influenced international scholarship on the subject in a very positive way. With the publication of this current report, I would like to express not only my congratulations but also the hope that the research results will be fully employed in actual practice.

Chen Yuan
Chairman of the Board of Directors
China Development Bank
2 August 2010

Acknowledgements

After a year and a half of concerted effort, the *China Development Report 2010* can finally be presented to its audience. This year's Report has chosen to focus on the topic of 'China's urbanization' for the reason that this subject is of immediate but also ultimate significance to China. Urbanization has not only propelled rapid economic growth in the country and profoundly changed its social and economic structures in the process, but also affected the course of development in the rest of the world.

After experiencing the impact of the global financial crisis, people in China are fully aware of the significance of urbanization in general, but fierce debate continues as to how to accomplish it and what kind of urbanization it should be. The title of this Report is *Strategy for a 'New Style of Urbanization that Enhances Human Development'*. The aim is to emphasize that, while land, water, financing, and basic infrastructure are important, at the end of the day, 'urbanization' relates to human beings. Most importantly, it relates to those people who are newly coming into cities, and specifically to the provision of public services for rural migrant workers.

This Report combines theory and practice with respect to many aspects of this primary subject. These include turning rural migrant workers into 'urban citizens', evaluating the spatial configuration of cities and the main forms that urbanization might assume, evaluating industries and employment, the provision of public services, the 'greening' of urban areas, and effective ways to manage and govern urban areas. We hope that the Report will make a definite contribution to both academic discourse and the formulation of policy.

The smooth completion of this Report is due to the hard work put in by all members of the core team as well as the strong support of many outside authorities and entities. The two authors of the main part of the Report are Yang Weimin, Secretary-General of the National Development and Reform Commission, and Cai Fang, President of the Institute of Population and Labor Economics of the Chinese Academy of Social Sciences. The depth of their professional knowledge and experience in this field, their hard work, and their extensive experience in the actual practice of policy formulation, provided a firm basis for successfully completing the Report.

Wang Mengkui, former President of the Development Research Center of the State Council and Chairman of the Executive Board of the China Development Research Foundation, carefully read the entire text of the Report four times and offered important guidance. As Project Leader, Tang Min, Secretary-General of the Foundation, was thoroughly engaged in the drafting and editing of the different sections of the text.

This Report also represents the crystallization of the cooperative efforts of people from many disciplines. The China Development Research Foundation asked scholars from a number of government departments and academic institutions to prepare 17 Background Reports as part of the preparatory process. Much of the information, analysis, and recommendations from these reports has been incorporated into this master Report. The Background Reports and their authors are as follows:

- Liu Minquan and Ji Xi: *Theories of Urbanization and Human Development*
- Li Shantong: *The Impact of Urbanization on Economic Growth*
- Gu Chaolin: *The International Experience of Urbanization, Including Policies and Trends*
- Gu Chaolin: *Spatial Configuration of Urbanization in China, and Determining Mechanisms*
- Zhang Zengxiang: *Report on Monitoring of China's Cities through Remote Sensing*
- Han Jun: *Turning Rural Migrant Workers into Legitimate Urban Residents: Current Status and Future Prospects, Including Policy Options*
- Liu Shouying and Liao Bingguang: *The Urbanization of Land: Moving from a 'Sprawl' Mode to More Rational Growth*
- Yue Xiuhu: *Urbanization in China as Seen from the Perspective of Human Development: A Review of Events to Date and Discussion of Challenges Ahead*
- Du Yang and Wang Meiyan: *People, Industrial Development and Jobs in the Course of Urbanization*
- Wang Yanzhong: *Improving Social Welfare Systems in the Course of Establishing China's 'New Form' of Urbanization*
- Chen Huai and Pu Zhan: *Improving Urban Housing Systems in the Course of Urbanization*
- Liu Jingsheng, Li Ming, and Yang Hao: *Meeting the Challenge of Building Urban Infrastructure That Is Going to Cost Some RMB 18 Trillion*
- Pan Jiahua: *Creating a Habitable Urban Environment.*
- Ye Xiafei: *Creating Rail Transport Systems That Enable Urban Development*
- Li Shi: *2010 China Human Development Index*
- Du Zhixin: *China's Strategy for a 'New Form' of Urbanization, and a Comparative Analysis of China, Japan and South Korea*
- Yu Jiantuo: *The International Experience with Respect to Urbanization*

The above authors of Background Reports also participated in discussions at various stages of the project, and provided invaluable comments and advice.

In August 2009, the Project Team conducted field investigations in order to gain a more accurate grasp of the problems and processes accompanying China's rapid urbanization. The first was in Guangzhou and the second in Chongqing, and the municipal governments of those two cities provided strong support to the project. In addition, three other municipalities provided the Team with their assessments of the actual costs of transforming 'rural migrant workers' into 'urban citizens'. Those three were Wuxi in Jiangsu Province, Shuangyashan in Heilongjiang Province, and Yantai in Shandong Province.

A number of other authorities within China also participated in the discussions at various points and provided very valuable and constructive ideas and recommendations. Among others, these included Lu Dadao, Lu Xueyi, Zhao Renwei, Niu Fengrui, Li Tie, Wang Xiaolu, Han Wensiu, He Yupeng, Mao Qizhi, Huang Luxin, Ni Pengfei, Feng, Changchun, Ye Jianping, Lu Ping, Zhang Wenzhong, Fang Chuanglin, Xie Yang, Lu Fengyong, Shen Bing, Wang Zeying, and Wang Xiaoming.

In order to draw on the experience of countries within the OECD with respect to urbanization, the Foundation invited the OECD to write a study on *Urbanization Trends and Policies in OECD Countries*. This was the first time the Foundation had ever invited an international organization to contribute a Background Report to its annual *China Development Report*. The team preparing the study was led by Ms Lamia Kamal-Chaoui, Head of the Urban Development Programme of the OECD. The Background Report was jointly prepared by Javier Sanchez-Reaza, Tadashi Matsumuto, Olaf Merk, Daniel Sanchez-Serra, Mario Piacentini, Alexis Robert, Dorothee Allain-Dupre, Michael Donovan, Wang Xiao, and Kasuko Ishigaki. It provided large amounts of information on the latest trends in urbanization in OECD countries, as well as information on the actual practice of formulating policy. Much of the useful experience as described in this Background Report has been incorporated into the *China Development Report 2010*.

On 26 June 2009, the Project Team held a forum on 'China's Urbanization' with OECD representatives. On this occasion, a number of authorities provided critiques and described the OECD experience, including Mark Drabenstott, Federica Bussillo, Jeong Ho Moon, Marco R. Tommaso, Lamia Kamal-Chaoui, and Olaf Merk. Irene Hors did a tremendous amount of work in coordinating the proceedings, culminating in a very successful cooperation. In addition, Professor Dwight Perkins and Professor Alan Altshuler of Harvard University in the USA offered constructive opinions on the *Report*.

The China Development Research Foundation assumed all responsibility for organizing the actual work of preparing the Report. Du Zhixin, Yu Jiantuo, and Du Jing did a wonderful job not only of organizing but also of assembling materials, conducting supplementary research, and editing.

The China Development Bank provided generous funding for this project. In addition, starting in 2008, the China Development Research Foundation established a 'China Policy Research Fund' in order to support its annual Reports and associated research. The Starr Foundation in the USA and the Vodafone Group provided strong financial support for the fund in the years 2009 and 2010.

The company GTZ in Germany provided enthusiastic funding for the English publication of this Report.

On behalf of the China Development Research Foundation, I wish to take this opportunity to express appreciation to all members of the Project Team and all the individuals and organizations involved in bringing this Report to successful completion!

Lu Mai
Secretary-General
China Development Research Foundation
25 August 2010

Introduction

More than 2000 years ago, Aristotle is said to have noted that people come to city-states in order to make a living and then stay there in order to enjoy a better life. The 'city-states' of Aristotle's day differ from today's municipalities, and New York may be quite different from Guiyang, but it is an indisputable fact that more and more people around the globe are saying farewell to the countryside and gravitating into cities.

With its 5000 years of civilization, China was one of the earliest states to develop cities of a certain size and number. The historic cities of Chang'an, Bianling, Luoyang, Jinling, and Beijing were among the most notable on earth for hundreds of years. Starting in the nineteenth century, however, China's urban development fell behind that of the world's advanced industrial nations.

Since the establishment of the People's Republic of China, urbanization has passed through a somewhat erratic development process. Development was very slow in the 30 years preceding the start of 'opening up and reform'. In the 30 years since that process began, urbanization has been taking place at a pace that has been unprecedented in the history of humankind. The speed with which China is urbanizing makes it one of the fastest-urbanizing countries on the globe.

This rapid urbanization has provided a powerful impetus for China's social and economic development. Economies of scale in China's cities and the 'concentration effect' have tremendously improved the efficiency with which resources are allocated. They have propelled economic growth and raised people's standard of living. In addition, the process of urbanization has contributed to improving public services for urban residents and to narrowing income disparities between urban and rural areas.

Even more important, however, is that the process of urbanization has created tremendous job opportunities. It has released hundreds of millions of Chinese farmers from having to depend on the earth for a living, generation after generation. It has allowed them the right to live and work in urban areas. As a result, upwards of hundreds of millions of 'rural migrant workers' have 'turned their backs to the old well and left their homeland' to start a new chapter and try to realize their dreams in China's cities.[1]

All the products 'made in China' have been created through their hard work; the splendour of China's cities has been the result of their sweat. These people are the ones who have created the extraordinary achievement of China's economic growth.

And yet, even in the midst of rapid urbanization, China faces unprecedented challenges as well. Rural migrant workers may be living and working in cities, but their children do not receive equal educational opportunities, and they themselves are accorded a different class of treatment when it comes to compensation, social security, and housing. They lack such political rights as the right to vote and the right to be elected. They exist in a kind of 'quasi-urbanized' status and are unable to truly enter into urban society. Although they are physically living in cities, modern urban life is far removed from their reality. One could say that they already have 'one foot over the threshold', and yet the other remains excluded from the benefits of urban prosperity.

Urbanization brings with it other challenges as well. Changes in how products are produced and in how people live are leading to increased use of land for urban purposes, increased energy consumption, environmental pollution, and climate change. Accelerating urbanization requires ever more job positions and a changing industrial structure, which puts its own demands on China's industrial makeup in the future. It also may lead to a worsening of such urban syndromes as increased traffic congestion, crime, social conflict, and urban poverty. All of these require innovative approaches to forms of urban governance that are in accord with China's circumstances at this specific stage of its development.

This Report proposes a strategy for a 'new form of urbanization' that focuses on enhancing human development. The strategy is grounded in the idea of 'taking the human being as fundamental'. It aims to promote the process of urbanization on the basis of social fairness and equity and 'harmonious development'. The main features include furthering the process of turning rural migrant workers into urban citizens in an orderly way, creating a link between 'people' and 'land' in how land is used in urban areas, with rural migrant workers included among the people under consideration; creating a link between 'people' and 'funds' in terms of fiscal expenditures; making 'urban clusters' the primary shape or form of urbanization; planning for a spatial configuration of urbanization in China that is distributed along what are called the 'two horizontal axes and three vertical axes', while regional characteristics and diverse industrial and employment features are taken into account; strengthening a more equitable distribution of municipal public services; and using innovative modes of urban management and urban governance in order to accelerate the 'new form' of urbanization in China and achieve more harmonious social development.

The most important goal of the strategy to develop a 'new form' of urbanization involves promoting human development. The crux of this issue lies in transforming the 'social status' or *shenfen* of several hundred million rural migrant workers. Taking a proactive stance in turning rural migrant workers into urban citizens is necessary in order to address urban–rural discrepancies and improve social equity. In addition, it is through this process that China will be able to increase domestic demand and stimulate social and economic development. 'Promoting human development' must be made manifest in specific ways. All citizens must have the guarantee that they will be able to enjoy the fruits of urban development. They must know that the development potential of each new generation will be enhanced by the process of the country's urbanization.

By the year 2030, China is expected to be 65 per cent 'urbanized', that is, its 'level of urbanization' should reach 65 per cent. We anticipate that the problem of 'quasi-urbanization' will be resolved over the next 20 years, starting with the beginning of the 12th Five-Year Plan. That is to say, at an average rate of 20 million people per year, within 20 years, China should resolve the issue of 'urban citizenship' for some 400 million rural migrant workers. Rural migrant workers should be able to take up true residency in cities, with all the rights that residency entails. 'Rural migrant workers' should include those already in cities and those moving into cities, and it should include family members who wish to accompany these workers.

By 2030, all rural migrant workers living in urban areas should be receiving the same treatment in terms of public services as those originally living in the cities. At the same time, during this period of two decades, the country should make every effort to improve public-service systems for all urban inhabitants. It should create environments that are conducive to urban life; it should broaden the range of people's basic rights, increase participation in public affairs, and improve the quality of urban life in general. Only when this is accomplished will a society that has been agrarian for thousands of years give way to one that truly represents a modern urban society.

China is in a period of very rapid urbanization. The transformation from 'quasi-urban' to 'fully urban' is a task of unprecedented significance and difficulty in the history of humankind. The magnitude of China's population and the scarcity of the country's resources require that the country proceed along a path that is unique to itself. It must turn population pressure into an engine for development and it must focus on human development as the core task, if it is to be successful in its process of urbanization.

Note

1 The concept of rural migrant workers is related to China's household register system and refers to the people who have their household register in rural areas but work mainly in non-agricultural sectors in urban areas.

1   Urbanization in China

Process, trends, and challenges

A process of 'urbanizing' has been going on in human societies for thousands of years, but 'urbanization' in the modern sense began only with the Industrial Revolution in the mid eighteenth century. Similarly, China has had a long history of urban civilization, but in the modern sense urbanization began only after New China was founded [in 1949]. Over the past 60 years, and particularly in the period of rapid economic growth after the start of the programme of 'reform and opening up', China's level of urbanization began to increase dramatically. By now, the process can be said to be in a middle stage of development.

The urbanization that has been accomplished to date in China, however, is mainly represented by what can be seen in material form. It can be recognized in such things as an increase in the number of cities, the increased amount of land being used, the host of buildings being constructed, and so on. The kind of urbanization that focuses on human development is still in its infancy, and this second kind of urbanization is where the real challenges lie. It is also where China will find the ability to increase its domestic demand and thereby drive the country's ongoing development.

Urbanization and human development

The term 'urbanization' indicates the process by which a population of people concentrates in cities. This process can be manifested in two ways: by an increase in the number of cities and by an increase in the populations of each city (*Encyclopedia Britannica*). Urbanization accompanies structural changes, namely a decline in agricultural activities and a commensurate rise in non-agricultural activities, and a gradual shift of the population from rural to urban areas. The process includes further socialization, modernization, and intensification of both the social and economic aspects of cities (Gu Chaolin, 2009).

Each step in the process of urbanization is a product of human effort and intelligence. Human actions permeate every aspect of the formation, expansion, and shaping of cities. At the same time, from the moment a city begins to form, that city itself also begins to shape and profoundly change the ways in which human society is organized. Cities change how goods are produced and how lives are lived.

The positive effects of urbanization

International experience indicates that urbanization is closely related to levels of human development. Figure 1.1 is a graphical presentation of the positive correlation between a human-development index and rates of urbanization in 171 countries and regions around the world.

Among 78 countries that are considered to be more highly developed (in which the human-development index is 0.8 or higher), 72 have an urbanization rate that is more than 50 per cent. Only one-tenth of these more highly developed countries have an urbanization rate of less than 50 per cent. Of the 77 countries and regions that have an even greater urbanization rate of more than 60 per cent, only two are low to middling in terms of development, with a human-development index of less than 0.8.

Urbanization is a major driving force behind modern economies. Urban concentrations of people have a pronounced effect on economies of scale, which dramatically reduce the average per capita investment and the marginal investment required of both individuals and the public in any given activity. Urban concentrations create larger markets and higher profit margins. As both human populations and economic activities concentrate in cities, market demand rises swiftly and also diversifies, spurring a division of labor and specialization that again improves economic efficiencies (World Bank, 2009).

With the ongoing globalization of economies, many industries and activities are increasingly dependent on cities for growth and expansion. Vital urban contributions include such things as research and development, modern service industries,

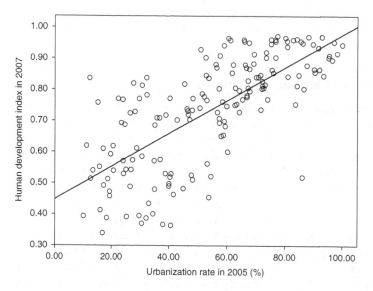

Figure 1.1 Urbanization and human development index.
Source: UNDP: *Human Development Report 2007/08* (2009).

finance and insurance industries, and information and computer services industries. Moreover, higher returns on urban industries attract more investment, technology, and human talent, which stimulates new technical innovations and transfers. This in turn stimulates the formation of whole new industries, making cities the most dynamic zones of activity in modern economies (OECD, 2010).

One can see at a glance the impact that concentrating populations has on economic growth by looking at a map that compares the economic densities of urban areas.[1] Figure 1.2 shows the economic densities of various regions in Japan. The cities of Tokyo, Osaka, and Nagoya have the largest populations in the country and their economic output per square kilometer is also greatest. A similar pattern applies in other industrialized countries around the world, including the USA (World Bank, 2009).

Urbanization contributes to more widespread application of public services, as well as to improved quality of those services. As a result, it contributes to better levels of education and good health. Average costs of providing basic public-service infrastructure, education, medical and healthcare services and so on are dramatically reduced by having populations concentrated in cities. The quality of such services is also clearly improved over what is found in rural areas. This is due not only to a better economic base in urban areas, but also because such areas concentrate superior human resources.

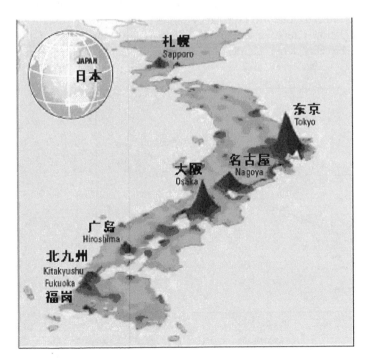

Figure 1.2 Economic densities in Japan.
Source: World Bank: *World Development Report 2009*.

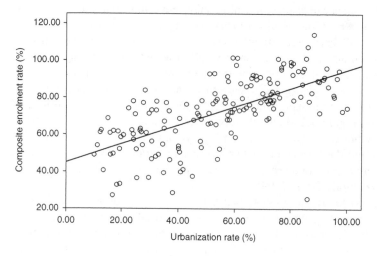

Figure 1.3a Urbanization and education.

Figure 1.3a indicates that the overall enrolment rate in school rises progressively with increases in the urbanization rate. Once urbanization rises above 60 per cent, only a very few countries exhibit an enrolment rate lower than 60 per cent. Figure 1.3b indicates that life expectancy shows a similar trend. Moreover, when the urbanization rate of a country is relatively low, the range of life expectancy can be very large, scattered broadly between 40 and 70 years.

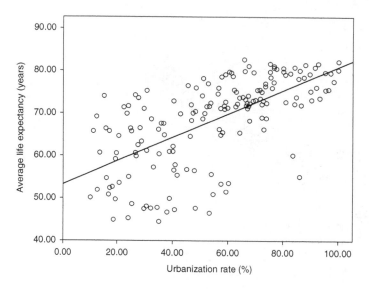

Figure 1.3b Urbanization and average life expectancy.
Source: UNDP: *Human Development Report 2007/08* (2009).

When urbanization rises above 60 per cent to 70 per cent, however, a sample of such countries shows the average life expectancy to be confined to a band of 65–80 years. This indicates just how important urbanization is in mitigating health risks.

Urbanization also plays a constructive role in improving governance. Once a farming population leaves rural areas and begins to concentrate in cities, it has a far greater opportunity to influence the conduct of government. Urbanization shortens the distance between the government and the 'people'. Every action taken by government and by officials is far more susceptible to scrutiny and oversight. Concentration of populations contributes to greater organization and division of labour in terms of all socialized conduct, and the 'will of the people' similarly is expressed with greater specificity and professional focus.

The costs of transmitting public opinion are vastly lower in cities and it becomes easier for people to carry out collective actions in asserting their opinions. Rural populations in developing countries may be larger in terms of actual numbers, but they also face very high transaction costs when it comes to collective actions since their homes are more dispersed. As a result, farmers lack the influence of urban people when guiding policy, even though a farming population may be far greater in actual numbers. (Olson, 1985).

Over the long run, urbanization can contribute to improvements in social equity and can gradually reduce disparities between urban and rural as well as among regions. As long ago as 1776, Adam Smith (in Volume 3, Chapter 4 of *The Wealth of Nations*) made a penetrating observation about the effect of urban commerce on rural reform. He believed that industrial and commercial cities provided ever greater markets for rural products, and also provided urban markets that were more convenient to access. This spurred greater development of land resources in rural areas. It also enabled rural areas to break through traditional constraints, which contributed to more conscientious and better organized governance, as well as to greater personal safety and freedom for individuals.

Korea urbanized at a very fast pace between 1975 and 2005, during which period the rural population declined by 76 per cent. The amount of land used in farming also fell by 16 per cent, yet grain production rose by 61 per cent. This can be attributed to more consolidated management of land, dramatic improvement in the level of education of the rural population, the adoption of agricultural technologies, and greater mechanization (Spencer, 2010).

Many countries experience increasing income disparities in the early period of urbanization, but these disparities gradually decrease as urbanization continues. Differences in urban and rural incomes, consumption, and general benefits begin to decline. In the Philippines, for example, although the overall difference between urban and rural incomes is still fairly large, regions with a higher level of urbanization show a gradual income convergence between urban and rural populations. The higher the level of urbanization of a given country, the smaller the disparities are in such things as availability of potable drinking water and healthcare facilities (World Bank, 2009).

The negative effects of urbanization

The positive effects of urbanization notwithstanding, a high degree of urbanization does not necessarily signify a more advanced level of human development.
The Republic of Djibouti in Africa has an urbanization rate that actually exceeds
86 per cent, but its human development index is only around one-half of what it
is in New Zealand, a country with a comparable urbanization rate. Trinidad and
Tobago and Burundi both have urbanization rates of less than 16.5 per cent,
which is roughly equivalent to the world average back in 1900. The human
development index of Trinidad and Tobago is 0.84, however, whereas that of
Burundi is 0.4. These examples show that urbanization is not the sole factor
influencing human development (Liu Minquan and Ji Xi, 2009).

Urbanization is sometimes accomplished at the cost of unbalanced development, and sometimes also at the cost of sacrificing the interests of certain
segments of the population.

In the course of industrializing and urbanizing, some countries achieve fast
economic growth while overlooking or failing to provide adequate public services.
They also lack rational planning mechanisms for urban development and environmental protection, which then leads to an increase in urban poverty, environmental
degradation, higher incidence of contagious diseases, and more crime. In England,
for example, the terrible situation with regard to public health services in the early
period of industrialization and urbanization led to a dramatic increase in the mortality rate, to the extent that it was higher in cities than it was in rural areas (Davis,
1965). Farmers who had lost their land, and other vulnerable groups, generally were
most directly affected by urban syndromes due to their lack of any social security.

Negative aspects of urbanization are also manifested in social changes. When
farmers leave rural settings and begin to work in factories and live in cities, this
profoundly changes the entire organizational structure of society, as well as its
underlying systems. Social relationships that formerly existed are now disrupted
and the former social order disintegrates. This leads to disorientation among 'new
urban people' with respect to a sense of values and it can lead to aberrant behavior. Social ties among people become more attenuated, to the point that confron-
tations and conflict occur more easily. Individuals in industrialized societies are
susceptible to feelings of isolation and helplessness, given the faster pace and
greater stresses of urban life, which can have a negative impact on mental health.
Crime rates and suicide rates can increase. Side-effects of urbanization in many
countries can include an increase in the numbers of people suffering from a
prevailing sense of anxiety and depression (Lin Minquan and Ji Xi, 2009).

Urban slums represent a concentrated reflection of unbalanced and unequal
development in the course of urbanization. In many cities, poverty is an unavoidable consequence of urbanization. According to a World Bank estimate, in 2002
there were 746 million people living in poverty in the cities of developing countries (this figure is based on the international poverty line of US$2 per day per
person) (Ravallion et al., 2007). The term given to concentrated populations
living in poverty-stricken conditions is 'slums', These are characterized by crowded
living conditions, a shortage of housing, a severely polluted environment, a lack

of clean drinking water and other social services, and a high incidence of crime. These are common features of urban slums around the world, but the problems in developing countries are more pronounced and more urgent.

The formation of slums is related to a host of economic and social factors. First and foremost is the matter of how land is distributed and managed. In many Latin American countries, annexation of land has caused large numbers of farmers to lose their land, forcing them to migrate into cities as a result. Once in cities, unable to find jobs or receive public services, they have no alternative but to assemble in certain areas and live in crowded shacks (Gu Chaolin, 2008). Secondly, the chaotic way in which land and housing is managed in many cities also contributes to the development of impoverished slums. In India, most slums start out in places where people simply occupy public land or privately-owned land.

The vast slum area next to the World Trade Tower in Mumbai, for example, was initially the location of workers' quarters when the workers were building the Tower. The rent-control system of the government created a shortage of rental housing in Mumbai, which was one of the important reasons for the spread of the slum. It has been 15 years since the city of Mumbai built any new rental housing. Even as seven million people are living in worsening conditions of impoverished slums, 400,000 living units are standing empty (Yao Yang, 2007). The scale of Mumbai's slums also reflects the inadequacies of public policy in terms of equity and inclusiveness. When large numbers of people who are poorly educated and unskilled come into cities with only the most modest resources, or even when they are utterly destitute, a swift expansion of slums is unavoidable if the government does not provide basic education, job training, and health insurance in addition to safe drinking water and health facilities.

Looking back over the course of more than two hundred years of urbanization, worldwide, it can be seen that the process has provided people with a tremendous potential for overall human development. Positive aspects can include propelling economic growth, raising people's standard of living, broadening the provision and quality of public services, improving social governance, narrowing disparities between urban and rural and among various regions, and so on. Nevertheless, whether or not this potential can be turned into reality depends to a large extent on the guidance of a country's government and its public policies. Such policies include those that govern land, those that determine mode of economic development, and those that relate to the provision of public services, including employment, housing, and social security.

The experience of urbanization in China, and its main accomplishments

Urbanization prior to the founding of New China

China's cities are nearly as ancient as the history of China itself. Until the start of the Industrial Revolution in the West, China's cities generally set the record for global urban population statistics, in each of China's succeeding dynasties. These cities developed under the aegis of an agrarian civilization and so occupied a unique position in the world history of urban development. Cities in the earlier part of China's history were generally fairly small, but once the Qin unified the country, social developments and the evolution of a centralized political system led to rapid increases in the populations of important economic centers as well as the capital cities of each dynasty.

The population of the capital of the Han dynasty, Chang'an, totalled between 400,000 and 500,000 people. By the Tang dynasty, it is estimated that the city of Chang'an had no fewer than 800,000 people and may have contained more than one million people at its height. During the Southern Song dynasty, the city of Ling'an (today's Hangzhou) contained more than 300,000 'households', from which the population can be estimated to have been around 1.5 million. During Ming and Qing times, three cities had populations of more than one million, namely Beijing, Nanjing, and Suzhou. In addition, more than ten regional 'core cities' had populations that totaled between 500,000 and one million.

In contrast, Western cities were much smaller at the time. Until the fourteenth and fifteenth centuries, only a few cities north of the Alps had populations that exceeded 50,000. These included Paris, Cologne, and London. The industrial and commercial centers that were to become famous later still only had populations on the order of twenty or thirty thousand, including Brussels, Nuremberg, Lübeck and Strasbourg (Zhang Guanzeng, 1993). Chinese cities of this time [prior to the Industrial Revolution], were around 20 times larger than the feudal cities of the same period in western Europe, whether one compares only the largest cities or the second tier of regional centers (Ma Jiwu and Yu Yunhan, 2004).

After the conclusion of the Opium War, China's traditional industries and mode of commerce in cities began to be bankrupted by the combined impact of foreign capital and an industrial mode of production. Cities in the interior, in the meantime, faced problems of inconvenient transport and unstable political conditions, which often led to stagnant economies or outright decline. The population of Xi'an in 1930, for example, was a mere 125,000 people, barely one-tenth of what it had been during the height of the Tang dynasty. Chengdu's population in 1930 was just 350,000, yet it had been 500,000 at the height of the Tang dynasty.

Meanwhile, such centers as Shanghai, Tianjin, and Guangzhou began to develop into ultra-large cities of over one million people as a result of their advantageous geographic conditions and the resulting commercial advantages. Generally speaking, however, urbanization developed only slowly in China prior to the founding of New China. This could be attributed to the slow pace of industrialization, the political turbulence, and other factors including geography and culture. China's urbanization rate when New China was founded in 1949 was only 10.64 per cent,[2] far lower than the world average at the time, which was 28 per cent, and also lower than the average developing country at the time, which was 16 per cent.

The process of urbanization once New China was founded

Urbanization prior to the start of reform and opening up

China's government focused on industrial development once New China was founded, in order to create a national economic and industrial structure that could be relatively complete and therefore independent. The government also began the process of urban development. The First Five-Year Plan period lasted from 1953 to 1957, during which time 156 'key projects' were fully launched. This brought large numbers of farmers into cities to work in factories and also into mining districts. By the end of 1957, the number of cities in China had increased to a total of 176, or 44 more than there had been in 1949. The urban population in the country had increased to 99.49 million, bringing the urbanization rate to 15.4 per cent.

The Great Leap Forward, a three-year event that began in 1958, 'blindly' went after high-speed economic growth. This brought a surge of the agrarian population into cities to 'build up industry', which caused an excessively rapid and explosive style of urbanization. During the period of the Great Leap Forward, China's urbanization rate increased at a rate of 1.5 percentage points per year. In 1960, the urban population reached 130.73 million people, a net increase of 31.24 million over 1957, and the urbanization rate reached 19.8 per cent.

The failure of the Great Leap Forward, together with natural disasters, forced the country to carry out adjustments to the national economy. The super-fast increase in the urban population had clearly exceeded the capacity of grain supply at the time. Starting in 1961, a large-scale effort began to reduce the urban population in an attempt to mitigate famine. Urban populations were 'mobilized' and returned to rural areas. The urban population was reduced by roughly 20 million in the two years of 1961 and 1962. The urbanization rate declined from 19.8 per cent in 1960 to 14.6 per cent in 1964. Only in 1965, by which time the national economy had basically recovered, did it rebound to 16.8 per cent.

The Great Cultural Revolution began in 1966, again damaging a national economy that had just recovered. The urbanization rate in 1966 was 17.8 per cent and it hovered around the same level for the next 12 years, reaching 17.9 per cent in 1978. During this period, between 1968 and 1972, around 40 million 'educated youth', cadres, and other urban dwellers were 'sent down' to the countryside. This was done to resolve employment problems in cities and also for other considerations. The process led to a successive decline in the urbanization rate over those five years.

Viewed overall, urbanization in China between the founding of the country and the start of reform and opening up went through a circuitous process that included speedy recovery and rapid growth and then stagnation. During this period, urban structures also changed. Medium- and large-sized cities expanded, while resource-based and industrially based cities were set up to integrate energy and mineral resources. Cities were also built in what were called 'third-line' areas [in the interior of the country, for strategic defense].

A household registration policy was strictly enforced, however, which limited movement of the rural population into cities. This, in addition to an economic policy that emphasized heavy industry, led to severely retarded levels of urbanization. The 'people's commune' system, and the restrictions placed on selling agricultural goods, meant that many smaller cities and towns declined. Meanwhile, in terms of urban construction, the bias was towards industrial building rather than urban housing and services, so that those functions remained under-developed. The development of service industries was grossly inadequate and many cities had highly incomplete urban functions.

Urbanization in China once reform and opening up began

The emphasis of the work of the Party and the State again shifted toward building up the economy ['economic construction'] once reform and opening up began to be implemented in 1978. Economic reforms in rural areas were highly effective in releasing their productive capacities. What were called 'town-and-village enterprises' began to flourish, which led to ferociously rapid growth of smaller towns and villages. The 'opening' [or allowing] of collective markets in these places drew in large numbers of farmers who now began to migrate toward the cities. In addition, a series of policies that were implemented from around 1979 now permitted those 'educated youth' and 'cadres' who had been 'sent down to the countryside' to return to the cities. All of these factors led to a swift rise in urban populations.[4] In the six-year period between 1978 and 1984, the cities swelled by more than 100 million people and the urbanization rate rose at an average annual rate of 0.85 percentage points to reach 23 per cent.

Starting in 1984, the emphasis of economic structural reform shifted from rural to urban areas. 'Urbanization' now began to feature the rapid development of coastal cities and what had been small towns. As the rural economy prospered, the problem of what to do with an excess labour force in the countryside again became a pressing concern.

In 1984, the State gave its approval and support to policies favouring the development of small towns. A strategy of 'opening up' coastal cities was put into effect that now established 4 'economic zones' and 14 'open cities'. This brought substantial and swift change to the growth of cities along the coast. In the decade between 1979 and 1991, a total of 286 new cities appeared in China, a number that was 4.7 times the entire number of cities created in the country prior to reform and opening up. By 1991, the urban population had increased to 312.03 million, an increase of 80.9 per cent over 1978, and the urbanization rate had reached 26.9 per cent.

In 1992, as symbolized by the 'inspection tour of the south' conducted by Deng Xiaoping, China's reform and opening up entered a whole new phase. Since cities occupy a core position in market economies, their standing and role in China now came into full play. In May 1993, the State went further in 'adjusting and improving' the standards by which cities could be established. In that year, it approved the declaration of 48 new cities, administered at the county level. By 1995, there were a total of 640 'cities' in the country, while the number of 'administered towns' had increased to 17,532. The total urban population was 351.74 million, and the urbanization rate had risen to 29 per cent.

China's process of urbanization entered a period of rapid growth upon moving into the twenty-first century. The Tenth Five-Year Plan, begun in 2001, specified that the country would be following a path of 'coordinated development' of large, medium-sized, and small cities as well as smaller towns. Between 2000 and 2009, urbanization on a nationwide basis rose from 36.2 per cent to 46.6 per cent (see Figure 1.4.) Large urban clusters in the eastern part of the country, as well as 'core cities' in the middle and western parts, began to grow quickly.

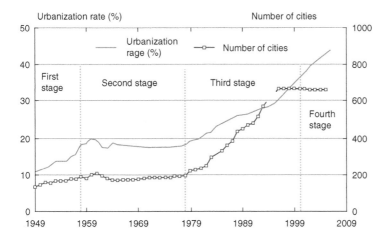

Figure 1.4 Level and number of China's cities.

Source: Li Shantong and Xu Zhaoyuan: *Options for China's Urbanization Road, China 2020: Development Goals and Policy Options.* China Development Publishing House, 2008.

Specific features of the process of urbanization in China

Scale and speed of growth

The process is characterized by large-scale, high-speed, growth. In the 30 years since the beginning of reform and opening up, China's scale of urbanization has risen dramatically, with the urban population increasing to 607 million people. Urbanization has increased at an annual rate of 0.9 per cent, making China one of the most rapidly urbanizing countries in the world. China's urbanization is in fact an event of epic proportions, a human migration of enormous magnitude. The flow of several hundred million rural residents from countryside to cities is unprecedented in the world.

Population distribution

The process is also characterized by having a population distribution that is 'large at both ends and small in the middle'. China's urban system is in the early stages of forming a structure that has 'extra-large cities' as the main component, with medium-sized and smaller cities as well as smaller towns as the 'foundation'. (See Figure 1.5.) At the end of 2007, there were 140 'extra-large cities' and 'large cities', the extra-large cities having populations of over one million people, and the large cities having populations between 500,000 and one million people. There were 232 medium-sized cities with populations between 200,000

- Ultra-large city
- Large city
- Medium-sized city
- Small city

South China
Sea Islands

Figure 1.5 Map of structural distribution of grades and scales of urban populations.
Source: Gu Chaolin: *Background Report, 2009.*

and 500,000. There were 283 small-sized cities with populations under 200,000, and there were 19,234 'small towns' that are now termed 'towns that have set up administrative systems', referred to below as 'administered towns'.

In terms of the distribution of China's urban population, it can be seen that there are more people in extra-large cities and small towns, and relatively fewer in medium-sized and small cities. Two metrics can be used to measure the size of China's urban population. One is a looser measure of 'urban populations in general', which includes the number of people in all cities as well as administered towns. The other is a stricter measure of just the 'urban' populations living in the 655 'cities'. Using the looser measure, there are just 316 million people living in the 655 cities, while a total number of 268 million people reside in county-level cities and administered towns. People living in county-level cities and administered towns therefore comprise 45 per cent of the total urban population of some 600 million.

Using the tighter metric, which adds up to a total urban population of 360 million, 47 per cent of the urban population live in extra-large cities that exceed one million people. An additional 17.7 per cent live in large cities that encompass more than 500,000 people. Added together, these two come to 65 per cent of the urban population of 360 million people. (See Table 1.1.)

Table 1.1 Population distribution in cities of different sizes (2007)

City scale	Number of administrative cities		Urban non-agricultural population		
	Number	Ratio (per cent)	Population size (10,000 people)	Ratio (per cent)	Average size (10,000 people)
>1,000,000	58	8.85	14,830.12	46.93	255.69
500,000~1,000,000	82	12.52	5,601.53	17.73	68.31
200,000~500,000	232	35.42	7,410.09	23.45	31.94
<200,000	283	43.21	3,760.12	11.90	13.29
Total	655	100	31,601.86	100.00	48.25

Note: Gu Chaolin: *Background Report 2009*; data originate from the urban-rural planning department of the Ministry of Housing and Urban-Rural Development: China's Cities and Population Statistical Data in 2007.

Regional distribution of population

China's urbanization is characterized by having a highly uneven regional distribution of population. Figure 1.6 shows the regional disparities in population in the country in the year 2008. Seen in overall terms, the urbanization rate becomes progressively less as one views the country from east to west. The three centrally administered cities of Shanghai, Beijing, and Tianjin rank as the top three in the country, with urbanization rates of 88 per cent, 85 per cent, and 77 per cent respectively. The regions that contain the fourth- to tenth-highest rates of urbanization are: Guangdong, Liaoning, Zhejiang, Heilongjiang, Jiangsu, Jilin, and Inner Mongolia. All of these are in the eastern or northeastern part of the country, with the exception of Inner Mongolia, which is considered to be in the 'western region'.

Using a simple average, the urbanization rate of the top ten regions in the country comes to 64.64 per cent (which does not take into consideration regional differences). The bottom ten regions, those that rank last in terms of 'urbanization', show a markedly lower rate of merely 34.95 per cent. These include Qinghai, Anhui, Xinjiang, Guangxi, Sichuan, Henan, Yunnan, Gansu, Guizhou, and Tibet (Gu Chaolin, Background Report, 2009).

Social and economic development

Urbanization in China is providing an extremely powerful engine for driving social and economic development.

To a large extent, the fast pace of social and economic development in China since the start of reform and opening up can be attributed to the speed with which industrialization and urbanization are proceeding in the country. Figure 1.7 shows the positive correlation between urbanization rates in all provinces of the country and the 'human development index'. The higher the level of urbanization

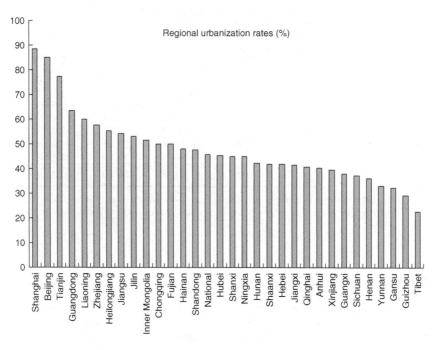

Figure 1.6 China's provincial urbanization rates in 2008.

Source: *China Statistical Yearbook 2009.*

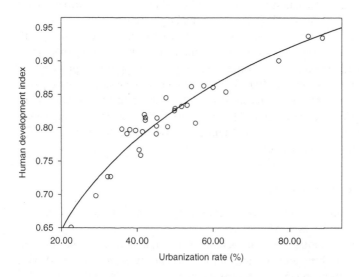

Figure 1.7 China's provincial urbanization rates and human development indices in 2008.

Source: The data about urbanization rates originate from the *China Statistical Yearbook 2009*, while the data about human development were produced by Li Shi for this report.

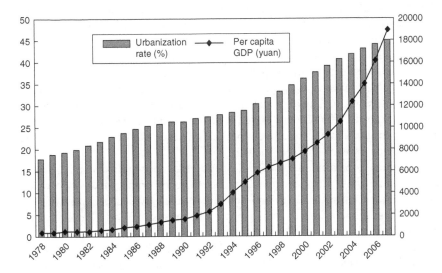

Figure 1.8 Relationship between urbanization and GDP growth.
Source: *China Statistical Yearbooks.*

in a given province, the more notable its accomplishments in terms of human development.

The role that urbanization plays in spurring human development relates not merely to the way in which it drives economic growth but also to the way it leads to improved basic public services and to reducing disparities between urban and rural within any given region.

Urbanization has brought with it rapid economic growth. Indeed, the speed of economic growth since the start of reform and opening up has been closely allied with the whole process of urbanization (see Figure 1.8). The 'concentration effect' of cities, combined with economies of scale, has had a powerfully stimulating effect on the economy. In the first place, urbanization has made a massive contribution to improving the efficiency with which resources are utilized. It has led to efficiencies in how land is used, including land for production, land for housing, and land for other facilities. It has enabled public use of basic infrastructure and improved the 'public usage rate' and 'comprehensive usage rate' of public services. It has enabled pollution-control efforts to be more concentrated, thereby reducing costs, raising efficiencies, and improving levels of pollution-control results.

In the second place, urbanization has generated a huge amount of consumption and investment demand, which has propelled economic growth. Rural labor has migrated into cities in large numbers, with a corresponding increase in consumer demand. For every 1 per cent increase in the number of people migrating from rural areas into cities, China's total personal consumption goes up by between 0.19 and 0.34 percentage points (Cai Fang, 2006). Statistics indicate that expenditures on personal consumption on average in China in 2008 came to RMB 3661.

Random-sample surveys show that average annual consumption in county-level cities came to RMB 8869, while average personal consumption in 36 large and medium-sized cities came to RMB 14,326.

At the same time, an increase in urban populations requires a corresponding increase in investment for municipal infrastructure and urban housing. Investment in real estate and basic infrastructure in urban areas has maintained rapid growth over recent years in China, which has played a major role in 'pulling forth' economic growth. The virtuous cycle [or positive reinforcement] created by this kind of consumption and investment provides a very powerful inherent impetus for economic growth.

In addition, urbanization has been furthering the process of economic restructuring. Rural labour, once employed in low-efficiency primary-industry occupations, has now shifted to secondary- and tertiary-industry occupations, which in turn has also stimulated economic growth. The results of World Bank research indicate that this shift in the labor force may account for as much as 16 per cent of China's GDP growth. (World Bank, 1998). Some Chinese scholars feel that the shift in the labor force may be contributing as much as 20 per cent to GDP growth every year. (Cai Fang and Wang Dewen, 1999).

Urbanization has played a positive role in reducing development disparities between urban and rural populations in China. Since the start of reform and opening up, income disparities have maintained a constantly increasing trend overall, but on a provincial level we can see that those provinces with a higher degree of urbanization are those that have smaller income disparities between rural and urban areas. Figure 1.9 shows the relationship between income disparities in provinces and urbanization. The higher the level of urbanization, the smaller the

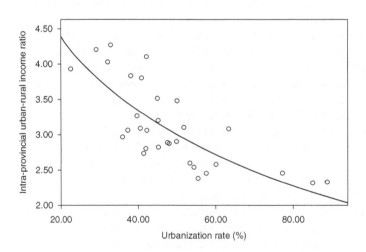

Figure 1.9 Urbanization rate and urban-rural income gap.

Source: The data about urban and rural per capita incomes originate from the *China Statistical Yearbook 2009* and the data about human development were produced by Li Shi for this report.

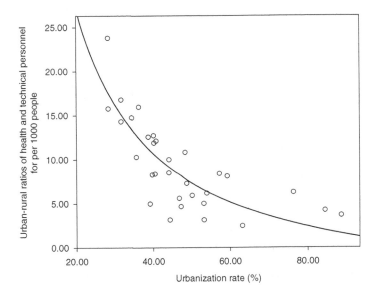

Figure 1.10 Urbanization rates and urban:rural ratios of health and technical personnel per 1000 people.

Source: The data about the urban:rural ratio of health and technical personnel per 1000 people originate from the *China Health Statistical Yearbook 2007*, and the data about urbanization rates originate from the *China Statistical Yearbook 2008*.

contrast between urban and rural incomes. This finding is consistent with World Bank conclusions on the subject as well (World Bank, 2009). At a time when China is putting considerable effort into narrowing income disparities, speeding up the process of urbanization provides greater room for different kinds of policy options.

The role of urbanization in reducing development disparities can be seen not only in terms of income but also in terms of public services. Figure 1.10 shows the relationship between urbanization and the number of health and technical personnel per thousand people in various provinces. It can be seen that the greater the degree of urbanization in a region, the lower the differential between health personnel in urban and rural areas.

Urbanization has proved helpful in spurring an improvement in China's basic public services. Government departments in cities have a better economic base and more access to high-quality human resources. This, plus the fact that policies have favored cities for a long time, means that public services enjoy a clear advantage in cities, as opposed to rural areas. This holds true in both quantitative as well as qualitative terms. Many public services and products share the nature of 'public goods' to a certain degree, which means that the concentration of people in any given place enables more individuals to enjoy the benefits of public services. Healthcare services in 2008 can serve as an example. The higher the level of urbanization in a given region, the more healthcare personnel are available to attend to every 10,000 people (see Figure 1.11). In Shanghai, which has the highest

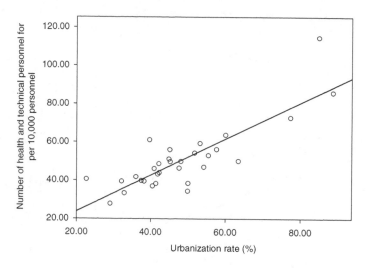

Figure 1.11   Urbanization rates and medical and health service popularization.
Source: *China Statistical Yearbook 2009.*

urbanization rate in the country (approaching 90 per cent), there are 86 healthcare personnel available for every 10,000 people. In contrast, Guizhou, which has an urbanization rate of less than 30 per cent, has only 28 per 10,000 people.

Challenges facing urbanization

The problem of 'quasi-urbanization'

By the metric by which we currently measure urbanization statistics, urbanization since the start of reform and opening up has been happening very quickly. Many rural migrant workers are included in these statistics as urbanites, however, since they have worked and lived within cities for a long time. At the same time, they and their families fail to enjoy the public benefits and political rights that are associated with urban household-registration status.

This is demonstrated in two primary ways. First, the way we currently account for urban residents in our statistics is to say that anyone who has lived in a city for more than six months is considered part of the 'urban population'. Rural migrant workers who live in cities for more than six months are therefore 'urban people', which means that rural migrant workers now constitute 26 per cent of China's total urban population.

Under China's current governing system, however, while these people are indeed living and working in cities, they are not allowed to receive the same treatment as 'regular urban people' in terms of workers' compensation, their children's education, social security, housing, and so on. They do not have political rights, such as being entitled to vote or to be elected to office themselves, and they are in fact far from truly being absorbed into urban society.

Secondly, by our current methods of statistical analysis, a considerable number of people are incorporated in the 'urban population' of 600 million in the country, even though they are in fact living in suburbs and working in agricultural production.

Based on the 2000 population census and a 1 per cent sampling survey undertaken in 2005, 71.8 per cent of China's increase in urban populations over the past five years can be attributed to rural migrant workers who still have rural household-registration status but are coming into cities to work. A second component can be attributed to people engaged in agricultural production who are living in suburban areas. Figure 1.12 demonstrates that the gap between the 'urbanization rate' and the rate at which people are becoming 'non-agricultural households' is constantly growing. By 2007, the gap was 12 percentage points.

Seen from this perspective, a certain amount of China's economic accomplishments have been gained by sacrificing the human development potential of rural migrant workers. The low incomes of rural migrant workers have resulted in low standards of living and poverty. Dreadful working conditions have resulted in occupational diseases. Children have been left behind while parents migrated into cities to work, or have accompanied parents but then been unable to access equal educational opportunities, which has led to psychological problems in addition to learning and living problems. Separation of families has had highly unfortunate consequences.

Second-generation rural migrant workers are now gradually becoming the main component of the rural labor force in cities. In addition, more and more children of rural migrant workers are now also coming into cities. If we cannot provide these people with adequate public services, and invest in their human capital, the inescapable result will be a lowering of China's quality of labor. This will then have an impact on the future of our industries, and the competitiveness of our cities and our country.

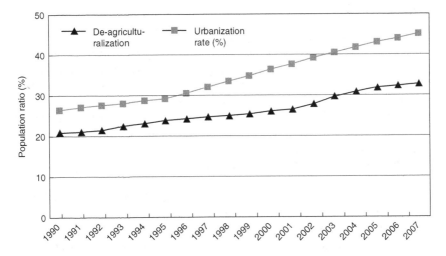

Figure 1.12 Population's urbanization rate and de-agriculturalization rate.
Source: *China Statistical Yearbook 2008.*

At the same time, if we cannot help rural migrant workers become truly integrated into urban life, in the future we will unavoidably be paying a heavy price in terms of socioeconomic problems, including social conflict and social unrest.

The full significance of 'urbanization' in China should include a real transformation of 'rural populations' into 'non-rural populations', such that farmers who come into cities can truly take up residence and enjoy the full rights of urban residency. Farmers, or rural migrant workers, should not remain 'rural' in terms of their household registration status, while becoming 'workers' in terms of just their jobs. They should not be 'urban' purely in terms of their geographic location but still 'farmers' in terms of their 'status'. Moreover, they should not be consigned to a life of finding transient jobs, especially since this status in life persists not just for one generation but for generation after generation.

In human history, any nation that is industrializing has to go through the historical stage of shifting its farming population from working on the land to working in industry. At the same time, it has to turn farmers and their families into an urban population. China has a unique set of issues, however, that surround what could be called large-scale, enduring, 'quasi-urbanization'. These issues can be attributed to the country's special system of household registration, together with all the systems that attach to the household-registration system. These include housing, compulsory education, social security, and so on. China's household-registration system has cut itself off from the logic of having concentrations of 'labor' accompany concentrations of 'population'. That has generated a rather special phenomenon in the country.

Box 1.1   Japan spent 20 years to convert its own rural migrant workers to urban residents

Japan's economy grew at a fast pace between 1955 and 1975, and, during this same period, a rural labor force of approximately 725,000 people every year moved into cities and took up non-agricultural jobs. After 20 years, the numbers of such people constituted 64 per cent of Japan's total number of employed people. At the outset, the great majority of these rural immigrants also were employed in the construction industry and in manufacturing. Within twenty years, however, Japan was able to turn its rural labor force into an urban population.

There were a number of reasons behind this:

- First, Japan did not discriminate between people holding a so-called 'urban residence' and those holding a 'rural residence'. It had only what was called a 'household transcript'. Japan's system of household registration permitted free movement, and to a considerable degree this facilitated the mobility of the labor force. It enabled economic development.

- Second, Japan's system of housing in urban areas permitted a rural labor force to take up long-term residence in cities. Japanese cities offered publicly managed housing and public housing estates, which offered secure housing for low and middle-income families. Some of this housing was made specifically for the rural labor force as it migrated into cities.

- Third, Japan adopted a system of national insurance that covered all Japanese citizens. As rural workers came into cities, they were obliged to join into various insurance programs, including pension systems, healthcare insurance, workers' injury insurance, employment insurance, and so on. At first glance, such a comprehensive form of insurance might appear to put onerous costs on an enterprise. In fact, it helped guarantee a source of labor for the company and ensured that it would not have to face a scarcity of labor.

- Fourth, and most important, was Japan's educational system. Japan instituted a nine-year compulsory education system. School-age children had to report to school within three days of accompanying parents into cities from the countryside. The schools then organized their enrollment in classes. These children therefore did not have all the problems of paying fees for being 'transient students', or 'sponsor-ships' just in order to be admitted, and they certainly did not have to return to their 'home' residence in the countryside in order to take the exam for higher education.

Source: *International Online: World News*, 11 March 2010, http://taobao.cri.cn/27 824/2010/03/10/4545s2779848.htm.

Land, and the issue of the forms or shape of urbanization

Since the start of reform and opening up, but particularly since the turn of the century, the 'urbanizing of land' has had a driving role in China's economic growth. Enormous revenues have been derived from turning farmland into land used for urban construction. This has been a massive temptation to municipal governments, which generally lack any stable revenue streams with which to undertake urban development.

The negative consequences of this process have been as obvious as the positive benefits, however. Such things as 'operating a city [like a business]', 'getting rich off land', and 'using land as the source of public revenues' have led to an extremely rapid expansion in the size of cities. This has happened so fast that the pace of 'land urbanization' has outstripped that of 'population urbanization'. The density of urban populations has fallen dramatically in the process. When it is considered that the current statistics for the 'urbanization rate' include 145 million rural migrant workers, a population that has not in fact been fully integrated into the urban population, the unbalanced way in which land is being urbanized faster than people are being urbanized becomes even more extreme (see Figure 1.12 and Chapter 6).

*The unbalanced spatial distribution of cities and the various
forms or shapes of urbanization*

Over the past three decades of rapid urbanization in China, most new cities have been concentrated around a relatively small number of areas, including Guangdong, Fujian, Zhejiang, Shanghai, Jiangsu, and Beijing. In 2008, the urbanization rate in the eastern part of the country was 56.2 per cent, which was 13.2 per cent higher than in the middle part of the country and 17.9 per cent higher than in the west. Problems attending this spatial distribution of cities have already become apparent.

First, the spatial distribution of cities is incompatible with the availability of resources as well as the carrying capacity of the local environment. The carrying capacity of the resource environment around the Yangtze River Delta area, the Pearl River Delta area, and Shanghai has already begun to decline. At the same time, some cities in the middle and western parts of the country that have relatively good natural conditions remain underdeveloped.

Second, regional disparities in how cities are distributed around the country are not only detrimental to balanced regional development but even contribute to further disparities. Third, the wholesale movement of rural populations from middle and western parts of the country, towards just a few areas in the east, has caused major adjustments not just in population but in resources, leading to extremely high social costs.

'Urban clusters' in China are insufficiently developed. The formation of urban clusters has already become the dominant trend in the process of urbanization. Several such urban clusters are making good progress in China but, seen overall, the number of these and the quality of their organization is too low, and their development is still at a very preliminary stage.

One thing preventing the integrated development of urban clusters is the socioeconomic 'control system' in China, which is based on the 'administrative district' as the main unit. Within a given cluster, each 'city' still lacks a well differentiated set of functions.

Industrial structures and the positioning [or definition] of functions is still identical in all parts of a cluster so that ferocious and harmful competition between cities is the rule. Meanwhile, inadequate infrastructure makes communications of all kinds inconvenient. Many regions that claim to be 'urban clusters' are in fact merely administrative measures or planning designs. They have not truly become urban clusters in terms of functions, comprehensiveness, and networks.

Severe shortage of land resources

The per capita amount of 'usable land' in China is 0.8 hectares, which is only slightly more than one-quarter of what it is worldwide.

The per capita amount of 'arable land' in China is less than 43 per cent of the comparable global figure.

In addition to the fundamental scarcity of land, other 'land issues' relate to the speed at which land is being 'urbanized' and the way that land urbanization is exceeding population urbanization. The shape that urbanization is taking is not concentrated in specific areas, nor is its distribution concentrated. Instead, the trend is toward low-density [high-sprawl] urbanization. In addition, China as a country has not yet reached peak population so that the contradiction between people and available land will only intensify in the future.

Different paths toward 'urbanization' put different demands on land use. Table 1.2 presents three different scenarios. The first distributes the anticipated new urban population of four hundred million people evenly across four different types or 'forms' of cities, namely extra-large cities, large cities, medium-sized and small cities, and small towns. Each is allocated 25 per cent of the total. In this scenario, in order to meet the demands of urbanization over the next 20 years, a total of 39,000 square kilometers will have to be newly 'occupied' by urban land use.

The second scenario assumes that extra-large cities will become the dominant form of urbanization, and that 50 per cent of urban populations will be concentrated in existing extra-large cities, with 20 per cent in large cities and medium-sized and small cities, and only 10 per cent absorbed into small towns. In this scenario, a total of 34,000 square kilometers will have to be put to urban land use. As compared with scenario one, this scenario therefore results in conserving 4760 square kilometers of land.

The third scenario envisages taking the path of 'small town development' as the primary mode of urban development. It mainly relies on small towns to absorb the increase in urban populations. It assumes that small towns will absorb

Table 1.2 Urban land requirements for different urban population distributions

	Per capita land occupa-tion[a] (m²)	Scenario 1		Scenario 2		Scenario 3	
		Popula-tion dis-tribution	Newly added urban land use (km²)	Popula-tion dis-tribution	Newly added urban land use (km²)	Popula-tion dis-tribution	Newly added urban land use (km²)
City with more than 1 million people	73	25%	7,300	50%	14,600	10%	2,920
City with 500,000–1,000,000 people	81	25%	8,100	20%	6,480	20%	6,480
Small and medium-sized city	93	25%	9,300	20%	7,440	20%	7,440
Small town	143	25%	14,300	10%	5,720	50%	28,600
Total land use (km²)			39,000		34,240		45,440

[a] The 'land' in 'per capita land occupation' refers to the built-up area of cities and administrative towns and the 'population' refers to the population with city household register and the permanent population, namely rural migrant workers, who have lived in urban areas for more than six months.

50 per cent of the four hundred million new urban residents, while large, medium, and small cities will absorb 20 per cent, with mega-cities absorbing only 10 per cent. Under this scenario, 45,400 square kilometers of land will be needed for urban land use purposes. This scenario therefore uses 6440 square kilometers more than scenario one, and 11,200 square kilometers more than scenario two.

It is obvious that different paths to urbanizing the country will result in different land-use pressures, since intensive land-use practices can be used only to varying degrees by different sizes of cities.

Water resources, energy resources, and environmental pressures

China's water resources rank among the scarcest in the world. Available water per capita is one-quarter the average in the rest of the world.

Moreover, water is highly uneven in terms of geographic distribution and seasonal availability, and the mismatch between concentration of cities and concentration of water resources makes this problem even more pronounced. Many cities have begun excessive mining of their underground water, which has led to constantly falling water tables and to the subsiding of the surface areas of cities, a trend that is getting worse by the day.

At the same time, the problem of polluted water in cities is acute. More than 90 per cent of urban water areas [sources] are severely polluted; close to 50 per cent of the water sources of key urban areas are not in compliance with drinking water standards. Given ongoing rapid urbanization and the trend towards ever more concentrated and large-scale use of water, the problem of not having enough water where it is needed is only going to intensify.

In 2008, the per capita use of water in China in urban areas came to 178.19 tons. Using this figure, if 15 million people are added every year to urban areas, the increase in urban populations will bring with it an additional 267 million tons of water demand every year. China's extreme shortage of water is going to be the constraining factor or bottleneck holding back the development of many cities.

Urbanization brings with it radical changes in people's lifestyles, particularly in the age of the automobile. In China, the process will greatly increase the consumption of energy resources. Meanwhile, as urbanization brings both people and production into closer proximity, it also aggravates environmental problems in the ecosystem in which urbanization is occurring. Measurements are indicating that the density of sulfur dioxide in the air above China's northern cities is, on average, 30 per cent higher than allowable standards. In southern cities, the sulfur dioxide is 19 per cent higher than standards.

Piles of accumulated garbage in China, collected over years, now amount to an aggregate figure of some six billion tons. The area of 'land-use' required for this garbage now comes to 500 million square meters. The garbage is already causing extreme damage to the soil, as well as to underground water and to the atmosphere. If we persevere in our current mode of production and our current lifestyle,

China's ecological systems will face a monumental challenge as levels of urbanization continue to rise.

The challenge of satisfying the diversifying demands of China's urban residents

Given rapidly transforming social and economic modes, the demands being placed on public services by citizens are also undergoing profound change, both in level and in specificity.

Economic growth has led to changes in the level of citizen's demands, such that people are transitioning from a basic subsistence mode to a growth mode in their needs. Now that their material needs are basically being met, other demands are coming to the fore, including physiological, psychological, and spiritual. Focal points of public attention are now including social ethics, public safety, and environmental protection, in addition to earlier concerns, including healthcare, education, and social security.

At the same time, a transitioning society is creating changes in the composition of citizen's demands. Those demands are becoming more diversified, more individualistic, and more based on legal systems. The trend is towards pursuing lives that embody a sense of wellbeing, that are quality-oriented, that call for equal opportunity. Citizens have begun to be aware of their rights, their political, economic, social, and cultural rights, and they are now seeking more high-quality and individualized public services and products.

Box 1.2 Analysis of the various demands being placed on public services by different kinds of urban groups

Western authorities who have studied urban issues conducted a survey that evaluated the expectations of different interest groups in urban areas, with respect to the performance of their cities. They then consolidated the results (Table 1.3). Generally speaking, lower-income groups in urban areas were concerned about whether or not cities could provide them with opportunities to improve their own situations. They were also concerned about prices of goods, the educational opportunities available for their children, and so on. Middle-class people were more concerned about the quality of life, whether or not it was outstanding, whether or not taxes were relatively low, whether or not there were adequate benefits that justified pursuing education. People who were not long-term residents in cities, including merchants and professionals who for one reason or another were only residing in the city for a short time, were most concerned about the opportunities for advancement in the city, whether or not the political situation was stable, whether or not one could spend a minimum amount of money in return for the highest quality of life. In brief, the demands of different kinds of people on public services were quite different.

Table 1.3 Analysis of different urban public demands of different social groups

Interested group	Related city functions	Main urban concerns
Poor class	Cities are still relatively better than the countryside, although life is difficult; some money can be saved to purchase land; children can have a better future through formal education	Income opportunities, affordable prices, education opportunities, housing, and transportation
Rich and semi-rich class	Cities are ideal places to live, mean better services, make it easier to establish links with businesses and governments, and are gateways to the outside world	Social status, income, security, cheap labor, quality of life, and quality–price balance of goods and services
Non-citizen businessmen and professionals	Cities are bases to make the highest profit in the shortest time, ideal places to enter corporate and institutional headquarters, and places to spend less for a decent life	Political and social stability, security, urban services, educational opportunities, housing, social intercourse, labor market, service availability and reliability, and product quality. Price is not a big problem
Visitors and tourists	City atmosphere, relaxed environment, good shopping environment, and all factors to ensure holiday and short-term comfort	Food, accommodation, transportation, security, comfort, shopping environment, tourist resources, and availability of special goods and services

Source: Yin Jizuo: *World Cities and Innovative Cities: Theory and Practice in Western Countries*, Shanghai Academy of Social Sciences Press, 2003, pp. 38–9.

Challenges brought on by the demand for housing

The experience of other countries indicates that many countries face a serious problem of 'slums' once their population becomes more than one-half 'urban'. Within the next few years, China's urbanization rate will also exceed 50 per cent. It may be very hard for the country to meet the additional demand for housing by using existing modes of housing supply and housing consumption.

Right now, the housing standards for rural migrant workers are quite low, sanitary conditions are poor, there are numerous safety hazards, housing lacks proper facilities, and so on. Rural migrant workers engaged in construction work live in two square meters of 'housing' on average. Given the housing needs anticipated for an additional two hundred million people within the next ten years, China's urban housing faces a massive shortage. As calculated at the standard per capita living space of 15 square meters, China will need nearly three billion more square meters of housing within a decade.

Box 1.3 Housing conditions of rural migrant workers in Hangzhou

Hangzhou's rural migrant workers resolve their housing problems mainly by renting from other farmers who have settled down in what are called 'villages within cities'. Some 62.3 per cent of all rural migrant workers lives in this kind of housing; another 15.8 per cent live in collective dormitories, 16 per cent live in sheds on construction sites, while 4.7 per cent rent from urban residents. Still another small percentage live in storage rooms of stores and restaurants, and some in hospital wards, as nurses accompanying patients.

Only 15.2 per cent of those surveyed expressed satisfaction with their living conditions. Most were unhappy with various aspects, including rent and the environmental conditions.

A further survey was conducted of the 169 individual rural migrant workers who had expressed dissatisfaction with living conditions. Of these, 30.1 per cent felt that rents were too high; 29.7 per cent felt that housing conditions were deplorable. One notable response was that 7.9 per cent felt that the place was not for long-term habitation. It was apparent that rural migrant workers have a sense of disorientation [or 'loss'] in not having any long-term housing or place to stay.

Source: Policy Research Center of Ministry of Housing and Urban-Rural Development: *Housing Problem of Peasants Living in Urban Areas*, 2001.

Challenges facing the whole issue of social governance in cities

As levels of urbanization in China continue to rise, municipal social governance is going to become one of the most crucial issues facing the country as it modernizes.

In the context of modern urban societies, such things as open social structures and the tremendous mobility of populations mean that social control systems that were based on ethics will become less and less effective. Economies are globalizing and municipal management and urban governance will soon be facing ever more intense market competition. Challenges include such things as the speed with which capital now circulates, the constant fragmentation of interest groups, and the rise of civil society.

Contemporary municipal 'governance' must now cover a broad range of tasks, from political administration to economic operations, cultural activities, and environmental protection. Municipal governance has become a very complex form of systems engineering. It requires the ability to manage many kinds of social issues, and at present China is far from being able to meet the demands.

Right now, problems of municipal management are not merely reflected in such things as traffic jams, cleaning up residential districts, and keeping social order. More importantly, they are reflected in the fact that the very systems required for modern social governance have not yet been established.

Notes

1 Economic density, a measurement of economic output per square kilometer, reflects the level of briskness and development of a regional economy. If a region has a higher economic density, its elevation in the map is also higher.
2 *China Statistical Yearbook 1983*. Henceforth, data originating from or based on *China Statistical Yearbooks* will not be specifically attributed.
3 The urbanization rate before the reform and opening up was basically computed on the basis of city populations, but the rate after the beginning of reform and opening up also included the populations of administrative towns. That is why 'city population' is used here for the period before reform and opening up and 'urban population' for the period after the beginning of reform and opening up.
4 The urbanization rate before the reform and opening up was basically computed on the basis of city populations, but the rate after the beginning of reform and opening up also included the populations of administrative towns. That is why 'city population' is used here for the period before reform and opening up and 'urban population' for the period after the beginning of reform and opening up.

2 Converting rural migrant workers into urban residents in the course of urbanization

Rural migrant workers are a unique component of China's contemporary society. These people leave their homeland and families to work in unfamiliar cities where their work becomes the 'core competitiveness' of all that is made in China. The sweat of their brows has watered the growth of China's myriad skyscrapers as well as creating the products sold around the world. Their contribution to China's economic growth over the past 30 years has been immeasurable, for they have contributed their very youth to the process of building China. Despite crippling work, however, these people have no permanent place of residence and no security, they live apart from their families, and they have extremely difficult lives. As we celebrate the rapid growth of China's economy, and pride ourselves on becoming a middle-income society, it behooves us not to forget this vital group of people. Indeed, this specific group of people is most in need of our public policy consideration.

The crux of the issue of rural migrant workers is the process of turning them into legitimate urban residents. That means enabling those employed workers who are already long-term residents in cities, and their families, to obtain the 'status' [*shenfen*] of 'urban resident'. It means enabling them, on a voluntary basis, to enjoy public services and political rights that are equal to those enjoyed by existing urban residents, as well as to assume the civic duties of urban residents and to become urban 'citizens' in the true sense of the word. This process of converting rural migrant workers into true urban citizens is the key task for the country at this immediate stage of promoting urbanization.[1]

The current state of affairs and the difficulties the country faces in converting rural migrant workers into urban citizens

After the start of reform and opening up [in 1978], the country's initial response to the movement of rural migrant workers into cities was passive acceptance, which then turned into a gradual loosening of restrictions on mobility. In the 1980s, policies exhorted surplus labor in rural areas to 'leave the soil but not the homeland, go into factories but not into cities'. The idea was to resolve surplus labor problems in the countryside by creating jobs *in situ*; farmers were not encouraged to migrate to cities, and indeed policies prevented them from doing so.

Since the 1990s, however, the movement of labor into cities, and from inland provinces toward coastal regions, has become an inexorable tide. To use the phrase of the time, the magnitude of the 'flood of peasant labor' clearly showed that the new situation could not be dealt with by trying to 'shift labor' to new jobs in the same rural localities.

After the 1990s, attitudes gradually began to change with respect to how to shift rural labor into new jobs, and policies began to accept the migration of workers into cities, and even to encourage it. Policies fundamentally changed on the issue in the twenty-first century. In 2002, a 'guiding precept' stated that, with respect to allowing rural migrant workers to find jobs in cities, policies were to 'provide fair [equal] treatment, reasonable guidance, sound management, and improved services'. This led to the removal of previous regulations that had allowed discriminatory practices, including unreasonable fees placed on rural migrant workers.

As the numbers of rural migrant workers in cities grew ever larger, the whole issue became a focal point of public debate. Another key breakthrough in policy came after the 16th National Congress of the Communist Party of China. In 2006, the State Council issued an 'Opinion on Various Issues to do with Resolving the Problem of Rural Migrant Workers'. Each level of government was now charged with the task of dealing with the issue.

Nevertheless, the critical aspect of enabling rural migrant workers to become legitimate urban citizens, to work and live in cities as normal city residents, was left completely unresolved. Policies with respect to this aspect of the problem were not changed one iota. As a result, the two different policies coexisted: encouraging rural migrant workers to come work in cities, and preventing rural migrant workers from receiving the legitimate rights of urban citizenship. Together, the two have led to the massive and uniquely Chinese problem that we have today: the 'rural migrant worker' problem.

Overall size of the rural migrant worker population, and its regional distribution

The direction of the movement of people, and size of the population, have undergone three main stages over the course of changing policies and a changing economic environment. The first stage was in the 1980s, when *in situ* employment predominated. Town-and-village enterprises provided the main source of jobs for rural migrant workers. During this phase, the number of workers rose swiftly from around 2 million in the early 1980s to 30 million in 1989.

The second stage occurred in the 1990s and was characterized mainly by cross-regional flows of people. Cities now became the main location of jobs for rural migrant workers. The size of the rural migrant worker population swelled to around 100 million at the start of the twenty-first century. As the range of movement broadened out, the percentage of people migrating across regions rose dramatically. The third stage has been occurring in the twenty-first century as the overall size of the rural migrant labor population began to stabilize and the rate of increase began to slow down. Between 2002 and 2006, the annual increase in the number of rural migrant workers has been an average of 6.78 million, a figure that has been growing at around 6 per cent. This is far lower than the average annual increase of 15 per cent in the 1990s.

Currently, there is still a surplus labour force in rural areas in overall terms, but the supply-and-demand situation is growing more complex. From a long-term 'over-supply', it is moving in the direction of 'structural shortages in the midst of overall surplus of labor'. Supply of rural migrant workers with special skills is inadequate in some areas, so that there have even been instances of labor shortages along coastal regions in peak seasons.

The total number of rural migrant workers in 2009 came to around 230 million people. Of these, 145 million were workers who had left their native towns and townships to seek work elsewhere; while 84.45 million were workers who were employed within their native regions.[2]

The flow of rural migrant workers has been mainly in the direction of the fastest-growing economies along the east coast. The National Bureau of Statistics

Table 2.1 Regional distribution and change (%) of rural migrant workers[a]

	East region	Central region	West region
2003	69.9	14.9	15.2
2006	70.1	14.8	14.9
2009	62.5	17.0	20.2

[a] With regard to the distribution of the destinations of rural migrant workers, 0.3% of rural migrant workers are working in Hong Kong, Macao, Taiwan, and foreign countries in addition to those working in the east, central and west regions.

Table 2.2 Distribution and change (%) of rural migrant workers in different types of cities 2001–2006

	2001	2002	2003	2004	2005	2006	2009
Centrally administered municipalities	8.2	8.4	9.5	9.6	9.9	9.4	9.1
Provincial capital cities	21.8	21.2	19.6	18.5	19.1	18.6	19.8
Prefecture cities	27.2	27.2	31.8	34.3	36.1	36.8	34.4
County cities	21.0	21.1	20.4	20.5	19.7	20.2	18.5
Administrative towns	13.0	12.9	11.6	11.4	10.0	9.9	13.8
Other regions	8.8	9.2	7.1	5.7	5.2	5.1	4.4

estimated in 2006 that some 70.1 per cent of all rural migrant workers were employed in the eastern part of the country, while 14.8 per cent were in the central part of the country and 14.9 per cent were in the western part of the country. The number in the east had increased slightly over 2003, while those in other parts of the country had gone down slightly.

By 2009, this distribution of workers had changed considerably due to two factors: the impact of the international financial crisis on eastern regions, and the accelerating pace of economic development in the central and western regions. In 2009, therefore, the percentage of workers in the east dropped to 62.5 per cent, to total 90.76 million. Numbers working in the central part of the country rose to 17 per cent, to total 24.77 million people, and those in the west rose to 20.2 per cent to total 29.4 million people. As compared with 2006, the number in the east fell by 7.6 per cent, while the number in the central and western regions rose by 2.2 per cent and 5.3 per cent respectively.

Next-generation rural migrant workers are now presenting a new set of issues to policy makers. These younger people, 23 years old on average, now constitute 60 per cent of all rural migrant workers. They were born and raised after China began 'reform and opening-up' policies, and their demographic profile is different from that of their parents. They have somewhat higher levels of education and skills training; they mostly have never engaged in agricultural labor, and they have a better sense of their own value. Work motivations of this new generation are shifting from 'merely making a living' to 'realizing hopes and dreams'.

This new generation of rural migrant workers is looking for longer-term opportunities and is very much hoping to settle down permanently in cities. The younger generation has a far better sense of its rights, and hopes to engage in life intellectually and emotionally (All-China Federation of Trade Unions: *Study Report on New-Generation Rural Migrant Workers*).

Problems relating to this new generation of rural migrant workers have been accumulating and are now beginning to affect political and social stability in the country. The problems are beginning to have a negative impact on sustainable economic growth. Targeted policies that address these issues are becoming an urgent imperative if China aims for ongoing social development.

Main issues facing rural migrant workers

The problems that rural migrant workers face are ever more apparent as their numbers increase. The government has therefore been applying a range of policy measures to various issues, seeking to address such things as poor working conditions, delayed payment of wages, no social security, deplorable housing, inadequate children's education, difficulties in getting medical attention, and so on. There has been no action at all with respect to the core issue, however – that of converting these workers into legitimate urban citizens. These workers and their families are still quite clearly receiving discriminatory treatment in many aspects of life, including 'compulsory' education, university entrance examinations, job assistance, medical care, guaranteed housing, social welfare, and political rights and benefits. [Each of those issues is discussed below.]

First, children of rural migrant workers are not able to receive educational services on an equal basis [with regular urban citizens]. Equal opportunity in receiving an education is the fundamental basis for an equitable society. The national government currently mandates that all children of rural migrant workers must be taken into the public school system [at the primary and middle-school level]. Nevertheless, quite a large percentage of children who are already living in cities do not, in fact, have any way to enter the school system and instead are forced to be educated at schools that are privately run for the children of rural migrant workers. Conditions at these private schools are generally poor. Fees are charged, which are not in any way standardized. According to the National Bureau of Statistics, in 2006, 17 per cent of rural migrant workers had brought their children with them into cities and had them study in local schools, and 70 per cent of these children were studying in public schools while 10 per cent went to 'schools for children of rural migrant workers and 20 per cent went to other types of private schools. The great majority of schools run specifically for children of rural migrant workers receive no support from public funding. Costs of the 'compulsory education' of these schools have not been included in public budgets, and the schools rely on fees for ongoing operations. This has an impact on the quality of the education and also adds to the financial burden of workers.

Another problem that deserves much greater attention is the discrimination against children of rural migrant workers in education at the levels of high school and above. Even if these children receive absolutely equal education at the compulsory education level [primary and middle school], once they enter the stage of non-compulsory higher education, they receive different treatment. They are obliged to return to the place of their household registration for high school. They cannot partake in the superior education offered to high-school age students in cities, and they must be located back in their original place of residence in order to sit for the college-entrance exam. The problem of unequal education for the children of rural migrant workers is one of the primary manifestations of inequality in educational opportunities in China in general.

When either one or both parents leave home to work in some other place, those children that they leave behind are generally called by a short-hand phrase that means 'children left behind to be cared for by others'.

There are around 58 million such children in China, according to statistics assembled by the All-China Women's Federation. This figure represents 28.29 per cent of all rural children. Among these children, more than 40 million are under the age of fourteen.

A variety of studies indicate that 'children left behind' suffer from a number of problems as compared with other control groups. These include malnutrition, poor study habits, bad performance in school, and so on. (Gao Wenshu, 2009; Su Fengjie, 2009). Many of these children suffer from psychological problems due to emotional deprivation. They are impassive, mentally closed, and defensive.

Box 2.1 Education of the children of rural migrant workers
under a state of 'quasi-urbanization'

Yang Yang's story: Yang Yang came to Shanghai along with her parents
when she was five years old. She first enrolled in a school run exclusively
for the children of rural migrant workers. In 2006, the school's building
was taken away from them and Yang Yang and her younger sister were
transferred to a public school. In this middle school, however, children of
rural migrant workers were taught in a separate class. The registration
number of this class was '5', and the class lumped children from a
preschool age up to grade 3. As a result, '5' became the code name for the
'class for peasant children'. In 2008, at the time Yang Yang was graduating
from junior high school, the Shanghai municipality issued a policy stating
that the children of rural migrant workers could attend mid-level vocational
secondary schools for free. Yang Yang's dream in life was to be a
supremely fine street dancer, but instead she enrolled in a certain vo-tech
school and opted for a course in hotel management. The reason was there
were only three courses in this school that actually had positions for children of rural migrant workers, and the other two were in digitally controlled
machine tooling and cooking. Among the other students who graduated
from middle school with Yang Yang, five boys and one girl elected to
enroll in vo-tech education in Shanghai. Three other boys elected to return
to their home towns for a high-school education. Another three girls felt
that it would be a waste of time to go to school and not make any money
in the process, so they apprenticed themselves to different trades. In the
second half of 2009, Yang Yang became embroiled in a dispute between
different 'gangs' in her school and was ordered to leave the school by the
authorities.

This is only one example of the situations faced by the children of rural
migrant workers, but it illustrates some of the issues that occur and that
lead to dropping out of secondary vocational school. This specific example
is by no means an exception.

'Children have an invisible ceiling above them, once they graduate from
middle school', remarked the principle of a school run exclusively for the
children of rural migrant workers.

Current policies that relate to continuing education state that, once the
children of rural migrant workers have graduated from middle school, they
must return to their original place of residence to attend high school. They
also must return to their original homes to sit for the national college
entrance exam. Many of these children were raised in the city, however.
Many were even born in the city or came when they were quite young.
They are essentially urbanites, and they face multiple problems when
returning to life and schooling in the countryside. Often, children find the

option unacceptable, yet they are barred from further education in the city and they are still too young to be hired for proper jobs. As a result, they give up school altogether and become aimless. They spend time in internet cafes, or game rooms, and some turn to a life of crime.

Bibliography

Xiong Yihan: *Grass-roots, schools and class reproduction*, The Opening Age, 2010, issue 1.
Zhang Kezhen: *Find solutions for these children*, People's Daily, March 23, 2007.
Zhang Yulin: *China's education: inequity expansion and its impetus*, 21st Century (online version), 2005, May issue.

They lack self-confidence and distrust others. In addition, their safety is at risk since they easily become vulnerable targets for harmful activity. This mishandling of human resources is generated by the whole issue of 'quasi-urbanization'. In the end, the problems can lead to poverty and to a form of social segmentation that is passed down from one generation to the next.

A second major issue relating to rural migrant workers involves healthcare. Children of rural migrant workers are unable to receive public healthcare and basic medical services on an equal basis with others, even though they live in cities. Children living in cities are immunized against diseases at only a very low rate. Rural migrant workers are not fully covered by the disease prevention and monitoring systems of urban areas, nor are they included in systems that offer birth-control services in urban areas. Rural migrant workers are not incorporated in urban medical assistance programs (for major illnesses), so there is no way they can receive the same treatment as urban residents. It is hard for people in general to get in to see a doctor, but it is even harder for rural migrant workers.

A third issue relates to overly low coverage of social security for rural migrant workers. First, the premiums are high, which creates a substantial barrier to entry; second, the mobility of workers prevents them from qualifying, given the one-year time requirement. As a result, very few rural migrant workers enroll in pension insurance. Moreover, management of pension plans in China is handled by different levels of government, while various regions have different and unrelated policies and systems. It is hard for mobile workers to transfer their plans and have ongoing coverage, another main factor affecting the participation of workers in such plans. In 2009, employers or 'units' paid the following percentages in to various kinds of insurance for rural migrant workers: 7.6 per cent of pension insurance, 21.8 per cent of industrial injury insurance, 12.2 per cent of medical insurance, 3.9 per cent of unemployment insurance and 2.3 per cent of childbirth insurance.

Relatively speaking, rural migrant workers who are engaged in the manufacturing sector are in a somewhat better position so far as social insurance is concerned. The construction industry is different. Occupational hazards are high in the construction trade, yet only 15.6 per cent of premiums for job-related insurance are paid for by the employer. This is far below the amount required by the *Regulations on Industrial Injury Insurance*. Meanwhile, the number of rural migrant workers choosing to pay for insurance of various kinds is extremely low: 1.8 per cent get pension insurance, 4.4 per cent get medical insurance, and only 1 per cent get unemployment insurance.

Box 2.2 Inadequate protection of the rights of rural migrant
            workers means that they are subject to higher rates of
            occupational disease

The great majority of rural migrant workers work in jobs that involve heavy labor and that are dangerous and dirty. Occupational hazards are common, yet most of the enterprises that hire the workers do not take preventive measures against occupational diseases. Some fail to monitor the dust and toxic materials emanating from the workplace; most fail to inform workers of occupational hazards and possible consequences, and they do not organize physical check-ups for workers or provide equipment to prevent potential problems. Many even evade their responsibilities by refusing to sign employment contracts with the workers and by constantly changing workers, sometimes rotating workers out every half year. These actions lower costs for the enterprise, but greatly increase the likelihood that workers will contract diseases. They transgress the legitimate rights and interests of workers, in terms of their safety and their health. In the end, the price has to be borne by the workers themselves and by society at large.

1   Two years ago, several dozen rural migrant workers contracted a 'strange disease' all at the same time. The workers had returned to their homes in Xiangjiaba Town, Shuifu County, Shaotong City, Yunnan Province, after working in a gravel plant in Fengyang County, Anhui Province. Twelve of them, strong young men, suddenly died one after another. The initial results of an investigation conducted by the Ministry of Health indicated that the cause of death was a lung disease called anthraco-silicosis. This is the most common kind of pneumoconiosis, and the kind that progresses most rapidly and does the most severe damage. Once the incident was discovered, the local government did check-ups on 400 other workers who had worked in the Shiying Gravel Plant in Anhui province, and discovered that 30 other men had also contracted the disease.

2   Starting in June of 2004, a rural migrant worker named Zhang
     Haichao worked in a variety of dangerous jobs at a materials plant
     in Zhengzhou City, Henan Province. He served as general laborer,
     rock crusher, and high-pressure drill operator, among other jobs,
     for three years, before he became ill and was diagnosed as having
     contracted pneumoconiosis. Several different hospitals made the same
     diagnosis, but the enterprise he had worked for refused to provide
     information on the case and the Zhengzhou Occupational Disease
     Prevention Center refused to agree that the problem was pneumo-
     coniosis. Instead, the Center said that it was merely tuberculosis. In
     order to get at the truth, this young 28-year-old went to the Hospital
     Number One associated with the Zhengzhou University, where he
     insisted that his chest be opened up to examine the true state of affairs.
     In this manner, he was able to publicize a very heart-rending story as
     a lesson to others.

3   The Ministry of Health issued a report in 2009, the *National Report
     on Occupational Diseases*. This report revealed statistics relating
     to the incidence of pneumoconiosis among rural migrant workers
     who worked in State-owned coal mines. As high as 4.74 per cent
     of those rural migrant workers who were given health examinations
     had contracted the disease. The shortest length of time recorded for
     contracting the disease was only 1.5 years, while the average length of
     time was 6.69 years. Among 'officially hired' workers in coal mines,
     the shortest length of time for contracting the disease was 25 years,
     and the incidence was 0.89 per cent. Occupational diseases among
     rural migrant workers are characterized by the very brief time it takes
     to contract a disease and by the high incidence of those who get the
     disease. Among occupational diseases, pneumoconiosis is the most
     prevalent.

     Most occupational diseases have a long latency period and a delayed
     onset of symptoms. Since rural migrant workers are highly mobile and
     tend not to take care of themselves, many of their diseases show up
     only after they have moved on to other jobs or returned to their native
     homes. This makes it hard for them to know where they contracted the
     disease and to press for compensation, let alone early treatment. The
     result is that not only is the person himself afflicted by the disease, but
     often his entire family has to bear a heavy financial burden.

Bibliography

Workers Daily, 25 May 2010.
*Rural migrant workers find it difficult to safeguard health rights after contracting
    occupational diseases*, Legal Express, 1 February 2010.

The fourth major issue relating to rural migrant workers involves the fact that they are not included in the urban housing-security system that applies to regular urban dwellers. In 2009, the National Bureau of Statistics issued a report, the *2009 Report on Rural Migrant Workers: Investigative Survey*. This report indicates that 33.9 per cent of rural migrant workers who were surveyed were living in dormitories provided by the employer or 'unit' involved; 10.3 per cent were living in 'work sheds' adjacent to construction sites; 7.6 per cent were living on-site in production facilities; 17.5 per cent were living in communally rented housing; 17.1 per cent were living in independently rented housing; 9.3 per cent were living in their own homes after working daily in locations outside their home town; and only 0.8 per cent were living in housing they had purchased.

Rural migrant workers who live in cities are a distinctly low-income group of people, and they therefore can only afford housing that is cheap and generally remote. On average, each person spends RMB 245 on housing, which is 17 per cent of the average monthly income. These figures vary slightly in different regions. In the Yangtze River Delta area, rural migrant workers spend RMB 350.78 each month on housing, which constitutes one-third to one-quarter of their income (these figures come from a survey of 16 cities, including rural migrant workers in Jiangsu, Zhejiang, and Shanghai). The standard stay in one place is 21.18 months, which is more than enough to qualify the workers for the six-month requirement for permanent residence in a city (Mo Jianbei et al., 2007).

According to a separate survey, conducted in Shanghai, Guangzhou, Wuhan, Chengdu, and Fuyang, the housing conditions of rural migrant workers are far worse than those of local urban residents.[3] Housing is crowded and miserable. Subsidized public housing has not been made available to rural migrant workers, and municipal governments in each place in fact are simply allowing the situation to take its own course, forcing rural migrant workers to take care of themselves as best they can. Their housing needs are quite separate from the whole system of guaranteed housing [or housing security].

How workers are housed has a severe impact on their quality of life. Housing is one of the greatest obstacles to enabling rural migrant workers to become normal urban citizens, and it is one of the toughest issues facing housing in China overall.

The fifth issue relates to the rights and interests of rural migrant workers, which are inadequately protected by safeguards. One problem that was outstanding several years ago has been improved to a certain degree, namely employers being 'in arrears' on their wage payments to workers. In 2009, the percentage of workers who were not being paid had come down to 1.8 per cent of the total. Other issues remain, however, such as the very long hours put in by workers. Surveys indicate that the average worker works 26 days of the month and 58.4 hours each week. Some 89.9 per cent of all rural migrant workers work more than the legally mandated 44 hours per week. A small percentage of workers sign actual contracts with employers – around 60 per cent do not have a contract.

Rural migrant workers 'roam outside the political life' of municipal governments, and so laws that protect their rights and interests are generally not a part of urban policy formulation. One very important point is that there is a direct link between the elections system and the 'household registration' system. According to current laws and regulations, rural migrant workers are not allowed to participate in elections outside their official place of residence.

A sixth issue relates to 'social protections' for rural migrant workers, which are very low. These workers are increasingly marginalized as a result and begin to constitute a social threat. In the process of urbanizing, many of the more developed cities are rapidly expanding in area and building up newly encompassed areas with extensive construction projects. The result is a large number of 'villages within cities' in such places as the Pearl River delta area, the Yangtze River delta area, the Bohai gulf, and the main centrally administered cities and provincial capitals.[4]

Since core-city rental prices are higher than workers can afford, most rural migrant workers live within these villages within cities, in appalling housing conditions. Although these areas provide rural migrant workers with a 'platform' on which to survive, the places themselves are often the 'dead corners' of cities, in that municipal governance scarcely enters into them. They feature high-density populations, poor sanitary conditions, grossly inadequate public facilities, and complex forms of maintaining social order. In addition to rural migrant workers, some college students also take up residence in such areas (see Box 2.3), since they too cannot afford the high rents of better districts. Marginalized, on the edges of urban life, the groups of people living in these areas have come to be known as 'ant heaps'.

Box 2.3 The current conditions of 'villages within the city of Kunming', and associated problems

At the end of 2007, there were 336 'villages' within an area of 249 square kilometers, a space that includes the main built-up area of the city of Kunming. The amount of space occupied by these villages covers 38.71 million square meters, a space that houses roughly one million people. The population density in these villages is around 50,000 per square kilometer.

Certain aspects of the villages located within Kunming's official 'planned municipal district' are as follows.

- Illegal use of land is rampant. 'Villages within cities' often take advantage of their proximity to city centers in order to make money from leasing land. The land is collectively owned. In 2004, the municipal government of Kunming cracked down on more than 8000 cases of illegal land use, involving nearly 130,000 mu [21,411 acres] of land. Most of these cases occurred within the 'villages within the city'.

- Illegally constructed buildings are commonplace and building density is extremely high. Given that occupancy is also high, removing people to do renovation work is difficult. When the municipal government decides to undertake demolition work, 'villagers' demand exorbitant compensation rates for extra floors that they have illegally constructed on top of buildings. The illegal construction has severely compromised the original harmonious architecture and layout of the villages. Building is done in a chaotic and ramshackle fashion.
- Municipal facilities are nil, with an impact on environmental quality. Moreover, the villages are aggressively expanding their building activities, so that any spaces for public activities (including 'green spaces') are disappearing. Roads in the villages are generally winding and lack public utilities, so that rainwater drainage and sewage flow together. Electric power and telecommunications lines are a mess; natural gas pipelines do not access the areas; the capacity of water supply lines is inadequate in terms both of delivering water and of draining out used water; other public-service facilities are lacking as well.
- Social problems are pronounced. Many of the original villagers are idle since they earn a living off rental properties. The younger ones become known as the 'four do-nothings' (don't farm, don't study, don't do business, and don't work). With no effective supervision governing a fast-growing population made up of outsiders, the rental properties of 'villages within cities' often become hotbeds for incubating various kinds of crime.
- Disaster prevention and relief systems are weak. Safety hazards abound. There is no control over building standards in the construction going on in the villages, so there are basically no fire escapes and no rescue corridors. Geological conditions are not taken into consideration when building, nor is the need for earthquake mitigation.

Source: *Largest People's Project in Kunming: Renovation of 'Villages in City'*, Kunming Daily, www.yn.xinhuanet.com/newscenter/2010-05/29/content_ 19922914.htm

Finally, the 'irrational' [or uncoordinated] way in which the labor force moves around is also distorting the structure of rural populations. China's current mode of urbanization operates on the basis of the long-term *de facto* urban residency of a mobile population, but since rural migrant workers and their families have not been given the option of establishing permanent official residency in cities, the age structure of urban and rural areas is gradually being inverted. The productivity of the urban population is rising, but at the same time rural areas are seeing an increasingly aging population. A structural change is therefore going on in urban and rural populations. What this means is that rural areas are paying the price for enabling cities to extend the period over which they enjoy a population dividend. [The population dividend refers to a limited window of opportunity in China when plenty of strong young labor is available for economic growth, due to the bulge of young people going through the demographics.]

The absolute necessity of converting rural migrant workers into urban residents

Over the course of nearly 30 years, the rural migrant worker phenomenon has moved into becoming a 'next generation', and new trends and characteristics are beginning to develop. The very reason we call these people 'rural migrant workers' is that we have always assumed they will one day be returning to the countryside. We have assumed that once they become too old or run into trouble finding a job, they will go back to their own original residences and use their 'contracted land' as their social security.

Even if this may or may not have been true in the past, it is no long in accord with what is happening now. Short-term jobs are no longer the primary form of employment for rural migrant workers in urban areas. The general situation now is that people who have moved from one region to another, in the course of leaving their original place of residence, have now transitioned from being 'part-farmer part-worker' to being 'full-time worker and not farmer at all'. A two-way flow between urban and rural in terms of human mobility has changed into full-time residence in cities. What was regarded as 'supplemental income' from urban jobs has now turned into 'lifelong employment'. More and more rural migrant workers are not only unwilling but unable to return to the countryside.

Rural migrant workers have turned into the mainstay of the national economy and are indispensable to its ongoing development. Economic operations require their contribution to creating wealth

According to data resulting from the Fifth National Population Census taken in 2000, rural migrant workers now constitute 58 per cent of the workforce in secondary industries and 52 per cent of the workforce in tertiary industries. They represent 68 per cent of the workforce in processing and manufacturing industries and 80 per cent of the workforce in the construction industry. Additional data from the National Bureau of Statistics shows that, in 2006, there were 47.124 million rural migrant workers engaged in processing and manufacturing and 27.06 million rural migrant workers engaged in construction work. As compared with 2002, these 2006 figures had gone up by 104.6 per cent and 55.7 per cent respectively.

By 2008, rural migrant workers had come to constitute 43.5 per cent of the entire employed workforce of non-agricultural labor. This figure was 8.4 per cent more than it had been in 2005 (*Center for Reform and Development of Cities and Towns of the National Development and Reform Commission, 2009*).

These statistics show how thoroughly rural migrant workers have become the primary body of labor in China's industries, and the primary force behind the creation of national wealth.

Given this *de facto* situation, it is no longer possible to imagine asking them to return to the countryside. The economy can no longer do without them. Without rural migrant workers, not only would the economy no longer function, but cities would cease to operate. The issues no longer relate to whether or not rural migrant workers should 'go back', but rather to how economic growth is inextricably tied to rural migrant workers.

The employment of rural migrant workers is far more stable than it was in the past, which considerably improves the ability of these people to 'stay on' in cities

A fairly large percentage of rural migrant workers have now completely disassociated themselves from agricultural production and live and work year-round 'on the outside', that is, away from their former homes. A considerable percentage of these people have taken their families with them and essentially moved away from the countryside, severing any ties to agricultural production but also any remaining links to rural society. Another component of rural migrant workers cannot be included among those who 'take families and head out', but rather belongs to a category that has married and had children in their new locale. Such people, both those who moved with families and those who created families after moving, have already been in an urban setting for a minimum of three to five years. Many have been in urban areas for over ten years.

According to a survey conducted by the Ministry of Agriculture, 57.8 per cent of those workers who had 'gone out' to find work in 2005 now had stable jobs. In 2009, the average monthly salary of a rural migrant worker was RMB 1417. Workers with incomes that exceeded RMB 1600 came to 27.3 per cent of those surveyed. Such workers, living year-round in cities either with or without their families, have been assimilated into urban life to a considerable degree. Their skills, income, and capabilities are now such that they can support an ongoing urban existence, albeit it at a fairly low level. Their ability to find employment is, in many cases, no less than that of legitimate urban residents. The only thing that differentiates them is their social 'status', that is, their inferior official standing as non-urban residents.

The percentage of next-generation rural migrant workers is constantly increasing, and these young people have a ferocious desire to be assimilated into urban life

Rural migrant workers are already in a period of transition from one generation to the next. They are in the final stages of shifting from the first to the second generation, in that the children of those workers who came into cities in the 1980s and 1990s are now beginning to constitute the main body of the workforce.

In addition, the workforce is shifting out of mere quantitative-type production into more qualitative-type production. The next generation, with higher levels of education, is helping transform the 'made in China' brand into one that is far more competitive.

In 2009, workers who were between ages 16 and 30 constituted 60 per cent of the rural migrant labor workforce, that is, they were born after the 1980s. This next-generation of workers shares the following characteristics. First, it is better educated. More than 26 per cent of workers who are under the age of 30 have received at least a high-school education. The percentage goes up to 31.1 per cent for those next-generation workers who are between the ages of 21 and 25. Second, next-generation workers have lost the ability to do any farming. By their household residency they are officially 'farmers', or 'rural residents', but in fact the great majority of them began to work immediately after leaving school and have never engaged in any kind of agricultural production. They lack any basic skills associated with agriculture. Third, next-generation rural migrant workers have quite attenuated feelings about 'the land'. Their mentality, lifestyles, and behavior, are thoroughly urbanized. Their city work is not regarded as something by which to earn extra income, in addition to farm income, but rather as their lifelong occupation. Not only do they not farm, but they have no concept of just how big a 'mu' is [0.1647 acre]. Next-generation rural migrant workers have a totally different concept of what their lives will hold as compared with that of their parents. Their parents intended to 'make a few bucks by working [in cities], then go back and build a home, get married, have children'. Instead, this generation has no intention of engaging in any kind of farming.

The phenomenon of 'landless' rural migrant workers has begun to mean that these people rely even more exclusively on making their living in cities

The term 'landless rural migrant workers' refers to those who no longer have any 'contracted land' that they can farm in the countryside. Two factors have caused this. One is having more children than family planning policies allow, that is, having what are called 'outside-the-plan children'. Policies prevent such people from being allocated a portion of collective land. The second is those children who were born after their parents signed 30-year contracts to farm specific plots of land now join the ranks of 'rural migrant workers' once they become adults.

The Labor and Social Security Bureau of Fuyang City in Anhui Province has gathered statistics on its local situation. According to its research, there are 600,000 'landless rural migrant workers' among the total of 2.28 million rural migrant workers in Fuyang. The number of 'landless' workers is now increasing at a rate of 100,000 per year. Based on the ratio of landed to landless as measured in Fuzhou, China currently has around 30 million 'landless rural migrant workers', nationwide.

In addition, land is being 'requisitioned' at low prices throughout China to the extent that more than one million farmers are losing their land every year.[5]

Table 2.3 Land conditions of rural migrant workers in the Yangtze River delta

	No. of samples	Landless		Land idling		Spouse-operated		Self-operated		Sub-contracted	
		No. of samples	%	No. of samples	%	No. of samples	%	No. of samples	%	No. of samples	%
Jiangsu	2836	911	32.12	214	7.54	296	10.43	822	28.98	593	20.91
Zhejiang	2036	512	25.14	—	—	158	7.76	736	36.15	630	30.94
Shanghai	2575	462	17.94	42	1.63	857	33.28	587	22.79	627	24.34
Total	7447	1885	25.31	256	3.43	1311	16.6	2145	28.8	1850	24.84

Source: Mo Jianbei et al. (ed.): *Integration and Development – An Investigation of Rural Migrant Workers in 16 Cities in Yangtze River Delta*, Shanghai People's Publishing House, 2007, p. 27.

Our justification for not allowing rural migrant workers to become urban residents has always been that farmland is the social security of these people, and can provide them with a job once they return. Where is the 'security' for a landless rural migrant worker? These people would find it very hard to 'return to the land', and are in fact facing a permanent future of living and working in cities.

Converting rural migrant workers into urban residents has an impact on the whole issue of 'modernizing' and 'building up' the country

A general consensus formed after the onset of the global financial crisis to the effect that China's main source of domestic demand in the future would come from cities and 'urbanization'. Without turning rural migrant workers into urban residents, however, cities cannot be a sustainable engine for ongoing economic growth.

In the past decade, China's urbanization rate has been increasing every year at the high rate of 1.2 percentage points. Domestic demand, and particularly consumer demand, has not increased at a comparable rate, however, and the fundamental reason is that 'urbanization' in the country has not included turning rural migrant workers into urban residents.

Everyone is talking about the various things that relate to urbanization, how domestic demand is insufficient, how service industries are lagging behind, unemployment is a huge problem, urban-rural income disparities are terrible, we have unbalanced regional development, we are taking over too much farmland for building purposes, and so on. Instead of saying that these things are all intimately related to urbanization, however, in China it is more accurate to say that they are intimately related to the issue of converting rural migrant workers into urban residents.

This is not a small issue. It cannot be encapsulated by the phrase 'three agricultures' [*san-nong*], or issues that derive from the three, namely agriculture, farmers, and rural areas. Instead, it is a far larger subject that must incorporate the question of the sustainability of China's mode of economic growth in the future. It must address the whole question of 'building up' and 'modernizing' China.

There are at least six advantages to converting rural migrant workers into urban residents, as described below.

1 'Converting rural migrant workers into urban residents' contributes to expansion of domestic demand, which facilitates the transformation of China's mode of economic growth

The 'demand-pull' economic function of increased consumption is an important part of transitioning to a new mode of economic growth. There are only three paths to expanding consumption. One is increasing the rate of employment, that is, turning unemployed people into people with an income who are therefore willing to increase consumption. The second is increasing the income of people who are employed, which involves adjusting the structure of employment distribution and increasing the percentage of the national income that goes into personal incomes. Once incomes are higher, consumption increases. The third is getting people with employment and an income to spend more. There are many ways to do this. They include improving the environment for consuming, increasing the availability of services-type consumption, and reducing anxieties that may attend spending more. This last involves improving governmental functions in providing public services, making consumers dare to spend more, enabling consumers to switch funds from the perceived need for future services that they have to pay for themselves to current spending on personal items.

In stimulating those people who are employed and have an income to spend more, the greatest potential lies in turning rural migrant workers into urban residents. In the past, our policies that were intended to increase consumption have focused mainly on investment. During the Asian financial crisis of 1998, the policy emphasis was placed on urban residents, and during the 2008 global financial crisis, the policy emphasis was on rural residents. Both times, however, policies aimed at stimulating demand overlooked the potential of a group with massive consuming potential, namely rural migrant workers who are neither 'urban' nor 'rural'.

Consumption demand depends on 'people' in order to be realized. Stimulating consumption can be achieved by focusing on people who already have higher intentions and ability to consume, or it can focus on expanding the numbers contained in that group. Since urban consumption basically relates to 'purchasing consumption', there is very little if any 'self-supplied consumption'. When urban and rural incomes are the same, therefore, urban 'purchasing consumption' will exceed the consumption of rural residents. To a country that is in the midst of economic development, expanding the size of the urban population is synonymous with expanding consumption.

In broad terms, it is not inaccurate to say that rural migrant workers consume less because they earn less. A deeper analysis shows that this conclusion is simplistic, however. Lower incomes are not the sole reason for less consumption. The lower consumption of rural migrant workers is also determined by the unique status of these people. They are subject to what can be called the 'four disassociations':

1   The 'household registration' [*hu-ji*] of a rural migrant worker is disassociated from his place of employment. He is registered in a rural area, but works in a city.
2   His actual place of residence is disassociated from the location of his 'home'. For most of the year, a rural migrant worker lives at the worksite, the place where he is employed. He also generally possesses a 'home' in his hometown. Workers who have 'taken their families along' with them to live in cities generally have vacant homes in the countryside for most of the year, except for the time they may be back to spend the spring-festival holiday period.[6]

3   Workers are separated from those they may be supporting. The majority of rural migrant workers are labouring 'solo' on the 'the outside', while the children or parents they are supporting have remained back in the countryside.

4   The place a person earns an income and the place he spends that income are different. Workers very rarely spent their income where they have earned it, in the city. Instead, the earnings are mainly spent back in the countryside, where they are used for such things as weddings and funerals, building or improving a residence, education and medical services, and for taking care of parents as well as being saved to provide for their own old age.

If rural migrant workers are permitted to 'settle down' by taking up permanent residence in the cities in which they are working, and if they are able to have the guarantee of the same housing, education, medical treatment, social insurance, and other public services as regular urban residents, they will gradually change their mode of consumption. Their consumption patterns will begin to resemble those of the existing urban population. They will either rent or purchase places in which they live more permanently; they will fix up the rooms, purchase the necessary household appliances, and, since they are now able to live together with family members, they will buy items for daily use and spend money on family recreation, entertainment, and tourism. Once they are no longer as apprehensive about taking care of their own old age, about losing their jobs, paying medical costs, paying fees for education, and so on, they will be more willing to spend their limited income on improving the immediate quality of their lives.

In conclusion, if rural migrant workers and their families are permitted to 'settle down' as regular urban residents in cities, they will consume more and will consume at levels more in line with their levels of income. Each person's consumption capacity may well be quite small and his personal contribution to increased consumption may be tiny, but the number of rural migrant workers, plus their families, is enormous. The potential for increased consumption overall is not trivial.

2 *'Converting rural migrant workers into urban residents' contributes to accelerated development of service industries which in turn relieves the pressures of unemployment*

Any fundamental resolution of the problem of the 'three agricultures', namely agriculture itself, farmers, and rural economies, must involve reducing the number of farmers and creating more non-agricultural jobs. To create non-agricultural positions, we must grow the country's service industries, and to grow service industries, we must promote the transformation of rural migrant workers into legitimate urban residents.

The crux of the difficulties involved in the 'three agricultures' lies in China's scarcity of land and water resources and its excessive number of 'farmers'. It is very hard to change the natural environment with respect to land and water, but the last consideration, an excessive number of farmers, is one that can be addressed.

Resolving the 'three agricultures', therefore, requires both conserving land and reducing the number of farmers. While decreasing the number of farmers requires the creation of more job opportunities, it does not imply that all rural labor needs to be shifted into industry. The experience of developing countries around the world has shown that, in the initial period of industrialization, industry has been the primary route to shifting a rural labor force into other occupations. Once industrialization enters a middle stage, however, and urbanization develops, service industries begin to supplant industry and become a major creator of employment positions. They become the primary sector absorbing the rural labor force.

In the early stage of industrialization in America, between 1820 and 1890, the ratio between a net increase in jobs in secondary industries and jobs in tertiary industries was 1:1.65. Between 1890 to 1998, the ratio changed to 1:3.72.

In China, between 1952 and 2008, the ratio between a net increase in jobs in secondary industries and jobs in tertiary industries was 1:1.21, even lower than it had been during the initial period of industrialization in nineteenth-century America.

Services industries are one important channel for expanding employment, but the scale to which these industries can be developed is closely related to the degree to which people are concentrated in certain areas. A key attribute of service industries is that the great majority of them are both produced and consumed in the same time and place. This is quite unlike industrial and agricultural products, which can be made in one place and used in another. A second key attribute of service industries is that they require a 'threshold population'. Only when populations reach certain levels can service industries be run like a business and become profitable. Only then can markets be further segmented, allowing for greater division of labor in society and a constant increase in services and employment positions.

Currently in China, on the periphery of certain extra-large cities and large cities, one finds a profusion of 'villages within cities' that are composed mainly of rural migrant workers. There is no industry to speak of in these areas. The reason people can live in them, and be employed, is that the density of the population has reached a size that enables it to provide services for itself and to provide employment positions for itself. A sufficient concentration of people is the prerequisite for service industries. If one disregards this rule, and separates out the process of industrialization from urbanization, and urbanization from developing service industries, then naturally it will be quite hard for service industries to grow.

The size of service industries is generally closely related to the degree to which a population is urban. Some 67 per cent of the value-added amount of China's service industries is created by 236 urban areas that are administered at the prefectural level and above. The value-added amount of service industries constitutes 52 per cent of the GDP ratio of China's mega-cities. The figure is 46 per cent for the country's 'super-large cities', 42 per cent for its 'large cities', 38 per cent for its medium-sized cities, and 34 per cent for its small cities. The percentage of employment contributed by service industries in mega-cities is 52 per cent, in super-large cities 48 per cent, in large cities 44 per cent, and in medium and small cities 45 per cent. In Liaoning province, 49 per cent of service industries are created in the two cities of Shenyang and Dalian. In Jilin province, 55 per cent of service industries are created in Changchun and Jilin City. In Zhejiang province, 27 per cent of service industries are created by Hangzhou and Ningbo. In Fujian province, 30 per cent of service industries are created by Fuzhou and Xiamen. In Guangdong province, 48 per cent of service industries are created by Guangzhou and Shenzhen. In Shanxi, Hainan, and Hubei provinces, between 40 per cent and 45 per cent of service industries are created by the capital cities of those provinces.

3 'Converting rural migrant workers into urban residents' is fundamental in helping narrow the income disparities between rural and urban areas

A three-pronged approach should be taken in narrowing the differential between urban and rural incomes. First, [we should] promote a shift of rural populations into cities that have greater job opportunities and higher income potential. That is equivalent to lowering the denominator. Second, [we should] do everything possible to modernize agriculture, which is equivalent to increasing the numerator. Third, [we should] set up sustainable mechanisms that actually achieve the stated policy intent of 'having urban areas pay back the investment put into them by rural areas, and having cities contribute to the support of the countryside'.

In recent years, attention has been focused on the second and third of these three measures, but policies addressing the first measure have been incomplete. That is, they have allowed the movement of farmers into cities to find jobs, but they have not allowed those farmers to 'settle down' there and become permanent urban residents.

The corresponding metrics for measuring urban populations have similarly been incomplete. When measuring 'urbanization', rural migrant workers have been included in the statistics as urban residents; when measuring income, they have been included in the statistics as rural residents and their income has been noted as that of 'farmers'. This erroneous statistical approach has led to the false impression of an ongoing and increasingly large disparity between rural and urban incomes. The practice is creating very considerable political pressures.

The gap between urban and rural incomes is too great [*guo-da*]. This is a fact. But is it similarly a fact that the gap between the incomes of 'urban residents' and 'rural residents' is increasing [*kuo-da*]? 'Too great' and 'increasing' are two separate issues. A deeper analysis of income disparities shows that if rural migrant workers and their families were permitted to 'settle down' officially in cities and take up permanent residence, it would resolve the issue of 'increasing' disparities even if it did not resolve the issue of 'overly great' disparities. The greater the population that is shifted into cities, the greater the rate at which disparities are reduced. If one assumes that right now there are a total of 300 million rural migrant workers and their family members, and makes the assumption that all 300 million settle down in cities, then the income of these people becomes counted as that of the urban as opposed to the rural population. One then finds that the metric as currently measured of 3.33 (with urban incomes being 3.33 times higher than rural incomes), goes down to 2.42.[7]

4 'Converting rural migrant workers into urban residents' contributes to more intensive use of land

Due to excessive loss of arable land, China is facing a massive challenge in guaranteeing its national food security as well as maintaining its capacity for sustained economic growth. Who exactly is 'occupying' the arable land? Much of the blame can be put on urbanization, the building of basic infrastructure, and the construction of all kinds of 'development zones'. At the same time, the amount of arable land being taken over by rural construction is considerable.

Between 1996 and 2007, the amount of arable land used for building cities was 6787 square kilometers. The amount used for building 'administered towns' was 6056 kilometers, while the amount used for building 'residential districts in rural areas' took up 1783 square kilometers. The latter two rural uses of land exceeded the amount used for city construction. Moreover, a large percentage of the arable land that has gone into construction has been used for housing, and the amount used for housing in rural areas has greatly exceeded the amount used for housing in urban areas.

More than a dozen times as much land is currently being used per capita to build housing units in rural areas than it is in urban areas. The reason is that rural migrant workers, unable to settle down permanently in cities and therefore unable to purchase or rent housing, are choosing to build in the countryside. If each of 145 million rural migrant workers built a home for himself in the countryside that occupied 180 square meters of land, it would require a total of 35 million mu of land nationwide. More significantly, if this generation builds, the next may well want to do the same. If one supposes that in fact 300 million rural migrant workers return home to build housing on that scale, the amount of land required may approach 100 million mu.

We doubt that such a situation will come to pass, for, if it did, it would be calamitous for China's long-term development as a nation.

When rural migrant workers are unable to become urban residents, the result is that they and their family members 'take up double space' in both urban and rural areas. China's land resources are insufficient to an extreme degree when it comes to satisfying the needs of economic development and urbanization. Both of these occupy land, but in addition, agricultural production requires that the country preserve at a very minimum 1.8 billion mu of arable land.

In addition, in order to satisfy the need for 'ecological goods', such as water and air, and to address such problems as water scarcity, climate warming, and resource and environmental issues, we absolutely must secure the conservation of an adequate amount of land for 'green ecology', and expand that amount if possible. There is only one possible solution among three difficult choices: we must adjust the spatial usage of land, we must use every inch in the most intensive ways possible in order to satisfy all the various demands on it.

Permitting rural migrant workers to settle down in cities is one way to conserve land, the reason being that land is used in a far more intensive manner in cities than it is used in the countryside and the amount occupied for housing is less. 'Urbanizing' migrant rural labor is a way to use a spatial reconfiguration of 'people' in order to adjust the structural use of land.

Wages of rural migrant workers are currently being adjusted and these people are seeing relatively large increases in pay. As a result, their purchasing power is entering into a critical period. If workers use their income as they have in the past, to build homes in the countryside, a calamitous situation as described above will be the swift result. There is no doubt about this. If, however, rural migrant workers become urban residents as a result of rational policy guidance, and they put this new income into consumption in urban areas, housing as well as other things, not only will this effectively conserve land, but it will increase domestic demand and therefore 'pull' forward economic growth.

5 'Converting rural migrant workers into urban residents' contributes to ongoing increases in the income of farmers, and to the development of modern agriculture in China

It is a mistake to think that all one needs to do to turn rural migrant workers into urban citizens is focus in a limited way on 'farming' and 'rural affairs'. The core issue of the 'three agricultures' is people. It is indeed farmers, their income, and the sustained growth of their income, but merely relying on 'agriculture' and 'rural issues' will not be sufficient to address the problems on ongoing increases in farmers' income. Moreover, the elasticity of demand for agricultural products, as well as income from agricultural products, is limited. There is very little margin for increasing income just by increasing prices. As a result, one cannot rely solely on increasing yields of farm products, and raising their prices, in order to bring the current income levels of farmers up to the levels of people in cities. Capitalizing rural land [turning it into an asset], can serve to increase the income of farmers, but at the same time this will vastly increase the costs of China's industrialization and its urbanization, as well as the building of its basic infrastructure. Moreover, capitalizing land can only resolve the income problems of a small number of farmers who live on the outskirts of cities.

We will not be able to increase rural incomes by focusing on improving the economies of rural areas alone. That is, we cannot grow county-level economies merely by developing town and village enterprises and creating small-town businesses. We have been hoping all along to solve problems of employment and improved incomes by doing these things, but after pursuing this approach for 30 years, we should recognize that some areas have indeed been successful but many others have not. Those that did well were those that were endowed with considerable resources or particular resources. The great majority of the top 100 counties in the country are either located in the mega-city areas or their neighboring regions, such as the Pearl River delta, the Yangtze River delta, and the Beijing–Tianjin area, or they have unique resources.

Nationwide, most other places do not enjoy these benefits. For those counties and towns that do not, not only will our exhorting them to do better not be productive, along with any preferential policies we extend, but will be counter-productive. It will in fact extract a heavy price. If we continue along this course, just the one consideration of the amount of land being occupied will become unbearable.

There are 2859 county-level 'administrative units' in China, nationwide. If each one of these sets up an 'industrial development region' of 5 square kilometers, the amount of land needed nationwide comes to 14,300 square kilometers. There are 34,369 towns and townships in the country. If each sets up an industrial district of 2 square kilometers, the amount of land used nationwide will be 68,500 square kilometers. Due to such land use, many regions will be unable to rely on agricultural production within their own localities to resolve the problem of ongoing increase in rural incomes.

The amount of arable land per capita in China comes to 1.37 mu [around one-fifth of an acre.] It is imperative that we use this precious resource in a highly efficient way. That is the minimum requirement for developing a modern form of agriculture, improving agricultural production, and increasing farmers' incomes. Similarly, in order to use land efficiently, at the very least we must have a labor force that is educated and manages this precious resource properly. At present, however, given our situation of 'quasi-urbanization', we have a farming population that is aging by the day. At the same time, given the uncertainties attending their inability to 'settle down' in cities, rural migrant workers are unwilling to let go of their contracted land, which prevents it from being consolidated and used efficiently.

Land currently cannot be farmed in quantities that allow for economies of scale, which makes it hard to realize any kind of modernized agriculture through mechanization and large-scale land use. This in turn forces the younger members of a farming community to leave the land in order to make a living. The aging of the farming population is further exacerbated, leading to a vicious cycle that is detrimental to improving incomes and modernizing agriculture.

6 'Converting rural migrant workers into urban residents' contributes to protecting the rights and interests of all China's people, and to furthering social harmony

Rural migrant workers have been marginalized for a long time now. They live on the fringes of cities. They are not accepted into communities and indeed are the object of discrimination, actual harmful behavior, and also neglect. The fact that they cannot assimilate into urban society and are deprived of their due rights has led to a host of social problems.

We have become aware of the fact that capital accumulation during the period of the planned economy in China was enabled by what we call the 'scissor-price differential' between industrial and agricultural products. Despite this recognition [of how farmers' labor was used to subsidize the industrializing of the country], we have failed to recognize the way in which 'quasi-urbanization' after the start of 'reform and opening up' similarly enabled a second wave of capital accumulation.

We have looked upon the supply of cheap and able-bodied labor from the countryside as being 'endless'. This labor supply accomplished the feat of turning China into a major exporter and a major global economy. Once the first-generation rural migrant worker population aged, however, and was unable to 'settle down' in the very cities in which it had paid for economic growth with blood, sweat, and tears, the aged and infirm among the generation has had no alternative but to return to their former towns and villages. As hundreds of millions of such rural migrant workers, now without any 'labor value', begin to return to the countryside, problems associated with their lack of any social security are going to be exacerbating social problems.

Most able-bodied youth of the next-generation labor force have by now migrated out of rural areas, leaving behind a population that is either old or very young. This has created a situation in which a large number of children are responsible for looking after the elderly, while elderly people are now responsible for the education and care of the children. As a result, many children are not in fact being educated or cared for and there is a certain vacuum when it comes to a proper upbringing. Many children have not seen their parents in years. Psychologically, they are growing up as orphans. Their personalities are solitary and they are estranged from their own relatives, to the extent that this too may result in social problems once they become adults.

A group of students from Wuhan University conducted a survey of the children of rural migrant workers. The survey indicated that 72 per cent of children chose not to go further with a high-school education upon graduating from middle school. Instead, 18 per cent chose to enter vo-tech schools to learn a skill, and 10 per cent elected to go directly into menial jobs. It is perhaps fine that children of rural migrant workers make their own decisions about their futures, but the fact that their educational level is grossly beneath that of urban children will not only lead to increasing disparities of income but it will be detrimental to the long-term development of these children. Apart from simply turning into 'rural migrant workers' themselves, these children should have other options.

The right to vote and the right to be elected to office are linked to one's place of 'household residence'. As a result, rural migrant workers who live elsewhere are unable to enjoy that right in their hometowns, nor are they allowed to participate in democratic elections in cities. They cannot participate in democratic decision-making, or management, or supervisory oversight. Their democratic rights are in fact in a state of suspension. They have all the conditions necessary to participate in urban elections except the fact that their electoral districts are defined as being back in the countryside. With no guarantee of their most basic rights and interests, they are unable to become 'urban citizens' in the full sense of the term.

Due to the way public policy is determined in municipalities, rural migrant workers are also unable to appeal effectively for their rights and interests. In their *de facto* places of residence, they are unable to participate in community self-governance. As a result, they have no sense of being 'members of the community' in those areas. Effective safeguards do not exist that ensure that these people are allowed to participate in community and municipal events, or the process of building their surrounding areas, or the process of managing their lives.

If we are to set up what we call a 'harmonious society', we must adhere to the principles of equity and justice. We must ensure that all members of the entire society possess equal rights and interests. Such rights and interests must include those of rural migrant workers, as well as members of their families. They should include the right to participate in the economic, political, cultural, social, and environmental improvement of the places in which they are working as laborers. Rural migrant workers too should enjoy the fruits of what we call the 'five great constructions', [or ways of 'building up' the country]. The 'harmonious society' that we are aiming for very clearly is not one in which several hundred million of our population fail to enjoy the rights of citizenship.

Orientation of policies that can turn rural migrant workers into proper urban residents

Converting a monumental number of people into urban residents is not only close to unique in the world's entire process of 'urbanization', and also a monumental challenge for China's ongoing socioeconomic development, but it is also a rare opportunity. The time is ripe right now for beginning the process. The 'carrying capacity' of cities is gradually improving. We should initiate action at the start of the 12th Five-Year Plan period in gradually resolving the issues of converting rural migrant workers and their family members into urban residents.

In the process, we should pay particular attention to the problems, demands, and new issues related to next-generation rural migrant workers. In this whole endeavor, the Central government must make its policies and terms of 'guidance' very explicit. While continuing to encourage each place to change its systems creatively and according to local realities, policy measures and objectives must now be made clear at the national level. Mere reliance on local initiatives and piecemeal, uncoordinated, efforts will lead not only to lack of clarity about this overall reform effort, but also to disparate policy approaches and a waste of resources. This will only create greater obstacles to reform in the future. Only by setting forth explicit objectives and laying out measures that are truly effective will we be able to accomplish our goals with the limited resources we have in hand. Only then will we be able to realize an orderly process of creating 'urban residents' and achieving full as opposed to quasi-urbanization. Only then will we realize the grand objective of creating a moderately prosperous society for all citizens.

1 Adopt principles that are voluntary, orderly, organized into specific categories, and yet coordinated by an overall plan

'Voluntary' means ensuring full respect for the wishes of rural migrant workers and their family members. Determination of a person's 'settlement locale' must be open and transparent and the rights and also obligations of rural migrant workers must be clarified on that basis. Those who are qualified to become urban residents and do so on a voluntary basis should be given urban-residency status. When rural migrant workers wish to remain 'part farmers and part workers', they should not be forced into becoming urban residents. It may be that the willingness of rural migrant workers to become urban residents will differ as their various conditions dictate.

For example, according to laws current in effect, if a rural migrant worker settles in a city that is administered at the prefectural level or above, he must surrender his contracted farmland. For people with uncertain employment prospects in cities, this may be an influencing factor. In addition, the willingness of people to become urban residents may be affected by whether or not they are incorporated into existing low-rent housing and the whole public-housing security system. In general, policies that are extremely transparent and explicit should be set up in order to clarify all conditions of 'settlement' [i.e., declaring one's place of residency], so that workers themselves can make rational decisions.

'Orderly' means gradually relaxing the conditions whereby rural migrant workers can declare an urban residency, and accepting a specific increase in urbanized rural migrant workers every year according to specific municipal conditions. Such conditions include the comprehensive carrying capacity of a city and its level of socioeconomic development.

It has taken a long time to arrive at our current figure of hundreds of millions of rural migrant workers. Resolving the issue of converting these people into urban residents will take a comparable period of time. We cannot deal with it in an overly rash way. We cannot, for example, simply abolish the 'hu-ji' system, allow 145 million rural migrant workers and their families to change their status overnight and 'settle down' wherever they are currently working.

Creating 'categories' means adopting policies that are tailored to specific situations in terms of the types of rural migrant workers, the regions in which they are living, and the actual situations of the municipalities in which they are located. It means formulating different categories of 'entry conditions' for different situations. It also means providing each region and each municipality with adequate autonomy in formulating policy, allowing it to craft entry provisions depending on its situation. Rural migrant workers may be divided into categories depending on their original place of residence, on their employment qualifications, on their occupations, and so on.

At an operational level, issues of rural migrant workers who hail from the immediate vicinity of a given city should be addressed first. In additional, priority should be given to those rural migrant workers and their families who have been in a city for many years, as well as those who have held licenses to operate businesses in cities for many years. Priority should be given to those who have stable long-term jobs and who have already signed long-term employment contracts. In terms of industrial sectors in which rural migrant workers are employed, priority should be given to those rural migrant workers who are in service industries and manufacturing. For example, workers involved in the construction industry have a high degree of mobility. Once the peak of building in any given area is finished, they may migrate to regions that have a larger market for construction workers, so it is acceptable not to give priority to converting this group of people into urban residents.

In addition to the above considerations, the carrying capacity of different regions and types of cities may be quite different. It is therefore not desirable to adopt a blanket nationwide approach to the conditions that should enable 'urban residency status'. The formulation of criteria should be at the municipal level or the local level. Each region and city should formulate different 'residency' conditions, with higher or lower barriers to entry as appropriate, depending on their specific circumstances. In the mega-cities of Beijing and Shanghai, for example, the carrying capacity is already severely overtaxed. Policies in these cities may be allowed to set relatively high standards for urban residency status. In places like Shenzhen and Dongguan, there are already huge numbers of rural migrant workers, and absorbing them all into urban systems would be quite difficult. These areas should also be allowed to set fairly high conditions on urban status.

'Coordination through an overall plan' means that overall consideration should be given to 'urbanizing' three main types of people: rural migrant workers, other transient populations who have come into cities, and the population of people living in what are called 'villages within cities'. It means approaching the reform of systems that handle these people in a comprehensive way, including fiscal policies, education, healthcare and medical services, and social security. It means evaluating issues from both an immediate perspective, but also from the need to set up long-term mechanisms that address both quantitative and qualitative issues.

The main substance of 'urbanization' has to do with converting rural migrant workers into urban residents, in terms of the 'human' element of urbanization. There are two other categories of people who should be taken into consideration when formulating policy, however. One is made up of college graduates who are concentrated in mega-cities and are already employed yet have not signed long-term employment contracts. Because of this, they have not been allowed to 'settle down' in their place of employment. This population segment includes a more transient population that has come into mega-cities from small- and medium-sized cities and county seats.

The second category of people who should also be taken into consideration includes farmers who have been dispossessed of their land as a result of the expansion of cities. Not only has their contracted land been requisitioned, but often their housing has been taken as well. In terms of their 'household registration status', however, they remain rural residents. Any governance applied to them is still that of the 'village' or the rural area. Problems involving these two additional demographic sectors should also be addressed through overall, comprehensive, policies.

2 Formulate a 'comprehensive plan' for converting rural migrant workers into rural residents

In light of the fact that converting rural migrant workers into urban residents involves so many different aspects, we recommend that a government body at the national level be asked to create an overall plan for furthering the process of urbanizing rural migrant workers. Such a plan should be approved by the State Council before being implemented, and it should be re-evaluated and revised on a regular basis. This 'plan' should incorporate policy but also be implementable and operational. It should result in actual resolution of problems. At the very least, it should encompass the following points.

1   Its principles should be explicit with respect to how to resolve issues of different regions, different cities, and different groups of people. For example, with respect to the classification of different sizes of cities, conditions for becoming an urban resident should be more stringent the larger the city, the greater the costs involved, and the more difficult the process. It should be possible to set up minimum entry requirements according to different regions and different types of cities and then let governments in each area formulate more specific regulations.

2   Any comprehensive plan must have feasible objectives. In looking at the correlation between international urbanization rates and GDP levels, when GDP per capita reaches around US$ 4000, the 'rate of urbanization' is generally at around 50 per cent. When GDP per capita reaches US$ 13,000, the average rate of urbanization, globally, approaches 65 per cent. In 2009, China's per capital GDP was around US$ 3800 and its rate of urbanization was 46.6 per cent. This was lower than the rate of economies at a similar level of development.

If China's per capita GDP grows at an average rate of around 6 per cent over the next 20 years, by 2030 it will reach around US$ 13,000. If we can gradually eliminate systemic obstacles to urbanization, as well as other types of obstacles, in line with the normal trend of market-economy growth, we estimate that China's rate of urbanization should indeed be able to reach a level of 65 per cent at that time. In this process, we should be increasing the urbanization rate at one percentage point per year in the decade between 2010 and 2020, and at 0.8 of a percentage point between 2020 and 2030.

The process of urbanizing rural migrant workers must be gradual and progressive. Starting right now, for the next 10 years we should first be focusing on people who have stable employment, who pay taxes, and who enjoy social security and a fixed residence. We should be turning this type of rural migrant workers and their families into 'urban residents'. At the same time, we should be lowering the barriers to entry for others, resolving issues for other workers and their families who are willing to remain in cities with their families and become permanent residents.

By 2020, we should first have resolved the issue of transforming the 'status' of around 200 million people. Between 2020 and 2030, we should address the issue of transforming the status of another 200 million people.

From now onward, we therefore will have to resolve the 'household residency status' of approximately 20 million people every year, which means resolving all the social benefits that go along with official urban residency.

Converting rural migrant workers into urban residents is going to require a massive investment in terms of funding. The report of the project team assigned to this specific subject indicates that we are currently spending an average of RMB 100,000 per worker on this process. In order to transform 200 million rural migrant workers into urban residents, China will therefore be investing something on the order of RMB two trillion. This spending will have to be distributed over two different levels of government, the Central government and local governments [which means both provinces and certain large cities], and also the market at large.

The Central government can cover the cost of RMB 500 billion by making transfer payments. These will be used primarily in support of education, medical services, and social security for rural migrant workers. Local governments will match that amount with RMB 500 billion from fiscal spending budgets, which will mainly be used on supporting the cost of building low-rent housing. The remaining sum of RMB one trillion should come through market sources, and will be used on such things as building basic infrastructure, a portion of housing, and on expenses for land. Since the cost of funding the urbanization of rural migrant workers can be considered a one-time expense, funding methods may include the issuing of bonds.

We estimate that the current problem of the 'quasi-urbanization' of rural migrant workers should be resolved, at least basically, by the year 2030. In addition to this overarching objective, however, we must have targeted objectives for each year and each region. These will include target figures for urbanizing a specific number of rural migrant workers and their families every year, nationwide, but also by region and city. Each region will have targets for resolving a specific number under its jurisdiction, including how many should be accomplished in every different type of municipality.

3   The comprehensive plan must have effective measures. It should be explicit about the basic principles and overall orientation of this reform, which is to change the dualistic structure of the urban and rural systems. Key aspects include creating systems to deal with household registration in the future, public services, social security, how contracted land of rural migrant workers can either be passed on to the next generation or transferred to others once people become urban residents, and how the land that rural housing sits on can be transferred [through a market]. They include setting up systems of public finance, and various reforms to deal with immediate issues as workers 'urbanize'. They include resolution of housing issues, where and how to source land and financing for housing, how to raise the large amounts of funding that will be needed for the social services required by the absorption of rural migrant workers into cities.

Given the extreme complexity of this whole process, we should set up pilot programs first and then expand upon them later. The national-level plan should specify where the initial pilot sites are to be located, as well as the principles to be followed, time allowed for the process, and deadline for expanding the program into other areas.

4   The plan should include measures that focus on the targeted group of next-generation rural migrant workers. The improvement of all systems, structures, mechanisms and so on should take the entire body of rural migrant workers into account, but the unique problems of next-generation workers should also be given close consideration. Aspects of particular concern to the next generation include job training, housing, social security, and public services. Specific measures should be targeted therefore at the standards that apply to acceptable thresholds for skills training, 'human capital' qualifications, social security premiums, and 'stable residence' qualifications.

Box 2.4 Various exploratory efforts in converting rural migrant workers into urban residents

Chongqing seeks to turn ten million farmers into urban residents by the year 2020

In July 2010, the Chongqing municipal government adopted an *Opinion on Overall Reform of the Household Registration System that Deals with Urban and Rural Households*, as well as a set of accompanying regulations. The aim was to turn the percentage of people within the city who actually possessed an 'urban residential permit' from the current 28 per cent to 60 per cent or 70 per cent by the year 2020.

This signified that some ten million 'rural people' were to be transformed into 'urban people' by that time. The key aspect of this reform involved setting up an experimental system that allowed for 'flexible withdrawal mechanisms' that ensured the legitimate rights and benefits of rural migrant workers, over a reasonable transition period, as they disengaged themselves from their contracted farmland and forest land and the land under their former housing. The initial group of 3.1 million rural people in the 'registration transfer plan' includes three components: local rural migrant workers, local middle school and vo-tech school students with a rural household registration, and 400,000 former farmers now being turned into non-farmers. The plan is to realize the transformation of all three groups into 'urban residents' before the year 2012. The ultimate goal is to have all ten million rural residents newly registered with urban residential permits.

The city of Nanjing in Jiangsu province intends to decrease its 'rural population' by one hundred million people in the next five years, under a comprehensive rural–urban development plan

In July 2010, the city of Nanjing in Jiangsu province issued an *Action Plan for Comprehensive Integration of Urban and Rural Development and*

Accelerated Regional Planning. This action plan specifically calls for 'three transformations' through the process of 'replacing three systems', namely, replacing the operating rights to contracted land with 'urban community security'; replacing the dispersed housing in the countryside with property rights to housing in the city, which would replace the previous property rights held as 'collective assets' with share rights in shareholding cooperatives; and replacing an agrarian mode of production, rural lifestyle, and rural registration 'status' with a rural lifestyle and status. The aim is to change the official status of around one million within six to eight years and thereby reduce the current 2.05 million 'rural people' in the city by 1 million.

Guangdong province plans to transfer 2.2 million people from rural to urban areas over the next 11 years

In early 2010, the Guangdong provincial government issued an *Outline for a Comprehensive Plan to Provide Equal Basic Public Services to the Population (2009–2020)*. This called for a strategy that actually moves populations of people to where public services are more available. The plan provides incentives for rural populations to move into cities, that is, from areas that are lesser developed in the Pearl River delta area towards those that are better equipped to bear the fiscal burden of providing services. The aim is to reduce the disparity in supply of basic public services between urban and rural areas, as well as that among various regions. In light of the complexities of shifting populations in this manner, and in consideration of the specific circumstances in Guangdong province, the plan envisages moving people only who currently have a Guangdong residential permit. By assimilating a mobile population into the urban development plans of the province, the plan aims to carry out two activities simultaneously, namely gradually liberalizing the 'household status' of people while also, in vigorous and realistic manner, providing them with basic public services. An estimated 200,000 people are to be moved every year from 2009, so that the total should come to 2.4 million by the year 2020. The goal is to keep disparities in the supply of public services in the region to within a band of some 20 per cent.

Generally, the plans described above focus on people who currently have residency permits that are local, that is, not from another city or another province. The plans are aimed at resolving local issues in converting rural populations into urban populations. The 'barriers to entry' are still extremely high when it comes to turning a more transient population into legitimate urban residents. Systems that relate to that transient population are as yet not being addressed, including land, housing, social security, and education.

Bibliography

Chongwing strives to turn 100 million peasants into urban residents by 2020, 21st Century Economic Report, 14 July 2010; Quoted from Chuancai Securities Net: www.cczq.com/VsInfo/0000002A071441.32.html.

Nanjing (0000) *to cut rural population by 1 million in five years and invest 100 billion yuan in building new cities and towns*, Netease News: http://news.163.com/10/0703/10/6ALL0FA0000146BC.html.

Nanjing (0000) *to make great leap forward in urban–rural integration by investing 100 million yuan*, Xinhuanet Jiangsu Channel: www.js.xinhuanet.com/xin_wen_zhong_xin/2010-07/09/content_20297702.htm.

Guangdong (0000) *plans to transfer 2.2 million people from rural to urban areas in 11 years*, SINA News: http://news.sina.com.cn/o/2010-01-04/092716875367s.shtml.

3 Adopt less stringent requirements for 'settling down with an urban residency status', in the process of turning rural migrant workers into urban residents

There are two different ways of thinking about how to turn rural migrant workers into rural residents – or one could say two different approaches. The first is to focus initially on pushing for greater equality in supply of public services. Once services are improved, policies can then begin to liberalize the process of unifying the two different types of residency status. The second is to maintain both systems as they currently exist, that is, the way public services are supplied and the household-registration system, but gradually broaden the definition of who can be an urban resident. The second therefore involves adopting less stringent requirements on urban residence.

The reasoning behind the first way of thinking is that a 'household registration' sets up an enormous dam-like barrier between people who have a rural status and those who enjoy an urban status, even though the registration itself is simply a piece of paper. The main obstacle in the way of turning rural migrant workers into urban residents lies in the many public-welfare systems, rights, and benefits that are associated with the piece of paper. As a result, this view believes that more effort should initially be put on equalizing the provision of public services. Rights and benefits should gradually be disengaged from the determining factor of a 'household registration'. Once human welfare systems are reformed, that is, once water on both sides of the dam is basically on an equal level, one can release restrictions on urban residency permits and the water will find its own channels.

Due to considerations of actual implementation and feasibility, this Report adopts the second line of approach. It favors a stair-stepped release of water, as it were, prior to full opening of the sluice gates. It recommends retaining the household-registration system, controlling the numbers of people [who are granted urban registration], loosening restrictions gradually and moving forward in a progressive fashion.

'Retaining the household registration system' means that, for this immediate stage, we should retain a system that provides for two different forms of urban and rural registration status. 'Controlling the numbers' means setting specific quotas per year in each different locality, depending on that locality's 'carrying capacity'. The number of rural migrant workers who are turned into urban residents should be kept within the ability of each locality's fiscal budget to pay for housing, public services, and basic infrastructure. 'Loosening restrictions' means relaxing the conditions by which rural migrant workers can be defined as urban residents, as according to the actual situation in each place. It does not mean, as has been the practice in some areas, 'enabling select candidates to have preferential treatment' at the provincial-government level. At the same time, equal-status public services must be provided to those rural migrant workers who are indeed qualified to become urban residents.

For example, with respect to the requirement to have a 'stable income', different localities can adopt different standards, so long as the rural migrant worker who is being enabled to 'settle down' as an urban resident has a certain source of income and an ongoing way to make a living in the city. With respect to the requirement about a 'fixed place of residence': it can be defined in different ways, including the purchase of housing that is 'owned as an asset', or living in government-supplied low-rent housing, or provided by the place of employment, or living in a rented place with a contract of more than one year, and so on. With respect to the requirement about 'stable employment', it can be defined as having an employment contract that has at least a one-year term, or it can mean obtaining a license to do business as an individual operator. 'Moving forward in a progressive fashion' means a succession of steps in accord with local conditions. In the first year, for example, a temporary residency permit can be extended; in the third year, a 'blue-card' residency permit, in the fifth year, an official urban residency permit. This enables the rural migrant worker to see that his hopes for residency are moving forward, while it also takes into consideration the carrying capacity of the municipality. It allows the process to be graduated and controlled within the capacity of municipal systems, so that they are not overstressed.

As described above, the four considerations in adopting a system that 'maintains the household registration system' should be acceptable to municipal governments. Right now, a number of cities and several provinces have adopted measures that enable a transient or 'mobile population' to gain residency permits if they meet certain conditions. Such cities include Shanghai, Beijing, Nanjing, Zhongshan, Changzhou, Wuxi, and Kunming, and the provinces include Guangdong and Jiangsu. Generally speaking, these measures are aimed at attracting highly qualified human resources, however. They are not really targeted at rural migrant workers. The barriers to entry to rural migrant workers remain insurmountable in such cases.

The basic instincts in these places are correct, and if the conditions are loosened to an appropriate degree, the methods can serve rural migrant workers as well. For example, the requirements for a certain level of education could be lowered given that most rural migrant workers are either middle-school or high-school graduates. Initially, the threshold could be set at having a high-school degree. The requirements for stable employment could be determined by the duration of a labor contract. As for those rural migrant workers who are engaged in their own individual businesses, localities should not require overly strict requirements. For example, requiring that a person have attained at least an 'intermediate technician' qualification should be regarded as excessively restrictive.

Such things as 'position', 'reputation', 'non-profit contributions', and so on should not be regarded as criteria for obtaining a residency permit. Nor should the size of a city be taken as the determining factor in allowing or not allowing a certain number of people to become urban residents. Not only do small- and medium-sized cities have to relax their residency requirements, but large cities and mega-cities must do so as well. In the central and western parts of the country, small- and medium-sized cities as well as smaller towns may be able to release restrictions quite quickly and provide all urban services to all residents. In theory, small- and medium-sized cities in the east should be able to loosen residency restrictions completely.

Large cities in the east, as well as mega-cities, will have to rely on their own specific conditions and overall carrying capacity in gradually relaxing restrictions. Those cities that are already over-populated may set slightly higher conditions on entry. Nevertheless, the whole issue of 'over-population' fundamentally relates to jobs and economic development and must be addressed from the standpoint of those issues. Industrial structure has to be adjusted, urban functions have to be modified; problems cannot be resolved simply by limiting populations.

As for those rural migrant workers who do not wish to 'settle down' where they are employed but would rather move back and forth between urban and rural settings, this is fine but municipalities must ensure that their rights and interests are protected. Labor should be fairly compensated, children should receive an education, and rights to social security, medical services and housing should be ensured.

When it comes to resolving the issue of providing public services on an equal basis, an approach that calls for 'first equalizing services and then later liberalizing household-registration terms for rural migrant workers on a nationwide basis' is not, in fact, feasible. The reason is that such an approach is both difficult to implement and lacks any binding constraints on [local] governments. Turning rural migrant workers into urban residents only after the benefits of an urban status are disengaged from that status is therefore not going to work.

Public services that go along with an urban residential status are quite different not only between urban and rural areas but among various parts of the country. Resolving those differences is not merely a matter of household registration but also a matter of levels of economic development and the readjustment of major interests. It is going to take a very long time. The process will not be accomplished within a few years.[8]

Box 2.5 Regulations in certain cities with respect to 'residency permits' and the 'settling down' of a transient population

The system relating to a 'permit to live in a place' is one of the key parts of the overall 'household residency status' system. Given that the economic circumstances of places are quite different, there is a diversity of approaches in this regard.

Shanghai

In February 2009, the Shanghai municipal government issued a document *Provisional Regulations with Respect to Extending Permanent Residency Status to Those People Who Currently Hold a 'Shanghai Municipal Residency Permit'*. This provided that those people meeting the following conditions could apply for permanent residency status in Shanghai:

1   They had held a Shanghai Municipal Residency Permit for a minimum of seven full years.
2   They had participated in the city's social security system for a minimum of seven full years, during all of which period the Residency Permit was valid.
3   They have paid income tax in the city during the full period in which the Residency Permit was valid.
4   They have been hired as or are recognized to be qualified at the level of 'intermediate professional' or higher, or have professional qualifications that are ranked at the level of 'technician' or higher (with a certificate of at least National Level Two). This includes confirmation that their employment has actually corresponded to their level of expertise.
5   They have had no record of misconduct. Such misconduct can include breaking national and municipal regulations to do with birth control; it can include any kind of criminal record that is at or above the level of being punished by the public-security management bureau.

With respect to the number of people being granted residency permits every year, Shanghai makes a year-end adjustment in the total number of permit holders that it will allow to apply for permanent household registration. Qualified permit holders must line up to be handled in proper sequence. Once the specified number of people to be handled that year has been reached, those who have not been considered will be put at the front of the line in the next year's consideration.

Jiaxing city, Zhejiang province

Jiaxing issues three different kinds of residency permits that come in two major categories. Each has different requirements, but the requirements for 'transient residency permits' are basically the same as the requirements for 'temporary residency permits'. Anyone who is a full 16 years old and has lived in a temporary place for more than 30 days must apply for such a permit.

The requirements for a 'general residency permit for a regular individual' are as follows: the person must be a 'new resident' who has held a valid 'temporary residency permit' for at least one year. The person must have a legal and fixed place of residence. He must have a legal and stable source of income. He must not have any record of misconduct, which includes disturbing public order.

The requirements for a 'residency permit for a person who is a professional' are as follows: he must be a 'new resident to Jiaxing', have an education that is at the level of a polytechnic degree, or high-school degree, or above, and he must be adept at a skill and/or have managerial experience. The review and approval procedure for this kind of residency is highly complex. It uses a point system, and only those with a full 150 points are qualified to apply.

Each of the three different types of residency permit has its own set of attendant benefits. For example, if the child of a person holding a 'transient residency permit' is seven years old or less, he or she is entitled to the immunization services of local health centers. If the child was born in conformity with family planning policies, he or she may have tuition and miscellaneous fees waived during the period of compulsory education.

Those people holding a 'general residency permit for a regular individual' can have one-half of the fees of compulsory education at a public school waived for their child. Children who have been born in conformity with family planning policies, and who also meet other requirements as stated in the application, may apply to enter both Jiaxin-administered middle schools and the medium-level vo-tech schools in the city.

Those people holding a 'professional residency permit' have the following benefits: children are allowed a full waiver of tuition and fees if they attend a public school during compulsory education years. Those residents who meet relevant conditions can apply for low-rent housing and 'affordable housing', and they can apply to purchase housing being built specifically for 'new residents' that is 'small-scale and affordable'. Those residents who have lived in the city for ten years are more are qualified to apply for a welfare program called 'minimum living security'. Those have lived in the city for 15 years or more are qualified to become 'urban residents' if they choose to do so.

Zhongshan city in Guangdong province

The 'point system' of Zhongshan city is made up of basic points, added points, and deducted points. The basic-point metric includes the individual qualifications of a person, his work experience, and his living situation. The added-point metric includes a person's basic circumstances, urgently needed personnel, patents and innovations, awards and special honors, donations to charities, amount of investment and paid-up taxes, family planning considerations, health and epidemic prevention, registration management, and the person's personal credit record. The deducted-point metric includes 'breaking the law' and 'other illegal behavior'.

The highest weighting is given to the consideration of a person's 'qualifications'. In terms of educational record, a person with a college degree is accorded 80 points, while a graduate student or above gets 90 points. In terms of skills, a person with 'high-level professional talents' gets 90 points, or the same number if he has qualifications that are 'grade 3 level' or above. A person who owns his own housing gets 10 points. In terms of the investment criteria, a person who invests a full RMB 500,000 gets one point, and an additional point for every RMB 200,000 invested after that. Tax payment of a full RMB 10,000 counts for 1 point, and there is an additional point for every 10,000 after that, but both of these considerations are capped at 10 points. Only when a 'transient worker' accumulates 100 points is he or she allowed to 'settle down' in the city.

Central-government regulations

At the Central-government level, the following actions were taken between 2007 and 2010.

- In 2007, the Central government raised the prospect of 'exploring the establishment of a unified national system of registration for 'household registration status', in terms of how such a system would be managed.
- In 2008, the Central government announced that it 'permitted those rural migrant workers who met the required conditions to settle down in cities'.
- In 2009, the Central government issued a statement about the 'principles' that would be applied to changes in the proposed system of services for transient workers and management of transient workers.
- In May 2010, the State Council approved and transmitted an 'Opinion' that had been drafted by the National Development and Reform Commission: the *Opinion on Key Aspects of Deepening Reform and Economic Restructuring*. It mandated that all parts of the country conscientiously implement the contents of this Opinion. The Opinion explicitly stated that the country would be 'deepening reform of the

household-registration system, accelerating the implementation of policies that related to small- and medium-sized cities, small towns and townships, and particularly county seats and core towns, with respect to liberalizing conditions for urban residency'. It [the country] would be 'going further in improving the registration system for a temporary population, and gradually adopting a residency registration system nationwide'.

The action taken in 2010 was the very first time a document issued at the State Council level had mentioned implementing a 'residency registration system' on a nationwide basis.

Bibliography

Li Gang (0000) *Zhongshan city in Guangdong province introduces point system for urban settlement*, People's Net: http://gongyi.people.com.cn/GB/10763790.html
Look into the real value of Zhejiang's household register reform, China News Weekly, 2007, issue 45.

Allowing rural migrant workers to enjoy full public services 'first' is a good start, but it also means that rural migrant workers will not be able to 'settle down' as a way to improve their condition. Promoting equalization of public services between rural migrant workers and proper urban residents is something that depends on a variety of factors. Some can be resolved by a piece of paper that calls for reform, plus a certain amount of investment. Others are not so easy, since they call for restructuring of the spatial distribution of cities, and for increased investment into land.

In some cities and towns, rural migrant workers outnumber the 'urban' population. In such places, if one were to lift the restrictions on urban residency in one stroke, very large numbers of school-age children of rural migrant workers would flood into cities in order to be enrolled in the urban education system. Building schools requires not only time and money but also land. Such cities and towns, however, are precisely the ones that are already over-built. Finding space for further construction of schools is going to be extremely difficult.

The issue of turning rural migrant workers into urban residents should be seen in the context of China's long-term socioeconomic development. All of the country's systems are in the process of being improved upon, including education, healthcare and medical services, social security, social 'relief' [welfare assistance], housing guarantees, and so on. All of these require policies and systems that are transitional in nature when it comes to rural migrant workers. Lowering the barriers to entry in China's cities does not mean lowering the levels at which services are supplied to rural migrant workers and their children. On the contrary, it means enabling more of them to enjoy the same services as 'urban residents'. The future direction of policies is intended to enable rural migrant workers to be assimilated into urban systems, in an incremental manner.

Policies are eventually meant to form an integrated society, including urban and rural, that functions as one unit.

4 Establish mechanisms that link the number of 'humans' to the amount of 'land'

Turning rural migrant workers into urban residents necessarily means that the population of cities will increase. This will put greater demands on public services and housing, and therefore greater demands also on urban land use. This requires that, in addition to the existing system of allocating specific amounts of land for urban use, we are going to have to allocate 'additional land quotas' for the process.

A mechanism that relates population numbers to land should be set up, in order to address the question of where the land is going to come from. In addition to the current 'base' amount of land that is included in land-use planning, the government at the national level [Central authorities] may add an additional 'quota' that is to be used mainly in addressing such issues as housing, basic infrastructure, public services, and so on for rural migrant workers. The increments would depend on the numbers of rural migrant workers to be assimilated into cities as residents. Places absorbing more people would receive larger land-use quotas. Places absorbing fewer people would get less.

At the same time, the density of populations in cities should be taken into account. When densities in existing cities are already quite high, for example, ten thousand people to every square kilometer for a city with a population of over 500,000, where the potential to add more people is already low, then more land would be granted. In cities with fairly low density and more potential to absorb people, less land would be granted.

Such an approach would help in mitigating the existing problem of having 'land urbanization' outpace the process of 'human urbanization' [that is, it would mitigate the problem of 'urban sprawl']. In this next great round of urbanization in China, it would contribute to economizing on land and using it more intensively. In addition, such an approach will provide incentives to municipal governments and encourage them to be willing to take in more rural migrant workers. At the present time, and for the foreseeable future, land is equivalent to money in the eyes of local governments until the whole public-finance system governing the Central–local division of taxes is changed. For now, so long as a locality has land, it has 'money'.

In addition, a mechanism should simultaneously be established that provides land-use quota to places that are less attractive to rural migrant workers. This could function in the following manner. The first step would be to state clearly that only people with stable employment in a place could gain residency there. The second step would be to set up a nationwide system of housing registration and, concurrently, a system of taxation on the management of that housing and on the housing itself. The more housing a person owned, the more taxes he would have to pay. The third step would be to establish a system that tied additional land quotas each year to the number of rural migrant workers who had been assimilated into the city the previous year, and that also took into account the density of the 'permanent-resident' population. If people moved out or migrated elsewhere, then the 'land quota' for that city would be docked a certain amount in the following year.

Increasing the amount of land used for housing of rural migrant workers in cities is not going to result in an overall increase in the amount of land required altogether. It is not going to increase the overall 'intensity' of land development. On the contrary, it should contribute to controlling the intensity of land development and help to protect and preserve arable land.

This approach [of tying land-use to numbers of people in cities] is in fact a kind of spatial reconfiguring. It turns land-use quotas for building housing in rural areas into land-use quotas for building housing in urban areas. The reason it conserves land in the final analysis is that rural migrant workers will continue to build housing in rural areas so long as they are not allowed to assimilate into cities. That takes up land, and in fact the amount of land used exceeds that used in cities.

5 Establish mechanisms that link the amount of 'money' to the number of 'humans'

It is imperative that we help municipal governments resolve their problems in raising sufficient funding or 'money'. From the perspective of a municipal government, any increase in the urban population signifies an increase in services and the need to fund those services. This puts a burden on municipal finances. This is the major reason municipal governments are unwilling to absorb rural migrant workers into their 'urban' populations.

Profound changes are going to have to be made in taxation systems, including setting up ways to increase taxes as the number of people increases, and not just as the value of industrial output increases. The tax base has to include both people and industries if we are to have urban mechanisms that give equal weight to attracting 'people' as well as 'business'. Fiscal transfer mechanisms are going to have to be established that increase as a city's population increases, instead of the current situation in which transfer mechanisms rely on the growth in public revenues.

At the present time, we might consider setting up mechanisms that link 'people' to 'money'. Public finance at the Central level and public finance at the provincial level could set up a system of transfer payments that uses the 'urbanization' of rural migrant workers as its determining factor. Subsidies would be extended to cities that absorbed a certain number of rural migrant workers into their 'permanent residence' status and that came up to performance levels over a certain number of years. These public-finance subsidies would be used primary on helping municipal governments set up social security systems for rural migrant workers and their families, for building medical facilities, compulsory education, and vo-tech facilities, for turning the existing schools for children of rural migrant workers into legitimate national-education-level public schools. They would be used to ensure that children of rural migrant workers could freely choose to attend either local public schools or the newly renovated 'children of rural migrant worker' schools. They would be used to pay for the building of low-rent housing, and for improving the supply of such things as electricity, water, gas, roads, sewage treatment, garbage disposal, public transport, and so on.

Funds that will be needed for turning rural migrant workers into urban residents are funds that must be used sooner or later. The sooner the process is started, the more the government will retain the initiative. As for the source of funding, one possibility is to issue specified national bonds for the purpose. Another is to extract a certain percentage out of the profits of State-Owned Enterprises.

6 Incorporate rural migrant workers into urban housing systems and urban rental-housing systems[9]

Any reform of the housing system in urban areas should take into consideration the needs of rural migrant workers. Any modifications of the real estate industry should also express the needs of rural migrant workers who come into cities for permanent residence. On the one hand, rural migrant workers should be encouraged to spend their incomes and savings on buying urban housing. On the other hand, since housing prices are excessively high in cities right now, and especially in China's mega-cities, the great majority of rural migrant workers cannot afford such housing which is a major constraining factor when it comes to their 'urbanization'.

First, methods should be devised that bring down the level of commercial housing overall. Doing this means increasing the amount of land available to cities while making sure that that land is used for residential housing and not for industrial purposes. In order to fund such housing, a property tax should be instituted as a stable source of income, and we should also research the possibility of allowing municipal governments to issue municipal bonds.

Second, more low-rent housing should be made available. Municipal governments should be encouraged by various means to build low-rent housing and to incorporate rural migrant workers into the criteria of people authorized to rent the housing.

Third, we should allow looking into the possibility of having collective economic organizations [businesses owned by collectives] use land approved for 'rural construction' as land on which to build high-rise apartments for rural migrant workers.

Fourth, we may want to lower the initial down-payment that rural migrant workers make when they buy either affordable housing or price-restricted housing. We may want to extend their repayment terms on loans, and extend preferential treatment when it comes to deed taxes and interest rates.

Fifth, we should encourage real estate developers to build 'social-purpose' housing that is appropriate for rental by rural migrant workers. In addition, we should encourage a market in small-scale rental units.

7 Explore the possibility of having rural migrant workers 'withdraw' from their land-use contracts once they have become urban residents

The purpose of turning rural migrant workers into urban residents is not to 'take their land', or to eradicate their land-use rights, including land that was under their former dwellings. On the other hand, however, if rural migrant workers have already settled down in cities for a long period of time, the land on which they hold contracts is sitting idle and the land under their old housing is not being put to use. This too wastes resources and is not conducive to economies of scale in agriculture. As a result, we should encourage farmers to pass on or transfer their contracts to farmland as well as to the land on which their housing is located. Institutional procedures should be set up to do this.

Certain principles must be observed, which include the following. First, the rights and interests of rural migrant workers in rural areas must truly be protected. Operating rights to land are an asset right that belongs to farmers. Even if farmers have moved into cities and taken up long-term residence, this right should not be expropriated in any capricious fashion. Any illegal adjustments to these land contracts are forbidden. Confiscation of land or forced transfer of land that is under contract to farmers is forbidden.

Second, rural migrant workers should be permitted to sell their contracted right to operate land through market mechanisms, if they are acting on a voluntary basis. Similarly, they should be allowed to sell the legally prescribed amount of land that attaches to their dwellings, and receive financial compensation. This should be one of the sources of funds that helps finance their entry into urban areas. The Central government, as well as governments at various levels, may also allocate a certain amount of funds to be used in the purchase of such contracted land. The land then would be provided to local 'collective economic organizations', for no compensation, in order to further the policy known as 'having cities help promote the countryside, and using industry to further agriculture'. The aim would be to improve agricultural practices and rural production as well as living conditions.

8 Ensure that political rights are respected by facilitating the assimilation of rural migrant workers into cities

Turning rural migrant workers into urban residents is one aspect of a major transition under way in Chinese society. Only when the political rights and interests of several hundred million rural migrant workers are effectively guaranteed and actually realized, only when these people are actively engaged in their own governance in urban areas and constitute an organic part of urban society, will it be possible to say that they have truly been assimilated into cities.

In order to accomplish this, therefore, we recommend a revision in election law. In order to resolve the problem of not allowing 'people who come in from outside', which includes most rural migrant workers, the right to participate in elections, we might change the 'election registration system' as follows. In addition to the base of the regular voting population that has urban status, the 'long-term residents who are from outside' could also enjoy a percentage of total voting rights. This would enable all citizens in the country, no matter where they might be living, to exercise their own civic rights.

At the same time, we should explore enabling rural migrant workers to participate in 'democratized governance of cities' on an orderly basis. This would involve setting up effective mechanisms and channels through which people can express their own rights and interests. It would stimulate cities to recognize that they have not only the obligation but also a willing interest in absorbing rural migrant workers into their governance structures. The residency permit could serve as the basis for such systems. Rural migrant workers who meet certain criteria could then participate in grassroots-level democratic affairs and exercise democratic supervision over government.

On the other hand, we should also mobilize governments, non-governmental organizations, and other diverse forces in order to enable communities to play an 'integrating role' in social affairs, and to facilitate the assimilation of rural migrant workers into cities. In areas of concentrated occupation by rural migrant workers, we should set up systems for regular opinion polls and residents' councils. We should strengthen the interaction among different groups of rural migrant workers so that they are aware of and concerned about community affairs and will want to participate in an enthusiastic and proactive way. We should involve rural migrant workers in the process of budgetary reform, in 'democratic forums', in public hearings for municipal residents, and in the various forms of urban governance.

Notes

1 Turning rural migrant workers into urban residents falls within the scope of the policy on population migration. But population migration includes both the employment and residence of peasants in cities and also the free population migration between different cities and towns. As China's higher education is being popularized, how to solve the employment and residence of university graduates has also become a very pressing task. But this report is mainly targeted on the employment and residence of rural migrant workers in cities.

2 Unless specified otherwise, all the data in this report about rural migrant workers originate from the monitoring and investigation report on rural migrant workers conducted by the National Bureau of Statistics.

3 The data from the 2005 investigation in Chengdu indicate that more than one-quarter of rural migrant workers had a per capita housing space of less than 5 square meters, and one-third of them had a per capita housing space of 5–10 square meters, which were far lower than the 16-square-meter per capita housing space for a difficult urban household in Chengdu. In Shanghai, the per capita urban housing space at the end of 2005 reached 15.5 square meters, but 74.9 per cent of the surveyed rural migrant workers had a per

capita housing space of less than 10 square meters. In all five cities, 66 per cent of the surveyed rural migrant workers had a per capita housing space of less than 7 square meters.

4 'Village in city' is a special phenomenon appearing in the course of China's urbanization. Rapid urbanization has drastically swelled the land used for municipal construction and included some villages and their farmland on the outskirts of cities in the scope of the land for municipal construction. While most collectively owned farmland has become publicly owned, the plots of the expropriated land, such as homestead land, private plots, private hilly areas, that have been returned to villagers continue to be collectively owned. The communities formed on these plots mainly for residential purpose are called villages in city (Miao Lining, 2008).

5 *More Than 1 Million Chinese Peasants Lose Land Each Year and Officials Vow to Strictly Protect Farmland*, People's Net, 9 March 2006.

6 According to the investigation by this author, an administrative village in Jiangxi Province has three natural villages: old village, middle village and new village. The new village is all made up of two-storey buildings that were planned and designed in a unified way by professionals and built by peasant households according to the 'five throughs and one -ization' (road, water, telephone, cable television, methane, and landscaping). Each household occupies 180 square meters of land, but only four of the 22 buildings are occupied. All others are vacant, because their owners are rural migrant workers working all the year round in urban areas.

7 The per capita disposable income of urban residents in 2007 was 13,786 yuan and the per capita net income of rural residents was 4140 yuan. The urban–rural income gap was 3.33-fold. If the 1596.22-yuan wage income of a rural migrant worker were fully the income of the rural migrant worker, the total income of rural migrant workers would be 1161.25 billion yuan after it was multiplied by the total rural population. And if this total income were added to the total income of urban residents, the total income of urban residents would be 9347.15 billion yuan. If this figure were divided by the new urban population, namely the 300 million rural migrant workers and their family members, the new per capita income of urban residents would be 10,458 yuan. If the 1161.25 billion yuan were deducted from the total income of peasants and if 300 million people were deducted from the rural population, the new per capita rural income would be 4329 yuan. So the new urban–rural income gap would be 2.42-fold.

8 The cities with more universities and other cities have a tangible gap in university admission rates. But this is not an issue that can be solved through household register liberalization. And once household register is liberalized, everybody can come and settle down. It is all possible that the cities with more universities have become overburdened before the arrival of rural migrant workers.

9 In the *China Development Report 2008: Establish a Development-Oriented Social Welfare System for All People*, the China Development Research Foundation made specific proposals from the perspective of social welfare on the establishment of a multi-level housing security system for rural migrant workers and meet the different-level housing demands of rural migrant workers in various forms. Please refer to the report for detailed contents.

3 Setting up a spatial configuration for 'urbanization' in China that features 'two horizontal lines and three vertical lines'

Urbanization involves changing both social and industrial structures. It also requires changes in the spatial configuration of a country's land. In this regard, the process is irreversible, since once farmland, forests, and water surfaces have been turned into city spaces, it is extremely hard to turn them back again into what they were.

Both international experience and China's own experience have made it apparent that it is of ultimate importance to guide the process of rapid urbanization in a clear and rational way. The State [or national government] must be explicit in defining the orientation that urbanization is to take. In line with an overall plan that involves developing the entire country, the government must have not only a rational plan for urbanization, but a plan for conserving agricultural spaces and ecological areas.[1]

Within the next decade or so, China will be creating a 'strategic pattern of urbanization' on the nation's 960 million square kilometers of territory. This pattern will be characterized by 'two horizontal lines' and 'three vertical lines'. In addition, the country intends to create a 'strategic pattern of agricultural production' that features '23 broad strips of land within seven regions', and it will be creating a strategic pattern of ecological areas that features 'two screens and three belts'.

The existing state of land development in China, and associated problems

The territory of a country constitutes the space within which its people must survive and continue to develop. In recent years, urbanization in China has taken up increasing amounts of space, particularly as large- and medium-sized cities have expanded outwards and as inner-city spaces have been rebuilt. China has considerable land and yet its area available for development is limited. When figured in terms of per capita, space is even less. Sixty percent of China's territorial space is either mountainous or on high plateaus, where the atmosphere is thin. Once the areas in the country that must be conserved as farmland and those areas that are already built upon are subtracted, the space available for future urbanization comes to only 3 per cent of the country's total land area.[2]

The fact that land that is appropriate for urbanization is minimal in China limits the country's choices as it evaluates how to carry out urbanization. The country is currently facing an urgent need to address a critical problem: how to manage the contradiction between pressures on land, as needed by rapid urbanization, and the very limited amount of land resources. It is confronting the problem of how to urbanize and still preserve sound and sustainable socioeconomic growth, while still creating an inhabitable environment in cities.

The experience of many industrial countries has been that urbanization used space in a way that was first 'centralized, then decentralized, and then recentralized'. This indicates that China's current plans for the spatial configuration of its urbanization must focus on efficiency, even as the plans continue to aim for fair and balanced development.

The spatial configuration of a country's urbanization reflects that country's fundamental policy orientation in terms of efficiencies, fairness, and sustainability. This orientation may be quite different in different periods of history. In the 1950s and 1960s, many industrialized nations emphasized the balanced development of their national territory in terms of both overall planning and urban planning. This was in order to prevent excessive concentration of populations in large cities and to balance out disparities among different regions and between urban and rural areas.

For example, in 1954, France began a policy of 'territorial adjustment'. It restricted further development of large cities and encouraged that of small- and medium-sized cities. The creation of satellite cities and regional centers became the main way the country sought to balance the development of its national territory.

Japan formulated its first 'comprehensive development plan' in 1960. This was done in order to prevent excessive concentration of people in the three major metropolitan 'hubs' and to reduce the economic disparities between these three areas and local [provincial] cities.

The process of economic globalization has meant that urban planning and the optimum use of national territory must now also focus on being globally competitive. Once Japan confronted the new situation of having to enter the arena of globalization, for example, the country continued to strengthen functions that turned Tokyo into a world-class city. At the same time, the country supported the development of individual, self-sustaining, regions. This made each region the large-scale hub of international commerce and communications. The idea behind use of national territory evolved from an initial attempt to limit over-concentration in large cities, to an effort to achieve balanced regional development through city clusters and several 'world cities'.

During China's own period of rapid urbanization, national conditions in the country dictate the need to strengthen functions that enable it to regulate land use in a strategic and macro-oriented way. While aiming for balanced development, the country must also seek 'efficiency' through rational urban planning and spatial configuration. In light of its current stage of development, China must, as soon as possible, formulate a rational strategic pattern of 'urbanization' as well as strategic patterns for agricultural and secure ecological use of land.

Box 3.1 Classification of types of national territory in China

Broadly speaking, if one classifies land according to the type of product it provides, a nation's territory can be divided into space used for urban areas, that used for agriculture and for 'ecology', and that used for other purposes.

'Urban space' refers to that which provides mainly industrial products and services. It incorporates space used for constructing the city itself and also that used for industry and mining. Space used for urban construction includes built-up areas for both the city and what in China are called administered towns, or 'towns that have set up administrative structures'. Space used for mining construction is mainly independent of the built-up areas of cities and exists in separate mining regions.

Urban space is the primary sphere in which contemporary human societies live and interact. With greater populations, greater concentrations of residences, they are relatively more developed, their industrial structure centers on both industry and services. Forms of human settlement include large cities, city clusters, city 'hubs', greater metropolitan regions, and so on.

'Agricultural space' refers to that used to produce agricultural goods as its main function. This includes space both for rural living and for agricultural production. Space devoted to agricultural production is mainly arable land, but it also includes gardens [parks, open land], and land used by agriculture in other ways. Space used for rural living includes both human settlements and space used for such things as rural public infrastructure and public services. In contemporary societies, the populations living in agricultural spaces are relatively smaller, residences are more spread out, the industrial structure is primarily focused on agriculture, and human settlements take the form of slightly more densely populated areas that concentrate in small towns and villages.

'Ecological space' refers to the space that functions mainly to provide ecological products or services. Depending on whether such goods and services are more or less, a further subdivision can be made into 'green ecological spaces' and 'other ecological spaces'. Green space refers mainly to forests, water surfaces, wetlands, and inland seas. While some of these are manmade, such as tree plantations and reservoirs, most are natural rivers, lakes, and woodlands. The category of 'other ecological spaces' refers primarily to natural environments that exist 'naturally' such as deserts, 'raw land', salinized land, and so on. Although some woodlands, grasslands, and water surfaces also have the function of providing products such as forestry products, animal husbandry products, and aquatic products, the main function of these places is still ecological. Over-reliance on their agricultural function may serve to damage their ecological function. It is for this reason that we define woodlands, grasslands, and water surfaces as 'ecological space'.

Relative to agricultural space, ecological space is more sparsely populated and it is far less developed. It has little in the way of business [its economic scale is small], and small towns constitute the very small number of human settlements.

'Other space' refers to the systems that crisscross the above types of space, including transport, energy systems, telecommunications and other forms of basic infrastructure, hydro-electric power systems, military facilities, and religious and other special uses of space.

Changes in China's territorial 'space'

China's territory has undergone tremendous changes since the beginning of 'reform and opening up' (Table 3.1). These have been brought on by rapid economic growth, industrialization, and urbanization.

In 2008, the amount of space occupied by all types of 'construction' came to 330,000 square kilometers out of a total 9.6 million square kilometers of national territory as measured by land mass alone. Of this amount, 165,300 square kilometers was occupied by rural housing, 40,600 square kilometers was occupied by urban construction, independently located mining territories occupied 41,500 square kilometers, transport routes occupied 25,000 square kilometers (not including rural roads), and arable land came to 1.2172 million square kilometers. Forestland occupied 2.3609 million square kilometers, and grasslands occupied 2.6183 million square kilometers, both classified mainly as 'ecological space' but also serving an agricultural function. See Table 3.2.

Due to changes in the way statistics are measured, it is not possible to provide comparable figures over a longer period of time, and we can only compare figures from the year 2000 to now. Data on spatial configurations of national territory in these years, however, should not affect our understanding of the trends that are dictating the long-term behavior of structural changes. The overall trends and directions are consistent with one another.

Table 3.1 Change of spatial structure (in units of 10,000 km²)

Year	Urban space		Agricultural space		Ecological space		Other space
	Space for urban construction	*Space for industrial and mining construction*	*Space for agricultural production*	*Space for rural life*	*Green ecological space*	*Other ecological space*	
2000	2.98	2.99	164.63	16.56	510.04	248.48	4.99
2005	3.61	3.66	159.16	16.57	515.41	246.92	5.35
2007	3.93	4.00	159.04	16.54	515.58	246.10	5.51
2008	4.06	4.15	158.95	16.53	515.53	245.91	5.56

Source: Calculated on the basis of the annual territorial reports of the Ministry of Land and Resources.

Table 3.2 Change of sub-classified territorial spatial structure (in units of 10,000 km²)

		2000	2005	2007	2008
Farmland		128.24	122.08	121.74	121.72
Parkland		10.58	11.55	11.81	11.79
Forestland		228.79	235.74	236.12	236.09
Grassland		263.77	262.14	261.86	261.83
Other agricultural land		3.81	25.53	25.49	25.44
Land for urban construction		2.98	3.61	3.93	4.06
Rural settlement		16.56	16.57	16.54	16.53
Independent industries and mines		2.99	3.66	4.00	4.15
Transport land		1.95	2.31	2.44	2.50
Reservoirs	Sub-total	3.53	3.60	3.63	3.65
	Reservoir water surface	2.66	2.72	2.74	2.76
Land for other construction purposes		2.18	2.17	2.18	2.18
Unused land	Sub-total	285.30	261.72	260.95	260.76
	Rivers and lakes	14.81	14.80	14.85	14.85

Source: Calculated on the basis of the annual territorial reports of the Ministry of Land and Resources.

Major changes between 2000 and 2008 include the following.

First, space used for urban purposes has expanded rapidly, given China's accelerated pace of both urbanization and industrialization. Between 2000 and 2008, the amount of space used for urban construction rose by 36 per cent, or by 10,800 square kilometers. Space for industrial and mining construction rose by 39 per cent or by 11,600 square kilometers. Land used to build up transport infrastructure also rose rapidly, from 19,500 square kilometers in 2000 to 25,000 square kilometers in 2008, which meant an annual increase of 28 per cent in the amount of land being occupied by roads. Land used for 'other construction purposes' did not change much, staying at about 21,800 square kilometers.

Second, space available for agricultural production continued to decline and the structural use of agricultural space also began changing, as follows. Between 2000 and 2008, 'agricultural space' in the aggregate declined by 56,800 square kilometers. Within that figure, arable land declined by the greatest amount, a decrease of 65,300 square kilometers or 5 per cent of total arable land in China.

During this same period, 'parkland' [or 'gardens'] increased by 12,100 square kilometers, which meant an increase of 11 per cent. Space used by human settlements in rural areas declined slightly overall. It had reached a peak in 2005, when the space used for human occupation reached 165,700 square kilometers. After that, it maintained a constant decline, actually going down over the entire period by 300 square kilometers.

Third, with the gradual increase of environmental protection measures, 'green ecological space' increased in overall terms. Between 2000 and 2008, forest lands increased by 3 per cent, or by 73,000 square kilometers. This was the result of reforesting land that had been used for agriculture, as well as planting trees in plantations. Grasslands, in contrast, decreased by 19,300 square kilometers. The reasons behind this included severe degradation of grasslands and desertification in some cases, but also the fact that certain municipalities began to encroach upon grasslands for industrial construction once the rules protecting farmland became more stringent. Rules over grasslands were less tightly controlled. 'Water surfaces space' increased by 9000 square kilometers, which was the result of major efforts put into developing hydroelectric power.

Problems that relate to 'developing' national territory

Structural changes in the use of China's territorial space, as described above, have contributed to China's fast economic growth and to the processes of urbanization and industrialization. At the same time, we should be aware of the problems that they have caused.

First, the way in which space has been used and restructured has been irrational.[3] This can mainly be seen in what could be called the 'three excesses and four scarcities'.

1   With respect to 'agricultural space' and 'ecological space', the irrationality has been manifested by a bias toward space used for agricultural production and against that used for ecology. There has been excessive 'opening up of new lands' and use of land for animal-breeding purposes, which has invaded land previously used for ecology. In recent years, action has been taken to redress this problem, through reclamation of forests from fields, the withdrawing of grasslands from excess grazing, and the reconstituting of lakes in places where they had been drained to create fields. This is beginning to return space that was formerly 'agricultural' into 'green ecological space'.

2   With respect to urban space, there has been a bias toward use for industrial production and against urban residential use. The amount of space being used for 'independently located mining operations' in China comes to more than 41,500 square kilometers. In addition, some 8035 square kilometers of space within cities is actually being used by industrial space. Most of the space in national-level and provincial-level 'development zones' is also put to industrial use, namely 9949 square kilometers. If one corrects for the overlap in figures, space used for mining and industry altogether comes to 50,000 square kilometers.

China has 40,500 square kilometers of 'urban built-up space', or urban areas that are 'built up' in one way or another. Of this amount, residential use of space comes to only 30.9 per cent. By this calculation, residential space in China's cities totals a mere 12,000 square kilometers.[4]

3   With respect to the living space available to people who live in cities as opposed to those who live in rural areas, there tends to be more space available in rural areas and less in cities. A total of 165,300 square kilometers of land in China is being used for human settlement in rural areas (this includes areas that are sparsely populated but does not include space covered by roads). The per capita living space available to rural people is an average 229 square meters. That available to urban people is 20 square meters, if one goes by the relevant 'standards' in China for urban living. (This figure includes space used by the residence itself, plus that for the neighborhood committee, the nursery school, smaller roads and any parks or green space in housing estates.)

Second, some areas are far over-developed.[5] The metric that measures 'intensity of development' in China is only 3.48 per cent right now, which does not seem very high. Given that only around one-half of the country's territory is suitable for development, however, this is not such a minor figure. In certain regions, the intensity of development is extreme. Shanghai, for example, is China's most developed urban region. GDP per capita in Shanghai exceeds US$ 10,000. The 'intensity of development' already comes to 29 per cent. (If one removes the area of Shanghai's three islands from the figures,[6] the intensity of development in Shanghai proper approaches 50 per cent).

Paris, London, Tokyo, Osaka, and Nagoya all have roughly the same 'spatial unit' as Shanghai. Greater Paris has a per capita GDP of US$ 63,000, however, and a 'development intensity' of only 21 per cent. Greater London has a per capita GDP of US$ 64,000, and a development intensity of only 23.7 per cent. The three metropolitan hubs in Japan have a per capita GDP of between US$ 37,000 and 42,000, and a development intensity of only 15 per cent. Tokyo has the highest development intensity, at 29.4 per cent.

Hong Kong, Shenzhen, and Dongguan also have roughly the same 'spatial unit'. Hong Kong's development intensity is 21 per cent, while it is 46.95 per cent for Shenzhen and 42.3 per cent for Dongguan.

The term 'high development intensity' implies certain things, including a dense concentration of people as well as economies of scale within a certain specific spatial unit. It also implies a reduction in the amount of 'agricultural space' and 'ecological space', leading to decreased production of both agricultural and ecological goods.

A major factor behind the excessively high 'development intensities' in some urbanized areas in China is the amount of waste and inefficiency in the course of developing land. High development intensities in some of China's cities are mainly the result of excessive occupation of land for use in industry, for use in rural construction, and for use in the building of housing in rural areas.

The amount of land used for industry in Shanghai comes to over 900 square kilometers, or 33 per cent of the entire amount of 'built-up land'. Township construction within the greater Shanghai area comes to nearly 400 square kilometers, or 13.8 per cent of total built-up land. Farmers' housing construction takes up 500 square kilometers of land, or 17.3 per cent of total built-up land. Added together, these three take up 64 per cent of Shanghai's total built-up land.

The reason industry uses excessive amounts of land in Shanghai is that the city has many industrial parks that are overly dispersed. Of Shanghai's more than 700 'parks', only 15 are administered at a national level and only 26 at the municipal level. The rest, more than 600, are administered at the district or township level, which means they are outside the scope of more stringent controls. Land occupied by such parks comes to 400 square kilometers.

Construction use of land in townships is not only excessive but also overly dispersed and poorly planned, with a floor area ratio (FAR) of only 0.3. Worse still, many factories are currently shut down.

Shanghai contains a total of around one million 'rural households'. Each of these occupies an average of 450 square meters. The city's 'rural population' comes to 2.15 million and the living space available to this population is around 230 square meters per capita. With no mountains or other kinds of terrain, the 'ecological space' available to Shanghai includes only its water surfaces and its arable land. Excessive 'development intensity' now means that not only is farmland decreasing, but ecological space is decreasing.

Third, irrational development is doing severe damage to the environment. Activities are damaging what was already a vulnerable ecology in China. In the process of 'development', including industrialization and urbanization, some places have shown reckless disregard for the carrying capacities of specific environments. This has led to the drying up of rivers, to receding and degrading of grasslands, to diminished wetlands, serious soil erosion, desertification, 'stony' [or Gobi] desertification, frequent geological disasters, and other ecological and environmental problems. As a result, less and less of China's own national territory is suitable and available for human habitation.

Within the space of just the past decade, the amount of land that was 'degraded' in China came to 20,000 square kilometers. Degraded land now covers nearly 2.64 million square kilometers, or 27 per cent of the total land area of the country. The area of desertified land in China comes to 1.74 million square kilometers, which is 18 per cent of the total land area of the country. Land that suffers from severe soil erosion comes to 3.56 million square kilometers. Land covered by sand [not mere desert] now comes to 1.74 million square kilometers. Land that has been 'alkalinized' [through poor land management practices] comes to 129,600 square kilometers. An additional 1.35 million square kilometers of grassland has 'retreated' due to degradation and salinization.

In 2008, there were 222 underground aquifers in China. Among these, 133 were at a fairly shallow depth, 78 were at deeper levels, and 11 were contained in karst cavities.

The aggregate sum of major pollutants being emitted by China is already exceeding the carrying capacity of the environment. Indeed, some 27 per cent of China's total national territory is now 'exceeding the carrying capacity of the environment'. Any rivers that flow through cities are predominantly polluted; the air pollution in many of China's cities is extreme. The long-term

Box 3.2 The 'impoverished' state of ecologies in China's
        western region

The 'western regions' were once an important incubator of the Chinese
civilization, for they had a pristine ecology in addition to a flourishing
economy. At one time, Xi'an was the nation's political, economic, and also
cultural center. It is generally felt that Xi'an started to decline after the
An-shi Rebellion [AD 755–763]. Only since the 1950s, however, has excessive development in the region became dramatically worse, as seen in
excessive use of water resources, soil erosion, and environmental degradation of all kinds. Authorities in the field believe that the rapid economic
growth of the west since the 1950s has consistently been accompanied by
deterioration of the environment such that sustainable long-term development of the area has already been affected. An 'ecological bottleneck' is
already constraining future growth. Meanwhile, China's overall prospects
for long-term sustainable growth rely on this region, and on protecting and
improving its ecology and its environment (Ahbulizi Yusupu and Chen
Zuqun, 2007).

   In these western regions, poverty and environmental degradation exist in
tandem. Together, they form a vicious circle. The type of poverty created
by the process is called 'ecological poverty'. According to statistics from
early 2002, 90 per cent of illiterate people in China were located in rural
areas, and 50 per cent of the total were located in western regions. The total
number of illiterate people in the country came to 85.07 million, a huge
figure. The impoverished regions in the west are mainly located in the
steppe area or in more remote mountains. These areas have severe desertification problems and areas of extreme soil erosion. The condition of
'nature' is terrible; destruction of the ecology is severe. The increase of
populations in the western regions in recent years has been very apparent.
This has exacerbated the problem of excessive development of land and
only contributed to further worsening of the environment.

   'Ecological degradation and lagging economic development are cause
and effect to each other, and their mutual intensification has augmented the
accumulated effect. A vicious circle thereby forms which could be
described as "worsening ecological environment – stunted economic development – further worsening ecological environment". This continues to
erode the potential base for economic development in the western regions.
Estimates show that direct economic losses that can be attributed to damage
to the environment in the western regions every year come to RMB 150
billion. This figure is 13 per cent of the region's entire gross regional product. As for indirect costs and potential losses, as well as the costs it will
take to restore the environment, the figure is many multiples of that' (Cha
Hongwang, Xiong Dongliang and Wang Maotai, 2005).

Source: Chen Tao: *Ecological relocation: a perspective of environmental sociology*, in Bing Zheng (ed.): *Reform, Opening up and China's Sociology: A Collection of Award-Winning Papers Presented at the Annual Meeting of the Chinese Sociological Association*, Social Sciences Documentation Publishing House, 2009.

effects of organic pollutants are beginning to be apparent. Land that contains severely polluted soil is expanding in area. Pollution of coastal waters is intensifying. All of these forms of pollution are already seriously threatening people's health.

Fourth, industrial concentrations are not spatially distributed in the ways that the overall population of people is distributed, which relates in part to the movement of rural migrant workers. As the main component of the transient population, these workers can only go where there are jobs. Often unable to take families along, they leave them behind, with elders tending the children. This leads to a separation of the working population from the population that is being supported by those workers.

Places that have the highest concentration of economic activity do not necessarily have the densest populations. To a certain degree, this has exacerbated the problem of cross-regional disparities in GDP per capita.

In 2009, the net flow of rural migrant workers out of central and western regions and toward jobs in the eastern part of China came to 44.64 million people. Within this total, 35.53 million workers did not take family members with them. If one were to assume that each rural migrant worker did take one family member with him, then the population of eastern regions would go up by 35.53 million and the per capita annual GDP of the region would decline by a certain amount. Specifically, it would go from RMB 39,800, as measured without taking family members into account, down to RMB 37,200. In corresponding fashion, the population of central and western regions would decline and their average GDP per capita would go up. Specifically, average GDP per capita would go from RMB 20,300 (in the central part of the country) and RMB 18,200 (in the west) to RMB 21,400 in the central regions and RMB 18,900 in the west.

The disparity in per capita GDP between China's eastern and western regions would then be far less. Instead of eastern incomes being 2.18 times larger than western, eastern incomes would only be 1.97 times larger than western incomes. See Table 3.3.

The disparity in GDP per capita between eastern and central regions would go down from the original 1.96 to 1.73 (eastern regions now earning only 1.96 times what central regions are earning). The degree to which the disparities are reduced depends on the number of family members who accompany the 'rural migrant worker'.

Provinces and cities that currently rank in the forefront of per capita GDP are also those attracting the greatest absolute number and 'net inflows' of rural

Table 3.3 Impact of turning rural migrant workers and their family members into urban residents on narrowing the inter-regional per capita GDP gap

	Current permanent population (10,000)	Net inflow of rural migrant workers (10,000)	Presumed total population	Per capita GDP based on current population (10,000 yuan)	Per capita GDP gap based on current population (1 for west region)	Per capita GDP based on presumed total population (10,000 yuan)	Per capita GDP gap based on presumed total population (1 for west region)
East region	52,761.75	4463.9	56,315.01	3.98	2.18	3.72	1.97
Central region	42,169.07	−2810.8	39,931.67	2.03	1.12	2.14	1.14
West region	36,729.69	−1653.2	35,413.74	1.82	1	1.89	1

Source: Based on the 2009 monitoring and investigation report on rural migrant workers and the national and provincial statistical bulletins. In particular, the presumed total population is worked out by adjusting the total populations in different regions, presuming that the net-flown rural migrant workers who have not brought their whole families with them (about 80%) will bring in one family member each.

migrant workers. The current trend is for economic activity to continue to concentrate in smaller numbers of specific areas. If we continue to account for people by 'fixing' their residence in their original administrative districts, we will only see an increasing disparity in GDP per capita among different regions. This will only contribute to unnecessary political and social pressures.

The physical separation of workers and their families, in addition to the irrational way in which public services are provided, has led to excessive discrepancies in the supply of public services among various regions. The areas into which rural migrant workers are 'flowing' are currently receiving both the taxes and the contributions to GDP of these workers. Areas out of which these workers have migrated, however, must still bear the cost of supplying public services to their dependents. Moreover, an 'insufficiently rational' fiscal system in the country inevitably leads to a sharp contrast in different levels of public spending and supply of public services.

Changes in the spatial configuration of cities

The ever-expanding use of space in the process of urbanization

The amount of space required for the 'build-out' of cities in China has been increasing at an accelerating pace ever since the start of 'reform and opening up' (Tables 3.4 and 3.5). This is evidence of the way in which urbanization is moving ever faster into a 'middle stage' of development. The 'built-up' area of cities, nationwide, went from 7438 square kilometers in 1981 to 36,000 square kilometers in 2008. This represented an increase of 3.88 times, or nearly a fourfold increase. Cities expanded at a rate of 6.3 per cent per annum. In the 1980s, urban expansion led to an annual increase in built-up area of only some 600 square kilometers, whereas in the 1990s, the annual increase came to 960 square kilometers. The pace of expansion has picked up dramatically in the new century, with the annual increase in built-up land coming to 1732 square kilometers.

The spatial configuration of cities and the distribution of populations are highly correlated with the distribution of economic activity in China. Major cities are mainly distributed along the eastern coastline. The pattern of urbanization in the country is therefore highly irregular. From an overall perspective, one can see a stair-stepped pattern of distribution that goes down from east to west, with fewer and fewer cities being located in the west.

As measured by the number of cities within each 10,000 square kilometers, the provinces and autonomous regions with the highest 'density of cities' as measured by the number of cities per 10,000 square kilometers are Jiangsu (3.86), Zhejiang (3.3), and Shandong (3.2).

The density of cities in Guangdong, Henan, Hainan, Liaoning, Hubei, and Fujian provinces ranges between 2.5 and 1.9. The range goes on down further to between 1.8 and 0.9 cities per square kilometer in Anhui, Hebei, Beijing, Tianjin, Jilin, Shanxi, Hunan, Jiangxi, Ningxia and Guangxi. The figure is between 0.8 and 0.5 in Guizhou, Shaanxi, Heilongjiang, and Sichuan (excluding Chongqing);

Table 3.4 Built-up areas (km²) of cities in China

Year	Built-up area	Year-on-year growth (%)	Year	Built-up area	Year-on-year growth (%)
1981	7,438.0		1995	19,264.2	7.38
1982	7,862.1	5.70	1996	20,214.2	4.93
1983	8,156.3	3.74	1997	20,791.3	2.85
1984	9,249.0	13.40	1998	21,379.6	2.83
1985	9,386.2	1.48	1999	21,524.5	0.68
1986	10,127.3	7.90	2000	22,439.3	4.25
1987	10,816.5	6.81	2001	24,026.6	7.07
1988	12,094.6	11.82	2002	25,972.6	8.10
1989	12,462.2	3.04	2003	28,308.0	8.99
1990	12,855.7	3.16	2004	30,406.2	7.41
1991	14,011.1	8.99	2005	32,520.7	6.95
1992	14,958.7	6.76	2006	33,659.8	3.50
1993	16,588.3	10.89	2007	35,469.7	5.38
1994	17,939.5	8.15	2008	36,295.3	2.33

Source: *China Urban Construction Statistical Yearbook 1990–2005*; *China Statistical Yearbook 2006–2007*.

below 0.5 in Yunnan, Gansu, Inner Mongolia, Xinjiang, Qinghai and Tibet; and below 0.2 in Inner Mongolia, Xinjiang, Qinghai and Tibet (see Table 3.6).

Special features of urban expansion in China

The impact of ongoing expansion of cities in China, and continuing acceleration of the pace of expansion, can be monitored by evaluating remote sensing images taken of 55 'representative' municipalities since the 1970s.

Table 3.5 Built-up areas (km²) of county cities and administrative towns in China

Year	Built-up area of administrative towns	Year	Built-up area of county cities	Built-up area of administrative towns
1990	8,220	1999		16,750
1991	8,700	2000	13,135	18,200
1992	9,750	2001	10,427	19,720
1993	11,190	2002	10,496	20,320
1994	11,880	2004	11,774	22,360
1995	13,860	2005	12,383	23,690
1996	14,370	2006	13,229	31,200
1997	15,530	2007	14,260	31,200
1998	16,300	2008	14,776	30,160

Source: *China Urban Construction Statistical Yearbook 2008*; No data are available for built-area of county cities before 2000.

Table 3.6 City density in different regions in 2007 (in number per 10,000 km²)

Region	City density	Ranking	Region	City density	Ranking
Heibei	1.61	11	Hunan	1.38	14
Shanxi	1.47	13	Guangdong	2.44	4
Inner Mongolia	0.18	24	Guangxi	0.91	17
Liaoning	2.07	7	Hainan	2.35	6
Jilin	1.56	12	Sichuan	0.66	21
Heilongjiang	0.67	20	Guizhou	0.76	18
Jiangsu	3.86	1	Yunnan	0.45	22
Zhejiang	3.30	2	Tibet	0.02	27
Anhui	1.69	10	Shaanxi	0.68	19
Fujian	1.92	9	Gansu	0.38	23
Jiangxi	1.31	15	Qinghai	0.04	26
Shandong	3.20	3	Ningxia	1.06	16
Henan	2.38	5	Xinjiang	0.14	25
Hubei	2.00	8			

Source: Urban–Rural Planning Department of Ministry of Housing and Urban–Rural Development: *China's Administrative Cities and Population Statistical Data in 2007.*

Note: Gu Chaolin: *Background Report, 2009.*

In terms of the spatial forms that urban expansion is taking, it is clear that the expansion of those cities located on plateaus or adjacent to mountains or rivers is not as affected by the local topography. They have a relatively greater amount of urban sprawl and generally cover more territory. They are expanding at a faster rate. A variety of factors contributes to their growth in concentric rings or radiating out along traffic corridors. More and more cities are taking a segmented shape of concentric circles, including Beijing and Zhengzhou.

Other cities, such as Tianjin and Shijiazhuang, are gradually expanding according to their original grid shape and radial patterns.

More and more cities located on both banks of major rivers are beginning to 'conjoin' with or merge into cities in the regions through which the rivers flow. One conspicuous trend is that cities which were originally on only one bank of a body of water are now expanding onto the other bank. Shanghai is a notable example.

Cities that have developed along valleys in mountainous areas are far more constrained by topography than those that have grown up on plains. In most cases, they have developed in the direction of the flow of the river. This is most obvious in the west, in cities such as Chongqing and Urumqi. As the perimeters of the cities expand outwards and approach a range of mountains or a neighboring river, what had been an 'open space' of undeveloped land between city and geographic feature now closes in. This has been the case with Taiyuan and Fuzhou. Such cities are now flanked by geographic barriers and their room for further expansion is 'squeezed' as a result.

Cities located along the coast not only have expanded along the coastal land surfaces but have also extended themselves out into the coastal waters. In these cases, urban spatial reconfiguration depends heavily on islands and coastal ridges.

The tendency to expand along coastlines is quite apparent. Qingdao is one example.

The speed with which cities are expanding is tremendous, but there are also huge differences in rates of 'built-up' expansion in different cities. Between 1973 and 2007, the built up area of Haikou expanded by 23.42 times what it had originally been. The area of the city took over an additional 100 square kilometers. The cities of Fangchenggang, Zhengzhou, and Ningbo all grew by at least five times. The place that changed the least was Chichihar. In 2008, its 'built-up area' was only 1.21 times what it had been in 1989.

Seven cities in China expanded at an average annual rate of 10 square kilometers per year, namely Beijing, Shanghai, Shenzhen, Nanjing, Guangzhou, Zhengzhou, and Chengdu. Among these, Beijing expanded to cover the most territory. For the past 30 years, the city has expanded at an average annual rate of 26.69 square kilometers. The average annual expansion of 11 other cities has been at a modest rate of less than one square kilometer per year, namely Shigatse, Karamay, Wewei, Yichang, Qiqihar, Nanchong, Lhasa, Lijiang, Xiangtan, Xining, and Bangbu. Among these, the city of Shigatse grew by only 0.25 kilometers per year.

With respect to how the size of a city affects its rate of expansion, we find that the larger a city is, the faster it grows. Among all cities included in the survey, those with populations that exceeded four million grew consistently at the fastest pace. Moreover, the rate at which these cities grew exhibited a stair-stepped pattern of four main stages over the course of a number of years. From the late 1970s to the early 1980s, the average annual expansion came to 5 square kilometers or less. From the late 1980s into the 1990s, annual expansion was stable at around 10–15 square kilometers. Cities began to expand ferociously in the twenty-first century, as their 'built-up' areas took off. Between 2001 and 2004, the incremental space needed for building up new urban areas came to more than 25 square kilometers per city every year. After 2005, the figure went down to 12.9 square kilometers, and has since shown a gradually declining trend.

Cities with populations that range between two and four million, as well as those with populations between one and two million, have also exhibited a two-step growth pattern but the rate of increase has been more modest. For cities in the first category, the initial stage of growth occurred between 1988 and 1993, and the second stage of growth came between 1998 and 2003. After 2005, growth gradually began to slow down. Cities in the second category of cities saw a more sluggish growth rate than those in the first category. The first stage of real growth only began in the year 2000, and the second stage in the year 2003. This growth spurt continued, however, all the way up to 2008.

In 1988, cities with populations in the range of 50–100 million started expanding at a rate of under 2 square kilometers per year on average, but this rose dramatically to 7.55 square kilometers in 2003. This high rate continued for only two years, however, before going back to under 5 square kilometers per year. As for cities with populations that are less than 500,000 in population, the rate of expansion has been quite steady, with only minor fluctuations. Only in 2005–2006 did the expansion rate exceed 1 square kilometer per city per year; for the rest of the time, it fluctuated but stayed under 1 square kilometer.

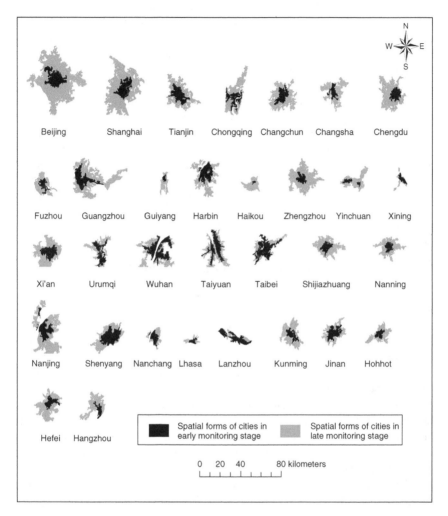

Figure 3.1 Average expansion speeds of cities in different scales.
Source: *Zhang* Zengxiang: Background Report, 2009.

With respect to the sources of land that are being used by the process of urbanization,[7] farmland, or 'arable land', is still the most important source of the 'built-up' new areas of cities. Arable land accounts for 57 per cent of the area used by the recent expansion of cities in China.

An additional 32 per cent of the total area of land being absorbed into cities was formerly classified as 'land used for construction'. 'Other' sources of land account for 11 per cent of the built-out areas, and these include forest land, marsh or wetlands, grasslands, and so on.

There are considerable differences in the percentages of the above several types of land that is now being put to urban uses. Most cities use more farmland than any other type of land for urbanization. Forty-six cities are indeed are using large amounts of farmland: the farmland being occupied in these cases constitutes between 42.5 per cent and 100 per cent of all land used for that particular city's construction.

A number of cities are using primarily the land on their peripheries that is classified as 'land used for other construction purposes' in order to expand. These cities include Beijing, Shenzhen, Harbin, Dalian, and Chichihar. As for the last category, 'land for other uses' that is now being absorbed into urbanization, cities occupying such types of land are mainly located in the western part of the country and certain regions in the south. Such cities include Karamay, which is expanding into grasslands, Yichang in Guangzhou province, which is expanding into forested areas, and Fangchenggang, which is mainly using land reclaimed from coastal waters. (Zhang Zengxiang: 2009).

Establishing principles that help define the spatial configuration of future urbanization

It should be recognized that the intent to 'urbanize' refers to the overall development of the country. It does not mean urbanizing at each level of governmental administration. Moreover, the pattern of urbanization that China now intends to take is one that uses only a very small portion of its national territory. The dominant share of territory should be put either to agriculture or maintained as 'ecological or natural space'.

To a large extent, problems that currently exist in China's development patterns, with 'development' covering the country with ubiquitous urban development and economic activity, are due to the fact that every single administrative district wants to 'urbanize'. This problem extends to every level of government and even governmental levels within a district. As a result, it is vital to begin to establish a rational pattern of urban spatial distribution in China. To do that, it is necessary to clarify some misconceptions and set forth certain principles.

1 The spatial distribution of urbanization should seek a proper balance among the human population, the economy, and an area's 'resource endowment'[8]

A variety of problems can result from unbalanced use of different types of land. These problems include the following, among others:

- excessive disparities in the living standards of people in cities and people in the countryside, as well as disparities in public services that each population receives;
- various social problems that accompany annual migrations of upwards of 100 million people;

- the acute loss of arable farmland due to 'blind expansion' of the built-up area of cities, as well as to the construction of 'development zones';
- excessive mining of underground water, such that large areas of ground are now subsiding;
- over-grazing on grasslands resulting in desertification and wastelands;
- over-development of marginal land in forests but also marshes, such that land is degraded and serious soil erosion results;
- the daily increasing pressure to have to transport water resources and energy resources across regions.

In evaluating the objective reasons for such unbalanced use of national territory, the ultimate cause comes back to China's scarce resources. These include, most importantly, land, water, and energy. In addition, the ultimate cause relates to the way in which economic activity, concentrations of population, and concentrations of resources are uncoordinated or out of sync. More subjective reasons would include the fact that insufficient attention has been paid to conceptualizing and creating principles that relate to the spatial reconfiguration of land. Such principles include those that must be followed in the course of economic development and urbanization.

It is highly important for China to establish concepts and principles that enable a balanced approach to land use if we intend to achieve sustainable growth. Such concepts and principles are also vital to the process of creating a balance in economic activity between urban and rural areas and among different regions.

If we do not establish such concepts and principles about balanced use of space, and if we do not seriously consider moving populations out from the most environmentally vulnerable places in the country, as a way to get at the root of the problem, we will not be able to prevent these areas from pursuing development. We will not be able to turn around worsening environmental conditions.

Once an ecosystem has been seriously damaged, there is no way to restore it without spending vast amounts of money. The process of trying to put back the forests after land has been destroyed by agriculture, or restore grasslands after they have been over-grazed, requires one massive engineering feat after another. We are aware of the costs already, as we are experiencing several examples: protecting and improving the ecosystems at the source of the 'Three Rivers', preventing the sandstorms that threaten Beijing and Tianjin by mitigating source problems, and reclaiming the stony desert that has developed on the Yunnan–Guizhou Plateau.

If indeed we do not establish such concepts and principles and thereby begin to control the intensity of the kinds of development that are threatening the most vulnerable of China's ecosystems, if we do not control problems at the source, where the carrying capacity of natural resources is already threatened, if we do not push through a change in the regional structure of industry that is already not able to match the carrying capacity of the resource endowment, we will not be able to keep people from wasting ever more energy resources, and ever more water, in the pursuit of development. We will also find it very hard to keep more pollutants from being emitted into the environment.

Once power outages and water shortages begin to affect people's lives, there is no alternative to spending huge amounts of money to redress the problems. The same is true once calamitous environmental disasters occur. Retroactive action includes batching in energy supplies, or diverting water from elsewhere, or trying to control environmental pollution through engineering projects.

Moreover, if we do not put severe restrictions on the burden of a human population in mega-cities that is already well over the capacity of those cities to provide for it, and control the problem at its source, it will be ever harder to prevent more people from swarming into these cities. If these cities do not properly deal with some of their urban functions but instead are allowed to continue all-out expansion in order to serve as 'economic centers', 'industrial bases', 'trade centers', and 'transport hubs', we simply will not be able to deal with the consequences. It will be impossible to keep housing prices from rising through the roof. It will be hard to deal with already unbearable traffic congestion, and with burdens on the environment that the environment cannot support.

China's population is expected to peak at 1.46 billion people. When that happens, we are proposing a concept of 'spatial balance' that is meant to distribute this population on China's 9.6 million square kilometers in a pattern that matches human presence with comparable economic activity, specifically the activity involved in generating a GDP of RMB 120 trillion.

Such a concept is meant to be strategic in how it plans for the nation to use its 1.8 billion mu of arable land, and its 2.8 trillion cubic meters of water resources. It is meant to promote a more harmonious development of humans and nature, and leave a 'home garden' for children and grandchildren, a place that still has blue sky, clear waters, and clean mountains.

China's 9.6 million square kilometers of national territory belongs not only to our immediate generation but to generations still to come. We cannot live in luxury just for our one generation alone if, in so doing, we irrevocably destroy a homeland that we in fact 'own' together with our children. This is all the more true if our aim is merely to create more immediate GDP.

2 The spatial distribution of urbanization should help preserve and strengthen the ability of ecosystems to provide 'ecological products'

Since reform and opening-up began, China has increased its ability to provide various products quite quickly, including agricultural, industrial, and service products. Generally speaking, however, the country has done poorly in terms of providing what could be called 'ecological products'. In fact, our ability to product superior ecological products has markedly declined.

Our national concept of development now involves 'taking the human being as the core concern'. Given this focus, the provision of ecological products must be an important component of overall 'development'. Development can no longer be regarded purely in terms of increasing the capacity to produce goods and services.

Box 3.3 The concept behind 'ecological products' and
characteristics of such products

While 'products' can be defined from a supply perspective, they also can and indeed should be defined from a demand perspective. Such things as clean air, pure water, a comfortable environment and a climate that is suitable for human beings can also be considered 'products' when thought of in terms of demand, since they are able to meet human needs.

Given the current backdrop of energy shortages, scarcity of resources, deterioration of ecosystems, worsening of environmental conditions, climate change and warming, frequent natural disasters, and the increasing need for clean air, pure water, and hospitable environments, it is time for us to define 'products' in a more substantive and inclusive way. It is time for us to set forth characteristics of things that we regard as 'ecological products'.

Ecological products are those that safeguard the security of ecosystems, that ensure that they continue to function properly, and that provide the 'natural factors' as well as the 'man-made natural factors', that supply a beneficial environment for human habitation. In addition to benefiting human existence in direct ways, ecological products also contribute to the needs of life in indirect ways. They absorb carbon dioxide, produce oxygen, sustain water resources, filter water and improve its quality, conserve soil moisture, prevent windblown sandstorms, moderate the atmosphere, clean the air, reduce noise, absorb dust, preserve biodiversity, and mitigate natural disasters.

In general, ecological products have the following characteristics:

1   They are regional in nature. They play an environmental role within a specific unit of space, whether that is in the atmosphere or on earth, and they have a pronounced regional quality. No matter how good the air is on Hainan Island, it cannot be used to improve the air over Beijing. When the waters of the 'Three Rivers' reach the mouth of the Yangtze and enter the ocean, the quantity of water may have been retained but the quality of water is distinctly different.

2   Ecological products are not easily measured. Unlike industrial and agricultural products, ecological products cannot be divided up into units of consumption by individual human beings, since their benefit generally accrues to an entire group of people. As a result, it becomes hard to measure, with any accuracy, just how much any given individual might have 'consumed'.

3   Ecological products are intangible. They generally are 'formless', and as a result could perhaps better be described as ecological 'services'. Forests, grasslands, and marshlands are the equivalent of the 'land' and 'machinery' that provide ecological services. They constitute the

'productive capacity' of ecosystems. They themselves, however, are not 'ecological products'. Once the productive capacity of the machinery is destroyed, both the quantity and quality of ecological products declines.

4   Ecological services are of a public nature. They are similar to such things as compulsory education, basic medical care, social security, public security, and so on, in that they belong to 'basic public services'. As such, they cannot be provided by individuals or private institutions but must necessarily be the responsibility of governments.

The most significant reasons that we need to develop the concept of 'ecological products' are as follows:

1   When we establish a concept of 'ecological products', this contributes to establishing a firmer understanding of the necessary harmony between man and nature. In exploiting and using nature, man cannot expect to override nature. The orientation of human behavior must be in alignment with the laws of nature.

2   Such a concept helps in defining the 'development rights' of any given ecosystem or ecological region. Ecological regions have people living within their boundaries who have the right to lead a better life and to develop their surroundings. The 'substance' of the development of ecological regions is different, however. It includes such things as providing ecological products by protecting nature and repairing ecosystems rather than creating agricultural or industrial products that take an actual form. This includes the idea of 'taking a scientific view of development' and adhering to the notion that a broader sense of 'development' is of primary importance.

3   Developing this concept of ecological products can provide the theoretical underpinning for the idea of 'ecological compensation'. Ecological products have a value, and therefore are something that can, theoretically, be 'sold'. The difficulty lies in dividing up and measuring exactly how much each 'producer' has contributed to producing the products, and how much each 'consumer' has consumed. As a result, ecological products can only be bought and sold through 'procurement' at the government or group level. That is, transactions can only function through various compensation mechanisms. In reality, a government represents all of the consumers of ecological products in 'purchasing' the services of ecosystems.

3 Respect the primary functions of different types of regions

The natural attributes of different kinds of space differ from one another. This determines the fact that the 'primary functions' of a specific unit of space can also differ from primary functions of other units of space.

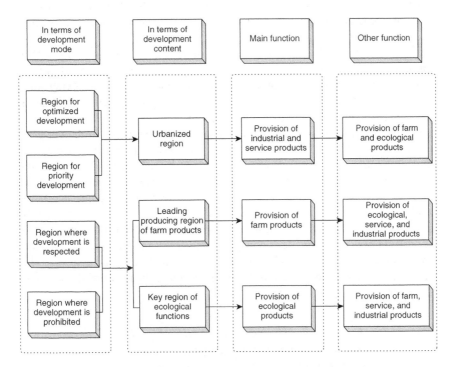

Figure 3.2 Classification and functions of main functional regions.

Different categories of space can be defined according to the 'products' that the space produces. Categories can also be defined by the contribution of a particular type of space to 'development', as broadly defined. Three primary functions of space can be used to define three principal categories of the use of land [or space], namely agricultural, industrial, and ecological.

Regions that are urbanizing are those that share the primary function of providing industrial products and services. Regions that are primarily agricultural share the primary function of providing agricultural products. Key 'ecological regions' are those whose primary function is to provide ecological services. [We feel that] the functions of various parts of China's national territory should be differentiated according to the 'primary function' involved. Once such functions are defined, the essential tasks and core substance of different kinds of 'development' can be more easily determined.

It is extremely important to differentiate 'primary functions' according to the natural attributes of a given region. When it comes to meeting the needs of mankind, all forms of space, including urban, agricultural, and ecological, are scarce commodities. Because they are so scarce, it is vital to choose development options in a way that respects the laws of nature.

The term 'primary function' is not the same as 'sole function'. Distinguishing a primary function does not exclude other functions. As one form of ecological 'space', grasslands that need to be preserved may not preclude grazing as part of their role. To define the 'primary function' of such grasslands in terms of their returns on livestock would be to relegate other vital functions to a secondary position, however, including such things as retaining moisture and conserving water sources, preventing wind erosion and sandstorms, conserving soil, regulating the atmosphere, maintaining biodiversity, and so on.

Returning farmland to forests, allowing grasslands to recover from over-grazing, restoring wetlands that were turned into fields, are all forms of 'restoring' the original function of an ecosystem, correcting a previously mistaken definition of the primary function of a particular space. The only way to conserve 'nature' in a fundamental way, and protect ecosystems, is to respect nature and make sure that human systems are aligned with it. This requires a prior determination of the primary functions of nature in terms of the specific natural attributes of a particular space. Then, economic development as appropriate to the specific attributes may be carried out. Among other considerations, this also means allowing only that concentration of people in a particular space that is in accord with the degree of economic activity in that space.

4 Give full consideration to the carrying capacity of local resources and the environmental carrying capacity in a given ecological space

Different spaces call for different primary functions. Each kind of space has its own quantities and varieties of resources and environmental considerations. Each has a different tolerance for human concentration and economic activity. Ecological spaces and agricultural spaces, for example, are not suited to large-scale and intensive industrialization and urbanization. As a result, they are limited in their ability to tolerate a high-consumption type of population. In such places, it is necessary for any excess population to be shifted, gradually, toward urban spaces with more jobs and higher incomes.

In a more agrarian period of history, people's consumption levels were not so high that a region could not sustain human occupation at a fairly low level. As the phrase went, 'each patch of land could support each patch's worth of people'. In an industrial age, however, or the age of service economies, people demand a higher standard of living. One patch of land can no longer suffice.

On the other hand, the resources and environments of urbanized areas also have their limits. Excessive populations and concentration of economic activity can bring pressures to bear on the environment that are hard to sustain. The quality of life begins to deteriorate. China has some areas in which the degree or 'intensity' of development is already over 40 per cent, as defined at the prefectural level in terms of the administrative unit. Further development of such areas has the potential to turn them into 'concrete boards' that are unsuited to human habitation.

Water is a key consideration. Water is a 'hard constraint' in areas that have scarce water resources, so that population, the size of economic activity, and industrial structure must be tailored to that resource and kept within the bounds of the available water. When large-scale industrial and urban development continues to be inflicted upon regions that are seriously short of water, eventually the supply of surface water runs short of demand. Only two options are then available. One is to tap into underground water. The consequence of this can be that the land surface subsides, damaging basic infrastructure in the area and even causing catastrophic damage to the entire city.

The second option is to transport water from one region to another over long distances. This is costly – the government needs to fund massive water transport projects – but it also has negative side-effects on the areas that are exporting the water. Consequences may be hard to measure. Moreover, the laying of pipelines required for water transport takes up space. It occupies land that is already highly limited.

5 Institute strict controls on the 'intensity of development' in different regions

Since the carrying capacity of any given unit of space is limited, it is necessary to limit the intensity of development in order to be able to satisfy the needs and demands of that area's ecosystem. Any expansion in 'built-up space' means that agricultural space and ecological space suffer a corresponding decrease. This inevitably affects the productivity of agriculture, but also that of the ecosystem.

When agricultural production in a given place is unable to meet demand, agricultural products can always be brought in from the outside and yields can generally be increased as science and technology advances. The same is not true of ecological production. As noted above, ecological products are 'regional' in nature and it is not easy to transfer them from one place to another. This means that development must be controlled to within the bounds of an ecosystem. The ecosystem must remain able to supply the basic minimum level of 'ecological products' for that district. This is critical in our age of erupting environmental crises. As we develop our economy, economic efficiencies cannot be our only consideration.

We are in need of more 'green spaces' in China, and more agricultural lands as well, in order to help purify the polluted air and water caused by man's activities. Animals and plants both need more space in which to 'take in sunshine' in order to ensure that the country has a stable source of food supply. As we engage in urbanization and urban development, we must also have a sense of self-restraint. We must retain sufficient space for farming and for ecosystems in order to leave at least a little 'space' for the generations to come.

6 Severely limit the 'low-efficiency' expansion of industrial production. Increase the percentage of land that is allocated for urban residences

At the present time, the percentage of space devoted to 'urban industrial production' in China is unduly high. This relates to various considerations, not just economic growth. It also relates to China's mode of economic growth, which is extensive rather than intensive, to having low-tech industries, and to the historic problem of focusing on 'production and not people's lives'.

As a result, China now needs to be proactive in restructuring its economy. It needs to transform its production methods, and create greater concentrations of industries and service industries. The country must avoid a mode of industrial development that calls for 'smokestacks in every village', which means it must improve the efficiency with which land is used for industrial production. It should engage in wholesale transformation of the current way in which industrial production occupies places that are more suited to human habitation. In sequence and over a period of time, industries currently occupying land that could be put into housing should be moved elsewhere. This will relieve some of the pressures to have more housing space in cities, without taking up farmland for that purpose.

At the same time, the country should increase its investment in the kind of basic infrastructure that supports human lives, and in public services in general. Such services should contribute to lowering commuting time and distances, raising the quality of life in cities, and improving the efficiency of economic operations. China should avoid having industrial production located in places that are at an irrational distance from where people live.

A proposed overall framework for thinking about the spatial distribution of urbanization

Thinking about a scientific spatial distribution of China's cities should be a comprehensive and centralized process that falls within the overall strategic pattern of development in the country. Such an approach not only must have a rational plan for urbanization, but it must protect and conserve agricultural space and ecological space as well. It must take into consideration the need to satisfy the country's demand not only for agricultural products but also ecological products. It must seek to minimize any industrial use of agricultural and ecological space.

Overall pattern of using China's national territory

Given that our point of departure is the desire to achieve ongoing and sustainable development for the nation through an overall approach to the use of its territory, we recommend that China establish what we are calling the 'three great strategic patterns'.

The first of these patterns incorporates 'three vertical and two horizontal lines'. The continental land corridor and the Yangtze River corridor would constitute the two horizontal axes. The coastal corridor, the Harbin–Beijing–Guangzhou corridor, and the Baotou–Kunming corridor would serve as the three vertical axes. Major urban clusters along these corridors would be primary supports for a system that linked other urban concentrations and cities into these hubs in a strategic pattern of urbanization.

The second of these patterns relates to agriculture and creates a strategic system of 'seven districts and 23 territorial belts'. The seven main agricultural producing areas in China are the Northeast Plains, the Huang-huaihai plains, the Yangtze River basin, the Fenwei plains, the Hetao Irrigated Area, the South China Region and the Gansu–Xinjiang Region. In terms of strategic use of space, this area fundamentally should be in 'basic farming fields', while other types of agricultural production form key components of the system as well.

The third pattern relates to what we are calling the 'two protective screens and three ecological zones'. The two screens [or shielding ecosystems] include the Qing-zang high plateau ecological screen and the Loess Plateau–Yungui Plateau [Yunnan–Guizhou] high plateau ecological screen. The belts include three zones with key ecological functions: the northeast forest belt, the northern desert-prevention belt, and the belt of hills in the south. Large rivers provide an important skeletal structure for these zones and belts, and they are supported by various other major ecological-function areas. Certain areas, distributed throughout these zones and belts, should become key places in which the State forbids the construction of any development zones.

Only once China has done adequate strategic planning on the 'three major strategic patterns' with respect to its overall territory will the country be able to bring various imbalances under control. Only then can it coordinate its distribution of economic activity, its human population, and its environment for natural resources and move toward greater concentration as well as balance. Urbanization will in the future be pursued on a very small portion of China's overall territory, and only on that portion that is suited to development. This will be done in order to enable industries and people to concentrate in certain areas, and to form a denser distribution of cities. The functions of the mega-cities clustered around the rim of the Bohai Gulf and in the Yangtze River Delta and the Pearl River Delta will continue to be enhanced in an effort to make these cities more internationally competitive. Based on this experience, other regions that are suitable for development should be guided to form several major urban clusters and regional city clusters as well.

The rural population will continue to migrate into cities. The living space that they now leave behind will be returned to farming purposes, as well as reforestation, rebuilding of grasslands, and restoration of water sources. All the various ecological functions will be elevated to major importance, including protecting and conserving the sources of water, preventing sandstorms and stabilizing shifting sands, conserving water and soil, maintaining biodiversity, and protecting natural and cultural resources. The various ecosystems, forests, water systems, grasslands, wetlands, deserts, farmland, and so on, will be stabilized as possible.

The spatial distribution of urbanization within China

Five different categories of China's future urbanization can be distinguished according to how cities are spatially arrayed in the country. The categories are mega-city clusters, large urban clusters, other urbanized areas (metropolitan areas, urban hubs, and urban strips), border cities that form 'port cities', and medium-sized and smaller towns that exist in a 'dotted' configuration.

This categorization takes into account the carrying capacity of the resource endowment for each category, the intensity of current development and further development potential, and political and ethnic factors. Urbanization plans will be implemented according to each category.

In the future, approximately one billion people will be concentrated within the space of these five different categories of urban areas. The areas will basically meet the needs of China for urban space in the year 2030, when we expect China's population to have reached a peak figure of 1.46 billion and the urbanization rate in the country to have reached 65 per cent.

Mega-city clusters

We recommend that the country give preference to 'optimized development' of its three mega-city clusters, namely the rim of the Bohai Gulf (including Beijing, Tianjin, Hebei, central and southern Liaoning province, and the Jiaodong peninsula), the Yangtze River delta and the Pearl River delta. These three areas are already intensely developed and the carrying capacity of their resource environments is beginning to weaken. While they should further increase their comprehensive economic strength, these areas should also focus on changing their economic structure. They should accelerate the pace at which they transform their mode of economic development. These areas should be made into 'key' focal points for China's international competitiveness. They should serve as the 'dragon heads' or leaders in stimulating the entire country's socioeconomic development. They should become leaders in innovation, and areas of global influence. They should also have the greatest concentration of population in the country, as well as its most densely concentrated economic activity. (See Chapter 4 for details.)

Major urban clusters

We recommend that China emphasize the development of eight major urban clusters. Specifically, these are the Harbin–Changchun region (the Harbin–Daqing–Qiqihar region in Heilongjiang Province and the Changchun–Jilin region in Jilin Province), the southeast Fujian region (the coastal region of Fujian Province), the Yangtze–Huaihe region (the Wanjiang region in Anhui Province), the Central Plains region (the central part of Henan Province), the middle reaches of the Yangtze River (comprising the Changsha–Zhuzhou–Xiangtan region in Hunan Province, the Wuhan urban hub in Hubei Province, and the Nanchang–Jiujiang region in Jiangxi Province), the Guanzhong Plains, the Chengdu–Chongqing region, and the Beibu Bay region.

Given that we expect China's peak population to be around 1.46 billion people, the country cannot resemble Japan or the USA in having only three large urban clusters, and it certainly cannot resemble England, France, or Korea in having only one major urban cluster. While aiming for 'optimized development' of the three existing mega-city clusters, therefore, the country should also guide the formation of a number of new large urban clusters.

These should be in areas that have the necessary conditions, namely a fairly strong carrying capacity in terms of resource endowment, fairly good conditions for concentrations of people and economic activity, a certain already-existing economic base, urban systems that have already been initiated, and a fairly dense existing population.

These large urban clusters should form areas that each contain between 30 and 60 million people. If we use an average number of 50 million people per cluster, then we can calculate that the eight new urban clusters will be able to accommodate an urban population of some 400 million. (See Chapter 4 for details.)

Other urbanized areas

We recommend that China nurture and develop 'other forms of urban areas' that include such things as metropolitan districts, urban hubs, and urban strips. In addition to undertaking 'optimized development' of the three mega-city clusters and the eight large urban clusters, China should nurture and develop a number of 'urbanized areas' in which cities will be fairly densely concentrated. Such areas would require some or all of the following characteristics. They should have resource environments with fairly strong carrying capacity. They should be fairly well endowed in terms of either energy or mineral resources. They should have conditions that allow for substantial concentration of both people and economic activity. They should be important to 'balancing' the development of China's built-up areas. They should be important in safeguarding the security of the national territory. They should have special significance in terms of ensuring that all ethnic groups are able to develop in tandem.

Such places will include the central and southern part of Hebei Province, the central part of Shanxi Province (the Taiyuan urban hub), the Hohhot–Baotou–Erdos–Yulin region in Inner Mongolia, the central part of Guizhou Province (the Guiyang urban hub), the central part of Yunnan Province (the Kunming urban hub), the central and southern part of Tibet, the Lanzhou–Xining region, the region in Ningxia along the Yellow River, and the northern slopes of the Tianshan mountain region in Xinjiang. Except for the central and southern part of Tibet and the region in Ningxia along the Yellow River, each of the other regions should be able to accommodate an urban population of between 10 and 20 million people.

Some of these regions do not actually have very strong carrying capacity in terms of their resource endowment. They do not have tremendous potential for highly developed economies or for concentrating large numbers of people. Nonetheless, they are important from other perspectives, including national security and ethnic solidarity. They too should be regarded as focal points and their development should be nurtured. If each of these urbanized areas does in fact absorb 10 million people or more, these areas should be able to accommodate an urban population that totals over one hundred million people. (See Chapter 4 for details.)

Port cities

We recommend that China strengthen the 'port cities' along its land borders. In order to meet the needs of further expansion of the program to 'open up' to the outside world, and particularly in order to be proactive in participating in all forms of international and regional cooperation, China should now expand and develop a number of inland port cities. This should be undertaken in concert with the building of international roads and transport lines. These cities should be built up as fast as possible in order to turn them into regional cities serving key functions. Such functions would include border trade, serving as ports, encouraging tourism, and becoming the central hub of communications lines. Cities to be considered would include Dandong, Tumen, Suifenghe, Hehe, Manzhouri, Erlianhot, Yining, Kashi, Shikatse, Ruili, Hekou, Pinxiang and Dongxing.

These cities should focus on expanding border trade and improving China's external relations. They should enhance the building up of their human carrying capacity. They should become 'bridgeheads' that are aimed at trade with northeast Asia, southeast Asia, and Central Asia. Their functions will include becoming processing bases and logistical 'nodes'. Their development should also help improve the spatial distribution of 'opening up' in China [which currently centers on the coastal regions].

Medium-sized cities and smaller towns

We recommend that China also develop a range of 'other' medium-sized cities and smaller towns, in a pattern that is 'dotted' around the country. The spatial distribution should be 'dots' and not 'sheets' of cities. Such cities will be located outside the scope of other urban areas as described above. They may be in primarily agricultural areas, or areas that have key ecosystem functions. In these instances, the policies to be implemented should focus on 'limited development'.

First, sufficient consideration must be given to the environmental carrying capacity and resource endowment of the existing cities. County seats, and those small towns with potential, can form 'dots', but not what could be called 'sheets' or 'tracts'. Such places should focus on developing their unique attributes. They should not seek to become 'comprehensive-type' cities without any kind of special features. They should develop into regional centers for public services, depending on the advantages and conditions of each local area. Some may become key transport nodes, or logistical centers in trade, or tourist sites or cultural and educational attractions or sports and health centers. Some may focus on being residential centers with beautiful surroundings. We want to avoid having each and every one try to become an 'economic center' with its own 'industrial base'.

Notes

1   The ecological function area refers to an area that takes the provision of ecological products as its main function. When we discuss the spatial pattern for urbanization, we must consider the issue from a 'three-in-one' perspective of the spatial pattern

for agricultural production, the spatial pattern for ecological products and the spatial pattern for urbanization. In keeping with the types of provided products, this report divides the territorial space into the areas for urbanization, the leading areas for farm products, and the key areas for ecological functions. The specific definitions will be offered in the following part.

2　According to the evaluation of resource and environmental tolerance made by the Chinese Academy of Sciences, China has only 1.8 million square kilometers of territorial space suitable for industrial and urban development. After the protected farmland and the area for construction are deducted, the country has only 280,000 square kilometers, or about 3 per cent of the total land territorial space, available for industrial and urban development. The 280,000 square kilometers cannot be all developed now, because necessary spaces must be reserved for our future generations.

3　Spatial structure refers to the composition of different types of spaces and their distribution in different regions. They include the ratio between urban space, agricultural space, and ecological space, the ratio between the space for urban construction and the space for industrial and mining construction in urban space, and the distribution of the urban space and the space for industries and mines between different regions.

4　Japan has the same industrial output value as China does. But its space for industrial production is only 1600 square kilometers. In the 40 years from 1965 to 2004, Japan's space for industrial production increased by only 700 square kilometers. Japan has a population of 130 million and its space for urban residence is 11,000 square kilometers. The per capita residential space was more than 80 square meters. The three metropolitan rims have an industrial space of only 600 square kilometers but have a residential space of 3700 square kilometers. The latter is six times the former. The Paris region in France has a total area of 12,000 square kilometers. It has an industrial space of only 205 square kilometers and a residential space of 1100 square kilometers. The latter is five times the former.

5　The development intensity refers to the ratio between the constructed space and the total space within a spatial unit. The constructed space comprises the built-up districts of cities and administrative towns, the independent industrial and mining areas, the rural settlements, the land used for the construction of transport, energy and water control (excluding water surface), and the land occupied by military, religious, and other facilities.

6　The three islands are Chongming, Changxing, and Hengsha. They have a total land area of 1411 square kilometers.

7　The urban land sources can be classified into three categories. The first category is the use of farmland. The second is the use of other land for construction purposes, namely the land for the construction of independent towns, rural settlements, industries, mines, and transport facilities outside the built-up areas of cities. The third is the use of other land, namely all land sources other than farmland and land for construction purposes. It includes forestland, grassland, water area, unutilized land. and sea.

8　Spatial balance means to realize a spatial balance between population, economy, and resource and environment within a specific spatial unit of the national territory, which is human-oriented and is based on the tolerance of resources and environment.

4 Making 'urban clusters' the primary form of urbanization in China

Determining the forms in which urbanization should occur is a key part of China's whole process of urbanization.

Within the next 10 years, China intends to turn 200 million rural migrant workers, together with their family members, into legitimate urban residents. It intends to turn another 200 million rural inhabitants into urban residents in the following decade. In doing this, circumstances dictate that the country cannot take the course of sprawling, diffuse, low-density urbanization. The country's lack of land and scarcity of resources mean that its urbanization must be tightly knit, densely populated, and highly concentrated. Urban clusters are therefore the primary form by which the country will be urbanizing. Regions with such clusters will be serving the function of coordinating development among other sizes of cities and towns.

China's options as it pursues urbanization

Compact Cities

Two models have characterized urban development in the West. One is the very compact model as seen in European countries. People and industries are fairly densely concentrated in cities, which lack much space. Land used for building up the city is conserved, which improves the efficiency with which land is allocated. The USA is representative of the second model, which is characterized by urban sprawl, lower densities of people, and higher consumption of energy resources than required by the more compact model.

The idea of compact cities was first proposed by George B. Dantzig and Thomas I. Saaty in a work published in 1973, called *Compact Cities – A Plan for Livable Urban Environments*.

In 1990, the Commission of European Communities (CEC) issued a *Green Paper on Urban Environments*. This reiterated the concept of 'compact cities', and presented it as a way to address residential and environmental problems. The *Green Paper* felt that the concept met the needs of sustainable development.

After this, the number of authorities exploring this concept of compact cities began to increase, and consensus was reached on the general features of such cities. They were seen as being densely populated, with mixed-use functions. They helped preserve the countryside. They reduced reliance on cars and lowered energy consumption. They supported public transport, walking and bicycling as modes of getting around. They made public services more accessible to a larger population. They allowed more efficient use of public facilities and basic infrastructure. They led to the revitalization of urban cores and the renaissance of cities (Fang Chuanglin and Qi Weifeng, 2007).

Compact cities can be analyzed from different perspectives. The forms that such cities take are characterized by a high density of buildings and population, by mixed usage in terms of urban functions that are intensified and compounded, and by 'intensification' in an overall sense.

In terms of spatial dimensions, compact cities can be measured at a macro level that looks at both cities and city clusters, and they can be measured at a micro level that looks at communities and residential districts. At the macro level, compactness is reflected in the high density of both cities and city clusters. At the micro level, it is reflected in the high density and high floor area ratio (FAR) for a residential zone or community. In terms of spatial configuration, compact cities are characterized by a single city center, as opposed to either multiple centers or sprawl (Gorden and Richardson, 1997).

When analyzed in terms of policy requirements, the building out of compact cities must receive the guidance and support of various types of policies, including social, economic, planning, transportation, and environmental. Only then can sustained development of compact cities be realized. (Fang Chuanglin and Qi Weifeng, 2007).

The size of China's population and the country's limited amount of territory determine that it should adopt the 'compact city' model of urbanization and not the American form of urban sprawl. Nevertheless, the country has in fact followed the American path, with low-density and low-volume modes of urban growth.

This has occurred under the influence of policies that promoted the growth of small towns and that encouraged the active development of small- and medium-sized cities. It occurred in the context of allowing townships to turn into towns, counties to turn into cities or districts, and prefectures to turn into cities, which is the main way urbanization came about. It came about because administrative districts were the primary guiding force behind economic growth, and it was enabled by a fiscal system that encouraged localities to use their local land as though it were money in the bank.

Meanwhile, the household registration system prevented rural migrant workers from becoming urban residents, which also contributed to the resulting pattern of urbanization. Sprawl or 'decentralization' is mainly a question of the spatial layout of urbanization, while 'low-density' relates to the form that a city takes, and a low FAR is closely linked to the volume capacity of the city's buildings.

The larger the city, the denser its population

Population density is one indicator that reflects the compactness of the build-up area of a city or an 'administered town' in an overall way.[1] Greater population densities indicate that a city is using land in more efficient ways. Lower densities indicate the opposite. Table 4.1 shows the population densities of various sizes of China's cities, county-administered cities, and town-administered cities, as measured by the 'static population'. As the table indicates, the larger the city, the greater the population density and also the greater the efficiency of land use. The greatest efficiencies came in mega-cities of over two million people in population. In 2008, the density of population in these cities was 11,500 per square kilometer. Extra-large cities had densities that were 23 per cent less than this. Large cities were 18 per cent less dense. Medium-sized cities were 32 per cent less dense, and small cities were 63 per cent less dense. 'Administered towns' displayed the least efficient use of land, with densities per square kilometer of only 4570 people.[2]

If all of China's urban population of 640 million people lived in small 'administered towns', the amount of additional space required for them would be 140,000 square kilometers. This is roughly twice the current amount of space being used by the built-up areas of China's cities nationwide.

Table 4.1 Population-density change in built-up areas of cities of different sizes (in units of persons/km²)

	Population density in urban built-up areas in 1981	*Population density in urban built-up areas in 2008*	*Density change between 2008 and 1981*	*Accumulated density change between 2008 and 1981 (%)*
Mega-city (with population of >2 million)	15,405	11,460	–3,945	–25.61
Ultra-large city (with population of 1–2 million)	10,973	9,302	–1,671	–15.23
Large city (with population of 0.5–1 million)	11,143	9,692	–1,451	–13.02
Medium-sized city (with population of 0.2–0.5 million)	9,663	8,652	–1,011	–10.46
Small city (with population of <0.2 million)	5,843	7,035	1,192	20.40

Source: *China Urban–Rural Construction Statistical Yearbooks 1981 and 2008.*

Population densities in China's cities have been declining since the start of reform and opening up

The direction in which population density is trending is a reflection of whether a city is becoming more compact or more dispersed. Taking the entire 30-year period since the start of reform and opening up as one period, the dynamic change in population densities in China shows that density has been going down in the built-up areas of all types of cities, nationwide.

In the period between 1981 and 2008, the density of population in built-up areas of cities nationwide went from 19,000 people per square kilometer to 10,000 (Figure 4.1).

The 30-year period can also be divided into three different stages, however. The first was during the 1980s, when population densities in built-up areas of cities basically increased at a stable rate. Densities went from an average of 19,000 per square kilometer in 1981 to a peak value of 25,000 in 1990. During this period, the density per square kilometer increased by 5943 people.

The second period was the 1990s, when urban densities began to fall. If one subtracts out the figures for 1991, however, which were suspect (it is not possible to believe that average densities went from 25,000 to 21,000 within one year), then the speed at which densities declined in this decade was not all that fast. It went from 21,000 people per square kilometer in 1991 to 17,000 in 2000, a decline of 3800 per square kilometer over the course of the decade, or an annual decline of 380 people per square kilometer.

The third period was the eight years between 2000 and 2008, when the density of people in built-up areas showed an accelerating rate of decline. It went from 17,000

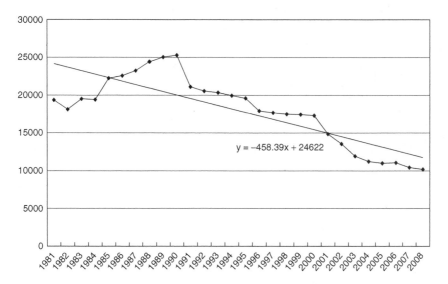

Figure 4.1 Population-density change of China's cities.
Source: *China Urban–Rural Construction Statistical Yearbook 2008.*

people per square kilometer in 2000 to 10,000 in 2008, an overall decline of around 7000 people per square kilometer and an annual rate of decline of nearly 900 people.[3]

Cities of different sizes exhibit different patterns.[4] Table 4.1 shows that the decline in density rates was greatest in mega-cities, that is, cities with populations of over two million. In 1981, their population density was 15,000 per square kilometer, which by 2008 had declined to 11,000 per square kilometer, a decrease of 3944 overall. The next-largest decline in population density rates could be seen in extra-large cities of between one and two million in population. In these, the figure declined by 1670 people. In large cities, the decline was 1,451 people, in medium-sized cities, it was 1011 people, and in small cities the density actually increased by 1192 people.

In 2008, the built-up area of 64 cities that have populations of more than one million reached 17,700 square kilometers. This was nearly one-half of the built-up urban area in the entire country. Since 1981, the number of cities with a population of over one million has increased by 46 and the built-up area of these cities is six times what it was in 1981. The built-up area of large cities has expanded by three times, that of medium-sized cities by 3.5 times, and that of small cities by 1.8 times.

In terms of aggregate figures, the changes in population densities of 'administered towns' and 'cities administered at the county level' have not been as pronounced as they have been in [provincially administered] cities (Figure 4.2). Population densities in the built-up area of county-level cities initially fell, but then rose back up again. Densities were 10,000 per square kilometer in 2000; these fell to 8000 in 2005 and then rose to 8800 in 2008. In overall terms, the population density of 'administered towns' has been constantly falling. In 1990, it was 7400 per square kilometer; by 2008, that had declined to around 4500, for an overall decrease of some 2000 people per square kilometer.

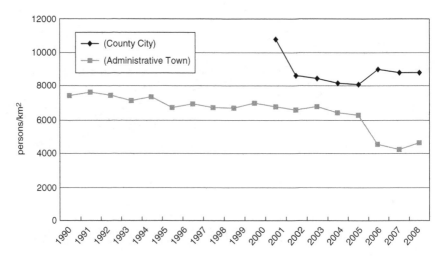

Figure 4.2 Population-density change of China's county cities and administrative towns.
Source: *China Urban–Rural Construction Statistical Yearbook 2008.*

To summarize the above, China's urbanization process since the start of reform and opening up has seen an overall decline in the density of urban populations. The decline in density has been fastest in county-level cities (2.8 per cent decline) and administered towns (2.7 per cent decline). The next-fastest decline in population densities has been seen in mega-cities of over two million in population (1 per cent decline). Extra-large cities, large cities, and medium-large cities have seen density declines in the range of 0.5–0.7 per cent. Small towns have exhibited two different trends: the population density is rising in one, and falling only slowly in the other.

Analysis of why population densities have been declining

The direct cause of the declining densities in urban populations is simple to diagnose. The 'official urbanization' of the human population has proceeded only slowly. The statistics used in this chapter to measure the 'population' aspect of 'population density' are limited in that they do not fully incorporate rural migrant workers. According to the *China Urban–Rural Construction Statistical Yearbook*, the transient population in 2008 was 35.17 million for 655 'cities' across the country, 10.79 million for 1635 'county-administered cities', and 25.31 million for 19,234 'administered towns'. The total was therefore 71.27 million, far less than the number of rural migrant workers as computed by the National Bureau of Statistics, namely 145 million.

The figures therefore exaggerate the impression of a decline in population density, but the trend is still in that direction. Figure 4.3 shows the change in

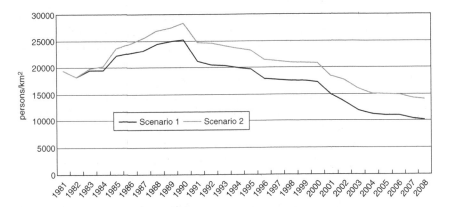

Figure 4.3 Urban population-density change when rural migrant workers are included.

Scenario 1 shows the urban population-density change based on the population with urban household register and the temporary population, and scenario 2 shows the urban population-density change when rural migrant workers are included.

Source: China Urban–Rural Construction Statistical Yearbook; the data about rural migrant workers originate from Han Jun: *Background Report, 2009*. The data for some years when data were unavailable were worked out on the basis of the data for other years.

urban densities in a way that takes into account rural migrant workers. The overall trend still shows a decline in densities, albeit one that is less dramatic. Urban densities dropped from 19,000 people per square kilometer in 1981 to 10,000 in 2008, when rural migrant workers were excluded. When these workers were included, they dropped from 19,000 to 14,000 people.

A second reason for the drop in urban densities of people is what we call the excessively fast 'urbanization of land'. There are objective and unavoidable reasons for this that relate to the stage of China's development. Urbanization is still in a 'middle stage' of development in the country, such that most cities are still pushing outwards to create the framework that can carry larger numbers of people. Cities are building out various urban functions, often in advance of an increase in urban populations.

At the same time, however, more important reasons for the excessive occupation of land by cities relate to governmental policies. Our current systems with respect to land and with respect to fiscal operations make such wasteful land use unavoidable.

First, we lack overall concepts and policies on urbanization. We have not instituted any kind of specific and detailed policy guidelines with respect to the forms and spatial configurations that cities should take. It is doubtless correct to encourage the growth of 'coordinated development of large, medium-sized, and smaller cities and towns', but precisely how to do has been left unclear. What constitutes 'coordinated' as opposed to 'uncoordinated'? How is 'coordinated development' actually manifested? Similarly, it is also correct to encourage the development of 'urban clusters', but we have not described where these should be, which cities should be included, nor how the process should take place. We lack specific and targeted policies in this regard.

The second concern relates to China's land and its fiscal systems. In China, the government has a monopoly on the primary market for land. When farmland is transformed into land for non-agricultural purposes, it must go through a process of 'requisitioning' by the government. Farmers must be compensated. The government then has a monopoly right on 'granting' that land out for other purposes. Three different kinds of procedures are used when land is to be used for 'operating purposes' [relating to business]. These are 'bidding', auctioning', and 'listing'. In the process of any one of these, the income is far greater than the compensation that was made to farmers. It is also far greater than the cost of developing the land. This profit margin constitutes a positive incentive for local governments to push out into neighbouring farmlands and expand the size of cities.

Meanwhile, under China's current fiscal systems, municipal governments lack any sufficient and stable source of funding with which to pay for public services and basic infrastructure. Municipal governments do have the right to determine how any revenues from land 'grants' are allocated. The tax system provides that any such income, as well as direct taxes on land and on real estate and buildings, should accrue mainly to municipal governments. This distribution of tax revenues also creates an incentive for governments to 'take over' land in the pretext of 'urbanizing'.

Table 4.2 Ratio of land-sale income to regional government's fiscal revenue and extra-budgetary revenue

	Net income from selling state-owned land (100 million yuan)	Regional fiscal revenue (100 million yuan)		Regional extra-budgetary revenue (100 million yuan)	
		Absolute value (100 million yuan)	Ratio of land-selling income to regional fiscal revenue (%)	Absolute value (100 million yuan)	Ratio of land-selling income to regional extra-budgetary revenue (%)
2003	1,799	9,850	18.26	4,566	39.40
2004	2,340	11,893	19.68	4,699	49.80
2005	2,184	15,101	14.46	5,544	39.39
2006	2,978	18,304	16.27	6,407	46.48
2007	4,541	23,573	19.27		

Source: China Land Resource Statistical Yearbooks 2004–2008; China Regional Fiscal Statistical Data (2004–2007).

What's more, in the last couple of years, local governments have been setting up what are called 'urban funding platforms'. To a large extent, the size of these platforms and their funding base rely heavily on the amount of land already 'occupied', as well as the still-available amount of local land.

Between 2003 and 2007, the total net revenue derived from 'granting' State-owned land came to RMB 1.38426 trillion, as shown in Table 4.2. Income from land grants plays a decisive role in the total public revenues of local governments.

The low floor area ratio (FAR) in China's cities[5]

Another cause of the decline in population densities of Chinese cities is that the buildings in these cities have a low FAR. As the country urbanizes at a fast past, land is severely inadequate but at the same time used in an extremely wasteful way. This can be seen in the striking figures that describe the low FARs in Chinese cities. At present, the metric used to measure this rate in China comes to an average of around 0.5. The figure is 0.75 for large cities and between 1 and 1.2 for 'core cities'. [6] These are far below the figures of 2 for Japan and 1.6 for Hong Kong (Wang Jian, 2010).

Given the lack of any constraints on how much land is being used by cities, and the lack of regulations with respect to land management, such a low containment capacity means that the problem of rampant land use is intensifying. China is now beginning to place stringent restrictions on conversion of farmland for urban uses, which means that problems of land use are going to be intensifying. The situation will have an impact on the total amount of housing that is available and will lower the per-household amount of living space.

China's unavoidable situation is that it has a large population on a small amount of land. This determines the fact that it cannot simply copy over western models for urban planning that allow for low densities of people. For China, the quiet and comfortable lifestyle of people in Western Europe is sheer luxury. Even places like Australia and Canada, with low populations relative to their land, are now attempting to use land in a more intensive way and to concentrate populations in cities.

There are those who criticize Singapore and Hong Kong for their high-density, high-volume approach to urban development, feeling that it leads to a lower quality of life. In fact, the approach shows how enlightened these cities have been. Hong Kong uses only one-tenth of its land for the built-up areas of the city. Not only does this raise the value of land and increase the efficiency of land use, but it gives the city considerable 'stamina' when it comes to future development. Through rational use of space, including three-dimensional transport systems and zoning for different urban functions, Hong Kong and Singapore have actually been able to improve their citizens' quality of life.

Raising the FAR in cities enables a limited amount of land to accommodate more people. For example, right now the FAR in cities in Guangdong province is around 0.52. Merely raising it to 0.57 would increase the 'built-up floor space' of the city by 200 million square meters. This is roughly equivalent to four years' worth of new housing requirements in the city.

Box 4.1 The situation in other countries with respect to incentives for improved FARs, and measures that deal with the granting of development rights

A *New District Planning Act* in the USA provides incentives to developers operating in high-density districts when they go beyond regular requirements with respect to creating public spaces and increasing the amount of floor space in a given building. In Manhattan's densest areas, for every one unit of public space that a developer provides on one side of the building, he is allowed to increase the floor space of the building by 10 units. Essentially all of Manhattan's high-rise buildings take advantage of this preferential treatment. In the dozen or so years following the establishment of the Act, considerable public space was created as a result. By 1973, in the lower Manhattan area, where every inch of land is precious, some 44,500 square kilometers of public space was created in the form of pedestrian malls.

Japan revised its *Law on Building Standards* in 1970. It too adopted an incentive system to reward the creation of more open space in the process of achieving greater floor area ratio. The new law provided that public open space could not come to less than 20 per cent of the area under construction. Incentives were provided at a certain formula if open space came to more than 20 per cent. Moreover, requirements and rewards for open space were pegged to different planned FARs. The higher the planned FAR of a project, the higher the incentives. By May of 1986, public space in the cities of Osaka and Kobe alone had increased by more than two hundred parcels.

Source: Yun Yingxia and Wu Jingwen: *Foreign floor area ratio reward and development right transfer measures*, Journal of Tianjin University, Social Science Version, Issue 2, Volume 9, 2007.

Maintaining strict controls on the size of large cities is contrary to the laws of economic development as well as the laws of urbanization

Since New China was founded [in 1949], it has consistently aimed for industrialization. The urbanization that might have accompanied industrialization has been neglected, however. In fact, the very subject was avoided until just prior to the twenty-first century. Not only was the development of large cities discouraged, but specific regulations controlled the size to which a city might grow. The experience of other countries and, more to the point, our own experience since the start of reform and opening up prove that it is now time to change this approach. It is time to start actively promoting the growth of large cities and large urban clusters.

The origins of the whole concept of 'urbanization' in China, and the process of developing an urbanization plan

In 1980, the State Council approved and transmitted a document, *Minutes of the National Conference on Urban Planning*. This set forth policies to 'restrict the development of large cities while encouraging the growth of medium-sized and smaller cities'.

In 1990, a law, *The People's Republic of China Law on Urban Planning*, was passed that incorporated this line of thinking and its resulting policies. It called for 'stringent controls over the size of large cities, and rational development of medium-sized and smaller cities'. Furthermore, it specified that the term 'large cities' referred to urban districts as well as neighbouring areas that had a non-agricultural population in excess of 500,000. Medium-sized cities were defined as urban districts and their surrounding areas with a population of no more than 200,000. Smaller cities referred to those with populations of less than 200,000.[7]

In the late 1990s, this approach to urban planning was modified slightly, with the formulation of what was called *China's Agenda for the Twenty-first Century*. This aimed at controlling 'any excessively fast growth of large cities'. The *Agenda* also called for developing satellite cities around large cities, and for developing medium-sized and smaller cities 'at an appropriate pace'.

Box 4.2 The debate on urbanization within academic circles in China

Academic debate on China's correct course of urbanization was extremely intense in the 1980s and 1990s. Discussions focused on several approaches, each of which argued for development of different sizes of cities. Debate also explored 'diversified development' and the development of urban systems.

The argument in favour of developing small cities

In 1983, an academic symposium was held to discuss urbanization in China, in which the unanimous opinion was that 'China should take a path of urbanization that conforms to its unique set of circumstances, a socialist path of urbanization that has its own attributes. ... The path of urbanization in each region should be appropriate to that region' (Wu Youren, 1983). In the concluding report of this symposium, attention focused on a 'vigorous attempt to restore and develop small cities and especially the great number of towns in rural areas'. It was felt that this was 'in line with a rational approach, and allowed for great vitality [in the process of urbanization]'. (Wang Fan, 1990). Once reform and opening up began, the realities of industrialization in rural areas and a policy orientation of 'strategic growth of small cities', combined with the restraints of a system that kept urban areas separate from rural areas, meant that this 'small-city approach' held sway throughout the 1980s and into the 1990s.

The argument in favour of developing large cities

At the same time, there were voices raised in favour of developing larger cities. Feng Yufeng (1983) felt that emphasis should be placed on 'developing those large- and medium-sized cities that had the proper conditions', as well as 'core cities'. Rao Huilin and Qu Bingquan (1989) explicitly noted that large cities could be developed far more efficiently than small cities. Wang Xiaolu and Xia Xiaolin (1999) believed that the optimum population size of cities in China, given the country's circumstances, should be between one and four million. Rao Huilin and Cong Qi (1999) pointed out that efficiencies relating to the scale of cities played a primary and decisive factor, and that China should loosen restrictions on large-city development to an appropriate degree. Zhou Ganzhi (1998) felt that China's more backward regions should first focus on developing large cities, in order to create focal points that would stimulate the growth of medium-sized and smaller cities.

The argument in favor of diversified development

Certain scholars attempted to strike a balance among these diametrically opposite viewpoints. They favored a path of urban modernization that was more 'diversified'. This argument favored the urbanization of rural areas but also the formation of urban hubs and the 'internalization' of cities in what was either a dual approach or a diversified approach (Ning Deng, 1997; Zhong Xiaoming, 2000). This approach highlighted the coordinated development of large, medium-sized, and smaller cities as well as a differentiated way of handling development in the eastern, western, and central parts of the country (Yu Xiaoming, 1999; Chen Bochong and Hao Shouyi, 2005).

The argument in favor of developing medium-sized cities

This approach was first proposed by the editorial board of the journal *Dynamic Economics*, in 1984.

The argument in favor of developing urban systems

As research into the whole subject of urbanization became more sophisticated, scholars began to feel that developing urban systems should be given more weight. Zhou Yixing (1988) pointed out that there is no universal rule about the optimum size of cities. Cities at all sizes and levels of administration share the need to develop systems. Hu Xuwei (2000), Deng Wei (200), and Zhao Daye and Cai Yu (2003) noted that urbanization models should, by nature, be diversified and should apply to cities administered at different levels of government. For all of these, urban systems should be the key focus.

Source: Gu Chaolin and Wu Liya: *Main results of China's urbanization studies*, City Issues, Issue 12, 2008.

China began to implement a system whereby 'municipalities' administered 'counties' in the early 1980s. The rationale behind this was that it would contribute to the stated policy aim of having urban areas 'bring along' rural areas. It would contribute to the development of small and medium-sized cities, and would enable them to 'radiate' their influence into outlaying areas.

A readjustment of administrative levels of government quickly began, which also involved setting up new systems. As a result, local areas soon began to turn themselves into 'municipalities' and the number of 'local-level municipalities' rose dramatically every year.

In 1978, there were 98 such municipalities. Between 2003 and 2008, there were 283, or an average annual increase of seven. Prior to the mid-1980s, county-level municipalities also increased, but at a stable pace of around 10 per year. In 1986, the authorities revised the standards for 'setting up municipalities', and the process of 'turning counties into cities' began to accelerate. By the time this process was stopped, in the early twenty-first century, it had been going for 15 years and 18.5 new county-level cities had been established on average every year. In 1993 alone, 48 new county-level cities were established.

The current system in place in China is one of 'municipalities administering municipalities' (which is to say, prefecture-level cities administer county-level cities). This change is the result of China's 15-year experience in having 'counties administer cities' and having 'localities convert themselves into cities'.

Once the conversion of 'counties into municipalities' was stopped in the late 1990s, localities now began to transform themselves into 'districts', in what was called 'counties converting themselves into districts'. The decline in the number of counties was basically matched by a corresponding rise in the number of 'municipality-administered districts' (Figure 4.4).

The larger the city, the faster it began to develop

Even as great efforts were being made to develop medium-sized and smaller cities, and even though there were constant attempts to control the size of large cities, such control, in fact, became impossible. The physical size of cities continued to expand and their populations continued to increase (Table 4.3).

Whether measured in terms of absolute numbers of increased population or the speed of increase, cities with populations of over two million led the way. Their built-up areas expanded more quickly and their populations grew more rapidly than smaller cities.

Figure 4.5 illustrates the changes in population and 'built-up area' during the period 1981–2008 for 207 'comparable cities'[8] in China. In the 32 cities with

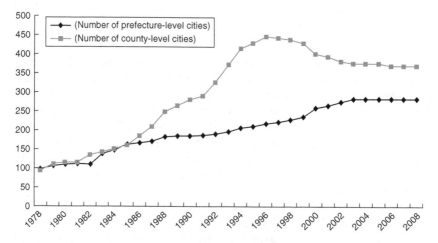

Figure 4.4 Change of numbers of prefecture-level and county-level cities.
Source: *China* Construction Statistical Yearbook 2008.

Table 4.3 Population growth and area expansion of cities of different sizes (1981–2008)

	1981		2008		Built-up area expansion (%)	Population growth (%)
	Population (10,000)	Built-up area (km²)	Population (10,000)	Built-up area (km²)		
City with >2 million people	4,676.6	3,035.7	14,426.3	12,587.7	414.7	308.5
City with 1–2 million people	1,376.9	1,254.8	3,694.8	3,971.7	316.5	268.3
City with 0.5–1 million people	1,937.4	1,738.7	5,341.0	5,510.8	317.0	275.7
City with 0.2–0.5 million people	762.4	798.0	2,147.5	2,482.0	311.0	281.7
City with <0.2 million people	81.1	138.8	187.2	266.1	191.7	230.9

Source: *China Urban–Rural Construction Statistical Yearbook 2008* and the statistical data for relevant years.

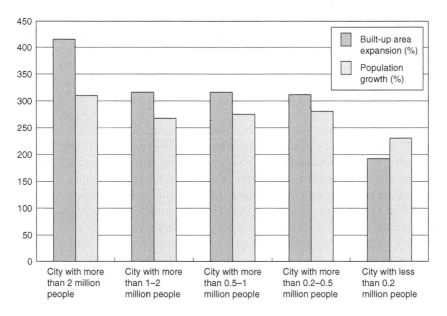

Figure 4.5 Growth of population and built-up area of cities of different sizes (1981–2008).

populations of two million or more, the cumulative increase in population came to 95.52 million people, or double what the populations had been at the beginning of the period. In the 175 cities with populations under two million, the cumulative increase in total population came to 72.12 million, not as much as the increase of just the 32 largest cities. The built-up area of the 32 larger cities increased by three times, specifically by 9552 square kilometers. The built-up area of the 175 smaller cities increased by 8300 square kilometers, also not as much as the increased area of the larger cities.

It should be noted that the increase in built-up area had a certain irrationality to it, so discrepancies also existed in the figures, and there was an overall decrease in the density of populations as analyzed in the text above. Both increase in built-up area and speed of population increase in the smaller cities, whether they were between one and two million, or 500,000 and one million, or 200,000 and 500,000, was roughly the same. Increases in all cases were notably below those in cities of two million or more in population but also notably higher than those in cities below 200,000 in population.

Urban economies are characterized by the way in which they have progressively increasing economies of scale, as well as progressively increasing economies of concentration. The larger the city, the more efficient it is.

Empirical analysis of large numbers of cities both inside and outside China shows that cities with the highest rates of efficiency are frequently largest. In the early period, town-and-village enterprises were mainly distributed throughout the 'home territory'. Later, as reform and opening up proceeded, such enterprises but especially those that had foreign investors, began to migrate toward the peripheries of large cities and urban clusters, where they invested in plant and equipment. This 'rational decision' on their part proves that the problems associated with 'urban syndromes' were more than offset by the benefits of the economies of scale.

Table 4.4 shows the circumstances surrounding the growth of China's 10 mega-cities between 1981 and 2008. The data indicates that the growth of these cities far outpaced the national average. It was much faster than the average rate of growth of cities altogether, but even faster than the growth rate of smaller cities.

According to urban policies that ostensibly placed strict controls on large cities, China's largest cities should have been tightly constrained, yet their populations increased enormously. Shanghai's population increased by 12.02 million, Beijing's by 9.72 million, Guangzhou's by 6.53 million, Chongqing's by 6.9 million, and Tianjin's by 2.58 million. The built-up area of these cities also expanded enormously, Shanghai's by 606 square kilometers, Beijing's by 376, Guangzhou's by 553, Chongqing's by 970, and Tianjin's by 289.

To a very large degree, urbanization is a function of the market. Large cities contain more jobs, higher levels of public services, and a relatively better environment for investment and innovation. As a result, they are the preferred option as a population migrates and flows toward opportunity. Trying to control the growth of large cities is simply not in accord with the realities of how cities develop.

Table 4.4 Development of China's top 10 mega-cities in 1981–2008

	Urban population in 1981 (10,000)	Built-up area in 1981 (km²)	Urban population in 2008 (10,000)	Built-up area in 2008 (km²)	Increase of built-up area (km²)	Growth of built-up area (%)	Increase of urban population (10,000)	Growth of urban population (%)
Shanghai	613.0	142	1,815.08	860.2	718.2	605.8	1202.1	296.1
Beijing	466.4	349	1,439.10	1,310.9	961.9	375.6	972.7	308.6
Guangzhou	233.8	162	886.55	895.0	733.0	552.5	652.8	379.2
Chongqing	190.0	73	879.96	708.4	635.4	970.4	690.0	463.1
Shenzhen	4.5	100	876.83	787.9	687.9	787.9	872.3	19,485.1
Tianjin	380.9	222	639.02	640.9	418.9	288.7	258.1	167.8
Wuhan	263.0	174	596.00	460.0	286.0	264.4	333.0	226.6
Zhengzhou	85.9	65	479.45	328.7	263.7	505.6	393.6	558.1
Nanjing	170.2	116	478.16	592.1	476.1	510.4	308.0	280.9
Shenyang	293.7	164	468.00	370.0	206.0	225.6	174.3	159.3

Source: *China Urban–Rural Construction Statistical Yearbook 2008.*

Certain countries have already basically realized the process of 'urbanization', and their experience shows that large cities still have the greatest attraction to people. Among OECD countries, large cities are where people increasingly live. More than 70 per cent of the population lives in areas that are administered by cities, and the growth rate of large urban populations is also the greatest (growing at an average rate of 0.8 per cent per year). Population growth rates of smaller cities (those with populations of between 100,000 and 500,000) are smaller than those of any other size of city. Their growth rates are also less steep (only some 0.4 per cent per year). Growth rates of medium-sized cities exceed those of smaller cities but are still lower than those of larger cities (OECD, Background Report, 2010). See Figure 4.6.

Metropolitan areas are continuing to grow in OECD countries. In some cases, the population in a given metropolitan area totals some one-half of the entire population of the country. Seoul, Randstad, and Copenhagen account for 44–48 per cent of the total populations of their countries. Since 1995, populations in the metropolitan areas of OECD countries have been growing at an annual rate of 1 per cent. Among major cities, Phoenix, Atlanta, and Toronto have been growing at a rate that is several times the rate of OECD countries overall.

The populations of a number of other metropolitan areas are growing at more than twice the rate at which the country's overall population is growing. Such cities include Luanda, Miami, Guadalajara, and Washington DC. The populations of Madrid, Seoul, Sidney, and Mexico City are growing at faster rates than the populations of their countries.

Ongoing population growth of large cities is the logical result of ongoing economic concentration. In 2005, the top 30 cities in the world as ranked by GDP accounted for around 16 per cent of global GDP. The top 100 cities

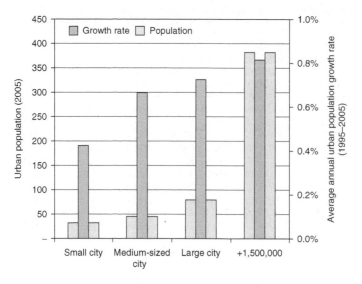

Figure 4.6 Population and population growth of cities of different population sizes in OECD countries (1995–2005).

Note that this analysis only uses city-led population area. 'Small city' refers to a population with 0.1–0.5 million people, 'medium-sized city' refers to a population with 0.5–1 million people, and 'large city' refers to a population with 1–1.5 million people.

Source: Based on OECD regional database.

accounted for 25 per cent of global GDP. The contribution of large cities to GDP is particularly high in some developing countries. In 2005, Mexico City occupied a mere 0.1 per cent of Mexico's area and yet provided 30 per cent of its national output. Luanda, the capital of Angola, occupied 0.2 per cent of the country's area yet also provided 30 per cent of national output. The largest cities in Hungary, Kenya, Morocco, Nigeria, and Saudi Arabia all accounted for 20 per cent of national output in 2005, though they occupied less than 1 per cent of their country's territory (World Bank, 2009).

The conclusion of the World Bank is that the greater the economic concentration of a country, the greater the density of wealth.

Urbanization is the process by which cities of all sizes are able to nurture their growth. Cities of all sizes have an imperative to grow, but some find it difficult to accomplish this. Critical conditions relate to specific circumstances, including the geographic setting of a city. Growth cannot rely solely on 'size'. It is therefore unscientific to call for developing cities of all sizes without taking all conditions into account, including regional industrial structure, capacity to provide employment, resource endowment, and carrying capacity of the environment. [Policy approaches that try to resolve complex problems with uniform solutions are to be avoided.]

Provide policy guidelines for small towns that are tailored to each situation, by classifying towns in a number of categories

Small towns are necessary as a supplementary form in the process of urbanization,[9] but on the whole they represent urbanization that is low-density, widely dispersed, and not compact. Policies should be tailored to various types or categories of small towns in order to guide their development. Those that are situated in urban clusters or near large cities should be encouraged to develop, to concentrate human populations, and to assume some of the special functions of 'functional urban clusters'. Those that have unique and irreplaceable resources should be encouraged to use their resource advantages in becoming distinctive and appealing in one way or another. Small towns located in the main agricultural parts of the country, or those in key ecological zones, should receive support for developing public services so that they become public-service centers for a given region.

The initial recommendation to develop small towns in China, and the evolution of the concept

China's reforms began in rural areas. From the late 1970s to the early 1980s, rural areas led the way in opening up markets for products and revitalizing the economy. The traditional market-centered commerce revived. Pervasive shortages of all products but particularly light industrial and textile products, gave town-and-village enterprises ample room for business opportunities. The 'household contracting system that tied production to compensation' was initially aimed at agricultural products, but when it was applied 'in an all-round way' to production in general, town-and-village enterprises grew tremendously. Surplus labour in the countryside was released to participate in the process.

These two factors, one commercial [the markets] and one industrial [the mode of production], rejuvenated places that held town and township governments in certain regions. One of the most notable of such regions was in southern

Table 4.5 Development of China's county cities and administrative towns (1981–2008)

Year	County city			Administrative town		
	Number (10,000)	Built-up area (10,000 km²)	Population (100 million)	Number (10,000)	Built-up area (10,000 km²)	Population (100 million)
1990				1.01	0.825	0.61
1995				1.5	1.3860	0.93
2000	1674	1.3135	1.42	1.79	1.8200	1.23
2005	1636	1.2384	1.00	1.77	2.3690	1.48
2008	1635	1.4776	1.30	1.7	3.016	1.38

Source: *China Urban–Rural Construction Statistical Yearbook 2008*. No data about county cities before 2000 are available.

Jiangsu province. While continuing their function as political centers in agricultural communities, on top of their educational and cultural activities, these places now became market centers with concentrations of town and village industries, in addition to playing a role in education and culture.

One scholar was acutely aware of the significance of what was happening. Fei Xiaotong [an eminent sociologist and anthropologist, who died in 2005], began to publish a series of articles based on his surveys and research.

Box 4.3 Fei Xiaotong and small-town development in China

Fei Xiaotong led his survey team to Jiangcun for a sixth visit on 2 May 1983. In September of the next year, he published an article, *Large issues regarding very small places,* in the journal *Outlook*. This turned China's rural reforms into a very hot topic. Mr Fei felt that emerging small towns could serve as 'nodes' in connecting similar towns throughout the countryside and also linking those towns in an organic way to cities. They could thereby serve as ways to connect two very different economies. From the standpoint of both theory and practice, he began a systematic description of how small towns in China could serve to revitalize rural economies and rural industry, could shift surplus labour away from agriculture, and could provide a solution to the huge population problem.

From 3 to 8 October 1983, Fei Xiaotong conducted a seventh survey in Rivertown. In the course of this visit, he pointed out that the resurgence of small-town economies could be attributed to rural industry. He also expressed his views on the ties between rural enterprises and urban enterprises, and on such things as the flow of surplus rural labour, the logistics of moving products, the nature of household sideline businesses, urban planning for the build-up of market towns, pilot-site reform projects for modifying administrative management systems, and so on. He later published these ideas in *Xinhua Daily* on 2 May 1984, in an article entitled *Another look at small towns*.

Fei Xiaotong paid his eighth visit to Rivertown between 21 and 23 October 1984. This time, his research focused on the ways that rural enterprises and regional economies could link up urban and rural areas. He felt that this was a breakthrough in terms of how China thought about small towns. Although research was at the most preliminary stage, he felt that town-and-village enterprises could serve the function of helping reform socioeconomic systems in China's cities. They could aid in taking the whole subject of 'social value systems' of urban areas to a deeper level. This was highly significant in the whole process of revitalizing small towns and researching the growth of town-and-village enterprises. It had major consequences for socio-economic development.

After leaving Wujiang, Fei Xiaotong visited Zhenjiang, Yangzhou, and Nanjing, after which he wrote a series of articles called *Small towns and new discoveries*, which were also published in *Outlook*.

> In 1984, Mr Fei published a number of articles that attracted the attention of the Central Committee of the Communist Party of China as well as relevant government departments. The articles included [four articles: Small Towns and Big Problems, Rediscovery of Small Towns, Small Towns Primary Exploration of North Jiangsu, New development of Small Towns].
>
> Source: Fei Xiaotong: *Rediscovery of small towns*, Xinhua Daily, 11 January 1984.

It is worth noting that Fei Xiaotong primarily discussed small towns in the context of rural affairs. He advocated the development of small towns mainly in terms of the emergence of the new force of 'town-and-village enterprises'. This may have been the result of a number of factors, including the 'combining of agriculture–industry–commerce' during the period of the people's communes, or fixed ideas about resolving all rural issues within the context of the countryside. Or it may have been due to the deep-seated belief that the rural population had to be kept from migrating into cities.

The result was that the country adopted policies to develop small towns and industries *in situ*, through a policy known as 'leave the earth but not the homeland, enter factories but not cities'. Given the above factors, this decision about how to modernize China's agriculture may have been inevitable.

Advocating the development of small towns was also brought on by two overseas considerations. The first was China's desire not to create the kind of slums that were afflicting some developing countries. In those cases, a rural population surged into cities, urban populations increased dramatically in a brief period, and the result was impoverished conditions in urban slums. The second overseas consideration was the phenomenon of a so-called 'counter-urbanization' in developing countries as people from cities flowed into suburbs, which then became bedroom communities. China felt that it could avoid this problem by having its own rural population move directly into small towns and cities.

Seen from today's perspective, the understanding back then was, to a degree, rather limited. The phenomenon of slums in some developing countries was due to a surge of population into cities just at particular times when that population exceeded the economic capacity of those cities, and the abilities of public services, housing in particular. One of the root causes of the problem in such countries was the system governing land in rural areas. Still, the very fact that people who had been dispossessed of their land would surge into cities was, by itself, an expression of the fact that cities had more job opportunities. In China, farmers will not simply take up and abandon their land for no reason at all. The State government and all other levels of government will also not tolerate farmers losing their land. As for the issue of 'suburbanization', this occurred in specific times in certain developed countries and was a temporary, exceptional, and non-mainstream phenomenon. Moreover, those who moved to suburbs were mainly from the middle classes, who did not move there to find jobs. The trend has already changed in recent years and there is now a tendency to move back into large cities.

China's national situation, in terms of a scarcity of land, dictates that it cannot allow people to move from cities into suburbs in order to live in a low-density spread-out way. This is simply not an available option.

Small towns and cities cannot become the main form of urbanization in China in the future

Many small towns are not equipped to handle the functions required of a city. The size of a city determines the services it should undertake to supply and the scope of duties it should aim to encompass. These might include being an economic center, a political center, a cultural or education or political center, a manufacturing base, a center for logistics, a trade center, and so on. Small towns are regional centers for political, cultural, and medical services, and for maintaining the public order. They can concentrate public services and serve as centers for such things as agricultural technology, and they can also develop certain primary-level services targeted at health or materials or other specific needs. Examples might be catering, warehousing, or certain kinds of commerce. Due to their limited size and the limited radius within which they supply services, however, small towns will find it hard to develop highly concentrated advanced services. They cannot grow industries that need a higher 'threshold of population'. This includes activities that deal with assets in one way or another, such as accounting, legal services, R&D, and the securities and investment industries. Small towns can also form concentrations of industry, but within certain constraints. Those that are far from cities must generally rely on the features or resources of their own locality. They cannot concentrate industry in any major way, or else they become large cities.

These specific functions of small towns mean that few of them will be able to create sizeable numbers of jobs in a sustainable fashion. No matter how supportive policies might be, they will not grow into large and powerful places. Policies in favour of indiscriminate development of small towns in places like China's sparsely populated far west or the northeastern part of the country have therefore been counter-productive. In trying to grow the economies and increase the built-up areas of such places, policies have contributed to 'blind' establishment of development zones, to blind development of industry, the occupation of huge amounts of arable, and 'growth' that has disregarded the public-finance resources to support it. We are already paying a high price for these mistakes.

A few small towns will indeed be able to develop and become vehicles for sustainable creation of jobs. Our own experience in the Pearl River delta and Yangtze River delta areas, as well as considerable international experience, shows that small towns on the periphery of urban centers can help them perform certain special functions. They can become a part of the larger regional economy or a part of the process of 'functional urbanization'. They can indeed become a major force in their own right, with some serving as processing bases for manufacturing, some as logistical centers for goods, some merely residential areas or places for recreation. In these cases, we do want to encourage the development of

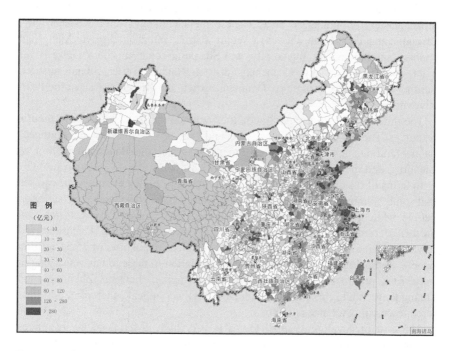

Figure 4.7 Gross regional product of China's Counties in 2007 (in units of 100 million
        yuan)

Source: Based on the county-specific economic statistical data of the National Bureau of
Statistics.

small cities by concentrating populations in these places and parceling out specified functions of the urban clusters.

In order to analyze the regional distribution of economic activity, we have
divided gross regional product [GRP] into nine discrete levels. Figure 4.7 shows
that the counties in the top level of gross income tend to be located in three
specific types of regions. The top 150 counties (which include county-level cities
and districts not administered directly by cities) are distributed as follows.

First, they are located in areas around mega-cities. They have become key
constituent parts of those cities. Foremost among them are counties that directly
service cities, such as the counties under the jurisdiction of Shanghai, Beijing,
and Tianjin. They include 'counties' that in recent years have been turned into
'districts'. Other examples include the Fanyu and Huadu districts in Guangzhou,
the Shapingba, Kiulongpo, and Yubei districts in Chongqing, the Xiaoshan
district, Tonglu county, Chun'an county, Jiande city and Fuyang city in
Hangzhou, the Pukou and Liuhe districts of Nanjing, and the Wenjiang county
and Changqing district in Chengdu.

The second type of front-ranking counties are located in relatively mature urban clusters or 'urbanized areas'. These include Jiangyin city, Kunshan city, Zhangjiagang city, Changshu city, Wujin district, Yinzhou district, Xiangshan county, Ninghai county, Yuyao city, and Shaoxing county in the Yangtze River delta, and Dongguan city, Chancheng district, Nanhai district, Shunde district, Sanshui district, Zengcheng city, Doumen district, and Xinhui district in the Pearl River delta.

The third type of front-ranking counties is made up of those that have unique resources. These include Fengrun district and Qian'an city in Hebei, the Zhungeer banner and Dongsheng district in Inner Mongolia, the Bayuquan district in Liaoning, and the Korla and Shihezi cities in Xinjiang.

In terms of the distribution of population in front-ranking counties, we can see that some 'administered towns' in certain districts have considerable attraction to people, while most do not. Using data from the *China Urban–Rural Construction Statistical Yearbook*, we can see that, in 2008, the total of 19,234 administered towns in China had a total 'temporary' or transient population of 25.31 million people. Some 46 per cent of the transient population in these towns was living in only four provinces (or cities), namely Shanghai, Jiangsu, Zhejiang, and Guangdong. While these had considerable 'magnet appeal', therefore, administered towns in other areas did not.

The cost of developing small towns is very high in terms of the resources required. China's fundamental situation, given its huge population, is that only a tiny amount of the country's limited land and scarce energy can be put towards space for human residences and development. If our policy orientation aims to develop small towns, we will see the phenomenon of each and every small town attempting to expand its built-up area by occupying more land. Even if each takes up only a small amount of land, in the aggregate, the amount will be considerable. If each uses only 1.6 square kilometers for its 'built-up' area, for example, the total will come to 30,000 square kilometers. Given that there are 138 million people in such towns, the population density will then be only one-half what it is in cities, on average.

Put in other terms, if all of this small-town population lived in larger cities, it would require just 13,800 square kilometers of space. This would conserve 17,000 square kilometers of land and would result in a far higher urban density nationwide.

China cannot afford to have its population live on the outskirts of large city centers, as people do in some countries, using multiple cars per family to get to jobs, living in houses that are separate from one another, commuting on highways that occupy considerably more land as well. The extensive sprawl that such of model of development entails is not feasible in this country. As a result, it is equally infeasible to have small towns serve as the main residential location of our urban population. Most of our urban population will have to be concentrated in compact cities, living in densely populated large-city urban centers.

The cost of developing small towns is also very high in terms of the social costs involved. Large cities have their 'urban syndromes', but small towns also have their ailments. If we were to allow small-town development to become our major form of urbanization, this would require the creation of tremendous numbers of job opportunities in small towns. This in turn would require growing the economies of such places, which would necessarily involve building a 'development zone' in each one. China has 19,000 'administered towns'. If each one of them were to build such a zone, occupying an average of two square kilometers to do so, the amount of land so occupied in the country would approach 40,000 square kilometers.

By and large, administered towns in China have poorly developed planning processes. They grow in a blind manner. Some very small places have highways going through them that have six or even eight lanes. Some have built themselves up to accommodate 150,000–200,000 people, when at the present time they only have 20,000 occupants. Some have planned for huge parks in the middle of town, thereby not only wasting precious farmland but also ensuring that they will be unable to realize overly ambitious ideas. In a country with such a huge population, indiscriminate development of small towns will result in turning the regions with developed economies and high population densities into places with no farmland, little in the way of green space, countless smoke stacks, congested traffic, and overflowing sewage. It will lead to a chaotic [un-zoned] mixture of industry and human habitation.

Small towns, as they are being generated spontaneously in China, have no scientific precepts when it comes to thinking about sources of drinking water, prevention of floods, earthquake mitigation procedures, and so on. Moreover, places that once had great cultural and historic value are losing their unique quality in the midst of the rush to 'build big, build fast, and do it now'.

Indiscriminate development of small towns, as one model of urbanization, is also environmentally disastrous. The cost of building basic infrastructure alone is monumental in terms of damage to ecosystems. Overly dispersed industry requires that infrastructure be built in a form described as 'mosquito-net build-out'. It requires high-voltage power grids that march in all directions. This then necessitates the building of high-voltage power plants throughout the land. The power shortages that characterize some regions are not generally due to lack of power, but rather to problems with the grid. Some places have already taken up all available space with factories, and it is hard to find space for the footprint for the electricity pylons.

In addition to the above considerations, another key factor argues against making small-town development the primary mode of urbanization in China. That relates to the country's unique way of dividing up administrative [governing] units. Continuing to put great effort into developing small towns, as we have been doing, means that we unavoidably continue the process of upgrading administrative levels.

China divides its governing units into multiple levels of administration, and each level gets heavily involved in business activity. 'Developing a small town' is therefore equivalent to developing one's own seat of government, developing one's own political center. However, when everyone can grow in size, nobody can. When everyone can do it 'all', nobody can. When everyone tries to attract in farmers to help build up their economy, nobody can.

China has now experienced years of having policies that support the development of small towns. Despite these policies, however, the great majority of small towns have not in fact grown in strength. The towns have indeed occupied land, built development zones, created fairly impressive basic infrastructure in many cases. They have extended preferential policies in order to attract investment, but the result is still an exodus of people moving to other places for jobs.

Between 1990 and 2008, the amount of land devoted to 'built-up areas' in administered towns expanded from 8000 square kilometers to 30,000 square kilometers. The number of people in these places went up at much more modest pace, from 60 million to 138 million. The amount of space being used went up by an average of 7.5 per cent per year, while the number of people went up by an average of only 4.6 per cent per year.

The increase in the 'total population in administered towns' has been caused mainly by the increased number of such towns. An average 'administered town' in the 1990s included around 6000 people, while the figure now is around 8000. Even this increase has been brought on in large part by the merger of adjoining localities as development spreads in all places at once. It has not primarily been due to the growth of any one individual town.

Meanwhile, the average population size of county seats has declined, from 85,000 people in the year 2000 to the current 77,000. By 2005, the total number of 'administered towns' had basically stabilized at 17,000. The total population in these towns had peaked at 148 million. In recent years, the total population of administered towns has been declining. It went from 140 million in 2006 to 138 million in 2008. This was a decline of over 10 million people within the space of three years.

'City clusters' should become the main form of urbanization in China

The Central Committee of the Communist Party of China presented its recommendation on the 11th Five-Year Plan, as contained in the document *Recommendation on formulating the 11th Five-Year Plan for national economic and social development*. This document brought out the following points.

'The Pearl River delta, the Yangtze River delta, and the Bohai urban hub should continue to play their leading role in stimulating inland economic development and in radiating their influence into neighbouring areas. They should further the process of creating a division of labour among cities and enabling each to support the others with their particular advantages. They should aim for increasing overall competitiveness of the clusters as a whole.

'In regions where conditions permit, mega-cities and large cities should serve as the 'dragon heads' in creating comprehensive urban plans for new city clusters. Land use should be kept to a minimum in these places, job opportunities should be maximized, capacity to concentrate factors should be quite strong, and population should be distributed in a rational manner.'

The 11th Five-Year Plan also notes, 'City clusters should become the main form by which urbanization is carried forward. The country should gradually set up a spatial configuration that has several urban clusters that are well coordinated and sustainable. The vertical axis of such clusters will include the Harbin–Beijing–Guangzhou rail line along the coast; the horizontal axis will follow along the Yangtze River and Longhai rail line. Other cities and small towns will be distributed in a 'dotted' pattern, separated by land that is permanently set aside as farmland and districts that are permanently declared to serve ecological functions. The urban clusters will be the focal points.'

The 17th National Party Congress went further in stipulating that, 'the country must cultivate a new axis of economic growth, with urban clusters exercising a strong radial influence, and relying mainly on extra-large cities. Strengthening carrying capacity in a comprehensive way should be the main focus.'

'Developing urban clusters' has already become a major policy initiative on the part of both the Party and the State government. Issues that remain relate to deciding exactly which cities to develop, and how to develop them.

The concept of 'city clusters'

The concept of 'city clusters' was first proposed in 1961 by the French geographer Jean Gottman, in a work entitled *Megalopolis* [in Chinese, this becomes 'large-city clusters']. Gottman used this term to describe the conjoining of five large urban hubs on the east coast of the USA. He regarded this as being the ultimate end of the process of urbanization.

After this initial presentation of the idea, definitions began to change as the field of urban development progressed, and a number of other conceptual ways to describe 'urban clusters' began to appear. These included metropolitan areas, metropolitan hubs, large urban hubs, greater metropolitan area, urban strips, urban spheres, city sprawl, and so on. The starting point for all these descriptions and concepts about urban forms may have been somewhat different, but the underlying substance of what they were describing was similar. Essentially, they all referred to the spatial configuration within which urban functions were carried out.

City clusters as defined by some Chinese scholars include the following characteristics.

Such 'clusters' have a certain number of cities within a certain prescribed area that differ in terms of characteristics, types, levels of administration, and size. They feature one or two 'mega-cities' as core cities. They maintain internal connections among cities by relying on modern transport and comprehensive logistical networks, as well as high-speed information networks. As a unit, they comprise a fairly complete urban agglomeration (Yao Shimou, 1992).

The term 'urban cluster' as used in this report refers to the ability to carry on commercial activity within a certain unit of space, with one or two cities serving as 'primary' or as 'centers', and with a number of small and medium-sized cities, or small towns, distributed around them but discrete and not conjoined. These smaller cities are separated by farmland, forests, water surfaces and other such forms of 'green space'. They are connected by highly effective networks of basic infrastructure (Ma Kai, 2006). As such, urban clusters are a highly evolved form of urban space and result only when large cities have developed to a certain stage.

Urban clusters have become the primary trend of urbanization throughout the world

Urban clusters are both the venues of job creation and places where people live. They support economic growth and so are central to any country's ability to be competitive on an international basis. In the great majority of situations, urban clusters exhibit a high level of productivity. This productivity is related to the degree of economic specialization in a given cluster, to density and composition of human and material resources, and to the degree of innovation.

Due to fairly high levels of productivity, such clusters generally have GDPs that are higher than the national average. Since they have multiple centers, urban clusters are able to avoid the problem of having overly concentrated urban functions and the 'urban syndromes' that can be brought on by having everything focused in one huge mega-city. Moreover, since they are a fairly concentrated expression of one particular region, they generally can be effective in lowering development costs. They can avoid the loss of land that goes with a more extensive or 'sprawling' form of urban development. They are therefore useful in conserving land and conserving ecosystems and natural environments. They lift the ability of the public to enjoy [higher] basic infrastructure.

The main modes and speeds of urban development in the world have been changing substantially since the 1950s. This has been the result of advances in science and technology as well as in urban industries on the one hand, which have brought populations, investment and technology into large cities and their surrounding areas at a very fast speed (Dicken, 1992, 1994). On the other hand, the speed with which transportation systems have developed has enabled cities to go from a long-term process of inward concentration to a more dispersed form of growth out towards suburbs. High-income earners have moved from urban centres to their peripheries, and as a result industries have also suburbanized. Suburbs have expanded dramatically, leading to the appearance of new cities on the edges of existing large cities (Meyer, 1991).

This two-way movement, with concentration towards the center and then dispersing towards the periphery, has propelled large urban clusters to expand at a rapid rate, or, one could say, it has made urbanization itself 'expand' at a rapid rate. It has led to conjoining of cities with their surrounding new cities, creating clusters that have large-city nuclei surrounded by areas with which they maintain close economic ties. The core city and its outer areas have maintained close interrelations, a certain degree of spatial differentiation, a regional division of labour, and distinct landscape features.

Since the 1980s, socioeconomic changes, but particularly the 'informatization' of society and the trend toward economic globalization, have also propelled changes in the forms of the world's urbanization (Castells, 1989, 1994). In recent years, the growth of large cities and urban clusters has been dramatic and represents the trend of urbanization globally. Moreover, each of these is now playing a key role in the broader global urban system.

Research indicates that America's three main urban clusters, namely the Greater New York area, the Greater Great Lakes area, and the Greater Los Angeles area, account for 67 per cent of America's GDP. Japan's three main urban clusters, namely the Greater Tokyo area, the Osaka–Kobe area, and the Nagoya area, account for 70 per cent of the country's GDP.

Places around the world that are generally regarded as urban clusters include the Greater London area, the Greater Paris area, the Berlin–Brandenburg area, the Randstad area (in the Netherlands), the Greater New York area, the Greater Los Angeles area, the Northern Ohio area, the three major urban hubs in Japan, the Greater Moscow area, the Toronto area and the Greater Vancouver area, and the Seoul urban hub.

By looking at global urbanization trends, one can see that the growth of urban clusters is closely related to shifts in the center of gravity of the world's economic activity. After the eighteenth century, the Industrial Revolution turned England into the center of world economic growth and, as a result, London and central England became a large city belt or urban cluster along the London–Liverpool axis.

In the nineteenth century, the emergence of the European continent as an economic force turned Western Europe into the center of world economic growth. Accordingly, urban clusters of varying sizes were formed in the Greater Paris area, the Rheine–Ruhr Area, and the central part of the Netherlands and Belgium. These centered on the large cities of Paris, Brussels, Amsterdam, and Bonn, and formed a Y-shaped axis of development.

In the twentieth century, the center of world economic growth shifted from Western Europe to North America. Accordingly, the Boston–New York–Washington urban cluster and the Great Lakes urban cluster formed in the northeast and central parts of the USA.

After the Second World War, the rise of the Japanese economy with its accelerated pace of industrialization and urbanization turned the eastern part of Japan into a giant urban cluster along the Tokyo–Osaka axis.

It is worth mentioning that the center of economic growth in the world is now shifting toward the Asia–Pacific region. In the twenty-first century, China is in the process of becoming a new 'growth node' in global economic development. One can foresee that the new urban clusters of the twenty-first century will emerge in China. They will be found in the Pearl River delta, the Yangtze River delta, and the Beijing–Tianjin–Tanggu Area [or 'Jing-jin-tang area']. (Wu Chuanqing, 2004).

The current process of developing urban clusters in China

Nearly 20 cities and regions in China have already formally declared that they intend to build themselves up into urban clusters, according to data that is still partial. Only three true urban clusters currently exist, however. These are the three centering on the Yangtze River delta, the Pearl River delta, and the Jing-jin-tang area.

Box 4.4 The evolution of various forms of urbanization in the
USA and Japan

In the USA, cities with a population of more than one million grew by 117 million people between the years 1950 and 2000. This represented 83 per cent of the incremental growth in urban populations in the country, and 90 per cent of the total growth in the population of the country at large.

Quantities of people flocked into the northeastern urban areas, including Boston, New York, Philadelphia, and Baltimore, and into the central Great Lakes area, including Pittsburgh, Cleveland, Toledo, and Detroit. The rapid development of large cities and ongoing growth of urban clusters turned these two areas into vast urban clusters. The two areas are made up of more than 20 large cities, each of which has a population in excess of one million. The two areas account for more than 70 per cent of manufacturing in the USA. These ultra-large urbanized areas have become the most industrialized and urbanized parts of the country and hold its highest density of population.

The Greater New York Metropolitan area is located in the northeastern part of the USA, on the west coast of the Atlantic Ocean. New York City serves as its core area but it extends across three states: southwestern Connecticut, the five boroughs of New York, Long Island, the lower reaches of the Hudson River valley, and northern New Jersey. The area includes 31 counties within its sphere of influence, covers 33,600 square kilometers, and contains nearly 20 million people.

While it covers only 1.5 per cent of America's total land area, this area encompasses 20 per cent of America's population. Its manufacturing constitutes one-third of all manufacturing in America.

Japan's urbanization occurred in step with the country's process of industrialization. Large numbers of people began to shift from small cities and rural areas toward the coastal regions along the Pacific. In the process of industrialization, four major industrial regions formed, centered on Tokyo, Osaka, Nagoya, and Fukuoka. In the 1960s, these accounted for 70 per cent of the country's gross industrial output at a time when heavy industry predominated in the country, but occupied only 12 per cent of the country's land. With structural changes in economic activity and the growth of cities, the eastern corridor gradually began to form three large metropolitan hubs. Tokyo serves as the center of the Capital hub, Osaka as that of the Kinki hub, and Nagoya as that of the Central hub.

In the years between 1955 and 1970, 7.5 million people flowed into these three metropolitan hubs. After the 1970s, as the growth rate of Japan's economy began to moderate, urbanization also began to slow down and fewer people flowed in to the three major centers. At that point, a more apparent trend was the practice of commuting back and forth between neighbouring regions and these urban hubs.

Since the second half of the 1980s, influenced by the 'great waves' of informatization and globalization, factories have increasing dispersed out of urban centers toward 'local hubs'. They have even dispersed away from 'local hubs' to production overseas. The urban functions of the Tokyo area have only been strengthened by this, however, since Tokyo continues to be a commercial center. Populations are therefore once again beginning to move closer to the city center.

Source: Wu Chuanqing: *Overview of world city clusters*, Ningbo Economics, Issue 04, 2004.

One can see from the data in Table 4.6 that these three urban clusters already occupy 3.25 per cent of China's total land mass. That is, they stand on more than 310,000 square kilometers of space. They hold a concentration of 200 million people, which is 15.16 per cent of the country's total population. In 2000, the number of people in these urban clusters was 15.08 per cent of the total, which shows that people are still moving toward these urban centers.

In 2006, the GDP produced by the concentrations of activity in the urban clusters came to RMB 9.1489 trillion, which was 40.32 per cent of the country's total GDP.

The density of population in these places reached an average of 643 people per square kilometer in 2006, which is still less than that in Japan's three major metropolitan hubs where, in 2000, density was 757 people per square kilometer.

In terms of density of population in administered areas, the Pearl River delta is the most densely populated of China's three clusters, with some 1258 people per square kilometer. This density is 1.5 times that in the Yangtze River area, and 3.4 times that in the Jing-jin-tang area.

By way of contrast, density in Japan's three metropolitan hubs is higher, with 757 people per square kilometer which is 1.23 times the density in China's urban clusters. From an overall perspective, it is clear that the process of concentrating populations in China's urban clusters has a ways to go. (Yuan Xin and Tang Xiaoping, 2008).

As noted above, the GDP generated by America's three main urban clusters contributes 67 per cent to the country's total GDP. That generated by Japan's metropolitan hubs contributes 70 per cent to its GDP. In China, the contribution of the three main urban clusters comes to only around 40 per cent of total GDP. Moreover, the role and contribution of the major cities in these areas is also on the low side.

New York accounts for around 24 per cent of America's GDP. Tokyo accounts for 26 per cent of Japan's GDP, London for 22 per cent of UK's GDP, and Seoul for 26 per cent of Korea's GDP.

Table 4.6 Development of China's three major city clusters (2006)

Region	Population		Administrative area		Population density (persons/km^2)	GDP	
	Quantity (10,000)	Ratio (%)	Quantity (km^2)	Ratio %		Quantity (100 million yuan)	Ratio %
1. City cluster in Yangtze River delta	8,471	6.41	100,242	0.10	845	38,149	16.81
Shanghai	1,815	1.37	6,341	0.01	2,862	10,366	4.57
Eight cities in Jiangsu Province (Nanjing, Zhenjiang, Wuxi, Changzhou, Suzhou, Nantong, Yangzou, and Taizhou)	4,037	3.05	48,512	0.51	832	17,346	7.64
Six cities in Zhejiang Province (Hangzhou, Ningbo, Jiaxing, Huzhou, Shaoxing, and Zhoushan)	2,620	1.98	45,389	0.47	577	10,436	4.60
2. City cluster in Pearl River delta	5,365	4.06	42,631	0.44	1,258	34,080	15.02
Hong Kong	681	0.52	1,068	0.00	6,376	13,980	6.16
Macao	50	0.04	16	0.00	31,250	1,116	0.49
Nine cities in Guangdong Province (Guangzhou, Shenzhen, Dongguan, Foshan, Zhongshan, Zhuhai, Jiangmen, Huizhou, and Zhaoqing)	4,634	3.51	41,547	0.43	1,115	18,984	8.37
3. City cluster in Beijing–Tianjin–Tanggu area	6,203	4.69	168,974	1.76	367	19,259	8.49
Beijing	1,581	1.20	16,808	0.18	941	7,870	3.47
Tianjin	1,075	0.81	11,920	0.12	902	4,359	1.92
Seven cities in Hebei Province (Tangshan, Langfang, Baoding, Qinhuangdao, Zhangjiakou, Chengde, and Cangzhou)	3,547	2.68	140,246	1.46	253	7,030	3.10
4. Total of three major city clusters	20,039	15.16	311,846	3.25	643	91,489	40.32
National total	132,179	100.00	9,600,000	100.00	1.38	226,905	100.000

Source: Yuan Xin and Tang Xiaoping: *City Rims: Japan's experience and development of China's three major city clusters*, Qiushi Journal, Issue 2, 2008.

In contrast, of the premier cities in China's urban clusters, Beijing accounts for only 3.5 per cent of China's GDP, Guangzhou for 2 per cent, and Shanghai for 5 per cent; that is, China's urban clusters contribute just one-tenth of the share that other country's urban clusters contribute to their economies. It is clear that there is tremendous opportunity for further growth in China's premier cities. In the future, these cities will be increasing their international competitiveness, participating in global economic activity and creating a whole new pattern of growth for China's economy.

China's three urban clusters are the mainstays that support China's rapid economic growth. The density of development in these areas is already quite high, however, and the carrying capacity of the resource environment is beginning to weaken. A World Bank study (Leman, Edward, 2005) notes that 29 per cent of the country's entire population lives within an hour's radius of 53 major cities.[10] This segment of the population constitutes 53 per cent of China's total urban population. Most of these urban areas have tremendous room to develop. Certain cities with relatively stronger carrying capacity in terms of their resource endowment may be able to grow into even larger urban clusters.

Box 4.5 Standards by which city clusters can be defined

The following basic determining factors could be used to distinguish urban clusters in China. These take into account a number of considerations, including international and domestic indicators and standards currently used to define urban areas, metropolitan hubs, urban clusters, and megalopolises. They take into full account the development stage of China's existing urbanization. They take into account the key position and international position China's urbanization takes at a time of economic globalization. They also take into consideration the fact that, in China, the government plays a guiding role in incubating and nurturing the formation of urban clusters.

1. An urban cluster should contain no less than three and no more than 20 major cities or urban hubs. Among these, at least one must be a 'nuclear' or core city, either an extra-large city or a mega-city, with an urban population of no less than one million people.
2. An urban cluster should have a population of no less than 20 million, among whom at least 10 million are 'urban residents'.
3. The per capita GDP of the city must exceed US$ 3000 and the degree of industrialization should be relatively high, generally in the latter stages of development.
4. The 'economic density' of an urban cluster should exceed RMB 5 million per square kilometer, and at least 30 per cent of the area's revenues must be oriented towards 'the outside'.

5. The density of the network of rail transport in urban clusters should be between 250 and 350 kilometers of line per 10,000 square kilometers. The density of the network of highways should be between 2000 and 2500 kilometers per 10,000 square kilometers. The networks should form a highly developed and comprehensive transport system.

6. The percentage production value that is non-agricultural in an urban cluster should be no less than 70 per cent. The labour force should be at least 60 per cent non-agricultural.

7. The level of urbanization in urban-cluster regions should be greater than 50 per cent.

8. The mean GDP of the core city of an urban cluster should be greater than 45 per cent of the cluster's GDP; the city should be able to perform urban functions that are cross-provincial.

9. The rate at which people from neighboring areas commute into the core city should be 15 per cent greater than the population of the core city itself.

10. An urban cluster should have the ability to dispatch buses at certain rates within certain rings or concentric economic zones around the core part of the city. For example, the dispatch rate should be every ten minutes within the half-hour inner ring of the city. It should be every 20 minutes within the one-hour ring around the city, it should be every 20 minutes within the two-hour ring around the city, and it can be more than 30 minutes outside the two-hour ring around the city.

Source: Fang Chuanglin: Research progress and basic judgement on standards for city clusters' spatial identification, Journal of City Planning, Issue 4, 2009.

Various measures that will be necessary in order to turn 'urban clusters' into the primary form of urbanization in China

The rapid development of China's urban clusters has come up against numerous constraints. These relate in part to China's overall stage of development and its unique systems and mechanisms. In addition, however, the process is hampered by a lack of overall planning. The spatial configuration of the process is irrational. As urban areas constantly increase, farmland is being lost at a serious rate. The build-out of basic infrastructure is moving slowly. The mode of China's economic growth is still 'extensive' as opposed to intensive, and industries are not highly competitive. Urban employment systems and public services are insufficient, and the problem of turning rural migrant workers into legitimate urban systems is pronounced. The imbalance between demand for and supply of natural resources is extreme and problems relating to the ecosystem are intensifying.

In order to address all of these problems and contradictions, we are going to have to adhere to policies that focus on human development. We are going to have to take a path of compact, intensive, and high-density development.

1 Make adjustments in the current spatial configuration

In overall terms, China's various forms of cities can already accommodate China's population, even when that population reaches its peak.[11] The problem we confront is the configuration of the space and the way space is used inefficiently. Right now, the total built-up areas of cities, county-administered cities, administered towns, independent areas engaged in industry and mining, rural settlements, and development zones, comes to a total of 300,000 square kilometers.

From now on, we should be able to keep from occupying more arable land for human settlement on a nationwide basis if the following list of considerations can be achieved: if land used for rural settlements can gradually be reduced as people become urban residents; if industrial and mining districts can come to be considered as 'urban spaces' and we intensify human density in them even as we intensify industry; if more 'administered towns' can be developed into small and medium-sized cities and thereby greatly increase their population density.

The critical issue is whether or not we can improve the efficiency with which we use space, whether or not we can shift the emphasis of our urbanization efforts towards optimizing the urban spatial configurations. The whole question of adjusting urban spatial configurations must be incorporated in our overall thinking about adjusting the country's economic structure.

2 Promote and nurture the growth of twenty urban clusters

China should continue to give preference to developing the three urban clusters that currently exist, namely the Bohai hub (which covers Beijing, Tianjin, Hebei Province, the central and south parts of Liaoning Province, and the Jiaodong Peninsula), the Yangtze River delta, and the Pearl River delta (including Hong Kong and Macao).

At the same time, the country should focus on developing eight additional urban clusters and nine urbanized areas. The eight additional urban clusters are the Harbin–Changchun urban cluster (the Harbin–Daqing–Qiqihar area in Heilongjiang Province and the Changchun–Jilin area in Jilin Province), the Southeast Fujian urban cluster (the coastal area in Fujian Province), the Jianghuai urban cluster (the Wanjiang city cluster in Anhui Province), the Mid-Yangtze River urban cluster (the Changsha–Zhuzhou–Xiangtan urban cluster in Hunan Province, the Wuhan urban hub in Hubei Province, and the Nanchang–Jiujiang area in Jiangxi Province), the Guanzhong Plains city cluster, the Chengdu–Chongqing urban cluster, and the Baibu Bay urban cluster (the southern part of Guangxi Region, the northern part of Hainan Province, and the eastern part of Guangdong Province).

These areas are chosen in light of their existing foundation, the carrying capacity of their resource endowment, and their potential for future development.

The nine urbanized areas include the urban hub in the central and southern parts of Hebei Province, the Taiyuan city rim, the Hohhot–Baotou–Erdos–Yulin urban hub, the Guiyang urban hub, the urban hub in the central part of Yunnan Province, the urban hub in the central and southern parts of Tibet, the urban hub in the Lanzhou–Xining region, the urban hub in the Ningxia Region along the Yellow River, and the urban hub along the northern slope of the Tianshan Mountain.

3 Adopt a more coordinated approach to the growth of large, medium-sized, and small cities and small towns, as urban clusters are being developed

China must necessarily take a path toward urbanization that features compactness, intensification, and high density. Consequently, it must regard the development of 'urban clusters' as the primary form in which urbanization takes place. Urban clusters have already been developing quite rapidly due to their unique advantages. They have begun to supplant unitary cities as the primary support for China's constantly accelerating economic growth.

At the same time, such clusters stimulate the growth of cities as well as new districts through their radial influence, and thereby spur the economic growth of larger regions. China's experience in its various urban clusters, as well as the experience of other countries, proves that small towns and cities can also grow quickly if they are situated within urban clusters or near their perimeters. Smaller towns and cities further away are different. Although they might be able to concentrate certain special industries and serve as 'service centers' for local communities, such places have only limited capacity to generate jobs for people. They will not be able to grow quickly and some may even decline.

4 Strengthen the extent to which urban-cluster planning is centralized and unified

Urban planning with respect to 'urban clusters' is on the order of 'hundred-year' planning. Highly significant, it nonetheless does not exist in any real sense in China at this time. The process cuts across administrative divisions and different sectors of the economy, which makes it highly complex. Given China's existing systems, it is extremely difficult to carry out coordinated strategic arrangements and comprehensive planning.

As a result, the overall plans for strategic development and general spatial configuration of urban clusters are, at present, in abeyance. All levels of government express strong interest in urban cluster development, including provincial, regional, and municipal, but plans are in fact limited to actions within the scope of provinces themselves. It is difficult to connect up cross-boundary links that must exist within the urban clusters themselves and to begin to define a division of labour.

Therefore, in the process of developing urban clusters in the twenty-first century, China must first conduct a scientifically based planning process that aims to make sure urban clusters develop in an orderly way.

5 Promote the integration of neighboring cities within urban clusters

Integrating neighboring cities within an urban cluster involves clarifying the functions of each and ensuring that each interacts with others in a way that creates a stronger whole. Positioning of industries should be mutually supportive; basic infrastructure networks should be interconnected; personnel should be able to move freely among districts. Any population that exceeds the carrying capacity of extra-large cities should, in appropriate fashion, at the same time, the functions of small and medium-sized cities should be strengthened, as well as their overall carrying capacity.

Regulations should be formulated that are unified and apply to the entire urban cluster. Comprehensive urban planning should be applied to the 'industrial positioning' [or zoning] of each city and to defining its key functions. Comprehensive zoning plans should apply to housing, public services, ecosystem patterns, and to the protection of open green space between cities. Unified arrangements should be made for systems that interconnect cities, including transport, energy, communications, environmental protection, disaster mitigation, and basic infrastructure. These should be 'built by all and built for all'. Systems should be as integrated, networked, and internally consistent as possible.

6 Advocate an 'intensive form' of growth for urban clusters

The planning process as it relates to urban clusters is an important tool in the overall process of regulating urban development. Zoning can help prevent cities from encroaching upon neighbouring farmland and ecological areas. It can help increase the density of built-up areas, and prevent land development in areas that are outside the defined 'urbanization areas'. New urban boundaries can be re-evaluated every 10–20 years, depending on new requirements.

New urban-development plans should emphasize the construction of mass-transport systems and the building of residential areas that lie within a reasonable radius from the stations of these transport systems. They should ensure the availability of office space, business services, and other functions. They should aim to reduce vehicle traffic and air pollution by establishing mixed-use urban city spaces and human-oriented designs. The main-stream development trends of urban clusters in the future should be characterized as 'intensive' and 'intelligent'. These should apply most importantly to land use, in order to ensure that ongoing development of living space for human beings in the future is sustainable.

7 Strictly control the spatial reconfiguration within urban hubs; raise urban floor area ratio (FAR) in a rational way

The average FAR of buildings in China's cities right now is only 0.75, yet it ranges between 1 and 2 for most places in East Asia. With far less land than

---

Box 4.6 The experience of certain countries in adopting 'compact' urban
          policies

The Commission of the European Communities (CEC, 1990, 1992) has
encouraged its member cities to become more 'compact', while staying
within quality-of-life standards and standards of environmental quality.
The British government has made 'compactness' one of the core elements
in its sustainable development policies, that is, it is focusing on the process
of making England's cities more compact (Ministry of the Environment,
1993). The government of Holland has adopted similar policies (Urban
Planning Administration, 1991). Most recently, the Japanese government
has introduced the concept of 'ecologically [sound] compact cities'. This is
now one of the top-priority policies with respect to its cities. (Ministry of
Land and Transport, 2009). The Australian government (Newman, 1992)
and the North American governments (Wachs, 1990; Chinitz, 1990) have
done the same thing. Compact-city policies are designed to intensify the
use of urban land by increasing residential density and concentration. They
encourage mixed use of land, and control the amount of development
outside specified areas (Churchman, 1999).

Source: OECD: Background Report, 2010.

---

that available for urbanization in Japan, China should have a higher volume-
capacity rate.

Depending on how urbanization proceeds in China, we might want to consider
imposing restrictions on residential buildings that have lower FARs, in conjunc-
tion with how we restructure the spatial configuration of cities. The goal is to
have a reasonable increase in the FAR. FARs of the older urban districts and
downtown areas should be set to strike a balance between economic and environmental efficiencies. Borrowing from international experience, we may implement
incentives for higher FARs and allow authorization of development rights based
on given FARs.

8 Build large residential areas and satellite cities

The course of urbanization is dictated by increases in urban populations.
Populations have increased with tremendous speed in the Yangtze River delta,
Pearl River delta, and Jing-jin-tang region, where urbanization has happened
faster than elsewhere. As a result, cities have exploded in size, exceeding
the existing capacity of urban systems. This has brought extreme pressures to
bear on such things as transport, overall population, residential space, resources,
and the environment.

There is now an urgent need for large-scale residential districts and satellite cities in order to ameliorate these problems, ease traffic congestion, and create better living conditions. We should consider injecting large-scale residential areas into the already-existing built-up areas of cities in order to make sure that increases in population do not cause cities to expand further into outlying land. This will allow us to achieve our goal of increasing human density.

In terms of the spatial arrangement of satellite cities, we should consider a gradual approach that starts with closer areas and then moves outward along subway lines or highways. Supervisory controls can be implemented through various policy mechanisms, including low-priced land, low-priced construction costs, preferential policies, and so on, to ensure that the housing being built remains within affordable levels. Meanwhile, service facilities that comply with high standards should be built in order to create a comfortable, clean, and convenient living environment. Such facilities should include stores, schools, hospitals and senior citizens centers.

9 Set up cooperative relationships among various levels of government

We will need to set up a variety of cooperative partnering mechanisms to deal with complex issues that are bound to arise in the course of urbanization, and particularly the development of urban clusters. These should be set up across various levels of government.

We may consider two different approaches. One would be to set up coordination mechanisms that extend across districts and municipalities. This would resemble the way nine county governments in the San Francisco Bay Area have formed a 'Bay Area Association for District Governments'. This Association is responsible for overseeing economic development around the Bay Area, as well as for environmental and ecological protection.

The second approach would be to set up vertically oriented cooperative relationships between government departments. The relevant Central-government department in an area would be in charge of formulating regulations and plans for that area. This would be similar to the way in which Japan has dealt with coordination problems. The Land Ministry in Japan formulated development guidelines for each of the major metropolitan areas in order to harmonize development within each metropolitan hub.

Notes

1 The size of a city as an administrative unit in China does not reflect that of the urbanized area, which is determined by the built-up area instead. A built-up area refers to land expropriated and developed for non-agricultural purposes. It includes continuous urban zones, and suburban zones that are closely associated with them and that, having access to a basically complete range of public utilities, serve the city's development purpose (e.g., the airport, marshalling station, sewage treatment plant, and radio communication facility).

2 Based on the *China Urban–Rural Statistical Yearbook 2008*.
3 After 2006, the *China Urban–Rural Construction Statistical Yearbook* included temporary population in its statistics. Therefore, the total population after 2006 included temporary population. Otherwise, the population density drop would have been more dramatic.
4 A large city has a more dramatic population density decline. The causes of this conclusion will be analyzed in the following part of this report.
5 The land-use volume rate = total constructed area/the land area used for construction.
6 The concept of the national central city was first introduced in 2005 by the Ministry of Construction when it was compiling a national plan for cities and towns according to the Urban Planning Law. The so-called national central city refers to a city that can perform leading, radiating, and distributing functions across the country. Currently, Chongqing, Beijing, Tianjin, Shanghai, and Guangzhou are defined as the five major national central cities.
7 The City Planning Law adopted in 1990.
8 China had 225 cities in 1981. But some of these cities adjusted their administrative divisions and some cities had visibly irrational data. Therefore, only 207 of these cities were comparable in 2008.
9 As its name implies, a small town is an area between urban and rural areas. In summary, the concept of small town can be interpreted in the narrow and broad senses. A small town in the narrow sense refers to the administrative town, including the county city, except in a place that has an administrative city. A small town in the broad sense also includes the rural town in addition to the county city and administrative town in the narrow sense. The small town in this report refers to the administrative town and county city.
10 Each of these city areas centers around a city with a non-agricultural population of more than 1 million, including the population of nearby cities or counties.
11 In 2008, China's built-up area totaled 300,000 square kilometers (some were repeated calculated; for example, a development zone with a population of 3000 was statistically included in the built-up area of a city). It included 40,600 square kilometers for cities, 14,800 square kilometers for county cities, 30,200 square kilometers and 41,500 square kilometers for independent industrial and mining areas, 165,300 square kilometers for rural settlements, and nearly 10,000 square kilometers for national and provincial development zones. Based on the total population of 1.46 billion, the urbanization rate of 70 per cent, the urban population of 1 billion, and the population density of 10,000 people per square kilometer, the space required for urbanization will be 100,000 square kilometers.

5 Industrial structure and employment considerations in the course of urbanization

Healthy urbanization is a process that extends its benefits down to the level of families and individuals in cities. The process must provide them with adequate job opportunities. China is currently urbanizing at a fast pace and cities are becoming the primary realm for job creation. At the same time, China is in a critical period as it restructures its economy and moves from being a lower-middle-income country to a higher-middle-income country. Whether or not China can address its employment issues properly is closely related to the success of this restructuring of urban industries and to the whole process of urbanization itself.

The current state of urban employment in China

From the late-1950s to the mid-1980s, China had a classic 'dual economy' with a strict separation between urban and rural areas. Employment in the two economic spheres was also strikingly dualistic. The majority of people with an 'urban household registration' worked for state-owned enterprises, while a minority worked in enterprises that operated under the collectively owned system. In the countryside, the majority of people were engaged in agriculture. This system prevailed for almost two decades, between the 1950s and the mid-1970s.

After this period, some rural residents began working in town-and-village enterprises and in private enterprises as those businesses began to develop, but even into the mid-1980s, only some 20 per cent of rural people were employed in non-agricultural jobs.

Starting in 1984, the system controlling the flow of the labor force from the countryside into cities was gradually relaxed. More and more 'farmers' began to leave rural areas for jobs in cities. People known as 'rural migrant workers' [*nong-min-gong*] became a key component of all people employed in cities (see Table 5.1). The large numbers of rural migrant workers flowing into cities began to have a profound effect on the structure of employment in cities, as well as on the total number of jobs.

Total size and distribution of urban employment

As China's population has continued to 'urbanize', the total number of urban jobs has increased together with the urban percentage of the country's total

Table 5.1 Scale of inter-regional flow of rural migrant workers 2000–2006

Year	Number of rural migrant workers (10,000)	Ratio of urban employment (per cent)	Ratio of employment in secondary and tertiary industries (per cent)	Ratio of urban-rural employment (per cent)
2000	7,849	36.9	21.8	10.9
2001	8,399	35.1	23.0	11.5
2002	10,470	42.3	28.4	14.2
2003	11,390	44.4	30.1	15.3
2004	11,823	44.7	29.6	15.7
2005	12,578	46.0	30.1	16.6
2006	13,212	46.7	30.1	17.3

Source: The number of 'rural migrant workers'originate from the rural social and economic research team of the National Bureau of Statistics: *China Rural Household Survey Year books*; the ratios are worked out on the basis of the data in the *China Statistical Summary 2007*.

labor force. In 1998, China undertook major reform of the employment system in its state-owned enterprises. This led to a tremendous increase in unemployment. Large numbers of workers lost their positions, the unemployment rate rose, and the 're-employment rate' of both workers and staff declined.

This then led to a false impression, however. It looked as though the total number of jobs in China had not increased since the 1990s, and indeed may have gone down in absolute terms. In fact, the total number of jobs in cities in China has been constantly increasing. Table 5.1 shows total urban employment and its percentage of total employment in the country. In 1990, the total urban labor force came to 170 million people. By 2008, the figure had increased by 77.3 per cent and now came to 300 million. The number of people employed in cities had risen by 7.32 million people per year and the urban percentage of total national employment had also increased, going from 26.3 per cent in 1990 to 39 per cent in 2008.

The ownership structure of entities in which urban people are employed has also changed enormously. In the early 1990s, state-owned enterprises and collectively owned entities accounted for more than 80 per cent of urban employment. By 1997, that figure had fallen to 67 per cent, not because employment by these entities had declined, yet, but because other forms of employment had increased. Other entities hiring urban residents included shareholding companies, jointly-operated entities, limited liability companies, and new types of entities invested in by businesses in Hong Kong, Taiwan, and other countries.

It was after 1997 that employment in state-owned enterprises and collectively owned entities declined precipitously, once their employment systems began to be reformed. The percentage of the total labor force employed by these entities also fell swiftly. By 2008, the percentage came to only 23.5 per cent. At that point, private [*si-ying*] and individually operated [*ge-ti*] enterprises employed 87.33 million people and accounted for 28.9 per cent of the total urban employment.

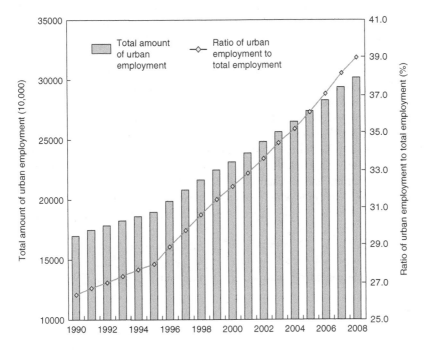

Figure 5.1 Total amount of urban employment and its ratio to total employment.
Source: Based on data from *China Statistical Yearbooks*.

In short, China's employment structure began to diversify, with a declining percentage of employment provided by state-owned and collective units. Various other forms of entities, as listed above, provided 48.63 million jobs and accounted for 16.1 per cent of total urban employment.

In addition to the various kinds of entities hiring labor in cities, as noted above, another category of employment should not be overlooked. It is one that is not included in China's traditional statistics. That category could be called non-formal [or informal] employment and it is quite substantial both in absolute terms and percentage of the total labor force. Non-formal urban employment rose quickly in the late 1990s and reached a peak in 2004, when it totaled around one hundred million people. At that point, it represented 38 per cent of total urban employment. The figure then declined slightly and in 2008 came to roughly 31.5 per cent of total urban employment.

The 'unemployment rate' in cities and the 'labor participation rate' in cities

The unemployment rate is the key indicator that reflects the overall situation in the labor market. The figure normally given by the *China Statistical Yearbook* is the rate of people who actually register as unemployed.[1] Several categories of people are not included in this statistic, however, including people who have reached retirement age and so do not 'register' their unemployment, people who do not have 'urban household registration status' and so cannot register unemployment, and people who either do not want to register or simply have not yet registered. As a result, this official figure often is not in fact representative of the unemployment situation.

We can, however, arrive at a figure for unemployment that is based on definitions of the International Labor Organization and that uses officially published statistics. With that, we can carry out international comparisons of the surveyed unemployment rate in China's cities. Given China's unique situation, such surveys include only a small percentage of the number of people living on a permanent basis in cities who have come in to work in them from elsewhere. As a result, the surveys mainly reflect the unemployment rate of people with an urban household registration.

As shown by Figure 5.2, prior to 1997, China's surveyed unemployment rate in urban areas was quite low, less than 4.5 per cent. After China's state-owned enterprises implemented reform of their employment systems in 1998, the rate

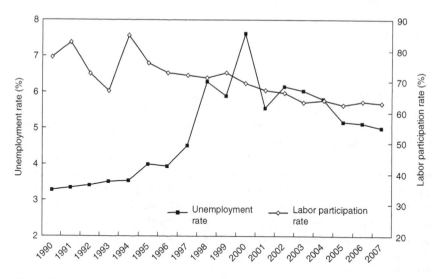

Figure 5.2 Statistics and estimates of surveyed urban unemployment rate and labor participation rate.

Source: The surveyed unemployment rate for the 1997–2004 period was based on data from the *China Statistical Yearbooks* and the *China Population Statistical Yearbooks*; the surveyed unemployment rate for 2005 was based on the micro data of the 1 per cent sample population survey conducted in 2005; the surveyed unemployment rate for 2006 and 2007 was estimated by the authors of this report;[2] the labor participation rate was based on data from the *China Statistical Yearbooks* and the *China Population Statistical Yearbooks*.

rose quickly and reached more than 7 per cent in 2000. Since then, the figure has been declining somewhat as the labor market gradually improves.

The 'labor participation rate' is another key indicator of the state of the labor market. It gives the number of 'economically active' people as a percentage of the population that is at a 'working age'. In most years since the 1990s, this figure has stayed at over 70 per cent.

Prior to employment-system reform, however, a very substantial number of people who 'worked' in state-owned enterprises and collectively owned entities were, *de facto*, unemployed. The great majority of state-owned enterprises were either bankrupt or semi-closed down, but the unemployed status of their workers was not reflected in official statistics.

After 2000, as the unemployment rate began to rise, the labor participation rate began to decline. This correlated to the situation in the labor market. When conditions deteriorated in terms of lay-offs of people, those who were already fairly old, and those who had lower levels of education, often stopped looking for jobs and dropped out of the official labor market. Meanwhile, new people coming into the market also found their prospects unfavorable and many gave up looking for official jobs, either temporarily or permanently.

In more recent years, the labor participation rate has been fairly steady, under the impact of two trends. One is a slight improvement in the labor market (which raises the labor participation rate), and another is the increase in the number of younger people going to school (which lowers the labor participation rate).

The structural composition of the urban labor force

During the entire period of China's reform and opening up, the economy has been undergoing a two-tiered process. One has been the ongoing growth in the 'dual economy', and the other has been the ongoing change of the overall economic system. In terms of the labor market, these things have created a coexisting situation of 'hidden unemployment', 'natural unemployment', and 'periodic or cyclical unemployment'.

The dual economy in the country [urban and rural] featured an 'unlimited source of labor'. That is, China was plagued by hidden unemployment, given the surplus of labor in the countryside as well as the surplus or redundant labor in China's urban enterprises. In fairly early days, people estimated the *de facto* unemployment in rural areas to be 30 per cent and that in cities to be 40 per cent. In addition, China had to face cyclical changes in employment given the fluctuations of its macro-economic situation, as well as 'natural unemployment' caused by structural factors such as advances in technology, the changing structure of the economy, and the function of 'friction' [in an imperfectly smooth job market].

The labor market has also undergone fundamental changes in recent years with ongoing restructuring of the entire economic system. A clear improvement in the problem of hidden unemployment has been one result. First, systemic obstacles that previously blocked the free flow of labor have continued to be removed, which has ameliorated the problem of surplus labor in the countryside. The rural labor force has shifted very considerably into cities. One consequence is that more than half of the remaining labor force in the countryside is now over the age of 40. This most recent financial crisis has also shown that the rural labor force is no longer an inexhaustible pool, however. Cities have now developed a 'rigid demand' for the rural labor force, which, now that it has 'shifted out' of the countryside, no longer has the possibility of returning to the land.

Secondly, reforms of the urban employment system and the 'breaking of the iron rice bowl' have accelerated the development of job markets. Urban jobs are finally being 're-allocated' through market mechanisms, and enterprises have realized a tremendous decrease in the numbers of [redundant] staff.

While there has been a noticeable decrease in hidden unemployment, the effect of natural unemployment and cyclical unemployment are now relatively more pronounced. Figure 5.3 shows the various pressures of the different kinds of unemployment over time, as reform of the economy has been carried out and as the economy has grown. Different groups have become more or less vulnerable to the risks of unemployment as the situation has changed. This targeted kind of risk has been affected by structural changes, government policies, the age structure of the labor pool in urban and rural areas, and the human-resource qualifications in the different places.

First, rural migrant workers have become the primary source of labor supply. Nevertheless, they have not received the kinds of protections that apply to urban workers, and therefore have been more subject to the volatility of economic cycles.

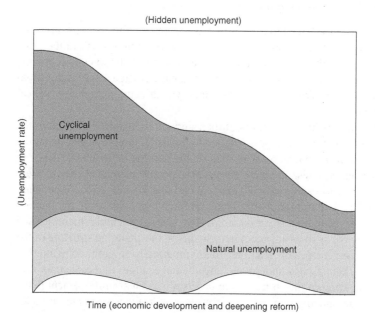

Figure 5.3 Types of unemployment and change along with deepening reform.

As macroeconomic prospects in the country go up and down, rural migrant workers have alternated between over-supply and shortage.

Second, there are those people who were formerly employed in urban areas: after labor-system reforms, many of those who were laid off were reallocated to new jobs through new employment systems. They therefore went from being 'hidden unemployed' to being employed. Those who had been born in the 1950s and on into the 1960s, however, were handicapped by the lack of any education during the years of the Great Cultural Revolution. This group of people, called '40s and 50s people' in shorthand, often became the first target of lay-offs and hence became unemployed. As time went on, they reached retirement age and gradually simply withdrew from the labor market.

Third, those young people who went to college after China expanded its college enrollments face the problem of 'frictional' unemployment, in the sense that they are qualified, in one way or another, but their qualifications now have to be matched up with the right jobs. In the long term, therefore, this group of people will continue to face structural kinds of unemployment. The number of college graduates who cannot find jobs will continue to increase, as numbers of graduates increase and the problem of matching them up with jobs continues.

Changes in the demographic structure of China's population, and consequences for labor supply in cities

The two determining factors in the potential supply of labor in an economy are the total quantity of the population and its demographic structure. When China implemented a strictly segregated form of 'dual economy', stringent barriers to labor mobility meant that changes in the structure of urban and rural populations only affected the situation in each locale. As such barriers were gradually eliminated, together with other restraining social and economic factors, the segregated nature of China's labor force was relaxed and changes in demographics began to have an overall as opposed to partial effect.

Trends in the changes in China's demographic structure

Major changes have been occurring among both urban and rural populations in China (especially among urban residents) with respect to the desire to have children and with respect to child-bearing behavior in general. These have accompanied changes in family planning policies, but also increases in standard of living and changes in lifestyle.

Between 1978 and 1987, China's birth rate rose from 1.82 per cent to 2.33 per cent. For the next 20 years, however, it consistently declined until it was 1.21 per cent. In the year 2000, 7 per cent of China's total population was over the age of 65 (State Family Planning Commission, 2010). China is already becoming an 'ageing society', but several features distinguish its 'ageing' from that in other developing countries (Office of the National Working Committee on Ageing, 2006).

First, China is entering the state of being an 'ageing society' at a far lower level of economic development than other countries. The average GDP per capita of developed countries when they reached a similar stage was between US$ 5000 and US$ 10,000. China's per capita GDP has just gone over US$ 1000, so it is 'ageing' at a much lower economic level. It is still in the ranks of lower-middle-income countries. In 2000, 6.8 per cent of China's population was over the age of 65. This was comparable to other countries in the world when they started to become ageing societies, but China's GNI per capita (gross national income) was a mere 17.3 per cent that of the world level when figured at the official rate of exchange of China's currency. When figured in terms of purchasing power parity, it was 56.3 per cent of the average world level. China therefore is distinguished by 'becoming an ageing society before it becomes a prosperous society'.

Second, the process of becoming an ageing society is accelerating in China. Doing a cross-sectional comparison of China and other countries shows this to be the case. Within an estimated 30 years (by the year 2030), the percentage of China's population that is over 65 will go from 7 per cent to 14 per cent. In France, the same percentage growth in the over-65 population took 115 years. In Sweden, it took 85 years, and in England and Germany it took 45 years. China's ageing process is expected to continue to accelerate for a long time, placing it in the forefront of the ranks of ageing countries (State Family Planning Commission, 2010).

Third, the ageing process in China is inverted when compared to the experience of other countries. That is, developed countries generally have an urban population that is ageing faster than the rural population, but the opposite is true in China. The birth rate is high in the countryside in China, but more and more young, able-bodied people are migrating to cities, leaving a countryside that is populated by older people. In 2000, the 'level of ageing' in the countryside was 1.24 times what it was in urban areas. This 'inverted relationship' is expected to continue all the way up to around the year 2040.

Fourth, China's ageing situation is progressively worse from east to west. The rate of ageing is notably faster along the more developed eastern coastal areas than it is in the underdeveloped west. Analysis has shown that Shanghai became an 'ageing society' in 1979, while Ningxia will only start to become an ageing society in 2012. This represents a time differential of 33 years.

From the latter part of the 1980s, China's natural population growth has been declining, partly due to the dramatically low birth rate and partly due to a gradually increasing mortality rate after the year 2002. In 1987, the natural growth rate of the population was 1.661 per cent. This was the highest it reached after the start of reform and opening up policies began; since that time it has declined and was 0.508 per cent in 2008.

The two factors of a declining birth rate and an increasingly ageing population will inevitably lead to a lower absolute number of working-age people in China, as well as a lower percentage of working-age people to the total population. In addition, specific features of the way China's population is ageing may pose severe challenges to the country's urbanization process in the future. The inverted numbers of older people in rural and countryside, and the way ageing is more intense in the east than in the west, mean that municipal departments in the east may well be affected by a shortage in labor supply in China's more developed regions. This will force municipalities and the eastern region in general to restructure industries faster than they otherwise might have done. Meanwhile, the acceleration of ageing in China and the fact that it is occurring at a fairly low economic level mean that social security systems will face ever more intense pressure in both cities and rural areas. Greater demands will also be put on urban capacities to provide social services.

Trends in the supply of labor

The supply of a working-age population in China has been increasing ever since the 1950s. Forecasts of the Chinese Academy of Social Sciences and the Institute of Population and Labour Economics show that this trend will continue until around 2015. By that time, the working-age population will have gone from 340 million to around one billion. After that point, the working population will enter a period of negative growth (see Figure 5.4).

The 'supply of a working-age population of labor' is a statistic that measures potential supply, since not all members of a working-age population will actually

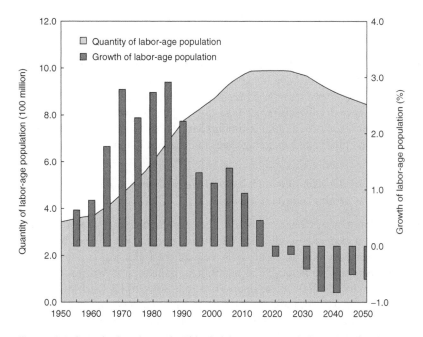

Figure 5.4 Quantitative change in China's labour-age population, 1950–2050.

Source: Wang Dewen: *Labour Market change and China's economic growth at low fertility rate*, Working paper of the Institute of Population and Labor Economics of the Chinese Academy of Social Sciences: www.aisixiang.com/download/6884_1_paper.pdf.

participate in the labor market. As a result, it is necessary to analyze the labor participation rate in order to have an accurate idea of actual labor supply. China's labor participation rate has been decreasing steadily since the 1990s. Between 1990 and 2004, it went from 85.6 per cent to 81.9 per cent. If the rate were to stay unchanged at the rate it was in 2005, then the effective labor supply (754 million in 2005) would peak in 2016 and start to decline. It would peak at 820 million people and decline to 817 million in 2020.

If, on the other hand, the labor participation rate continues to decline at the 1990-2004 rate, the labor participation rate may be down to 78.4 per cent by 2020, and the effective labor supply will peak in 2014 and then start to decline. It will peak at 790 million and go down to 775 million by 2020. Either one of these hypothetical situations concludes that the effective labor supply in China will peak by the year 2015. This is toward the end of the 12th Five-Year Plan period (Cai Fang et al., 2007; Wang Dewen, 2007).

Labor that will be required for the process of urbanization

One striking feature of urbanization is the fact that as economic activity concentrates in urban areas, it is accompanied by a concentration of labor. The migration of labor into cities is an increasingly obvious trend. In the course of social and economic changes associated with the changing urban–rural relationship in China, cities are seeing a constant expansion in job opportunities. These jobs and the inflow of labor are a key factor in the growth of China's cities, and are also a consequence of their growth.

As the overall size of China's economy has grown and as it has upgraded its industrial structure, cities have come to offer the greatest concentration of job opportunities in modern society. Cities are growing in size and industries are specializing and both of these things lead to greater economies of scale, greater benefits of concentration, and higher productivity. Division of labor among cities and also within cities is also enabling cities to create more jobs.

Restructuring of the economy in China and the consequent ability of the economy to 'absorb' more employment

Labor productivities of China's primary, secondary, and tertiary industries have all been given a tremendous lift since reform and opening-up policies began. In 1978, every RMB 10,000 worth of GDP required the following average investment in terms of human labor: 27.56 for primary industries, 3.98 for secondary, and 5.6 for tertiary. By 2007, these figures had gone down to 1.1 for primary, 0.16 for secondary, and 0.24 for tertiary. From these changes in labor productivity, and the changing differentials among the three industries, one can see the impact that urbanization and industrial restructuring are having on employment trends.

First, the percentage of the labor forced engaged by primary industries will continue to fall, and that fall will continue to accelerate. The percentage of the rural labor forced involved in agriculture has declined dramatically and the amount of surplus labour in the agricultural sector has also declined (Cai and Wang, 2008). Labor savings are increasingly the trend in agriculture, given changes in technology and growing efficiencies. The shift of labor away from agriculture will therefore continue, leading to a tremendous demand for new non-agricultural jobs.

Second, as urbanization takes place and industries are restructured, the distinct trend is towards an increase in tertiary industries. Service industries that provide for the needs of people will grow in particular, given that the urbanization of rural migrant workers will now become a key feature of China's urbanization in general. Since jobs in the service sector are far more elastic than those in second-ary industries, industrial restructuring will not necessary have to be done at the expense of jobs.

In overall terms, therefore, China's industrial restructuring will feature acceler-ated growth of tertiary industries and their absorption of large numbers of the 'new urbanites' as the country's urbanization progresses. In addition, the numbers of people being added to the labor market is growing at a slower rate year by year as the age structure of China's population changes. After 2015, the total number of people in China of working age will no longer increase. So long as China maintains its current economic growth trends, therefore, as well as a certain elas-ticity of employment, the future job situation in the country will not be character-ized by an over-supply of labor.

The ability of China's different regions to absorb employment: east, central, and west

Using statistics published in the *China City Statistical Yearbook*, we have calcu-lated the ability of various regions to absorb employment into non-agricultural industries (Table 5.2).

It must be pointed out, however, that corporate data on employment generally leaves out information on rural migrant workers and also local laborers. Data from small-scale and micro-scale enterprises is also not generally reflected in aggregate figures. The analysis as noted below mainly relates to formal employment. In point of fact, unofficial employment and employment in tertiary industries

Table 5.2 Employment-absorbing capacities of cities: jobs created per 10,000-yuan GDP

	Total non-agricultural industries	Secondary industry	Tertiary industry
Eastern region	0.048 (0.018)	0.047 (0.024)	0.056 (0.028)
Central region	0.074 (0.030)	0.074 (0.041)	0.088 (0.038)
Western region	0.066 (0.025)	0.058 (0.032)	0.094 (0.038)

Note: The figures in brackets are standard differences.

Source: National Bureau of Statistics: *China City Statistical Yearbook 2008*, China Statistical Publishing House, 2009.

along the coast is grossly underestimated. The ability of the coastal region to absorb employment is therefore much greater than the table below would seem to indicate. Nevertheless, the trends as they are exhibited in the data are accurate and also fairly significant.

First of all, to analyze the data in terms of regions: in the east, cities on average provide 0.048 job opportunities for every RMB 10,000 in GDP. Cities in the central part of the country that are industrializing at a fast pace provide 0.074 jobs per RMB 10,000 in GDP; the figure in western parts of the country is 0.066. There are two reasons for the lower figure in the east. First, less labor per unit of GDP is necessary in the east as a result of the more organic structure of capital and greater productivities. Second, figures for rural migrant labor are not included in 'official labor statistics' in the east, even though large amounts of such labor are being employed. This understates the number of jobs being provided per unit of GDP.

Second, analyzing the data in terms of job creation by type of industry results in a clear conclusion: service industries create more jobs. As shown in Figure 5.2, the number of jobs provided by tertiary industries in all three regions was greater than that provided by secondary industries. Structural changes in service industries are closely related to changes in the overall economic structure as an economy grows. In the process of rapid industrialization and urbanization, the concentration of people in cities generates its own demand for services. Such demand is concentrated in service industries that are labor-intensive and that therefore provide more jobs.

In addition, manufacturing and other industries generate a need for various kinds of services as an economy grows rapidly and industrialization proceeds, including new demands for such things as financing, information, insurance, and real estate. This precipitates structural changes in service industries in the direction of high-end capital-intensive and knowledge-intensive sectors. Such trends are already quite apparent in developed countries (Rosenthal and Strange, 2002).

China's service industries are conforming to the same trend. We regard financial, insurance, information, real estate, and R&D services to be what could be called 'high-end' service industries. As such, we have looked at the employment in those industries as compared to numbers of urban population and levels of economic development (Figure 5.5). The percentage of people employed in high-end service industries rises with levels of urban economic development. The scattered points in Figure 5.5 demonstrate a positive correlation (Cai Fang and Du Yang, 2003).

Third, China's eastern region is still the dominant force when it comes to absorbing rural migrant workers. Even though fewer jobs per unit of GDP are created in the east than elsewhere, the region is far larger in overall economic terms and far more able to absorb a larger workforce.

According to a survey undertaken in 2009, 66.8 per cent of all rural migrant workers who went 'outside' to work were employed in the east. That is, more than two-thirds of the total number of rural migrant workers was employed in the east. Guangdong province absorbed 27.8 per cent. Guangdong, Jiangsu, and Zhejiang

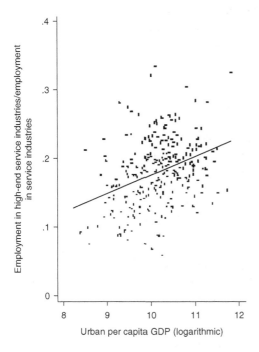

Figure 5.5 Employment ratio of high-end service industries and urban development.

Source: National Bureau of Statistics: *China City Statistical Yearbook 2008*, China Statistical Publishing House, 2009.

provinces together absorbed 43.7 per cent. China's central regions only absorbed 14.7 per cent, and the west absorbed 18.1 per cent (Sheng Laiyun, 2009).

The findings of this 2009 survey are consistent with earlier research (Cai Fang and Wang Meiyan, 2003). China's western region has grown at a faster comparative rate than the central and eastern parts of the country over the past decade. The national strategy to 'undertake major development of the west' and the strategy to 'undertake an emergence of the central part of the country' mean that non-agricultural employment capacities should be increasing in those two parts of the country in the future.

Employment as it relates to the concentration and diversification of industries

Rapid urbanization occurs in tandem with the shift of a rural workforce toward urban areas. In addition, however, economic activity increasingly concentrates in large cities. In 1997, cities that are administered at or above the prefectural level in China accounted for 42 per cent of the country's GDP. This percentage rose to 62 per cent in 2008.

In 2008, secondary industries in cities at this level [at or above prefectural level] accounted for 64.5 per cent of all secondary industries in the country, and for 71.4 per cent of all tertiary industries. Increasingly concentrated levels of economic activity in large cities mean that such cities are going to become the primary places in which China's employment problems must be resolved.

As noted above, employment in cities relies on ongoing industrial development. The allocation or presence of certain industries in cities determines the employment structure in those cities.

In China, manufacturing industries have been critical in providing jobs in cities to date, and manufacturing industries have determined urban employment structures. China consistently emphasized the development of heavy industries and chemical industries, and China's role in the overall international pattern of economic activities helped make secondary industries, and particularly manufacturing industries, primary in terms of urban industrial deployment. Figure 5.6 clearly reflects this relationship. One can see from the top part of the graph that the percentage of manufacturing increases as the size of urban populations increases, while the percentage of service industries actually begins to decline.

The relationship becomes even clearer when seen in terms of per capita GDP of urban populations (that is, level of economic development). As the level of

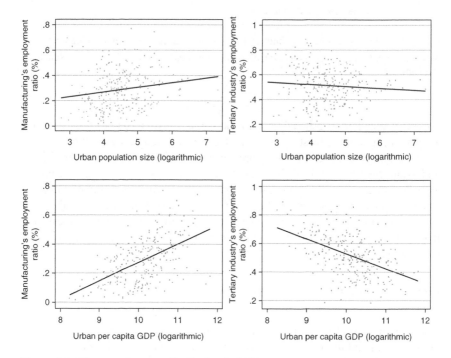

Figure 5.6 Urban employment distribution in 2007.

Source: National Bureau of Statistics: *China City Statistical Yearbook 2008*, China Statistical Publishing House, 2009.

economic development rises, employment is increasingly concentrated in manu-facturing industries while the percentage in tertiary industries declines. Combining the analyses above, we can see the following trajectory: as cities expand and their economies develop, employment moves from low-end services towards manufac-turing, while in a few large cities that are relatively more developed, employment moves from manufacturing toward high-end service industries.

Levels of economic development in cities and their industrial structure are determining factors when it comes to urban labor markets. This applies both to absolute numbers of people employed and the structure of employment. Other considerations or attributes of cities also play a role, however. For example, the level at which a city is administered as well as its population size and its location can influence its employment structure.

In the most fundamental sense, however, the way cities arise and develop in China depends on the concentration of the various factors of production, including the labor force. Such concentration in turn increases levels of speciali-zation and extends the 'chain of the division of labor', which ultimately results in efficiencies of scale. If the labor force is prevented from flowing from one type of industry to another, then this whole process of specialization is difficult to achieve. Moreover, even if urban economies are maximizing economic efficiencies, if employment is overly concentrated in certain sectors, that over-concentration exposes the entire labor market to far greater risks.

If core industries are impacted by external events, cities that have more highly concentrated employment in certain industries are far more vulnerable. In China, cities that have focused exclusively on resource development [extraction industries], for example, confront serious employment problems when their particular resource is depleted (Cai Fang, 2005).

From material showing the distribution of employment by industry in cities, we can evaluate the relationship between employment specialization or diversifi-cation and the growth of cities. Figure 5.7 shows the degree to which urban employment is distributed over various industries in a given city, depending on the per capita GDP of that city.[3] The larger the 'coefficient of employment variation', the more dispersed a city's population will be among various industries. The smaller the coefficient, the less dispersed. As the figure indicates, greater coefficients are associated with higher per capita GDP. The more developed the city, in economic terms, the more diversified its employment will be. The same correlation holds true for the size of a city's population: the larger the population, the more varied the employment.

This trend is quite apparent – the higher the level of economic development, the more diversified the employment – but it may be due to two different kinds of factors. First, during the planned-economy period in China, urban economies did not use market mechanisms to allocate industries. Instead, this was accomplished by the planning process. As a result, the later utilization of market mechanisms may have enabled urban economies to utilize their relative advantages, and may have broken down the old patterns of a division of labor among cities. Those cities with the liveliest economies generally have the highest levels of economic

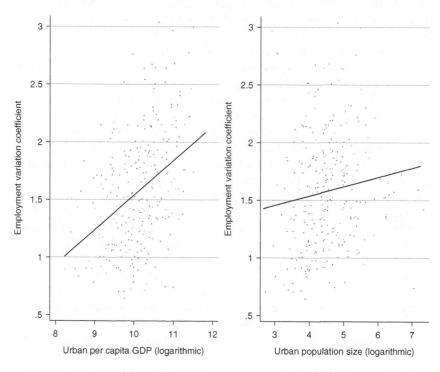

Figure 5.7 Diversification and specialization of urban employment, 2007.

Source: National Bureau of Statistics: *China City Statistical Yearbook 2008*, China Statistical Publishing House, 2009.

development and the phenomenon of diversification is more apparent. Secondly, economic development tends to draw forth new types of industries. The evolution and upgrading of industrial structures can also result in more diversified employment. The effect is all the more apparent in more developed cities.

Employment as it is affected by industrial shifts and urbanization

China's central and western regions still have considerable potential for urbanizing in the future. As labor costs rise, the more labor-intensive industries in the east will see a weakening of their competitive advantage. According to the traditional 'flying-geese theory', labor-intensive industries will progressively move to countries in which labor costs are lower.

In the meantime, the lower levels of development in central and western parts of China mean that these places will continue to have abundant labor supplies and relatively low wages. In other words, China can employ a 'flying-geese model' of development within its own borders, given its large territory and the way in which different regions differ in resource endowments.

Where conditions permit in certain parts of the central and western regions, labor-intensive industries may be able to grow, depending on local comparative advantages.

We can evaluate how industries have or have not shifted among different regions by looking at the changing distributions of primary, secondary, and tertiary industries in those regions. It is not hard to see from Table 5.3 that the eastern region held a dominant share of all industrial sectors in both 2000 and 2008. Western regions held the smallest share in all three sectors. In terms of aggregate figures, therefore, there still has not been any major shift in terms of secondary industries moving from east to west. Meanwhile, the decline in secondary industries in the middle part of the country has been only modest. Aggregations of regional data therefore fail to show that China's secondary industry is moving progressively from the east to the central and western regions

The above figures truly do not yet reflect any apparent inter-regional shift in industries. Nevertheless, the actual situation cannot be portrayed solely by using aggregate data. First, regional aggregate data may obscure changes that are taking place within the various provinces of a given region. An analysis of data from 31 provinces and comparable regions, during the same time period, shows considerable changes in the percentages of secondary and tertiary industries. The percentage of secondary industries held by Shanghai and Beijing fell during the period by 0.5–1 percentage points, for example, while the percentage held by Inner Mongolia and Henan rose by 1.0–1.5 percentage points. That of Gansu and Qinghai rose by 0.8–1 percentage points.

Second, industrial shifts have been occurring between provinces in a given region, as well as within each province, shifts that cannot be detected by looking at aggregate data. Many provinces along China's coastal regions still have inland areas that are relatively less developed. As industries shift from one place to another, it is natural that provinces first elect to shift industries to places within their own administrative jurisdictions that have suitable conditions.

Third, given problems with the way statistics are assembled, we cannot be more specific about structural shifts within the three different kinds of industries. Among secondary industries, lower-level sectors may well be shifting westward,

Table 5.3 Change in regional distribution of primary, secondary and tertiary industries (%)

		Eastern region	Central region	Western region
2000	Primary industry	42.96	34.43	22.61
	Secondary industry	59.80	26.32	13.88
	Tertiary industry	59.97	24.89	15.14
2008	Primary industry	39.71	35.84	24.45
	Secondary industry	59.91	26.48	13.61
	Tertiary industry	61.37	23.22	15.41
Change	Primary industry	−3.25	1.41	1.84
(2000–08)	Secondary industry	0.11	0.16	−0.27
	Tertiary industry	1.40	−1.67	0.27

Source: *China Statistical Yearbook 2009.*

while higher-end industries may be growing very fast, which puts an upward bias on the overall 'secondary industry' figures for the eastern region.

While overall trends may not be apparent in terms of industrial shifts among regions, certain movement can be seen in specific lines of business and specific regions. These were starting before but became far more apparent after the global financial crisis (see Box 5.1). Right now, 50 per cent of China's total volume of exports comes from processing industries along the east coast. Costs of making those products have been rising enormously, however, with increases in the prices of land, energy, and labor. Intense pressure from rising costs has led certain industries to shift *en masse* toward inland areas. These industries include shoe manufacturing, garments, textiles, ceramics, standard components, and so on from the provinces of Zhejiang, Guangdong, and Jiangsu (Wang Jici, 2010).

The ceramics industry in the city of Foshan, in Guangdong, can serve as one example. At its height, this industry had nearly 400 enterprises located in Foshan, and there are still 363 in the city. According to estimates of municipal authorities, however, more than 170 will either need to move out to less expensive places in 2008, or shut down. By August, 2008, Foshan's ceramics enterprises had signed contracts to invest more than RMB 25 billion in other provinces. This included money for 40,000 mu of land on which to build factories. The preferred place for these enterprises was now Gao-an in Jiangxi province, due to its advantages in terms of energy, resources, and human capital.[4]

Box 5.1 Foxconn shifts its operations inland

The municipal government of Hebi City, in Henan province, issued an emergency notification on its website on 25 June 2010. The substance of the notification was that the Foxconn Technologies Group was planning to invest in Henan province, build factories, and hire some 300,000 people. In the near future, it would be asking 100,000 people to start training at the company, in order to start sound operations at Foxconn in Henan.

Prior to this notice, a person within Foxconn had revealed that a plan to 'shift operations inland' would involve two-thirds of the production line at the company's current plant in Shenzhen. Employees at that plant would be reduced from the current 400,000 to 100,000. This June notification therefore was in accord with the earlier rumours. The future plant in Henan was to include some 300,000 people.

The future deployment of Foxconn has become fairly clear now, both as a result of the company's own information and reports in the media. The main manufacturing base currently located in Shenzhen will be relocating to Zhengzhou in Henan province. That facility makes computer connectors. The department that subcontracts the production of Apple products, as well as the staff at headquarters, will remain in Shenzhen. Employees there will be downsized to 100,000 people. Factories in Tianjin that are already producing cell-phone batteries and the external shells of cell phones will take over the entire cell phone production business. The computer department of Foxconn will be moving to Chongqing and Wuhan. According to reports, the first laptop computers were already being manufactured in Chongqing as of 18 May.

According to authorities responsible for the Zhengzhou labor market, by 14 August, Foxconn's Zhengzhou office had participated in nine special recruitment drives, hiring more than 200 people each time. Positions the company was hiring for included production group leaders, product-line managers, and product managers. More than 10,000 applicants were interviewed. On 14 August, Foxconn also set up nine recruitment stalls at the Henan provincial labor market. People lined up to apply for jobs, and it is said that the line was one kilometer long.

With close to 100 million people, Henan is China's most populous province. It has consistently been a primary source of rural migrant labor for the manufacturing centers along the coast. According to the data, close to 160,000 of Foxconn's total workforce of 800,000 are from Henan.

During this process, local governments in Henan have been encouraging people to find jobs 'on their doorstep'. The group organizing efforts have been effective in touching a chord in the hearts and minds of laborers.

Source: *Foxconn launches mass inland relocation and plans to build 300,000-man plant in Henan*, Beijing Youth Daily, 30 June 2010.

The transfer of industries [from east to west] is an expression of China's strategy to develop the economies of its less-developed regions, but it is also a way for the central and western regions to speed up their own urbanizing process. Commensurate with having relatively fewer secondary and tertiary industries, these areas are also less urbanized than coastal regions. The result has been that their populations have been shifting *en masse* towards the east.

Economic development in China requires the beneficial effects of concentration but it also requires coordinated and balanced development of various regions. The shift of industries and the formation of a spatial configuration of cities that are on a 'national' level must abide by similar economic laws.

As a result, it is inevitable that there will be a 'flying-goose-model' shift of labor-intensive industries towards central and western parts of China. Not all regions will be suited to accepting certain industries, but in overall terms this is the prevailing trend and it is one that will be beneficial to balancing out development among regions. At the same time, central and western regions must refrain from setting up excessive amounts of capital-intensive industries, which will only bias them against the advantages of labor-intensive-type business. They need to create a better climate for markets and investment so as to be able to receive the industrial shift from the east (see Box 5.2).

Box 5.2 Central and western regions should beware of falling
into the 'Mezzogiorno trap'

The term *'mezzogiorno'* refers specifically to the southern part of the Italian peninsula, including the islands of Sicily and Sardinia. More generally, it refers to the southern part of the country, which is considerably less developed than the north. The north–south discrepancy in Italy is unusual among developing countries. It is not unique, however, for Germany's situation has also produced a long-standing disparity in levels of development between east and west. Once Germany was reunified, that gap could not easily be bridged, creating a situation not unlike that of north and south Italy. Economists therefore often refer to Europe's 'two mezzogiornos'. Both of the lesser-developed areas enjoy substantial funding in the form of transfer payments from the central government, and are the object of special treatment, but this has had the effect of creating modes of development and industrial structures that are not fully suited to their own resources. It has led to insufficient employment opportunities and uneven distribution of income. Despite spurring growth to a certain degree, in the end the strategy has not been able to realize true unification. The phenomenon is referred to as 'falling into the mezzogiorno trap'.

The southern part of Italy began its 'catching-up process' from the position of being a traditional agricultural economy, while Germany began from the position of being a planned-economy system. These two areas are therefore a precise mirror of two transforming processes that are currently being faced by China's central and western regions. That is, the two regions in China are transitioning away from a 'dual-economy structure' and are 'switching tracks' from a centrally planned towards a market-economy system. Lessons derived from the 'two mezzogiornos' are therefore highly significant when it comes to implementing China's 'catch-up' strategy for its own central and western regions.

China's central government has implemented a variety of measures since the beginning of the twenty-first century to spur accelerated development of the central and western parts of the country. These include building up basic infrastructure, investing in production capacity, subsidizing public services and social security, and so on. The central government has invested large amounts in the two regions, through transfer payments as well as fiscal support of other kinds. This has changed the previous regional pattern of resource distribution to a considerable degree. It has spurred economic growth as well as social development and has been able to demonstrate the start of integration [or 'convergence'] with China's eastern region.

Unfortunately, the 'emergence' of China's central and western regions has not been characterized by an increase in labor-intensive industries. Instead, it has been accompanied by a swift rise in capital-intensive manufacturing. The speed at which capital-intensive industries have developed since 2000 is far greater than the speed of similar development along the east coast. The current amount of investment exceeds that along the coast. This phenomenon of 'capital intensification' is a kind of accelerated industrialization that is driven by government-led programs and by investment.

If we are to avoid the lessons of the mezzogiorno trap, we must now begin to modify our regional development strategy. We must, in timely fashion, ensure that these regions are pulled back onto the 'track' of using their own comparative advantages.

Urbanization, innovation, and economic restructuring

The process of 'urbanizing' in China is being done in tandem with ongoing restructuring of the entire economy. The two processes are interactive in that they affect one another. Above, we have discussed the relationship between urbanization and economic structure from the perspective of such things as 'concentration effect', 'scale effect' [economies of scale], changes in cost of labor, diversification of industries, and so on. We have looked at how such things affect urban employment. The link between urbanizing and economic restructuring is not, however, limited to these things.

Cities are increasingly the source of innovation in modern economies. Figure 5.8 shows the degree of innovative activity in 2008 among China's 30 provinces, major cities, and autonomous regions as charted against levels of urbanization. (Innovative activity is expressed in terms of expenditures per capita per year on research and development.)[5]

It is not hard to see the distinctly positive correlation between the two variables. The higher the level of urbanization, the more there is innovative activity within the economy.

One can also see a close relationship between levels of urbanization and the results of innovation. Figure 5.9 shows that those places with higher levels of urbanization also had higher levels of patent applications per 10,000 people at the end of 2008, and the innovative activities produced more results. The reverse was also true: lower levels of urbanization had relatively weaker innovative activity.

The close tie between urbanization and innovation is extremely relevant when it comes to addressing problems of urban employment. First, innovation spurs diversification of industries, which enables more diversified demand for employment. Second, it can also have a constraining effect on demand for labor, however, since innovation helps improve labor productivity and lowers the per-unit cost of labor – this is when the situation is viewed from a static perspective. Third, when viewed from a dynamic perspective, innovation still raises labor productivity, but in the process creates more competitive and vital urban economies,

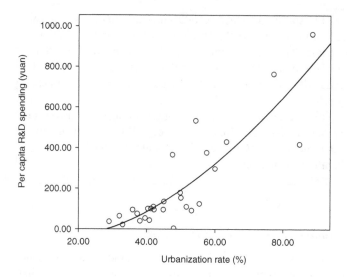

Figure 5.8 Provincial urbanization rate and per capita R&D spending.
Source: *China Statistical Yearbook 2009.*

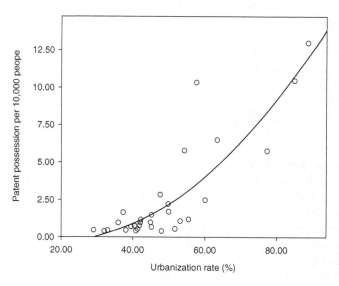

Figure 5.9 Provincial urbanization rate and patent possession per 10,000 people.
Source: *China Statistical Yearbook 2009.*

which over the long run draws more labor in to cities. Fourth, by its very nature, innovative activity is an indispensable link in the industrial chain. Innovative activity in itself creates tremendous numbers of job opportunities.

An excellent example is provided by Tokyo's TAMA. It shows how universities and research institutes in an urban area can cooperate with local industrial development (see Box 5.3).

Box 5.3 Tokyo's TAMA (Metropolitan Association for Advanced Technologies)

The Metropolitan Association for Advanced Technologies (TAMA) was established with the support of Japan's Ministry of Economy, Trade, and Industry. Set up in 1998, its main purpose has been to revitalize the Tokyo metropolitan area and industries in Tokyo's western region. TAMA aims to assist in developing new technologies, products, and services. It links nearly 200 enterprises with large numbers of other kinds of organizations, enabling cooperative activities that allow smaller enterprises to have access to new technologies, to market information, to product development and design, and to export information.

In setting up TAMA, the local business circles and government put great consideration into the capacities and actual situation of the local area, and they also took into account relevant international models. The TAMA district covers an area that includes 3 counties, 74 cities, more than 300,000 small enterprises, and around 40 universities. Among all of these, around 300 companies and 34 universities are actual members of the association. The association seeks to strengthen industrial interaction and industry–university ties through exchanges and cooperative research projects. (Traditionally, this kind of connection has been weak in Japan.) TAMA's overarching goal is to spur the research and development of new technologies as well as their commercialization. TAMA has set up a technology-licensing department to help with granting licenses to use technology for commercial purposes. The region covered by TAMA is particularly strong in machinery, electronics, instrumentation, and control systems. After 10 years of experience, TAMA has successfully focused the attention of decision-makers on companies in these fields, on the problems they face, and on setting up ties between the academic and corporate communities.

Source: OECD: *Trend and Policy of Urbanization in OECD Countries*, Background Report, 2010.

Finding solutions to issues of urban employment

Providing sufficient job opportunities is of ultimate importance to a healthy process of urbanization in China. The country must be proactive in setting up employment policies that integrate a number of issues and considerations, including demographic trends, changing industrial structures in different regions, and the way the labor market is segregated or 'compartmentalized'. At the same time, the country must accelerate the process of industrial restructuring in different regions, depending on the nature of each region's resource endowment.

[The following ten points provide an outline of possible solutions.]

1 Depending on the type of unemployment risk faced by different groups of urban and rural labor, formulate specific policies targeted at unemployment insurance and job creation

By now, China has basically addressed its problem of hidden unemployment in both urban and rural areas, but cyclical unemployment and natural unemployment are also now relatively more pronounced. Different employment groups are more or less vulnerable to different kinds of unemployment so policies should deal with each group as a specific category.

Rural migrant workers are more subject to the impact of cyclical unemployment. Proactive employment policies should be extended to them as we attempt to break through the way our systems segregate out this group of people, in terms of labor markets and public services. We must equalize social security and the ability of rural migrant workers to become legitimate urban residents.

As for people in cities who are not highly qualified and are facing unemployment, policies should focus on improving their employment capacities. In implementing social protection policies, we should improve the efficiencies of targeted programs. For college students who are not able to find jobs due to the increase in their numbers and the problems associated with matching qualifications with the right position, we should extend a proper degree of social protection as well as providing public services in the form of training and employment services. The aim is to shorten the painful process of finding a job.

2 Improve the statistical systems that measure urban employment

Our current way of accounting for employment in cities is inadequate. Many places lack accurate statistics about 'rural migrant worker' employment and 'unofficial' employment. This is detrimental to the accuracy of any policies aimed at providing employment services and support. It prevents rural migrant workers and 'unofficial employees' from enjoying the benefits of preferential government policies as well as the necessary government employment services. We should adopt international standards with respect to employment and unemployment in similar fields. We should improve our survey systems and statistical systems. We should make employment and unemployment figures the responsibility of local governments and also part of how the performance of local authorities is measured. We should ensure that accurate statistical measures receive greater weight in the system.

3 Adjust population policies at the appropriate time, as the country's demographic structure changes

In around the year 2015, China's effective labor supply will peak, after which labor supply will gradually begin to decline. We will go quite quickly from a 'population bonus' to a 'population deficit'. Fewer people will have to be supporting society at large in addition to their own families. The burden of caring for the elderly will be vastly increased. As a result, there is an urgent need right now for us to 'fix the roof before it starts raining', to improve our social security systems in both urban and rural areas. In addition, in certain areas that have the right qualifications, we can go a step further in relaxing policies that apply to family planning. This will postpone the arrival of the impending 'population deficit'.

4 Accelerate a geographic shift of industries in progressive fashion, depending on the labor-supply situation in different regions. Actively promote industrial restructuring and transformation of the types of industries in areas along the coast

To a certain degree, a decline in the effective supply of labor will mitigate problems of unemployment. Certain regions and certain sectors of the economy will be experiencing labor shortages. Since this will be more pronounced in aging populations in the countryside and in more developed coastal areas, the speed and absolute size of the labor migration into cities from the countryside will decline. Structural shortages of labor in labor-intensive manufacturing industries along the coast will mean that these industries see an intensification of labor shortages. This will increase the cost of labor in these areas and industries. We should therefore put considerable effort into restructuring industries. Industries along the coast should become more capital-intensive and the percentage of high-end service industries should increase.

5 Accelerate the process of developing service industries

A key prerequisite for achieving economies of scale in service industries, as well as for achieving a finer division of labor, involves greater concentrations of people in cities. The growth of service industries then also becomes the most important way to address employment problems in cities. We should ensure that more private capital is able to enter into service industries by breaking the monopolies that currently apply to telecommunications, airlines, railroads, and the postal service. Our aim is to accelerate the modernization of service systems and mechanisms. We should accelerate reform of financial-services industries, including banking, securities, and insurance. We should accelerate the globalization of China's financial-services systems and the process of integrating those systems with the rest of the world. We should accelerate reform of public services and the departments and units that supply those services. This includes rationalizing the pricing mechanisms for water, electricity, natural gas, and other such public products. At the same time, we must ensure that the most vulnerable groups in our urban populations are subsidized and protected.

We should seek to exploit all potential sources of employment in the traditional industries, by upgrading them and diversifying their traditional approaches. The intent is to extend the 'production chain' and thereby provide more jobs. In addition, we should actively promote reform of China's public-finance system. We should continue to explore the prospects of consolidating the business tax and the value-added tax, thereby reducing the double tax burden now being borne by service industries.

6 Ensure that regions employ their relative advantages in the course of developing their economies; abide by objective laws of industrial development in the course of urbanization

As industrial restructuring and upgrading takes place in the eastern part of China, labor-intensive manufacturing will move progressively toward central and western parts of the country. Those regions will then play a greater role in absorbing the rural population and providing it with employment. These places should therefore focus on labor-intensive industries as they develop heavy industry. They should avoid a tendency to neglect their comparative advantage in terms of labor-intensive types of business.

One very important policy adjustment will have to deal with how to accommodate the structural changes of industries in the east. Environmental protections must be strengthened as this happens, as well as provisions that relate to resource conservation. Laborers' rights and interests must be protected. The density of populations in the western and central parts of the country is lower than it is in the east. Small towns may not have a comparative advantage, and they also may lack much of any industry on which to rely. It is hard for them to create economies of scale or to extend out the industrial chain, so that their ability to absorb labor is reduced. It will therefore be necessary to form large cities in the west that are accorded fairly high status.

7 Maintain a diversified range of urban industries, in order to ensure the greatest 'absorption capacity' for jobs

We should take a lesson from the experience of the USA, the UK, and other developed countries, whose employment was hit hard by the global financial crisis. In the process of urbanization, we should be sure to maintain a certain degree of manufacturing, in order to keep demand for employment at all levels. This includes diversification in such mega-cities as Shanghai and Beijing as well (Yusuf, 2008).

8 Be proactive in finding ways to further innovation in technologies, products, and services

We should increase the strength of national budgetary expenditures on science and technology, and innovative approaches to products and services. We should strengthen centralized coordinating functions at the state level with respect to the whole process of scientific and technical innovations. We should carry out overall coordination of policies and implementations with respect to major science and technology plans and national science and technology development strategies. We should set up mechanisms for jointly held conferences for government departments involved in science and technology. We should strengthen the integration of state-level resources being put into public science and technology, and set up mechanisms for public benefit of the results of publicly funded science and technology.

We should support independently funded innovation, and improve our policies with respect to how independent technological innovations are managed. We should speed up the conversion of scientific results into commercial applications, and accelerate research that is strategically important to China's socioeconomic development. We should set up innovative systems that 'take the entrepreneur as primary'. That means encouraging and guiding entrepreneurs to increase investment in R&D and commercial applications of the results, through a whole range of policy measures, including tax benefits, financing, government procurement, and science and technology programs.

9 Put greater effort into improving the climate for investment and into fostering entrepreneurs

Entrepreneurs serve the function of reintegrating various kinds of innovative factors. They discover and open up new markets and they push forward new technologies. They are constantly developing products and services that are needed for economic and social development. Right now, we should be trying to improve the investment climate for entrepreneurship, which includes improving the necessary 'hardware' as well as 'software'. We should change the way in which many localities focus only on the hardware and not the software, which means protecting the innovative spirit of entrepreneurs, treating them properly by creating an atmosphere that is conducive to their setting up businesses and being innovative.

10 Actively find ways to help small and medium-sized companies grow

Small and medium-sized companies are the main channel for non-agricultural employment in China. They are also the means by which the country will transform its type of economic structure. We should make comprehensive use of policies dealing with financing, taxation, and fiscal measures to relieve bottlenecks that such companies face in terms of funding, technology, and personnel. We should actively foster the growth of technology-type and service-type companies, while at the same time guiding small and medium-sized companies to get rid of excess and outdated production capacity.

Notes

1 The registered urban unemployment rate refers to the ratio of the registered urban people without jobs to the total sum of the urban people with jobs and the registered urban people without jobs.
2 Although the Ministry of Human Resources and Social Security did not make public the data about the surveyed unemployment rate, it pointed out that in recent years this indicator had been converging with the registered unemployment rate. The former was roughly 1 percentage point higher than the latter. On this basis, we add 1 percentage point on top of the registered unemployment rate for 2006 and 2007 as the estimated values of the surveyed unemployment rate.
3 The specific calculating method is as follows: the standard difference and mean value of the employment in 13 industries are worked out on the basis of the employment in the 13 nonagricultural industries. Then by dividing the standard difference with the mean value, we can come up with the variation coefficient for the employment of a specific city.
4 Relocation without Pollution, South China Net: http://fs.southcn.com/fszt/bzh/bd/content/2008-08/13/content_5302770.htm.
5 Tibet is not included for lack of relevant data.

6 How to improve the provision of public services in urban areas

Urbanization is one important way to ensure that all people enjoy the results of economic growth and modern civilization. Providing public services within cities is a necessary part of ensuring the sound development of those cities. Right now, and for the foreseeable future in China, very large numbers of rural migrant workers are gradually being absorbed into cities. Whether or not the cities can provide adequate public services for existing urban residents, let alone new ones, is a great challenge for the government. The need for services challenges the government's capacity to provide them, as well as the methods and levels at which they are provided.

For quite some time after New China was established, cities were regarded as the medium for industrialization and for simply growing the economy. 'Urbanization' was a derivative of the concept of 'economic growth'. Under a model of development that turned 'consumption-type cities' into 'production-type cities', the provision of public services was slighted. This has changed dramatically since the start of reform and opening up, with improvements in the ability to supply services and in the establishment of urban systems, but there is still a distinct discrepancy between supply and demand.

Furthermore, we must also look to the future. Within 10 years, another 200 million rural migrant workers will become legitimate urban residents, putting intense demands on the need for public services. Improving the provision of public services is therefore one of the greatest challenges facing China as it urbanizes at a very fast pace. Providing public services is also critical if we are to avoid having slums and other 'urban syndromes' in Chinese cities.

The current state of public services in China's cities

Cities can be regarded as 'public service centers' when seen from the perspective of urban functions. To a large extent, the success of urban functions depends upon a city's capacity to provide public services. When public services are inadequate, whether due to poor capacity or to an urban population that exceeds the carrying capacity of the city, the very likely result is the appearance of urban syndromes and slums (see Box 6.1).

Box 6.1 Urban ailments: slums

Around one billion people in the world are currently living in slums, according to a United Nations report prepared by UN-HABITAT [the Human Settlements Programme at the UN], called *The Challenge of Slums*. This figure represents around one-third of all the people in the world who are living in cities. It represents one-sixth of the world's total population.

If effective measures are not adopted, the UN estimates that the figure might double within the next 30 years, to two billion. At that time, there will be at least 550 million impoverished people living in slums in Asia, some 188.7 million in Africa, some 128 million in Latin America and the Caribbean, and another 54 million living in around thirty of the world's most prosperous nations.

Slums are not a new phenomenon in the course of the world's urbanization. Dublin, for example, was 'one of the worst places in Europe in the nineteenth century', Paris too was noted for its slums. 'The French population increased from 29 million to 36 million between the years 1815 and 1851. Cities absorbed all those who were unable to find work in rural areas, and yet jobs were not available in cities either. Unemployment and excessive crowding created shocking living conditions. Only one-fifth of all urban households had access to running water. In 1832, a cholera epidemic took the lives of around 20,000 Parisians.' Other cities have also experienced dreadful slums, including Liverpool, Melbourne, New York, and Tokyo.

The first slums in the world appeared in England. Large numbers of the rural population began to flock into cities under the impetus of the Industrial Revolution. The first slum had appeared in London by 1820, and more began to form as the living conditions of the lowest tier of the city's inhabitants worsened. The UK government gradually began to explore measures to deal with the problems. In 1875, Parliament passed the 'Dwellings Improvement Act'. This was designed to eliminate slums and build low-cost housing. In addition to direct eradication of slums, the UK government passed policies aimed specifically at providing welfare-type housing for poorer families. For example, a 'council housing' system has been implemented since the 1950s and 1960s. The current welfare system in the UK has basically resolved the problem of actual slums. In order to deal with that portion of the population that is 'homeless', the UK has introduced measures to provide 'basic housing security'.

As an overall phenomenon, slums were a nightmare that western countries found unavoidable at the time. Only after the Second World War were slums dealt with in reasonably good fashion as western economies resumed growth and welfare policies were put in place. In fact, the appearance, growth, and eradication of slums is a process that moves in concert with a country's urbanization. The governments of all countries, and their major cities, have had to go through a transition from avoidance to acceptance, from ignoring the problems to emphasizing solutions. Given a necessary foundation of ongoing economic growth, the only way to eliminate slums is to link policies regarding slums to programs that reduce urban poverty. Such programs must address things like employment, income, health, education, housing, basic urban infrastructure, and public services.

Bibliography

UN-HABITAT (translated by Yu Jing et al.): *The Challenge of Slums – Global Report on Human Settlements 2003*, China Construction Industry Publishing House, 2006.
World Bank: *World Development Report 2009: Reshaping Economic Geography*, Tsinghua University Press, 2009.

The range of things regarded as 'public services'

China has been declaring that the country is aiming for 'constant improvement' in the provision of public services. It has set forth the goal of 'equalizing' the provision of public services, but as yet there is no explicit definition of what this concept of 'public services' means. There is not even a definition of what 'basic public services' entail. Any analysis of China's current situation and the challenges it faces with respect to urban public services must therefore first define the terms.

In this report, we divide all 'public things' that the government plays the leading role in providing into two separate components, public products, and public services. 'Public products' mainly refers to physical things that are provided and ultimately 'consumed', including roads, public buildings, basic infrastructure, and facilities. 'Public services' mainly refers to things with a 'service' component, such as public administrative services, education, health, social security, and so on.[1]

The definition of 'urban public services' incorporates four criteria. Such things must be 'basic', 'extensive' [or broadly applicable], 'urgent' [or meeting immediate needs], and 'feasible'.

The term 'basic' refers to public services that have a fundamental role in people's lives and the city's functions. 'Extensive' refers to public services that touch upon every household and every individual in the city. 'Urgent' refers to those public services that are of immediate and practical use to the great mass of urban residents, and that provide them with immediate benefit. 'Feasible' refers to the need to ensure that provision of services falls within the capacities of public finance and within the city's level of economic development. As an example, the great majority of cities in China right now can only provide nine years of compulsory education as a 'basic public service'. Education at the high-school level is still not considered to be within the scope of feasible public services.

In line with the criteria listed above, this chapter will address public services that relate to the following: 'the basic right to exist' of urban residents, 'basic respect' [or dignity], 'basic abilities', and 'basic health'. These things include such items as compulsory education, public health, basic medical care, and all kinds of social welfare and services. Other forms of public services will be addressed more specifically in Chapter 7, including public products that ensure the operating of city systems and functions, such as public transport, water supply, sewage, sanitation, environmental protection, and so on.

The current state of the development of urban public services in China

The long-standing problem of inadequate supply of public services in China has improved to a degree. The quality and effectiveness of services has risen markedly. Education, medical, and social security systems are gradually being set up and improved upon.

Compulsory education

Compared with the situation in rural areas, compulsory education in cities has now developed to a much higher level. Nine years of compulsory education is now available. The number of students in primary schools and middle schools in China's cities has basically been stable when comparing the years 2000 and 2007. The number of primary-school students is consistently around 17.61 million, and that of middle-school students is around 10.48 million. The number of actual schools has declined considerably, however. In 2007, there were 17,535 primary schools and 7,-594 middle schools (see Table 6.1).

Basic medical care

Public health and basic medical services in China mainly include the following components: disease prevention and control, health education, maternal and child

Table 6.1 China's urban compulsory education development

Year	Junior high		Vocational junior high		Primary school	
	Number of schools	Enrolments	Number of schools	Enrolments	Number of schools	Enrolments
2000	12,723	10,346,351	142	27,571	32,154	18,166,507
2007	7,594	10,475,859	13	8,104	17,535	17,610,813

Source: *China Education Statistical Yearbook.*

care, mental health, emergency treatment, collection and provision of blood, health supervision, and family planning. The vast majority of healthcare resources are concentrated in cities. China's total expenditures on healthcare increased by 68 times between the years 1980 and 2006, from RMB 14.32 billion in 1980 to RMB 984.33 billion in 2006. As compared with public spending on other types of public consumption, this was fairly low. Between 1998 and 2005, expenditures on public health and basic medical treatment constituted only around 4–5 per cent of total budgetary expenditures.

Social security

China has gradually set up basic pension insurance systems for urban workers that combine 'social pooling' of funds with individual accounts. The governmental level at which the funds are pooled and managed is constantly going up and the coverage of old-age pensions is gradually being expanded. At the end of 2008, the number of people participating in basic pension insurance plans, nationwide, came to 218.911 million. Among these, 165.875 million were currently employed workers, 53.036 million were retirees.

Urban medical insurance includes basic medical treatment insurance for urban workers [i.e., 'staff', a term that does not include labourers] and basic medical treatment insurance for urban residents. At the end of 2008, there were 199.956 million urban employees participating in such insurance plans. Pilot-site projects to extend insurance for major illness began in 2007.

By the end of 2008, a total of 40.68 million urban residents nationwide were participating in urban residents' basic medical insurance systems. The number of people covered by unemployment insurance, work injury insurance and childbirth insurance has also gradually risen. At the end of 2008, a total of 123.998 million people across the country were participating in unemployment insurance, 137.872 million in work injury insurance, and 92.541 million in childbirth [maternity] insurance.

In overall terms, however, China's urban social security system still suffers from a number of problems. These include inadequate coverage, 'pooling' at an administrative level that is too low, lack of mandatory rules on funding contributions, and low levels of management and the 'socialization' of services. Since the social security system was set up only gradually, after experimentation, it is managed separately and in different ways in different regions, which has led to differing levels of insurance. Distinct differences can even show up within a given city, since the standards relating to three forms of insurance are different. That is, there are different standards for people in government bodies, people in public institutions, and people in corporate enterprises. In addition, the great majority of rural migrant workers are excluded from any kind of system at all.

Housing security

Two documents came out in 2007 relating to housing: *Various Opinions of the State Council on Resolving Housing Problems of Low-Income Families in Urban*

Areas and *Administrative Procedures Relating to the Security Funds for Low-Rent Housing*. In 2007, investment in low-income housing nationwide approached RMB 9.4 billion. This exceeded the amount of funding that had been set aside for the purpose over the previous several years. New guaranteed housing units increased in that year by 680,000 units. By the end of November 2009, there were 18.5 million 'sets' of low-rent housing either being built or for which funds had been accumulated. Within this figure, 15.84 million units were newly constructed, nationwide, while 2.66 million more had been purchased or remodeled to serve the new function. Some 2.92 million people were receiving subsidized housing, among which 800,000 households were new additions. (Du Yu, 2010).

Currently, there are still around 7.47 million low-income people in China who live in less than ten square meters of space. This is 4 per cent of all urban households in the country.

According to the *2009–2011 Plan for Low-Rent Housing Security*, put out by a department within the State Council, 7.5 million units of guaranteed housing are to be built within these three years. If this plan is implemented as planned, the housing will cover all those currently living in less than 10 square meters of space. Overall, however, the construction of such low-rent housing has been proceeding very slowly because local governments are not enthusiastic about it. New housing being built that is devoted to low-rent housing currently comes to less than 1 per cent of the total. Moreover, plans are irrational in places, matching funding is not made available, standards for entry are too high, styles are too monotonous, and so on.

Public services for the migrant population and for vulnerable groups

China is currently undergoing a period of extremely rapid urbanization. At the same time, social mobility is also increasing, in line with socioeconomic structural changes, and the total number of the migrant population is increasing. In addition to rural migrant workers, this population of 'migrants' includes millions of college graduates who are newly certified with degrees and now looking for work, generally outside the place of their household registration. It also includes large numbers of people who have urban household residency status in one city but are living and working in other cities.

In 2012, the total size of the migrant population in China came to 210 million people. The flow was primarily in the direction of countryside to cities and from one city to another.[2]

Vulnerable groups of people in cities in China mainly include rural migrant workers and migrant children, and people who are poor, old, disabled, mentally ill, unemployed, or laid-off. They also include victims of disasters, and people who are 'in a weak position in terms of their employment'. This is a simplified list and also includes many people who belong to one or more of these categories.

Vulnerable people are the most in need of public services, since they are most lacking in the ability to care for themselves. To a degree, the level of public services extended to vulnerable people is an indication of the humanitarian concern of the municipal government. Looked at in overall terms, the way in which China cares for its most vulnerable populations does not come up to the mark. The country is not doing enough. Public services are inadequately targeted at these people, and indeed when the migrant population or members of vulnerable groups do partake of public services, they are subjected to various forms of social discrimination and outright exclusion.

Public services for the migrant population

Large numbers of people migrate to cities each year in China. Once there, they are unable to enjoy the benefits of urbanization, and particularly the social services that urban residents enjoy, due to either systemic factors or policy constraints. Not only is the unequal treatment they do receive with respect to jobs, education, and health detrimental to their own personal development, but it also damages all others in the city as well. It obstructs the effective allocation of human resources, it lessens the positive effects of concentrating people in cities, and it damages the quality of urbanization.

Labour market policy issues

Given the administrative system by which urban and rural people are classified in a 'dual' manner, according to the original location of their household registration, labour markets in China are also highly segregated. The migrant population is described in Chinese as 'labour from outside'. Discrimination that derives from the labour markets generally makes it impossible for the migrant population ever to find a 'decent job'. Since 'labour from outside' also lacks legal protections and systemic protections, it mostly works in jobs that involve heavy physical labour and are poorly paid. Moreover, 'different pay rates for the same amount of work' is a widespread phenomenon, as well as different rights applying to the same work. Such practices can be found within one enterprise.

Long-standing policies in China have been biased in favour of cities as opposed to rural areas, and have protected municipalities. Such policies have kept the rural population from enjoying the improvements in well-being that have come to urban residents in the course of economic growth and urban development. According to a survey conducted by the UNDP in some of China's provinces in 2009, low-skilled labour of migrant populations in a given place work half again as long, for the same pay, as local labour in those places.

The education of migrant children

Right now, there are more than 20 million migrant children in China who should by all rights be entitled to compulsory education. These children are scattered throughout cities in the country and the education that they are receiving in many instances is at an even lower level than what they would get in the country-side. Many are also forced to leave school, or do so voluntarily, as a result of poverty or because their parents are constantly on the move. Some cannot be placed in school at the right time when they come of school age, which means that they attend classes for much younger students when they are already young adults.

The policy guidance of the Central government with respect to the issue of compulsory education for migrant children is that the children should 'go primarily to public schools and should attend school primarily in the place to which they have migrated'. In terms of policy, therefore, migrant children are not prevented from going to urban public schools. In terms of the actual situation, however, all kinds of intangible restrictions as well as fees exist to prevent this from happening.

In many cities, publicly operated schools either completely refuse to take in the children of migrant people. or accept them but charge high fees on top of the normal miscellaneous school fees. Such fees are ostensibly for the special assistance needed by such children. As a result, many children have no alternative but to go to schools operated specifically for children of rural migrant workers. 'Rural-migrant-worker schools' lack the most basic qualifications to serve as schools, however. Their inadequate academic facilities also means that students have no guarantee of personal safety. The caliber of teachers is sufficiently low that academic quality is compromised, which again is detrimental to the long-term development of the child.

Local governments are not inclined to deal with the issues of schooling for migrant children. Right now, school budgets in China are determined according to the number of school-age children in the officially registered population of a given place. This means that migrant children who have left the locale of their 'household registration' find it hard to get equal treatment when it comes to public spending. The consequence is that 'compulsory education' in most places is *de facto* determined by the level of economic development in a city and by the state of the local government's fiscal budget.

Starting in 2008, Guangdong province has been receiving a special allocation for the education of children of rural migrant workers in the amount of RMB 100 million per year. This is still not sufficient, however, to reduce the tremendous pressure of funding education for these children. In 2009, children of rural migrant workers in the province accounted for one-third of all rural migrant workers' children nationwide. The number of migrant-worker children in Guangdong comes to six times the number in Beijing. Eighty-five per cent of these are concentrated in the Pearl River delta area, where one of every two primary-school students is a 'non-household-registered' student, and one of every four middle-school students is the same.

The fiscal revenues of Guangdong come to more than RMB 8 trillion every year, of which Guangdong has to 'hand up' 60 per cent to the Central government [national treasury]. Only somewhat more than RMB 2 trillion is left for various spending requirements, and this has to be spread over the needs of a population of more than 100 million people.

Health issues of the migrant population

China's social security system is linked in to the whole system of household registration. Cities have better health facilities and medical human resources than rural areas, but this does not mean that such facilities are available for taking care of a city's migrant population. The medical services enjoyed by the migrant population are far less than those enjoyed by the proper urban residents.

In China, Shanghai is considered a 'model city' when it comes to providing services for its migrant population. Nevertheless, in 2004, only two-thirds of migrant children in the city were vaccinated while all of the children of the officially registered population were vaccinated (UNDP, 2009).

Relatively speaking, living conditions for migrant children are miserable, which influences health in general and also contributes to the swift transmission of epidemic diseases. The cost of urban medical services is high, so when children get sick they are often sent back to the countryside for treatment. This prolongs the time they are sick, and extends the time needed for treatment.

Surveys have been done on the 'reproductive health' of the migrant population. This population is dominated by young adults who are at a sexually active age. Their level of education tends to be low, their physical work is intensive, and their living conditions are poor. They commonly engage in high-risk sexual behaviour and their awareness of the health consequences is quite low. These people therefore have a high incidence of sexually transmitted diseases and are in a high-risk category when it comes to reproductive disorders.

Some pregnant women among the migrant population fail to have regular check-ups prior to giving birth because they are poor, nor do they go to regular hospitals for delivery. This is unlike women who have official urban household registrations. Instead, expecting migrant mothers have no alternative but to seek cheap and inferior services. Some are sent to hospitals only when their lives are in danger. Due to tardy treatment, this leads to both maternal and perinatal mortalities (Sun Rongxi et al., 2008).

Migrant children are the most in need of health services among all vulnerable groups in China's cities. It is quite apparent that the treatment they actually receive, however, is less than what children of official residents of cities receive, as seen in their nutritional status, physical development, and overall health.

Public services for vulnerable groups

The urban poor

This term refers mainly to unemployed people who are poor, to elderly people who are poor, and to some people who are poor as a result of being sick. All of these people are in difficult straits because they have no source of income; they therefore generally need basic [or minimum] living allowance assistance either from the government or from 'society' at large. The number of unemployed poor in China's cities rose sharply towards the end of the twentieth century. This group gradually became the main source of 'urban poor' altogether.

The main social relief system that is aimed at the urban poor in China is called the 'minimum living allowance'. In 1999, the State Council promulgated a document entitled *Provisions for Minimum Living Allowances for Urban Residents*. This formally instituted the system, and since then the amounts of assistance have steadily risen.

The number of people benefitting from the system has also steadily risen, according to the *Statistical Report on Civil Affairs* put out by the Ministry of Civil Affairs (Table 6.2). The number increased nearly 10-fold between 1999 and 2008. In 2008, there was a total of 23.348 million people receiving benefits. The average amount each person received in these years was RMB 205.3 per month. Nevertheless, this minimum living allowance system only addresses the minimum caloric needs as calculated by the level of consumption in any given place. In fact, what a considerable number of poor people need is a more comprehensive social relief system.

The disabled

As a country, China has consistently shown concern for people who are disabled. Efforts to provide for them have grown rapidly, but people who are disabled still have trouble finding jobs and getting around, and it is undeniable that they are in a very vulnerable position. There are 82.96 million disabled people in China, according to the *Report on the second National Sampling Survey of Disabled People*. Only 2.608 million of these are enrolled in social insurance programs, however – just 3.1 per cent of the total number of disabled in the country.

Given the influence of planned-economy concepts, the mainstream view habitually regards social insurance as something to do with labour relations. The whole concept is mistakenly seen as a legal relationship built upon the foundation of labour relations.

Table 6.2 Numbers of China's urban residents receiving allowance and relief

Item	2004	2005	2006	2007	2008
Urban residents receiving minimum living allowance (10,000 people)	2205.0	2234.2	2240.1	2272.1	2334.8
Urban residents receiving temporary relief (10,000 person/times)	285.2	234.4	123.0	243.2	227.6

Source: *China Statistical Yearbook 2008.*

To a certain extent, this has impeded the 'socialization' of social insurance [meaning, it has impeded the spreading of risks and costs over the entire society]. It has relegated disabled people to remaining outside the scope of social insurance, not just in conceptual terms but also in terms of how systems have been set up. Quite apart from this, many cities have been remiss in failing to focus on disabled people as a group needing services. They have shown inadequate humanitarian concern.

The elderly

China has already entered into the status of being an 'ageing society'. By the end of 2008, the country had a total of 109.56 million people aged 65 and over, accounting for 8.3 per cent of the total national population in that year. Ageing has physiological causes, but it also has social causes. Retiring, for instance, often gives people a sense of being 'useless'. There are also systemic factors that relate to how older people in cities are increasingly vulnerable. For example, certain people who are at an older age receive quite low pensions and low levels of socially provided nursing services, which puts them in need of greater assistance.

Facilities for older people in cities are highly limited. Cultural events, recreation, rehabilitation services and health facilities, elderly care provisions, social institutions for the elderly in general are all essentially nil, and certainly cannot satisfy people's actual needs. At present, there are close to 38,000 'elderly care institutions' [nursing homes] at all administrative levels and of all kinds, including some that have private investment. There are more than 1.15 million beds, and more than 860,000 care providers.

To take beds as just one example, however, that number of beds can provide for less than 0.9 per cent of all elderly. This figure is far below the 5–7 per cent that is seen internationally.

At present, China has no systematic multi-leveled system to deal with services for the elderly. There is similarly no way to satisfy the differing needs of elderly people who have different levels of income. Moreover, the great majority of nurses who are tending to older people have relatively low levels of education. They lack any professional knowledge. Most institutions have no specialized personnel to deal with things like the psychology of the elderly, legal advice, social work, and so on. Such institutions find it very hard to meet the diversified and multi-layered needs of older people.

The challenges confronting the attempt to provide public services in China's cities

A number of things have contributed to setting up the conceptual basis for providing public services in China's cities, as well as the practicalities of providing such services. These include fast economic growth, ongoing improvement in the market-economy system, and the stated policy aim of 'taking the human being as the core element' in developing the country. At the same time, China is the

Table 6.3 Urban nursing and help institutions in China

Indicator	Number of beds (10,000)			Number of people accepted (10,000)			Year-end bed use rate (%)
	2007	2008	Change over previous year (%)	2007	2008	Change over previous year (%)	(%)
Nursing institutions	**251.0**	**279.4**	**11.3**	**200.0**	**221.9**	**11.0**	**79.4**
Welfare nursing institutions	241.2	268.0	11.1	193.3	214.1	10.8	79.9
Social welfare centers	18.5	21.6	16.8	14.2	15.5	9.2	71.8
Children's welfare centers	3.3	4.0	21.2	2.9	3.4	17.2	85.0
Social welfare centers	3.1	3.6	16.1	2.7	3.1	14.8	86.1
Urban welfare institutions for old people	33.0	41.5	25.8	22.6	29.0	28.3	69.9
Other nursing institutions	3.5	4.3	22.9	1.6	2.5	56.3	58.1
Community nursing institutions	**1.6**	**1.6**		**0.8**	**0.9**	**12.5**	**56.3**
Aid institutions	**4.7**	**5.1**	**8.5**	**2.6**	**1.7**	**–34.6**	**33.3**

Source: *China Statistical Yearbook 2008.*

largest country in the world in terms of population, and it leads the world in the massive scale of its 'urbanization'. These factors present unprecedented challenges to every level of government in the country as each attempts to improve urban public services and to satisfy diversifying social needs.

Challenges introduced by the needs of newly urbanized populations

Raising the level of urbanization in China will depend on developing cities' economies, but it will also depend on services that cities can provide. This includes both 'hardware' and 'software' services. An excellent set of public services can spur healthy growth, but the opposite is also true: poor services block further growth. Right now, China's problems of 'villages within cities' and 'urban syndromes' can be attributed to retarded development of public services. Many of China's cities are severely deficient in services. Add to that the anticipated additional 20 million people per year in China's cities and you come up with massive demand. Setting up municipal public-service systems that can meet the needs of urban development is going to be a heavy responsibility and a long and arduous task.

China is expected to reach its peak population in 2030, at which time the country's rate of urbanization will be some 65 per cent. In the next 20 years, another 400 million people are expected to become proper urban residents in China, and there is no question that these people will be generating tremendous demand for public services. Education is just one example. Despite the fact that the national government currently requires municipal governments to admit the children of rural migrant workers into their public school systems, a very large number of such children are unable to get into public schools. They have no alternative but to attend 'rural-migrant-worker schools'. According to a survey by the State Statistical Bureau, undertaken in 2006, 17 per cent of rural migrant workers are accompanied by their children and these children attend school in the local city. The ratio at which they attend rural-migrant-worker schools as opposed to public schools, however, is around seven to three.

Meanwhile, the number of school-age children that needs to be educated has already far surpassed the capacity of districts to provide schools for them, given the accelerating pace of urbanization. Housing is the same. Under our current housing system, both low-rent housing and affordable housing are aimed at only those people who hold a proper urban residency permit. The system has not been opened up to encompass rural migrant workers. The *de facto* approach of most places when it comes to housing for these people is to 'let the water flow where it may'. Housing for rural migrant workers naturally flows outside the bounds of the housing security system.

China may well be able to increase 'domestic demand' only through undertaking a 'new style of urbanization', but finding ways to fund the process is an enormous challenge. This is particularly true of funding public services or those semi-public services that take in minor amounts of fees for providing services.

Not only is funding a challenge, but the whole process of providing services involves the matter of fair distribution of resources among different cities and different groups of people, and it comes up against 'rigid constraints' such as the limited amount of land. We have to address not only these issues but also the ever-increasing demand of the existing urban population for better services. We are indeed confronting major challenges.

Challenges arising from ongoing increases in the demand for public services

People's expectations with respect to public services are constantly being upgraded as development levels improve. Right now, China's urban residents are moving from a state of 'subsistence' toward enjoyment-oriented living. Their range of needs and the 'substance' of their needs are constantly expanding, moving from quantitative to qualitative considerations, and also beginning to incorporate concepts of fairness, justice, and democracy. For example, when a population is still at the level of just trying to survive [staying warm and getting enough to eat], people are not focused on the quality of the air around them or their 'living environment'. By now, those things have already become part of people's 'basic needs'. Demands to clean up pollution are becoming ever more insistent. In an era when survival as opposed to 'good health' is not the main issue, people are more focused on such communicable diseases as tuberculosis, hepatitis B, and AIDS, while now they begin to worry about more chronic diseases such as heart disease, vascular diseases, and some kinds of cancer.

Back in the age of bicycles, when time was not the main concern, people complained about the crowded conditions of buses, not about their slowness. Now that private cars have entered into family lives and 'time is money', people worry about the time they have to spend finding a parking space. And so on. We are therefore facing new issues in the process of trying to improve public services while 'urbanizing' the country, namely how to maintain our focus on 'taking the human being as the core consideration' while meeting constantly rising expectations and still staying within the 'tolerance constraints' of limited amounts of funding.

Box 6.2 The public-service needs of empty-nesters

Not only is Beijing developing at a fairly fast pace, but its population is also aging fairly quickly. At the end of 2008, the city had 2.18 million 'elderly people' who were officially registered as urban residents, or some 17.7 per cent of the entire population. The rate of ageing in the city has now moved into a period of ongoing acceleration. We estimate that the number of elderly will reach 3.5 million by 2020, at which time they will be 20 per cent of the population. The traditional way of living is changing in the city due to ongoing socioeconomic development, implementation of national policies regarding family planning, improved housing conditions, and people's concepts about living space. The number of people in households is getting smaller, and 'empty nesters' are increasing. More and more adult children are choosing not to live with their parents, whether because they are working or studying elsewhere or for other reasons, which has changed multi-generational family units and household environments.

As a result, the need for public services that can care for empty nesters, and particularly elderly individuals who are living alone, is increasing. They need economic support, health and medical services, daily care, and emotional sustenance. They need new ways of providing services in order to cope with increasingly intense problems, including medical 'house calls', cleaning services, companionship, cafeterias, and day-care centers for the elderly.

Source: Sun Fei and Li Jianguo: *Care about 'empty-nest' old people and building nursing facilities for them*, www.xilele.com/xinwenzixun/ 43617.htm

Challenges brought on by changes in the spatial configurations of cities and changing 'types' of urbanization

Major changes in the spatial configuration of cities are occurring as urbanization proceeds in China. These present whole new challenges when it comes to providing urban public services to the population.

The population increase in the core parts of China's three main 'mega-cities' is now beginning to slow down as industries restructure and also as housing prices in these areas continue to rise. The three are the Bohai gulf region, the Yangtze River delta, and the Pearl River delta.

As a result, the functions of 'urban clusters' within these areas are being read-justed. New populations flowing into these clusters are creating a tremendous new demand for urban public services.

In addition, a number of new urban clusters will now be developing in China's central and western regions as the climate for investing in these areas improves. A greater concentration of industries will be attracting the existing rural population in these areas. Levels of public service are currently quite backwards in places that may possibly become new 'urban clusters', however, which means we are facing the tremendous task of building up entire new public-services systems. We are also confronting the need to finance those systems.

As 'super-large cities' continue to develop and as some of their functions are decentralized out into neighbouring areas, those areas are assuming the burden of functions formerly performed by the cities themselves. 'Small towns' may now be developing into 'small and medium-sized cities'. The great majority of these small towns lack any 'framework' for being cities, however. They are therefore facing the extreme challenge of constructing entire public-service systems.

As business continues to concentrate in certain areas and people continue to flow towards urban clusters, the ability of the great majority of small towns to attract people may well continue to decline. The number of small towns will not increase dramatically as it has in the past, and some towns may further decline as economic centers. The positioning or 'definition' of what a small town should be will become more of a challenge if such places are to serve as public-service centers for the neighbouring countryside.

Challenges brought on by systemic changes

China's existing system segregates 'urban' and 'rural', and practices a mode of reform that is characterized as 'incremental'. This means that the supply of public services is provided in segregated fashion to different groups of people. In addition, China's fiscal system 'divides up' the division of tax revenue in uneven ways among different areas. All of these systemic factors have created a situation in which China's current public-service systems are both fragmented and multi-tiered.

The kinds of issues that need to be addressed in upgrading public-service systems, therefore, do not relate merely to quantitative and qualitative considerations. They relate also to ensuring that there is a greater equalization of services between different kinds of groups of people and among different cities. They relate to the need to put different systems 'on the same track'. That is to say, satisfying the demand for public services in the process of urbanization in China will require a gradual transformation of government functions. In the course of improving urban public services, and in the process of urbanization, we will need to set up public-service systems and mechanisms that allocate resources more effectively and operate more efficiently.

New types of reform will therefore have to be mobilized. These would include, for example, reform of the dual administrative system that governs 'urban' and 'rural'. They would include reform of the revenue-sharing system and further improvements in China's system of public finance. They would include reform of the land system, and so on.

Areas that we have not yet vigorously attempted to address, or those needing the most in-depth reform, basically are precisely those that we regard as most difficult. They are precisely those areas that involve the hardest readjustment of interests. As a result, what we have done is adopt a policy of 'first develop and then apply reforms, first make the pie bigger and then divide it up'. We have felt that we can resolve issues of interest groups later.

Sometimes this approach is exactly the opposite of what is needed. Problems only grow larger as they are left unresolved. The difficulty of reform does not decrease – it increases. By now, it looks as though areas that need reform, or areas in which we reformed the 'branches' but not the root problems, are areas that cannot be resolved merely by making the pie bigger. That approach will no longer resolve problems of accommodating different interests.

Reforms that will be necessary do indeed involve massive readjustment in interests. It is going to be extremely challenging to handle the necessary reforms while still promoting a healthy process of urbanization in an effective way. We must not interrupt the historic process of urbanization in China by undertaking overly rash or zealous reforms.

We face extremely thorny problems. In order to complete this tremendous and complex task, we will need to rely on the political intelligence of the Party and on its ability to rule. We will need to take all factors into consideration, explore solutions that are realistic and feasible, carry out reform plans that are sequential and progressive in nature.

Going further in improving urban public services

Faced with a massive need for public services in the future, we are not going to be able to rely solely on methods we have used in the past. Providing excellent public-service systems depends on a variety of considerations including better urban economies and stronger budgets, more mature supply systems, governance that is standardized and efficient, the support of advanced technology platforms, and resource allocation systems that are both fair and rational. All these things require innovative improvements in systems and mechanisms. They require increasing the ability of cities to supply services and improving the levels of those services, and they mean picking up the pace of equalizing the provision of services. To promote further social equality and enhance social harmony, we must upgrade the overall operating capacities and efficiencies of cities.

Speed up the process of changing the underlying concept of 'urban public services'

The first thing to be done in the attempt to improve public services in cities is to change old concepts that are incapable of meeting the needs of the new era:

1   Urban public services need to be supplied in response to the needs of the public. They should actively reflect those needs, rather than being undertaken as a way to display the achievements of an area's government.
2   They should be supplied in response to the needs of society in general. Cities do not belong solely to the residents of that one city – they also belong to rural people and to society at large. Public infrastructure should therefore provide service to residents but also to farmers, to communities but also to whole regions.
3   Public services should be supplied for the majority of people, not any given minority. Those public services that are purely of a 'public' nature should especially be aimed at 'all the people'. They should be 'open', 'fair', and 'equal'.

4   Public services should be provided at levels that conform to the level of social development of a given place. Right now, and for some time into the future, we will only be able to ensure 'basic' public services. We are not setting up a welfare state.

5   The suppliers of public services should be determined by how well they conform to the attributes of that service. Governmental responsibilities should be determined by whether government is supplying purely public goods or semi-public goods. Attention should be paid to the efficiency with which public services are supplied and incentive mechanisms should be applied to more efficient practices. The aim is to conserve public resources and also lower costs.

6   The kinds of public services delivered should be determined by the needs of different types of people. We should not adopt a 'one size fits all' approach. Older people, children and young people, disabled people, and so on should be able to enjoy more services than able-bodied adults; there should be some distinction made between those who are poor and those who are wealthy, so that the burden of paying for different kinds of public services is balanced out.

In addition, care should be taken to harmonize the actions of government and non-governmental organizations. We should constantly seek to increase the rate at which citizens participate in their own urban governance. We should go further in defining the scope of public services, so that there is less chance of government's either over-stepping proper boundaries or not doing enough. This can occur when things are left unclear or insufficiently detailed. Such things as education, medical treatment, and particularly housing cannot all be swept into the category of 'public services'. At our current stage of development, nine-year compulsory education, basic medical treatment and public health, and low-rent housing are considered to be legitimate public services. Things beyond that of a 'service' nature should not be regarded as public services and commitments should not be made regarding their provision.

Define the boundaries of what should be included within 'public services'

Since we have failed to be clear in delineating the scope of public services, a certain degree of confusion has arisen in practice. This has occurred in the course of two major ongoing trends in China, namely 'urbanization' and the 'marketization' of the economy. Certain things that should have been handled by market forces have not been, while other things have been 'marketized' when they should in fact have been the responsibility of the government and supplied to the public for free. In some spheres, it may be that marketization has happened too quickly. Moreover, there are huge differences in the public services that different regions of the country have been providing, in terms not only of quality but also the actual kinds of services. Quality differences can be attributed to the different financial strength of localities, but differences in types of services are brought on by mistaken concepts of what should and should not be a 'public' service. It is imperative, therefore, that we define which kinds of things belong to the sphere of 'public services' and therefore cannot be supplied to the public via market channels, and which are legitimately within the sphere of market activity. We need to define exactly what 'basic public services' are, that is, those that the government must be fully responsible for providing.

There are two criteria for delineating the limits of 'public services'. One is the strength of the 'public' nature of the service, and the other is the ease with which the service can be segregated out or divided up. Using these two criteria, we believe that, at our present stage of development, China's urban public services can be divided into two types.

The first type is 'basic public services'. These are characterized by having a strong 'public' nature to them. They are not suited to marketization. They can only be provided by government as the sole supplier and they should be either free or provided at minimal cost. Naturally, the word 'free' is relative in this sense. Some basic public services can have individuals bear a portion of the costs, such as old-age pensions in which both individuals and corporations have to carry some of the burden. The purpose of charging fees or premiums, however, is to prevent the phenomenon of having excessive use because a resource is free. It is to improve efficiencies of the resource, not in order to retrieve the cost of the public service. Basic public services mainly include the following: compulsory education, public health and basic medical care, social security, social relief (including low-rent housing), job creation, poverty alleviation, disaster prevention and mitigation (including putting out fires), public security, public culture, basic science and leading-edge technology, non-profit technological research, national defense, and so on.

The second type [or category] includes 'other' public services. These have less in the nature of 'public' about them. Market-oriented methods can be used to build and operate them while the government serves as provider but not necessarily as sole provider. When other market entities are providers, the government can provide appropriate subsidies or can charge fees of the recipients of the services in order to cover the costs of construction and operation. Things in this category would include high-school and higher levels of education, special medical services, and affordable housing.

The above separation into types of services uses only two criteria. In fact, the ways in which other countries distinguish public services include many other criteria. Some services appear to be appropriate for market delivery, but could also be supplied by governments if funds were sufficient. A number of other considerations should therefore come into play when determining the scope of 'public services'. They include the ability of public finance to pay for certain things, the efficiency and quality with which government supplies the service, whether or not the price of government-controlled services can cover construction and operational costs, so that private enterprises can receive a justifiable profit from providing the service, while the poor still are adequately covered and basic human rights and sustainable development are given adequate attention.

Make rational adjustments in the relationship between Central and local governments [provincial governments and lower] in terms of both administrative responsibilities and the corresponding fiscal resources

Once the scope of public services is clearly defined, it becomes necessary to clarify exactly which public services are the responsibility of which level of government in China. Right now, the responsibilities are not clearly defined. The Central government, provincial governments, and the municipal governments that are under their jurisdiction are responsible for education, culture, science and technology, medical care, healthcare services, social security, and so on, but the lines delineating what each is responsible for are vague. As a result, local governments are far more inclined to take care of supplying public services to people whose 'household residence' is officially within their jurisdictions than they are to taking care of public services for people from elsewhere. This has already become a major obstacle to the healthy development of urbanization in China. We must now make explicit which responsibilities apply to the Central government, local governments, and municipal governments, according to the principle of 'separation of power' [this could also be translated as 'sharing of power']. Each should know the range of services for which it is responsible.

First of all, the Central government should be responsible for formulating rules and regulations about the scope of public services. It should be responsible for defining the types, the criteria, the principles and laws that apply to each, and it should be responsible for the 'plans' that are drawn up in some areas. Second, the Central government should be responsible for providing public services that cannot be divided up but instead accrue to the body of people as a whole. These things would include national defense, public security, public health, research in basic sciences and cutting-edge technology, as well as research that benefits the public at large. It should be responsible for cross-regional national disasters, fire prevention and mitigation, and poverty alleviation.

The question of exactly what role the Central government should take with respect to compulsory education, social security, social relief [welfare programs], job creation, and other basic public services, will depend on the results of fiscal reform and the eventual division of revenues between Central and local. Once the percentage of total national revenues that Central and local governments are entitled to has been determined, public-service responsibilities can be determined. If we retain the current percentages in the future revenue split, then the Central government should go further in increasing its spending on things that are basic to the people's livelihood. In brief, however, any allocation of responsibilities should be done in tandem with reform of the fiscal system.

The responsibilities of local governments should include the following: education at the high-school level, and that portion of higher education that is to be borne by 'government', social relief (which includes low-rent housing), job creation, regional disaster mitigation and prevention, public security, and 'public culture'. One-time expenditures that are required for public services for migrant populations should be subsidized by the Central government. Such things would include the building of schools and hospitals.

Press for reform of the modes by which public services are supplied in cities

On a superficial level, many of the problems that exist in China's realm of public services appear to stem from an imbalance in supply and demand. Deeper causes can be traced back to how reform of government administration has not progressed, however, and also how market-oriented reforms have not progressed.

In recent years, China has gradually picked up the pace of reform in the sphere of public endeavors. Certain service markets have been 'opened up' [to commercial participation]. Private investment [from society at large] has begun to enter service areas and we see the start of competitive mechanisms. Nevertheless, seen in overall terms, the transformation of government functions has been insufficient. Reform of administrative bodies has been inadequate, together with reform of enterprise systems. We must draw more on international experience in this regard, and look into setting up new models for how we deliver urban services. We should look specifically at a formula that could be described as 'service-type government + market-oriented operations + general participation by society at large'.

Accelerate the transformation of what is perceived to be within the sphere of 'government functions'

Within the realm of urban public services, 'government' should mainly perform the following functions: it should formulate rules of the market; it should procure public services on behalf of the public; and it should regulate and supervise market operations. The government should enable the full employment of market mechanisms, and stimulate the highest levels of public services, by using such things as price, fiscal, tax, and other incentive mechanisms and economic tools. In so doing, it should nurture the market, standardize it, develop it, and supervise it. If government is performing its functions properly, public services can call on a far wider range of 'social forces', and the provision of public services can become more diversified.

Promote the process of providing services through communities

Providing public services through communities has become an important trend in Western countries since the 1970s; it has been a major part of the administrative reforms of various governments. The term refers to methods, behaviour, and processes of delivering public services through the 'basic unit' of the 'community'. Such services are only those appropriate to the community, and the process is guided by the public interest and must be encouraged and supported at all levels of government.

As a new model for supplying public services, this features the following distinctions. It separates decision-making from execution of the results. It diversifies suppliers and encourages the recipients of the service to participate in the supply process. It focuses on setting up cooperative relationships among government, non-governmental organizations, and citizens. It makes the providing of public services something that is cross-departmental and shared by all concerned, including the public sector, the private sector, the not-for-profit sector, and the communities themselves.

Only a few public services in China are currently provided through communities in this manner. They include job training, nursing care for the elderly, public health, and basic medical services.

In the process of using communities as partners in the delivery of public services, the government is transferring a portion of its 'functions' to those communities. Governance functions thereby extend into grassroots-level social structures. This helps to eliminate unfairness in the distribution of public services. While still meeting a diversity of service needs, it allows for the provision of public services on a more equalized basis to the public.

Diversify methods of delivering urban public services

Ever since the 1960s, authorities in other countries have been proposing a diverse array of 'modes of delivery' of public services. Generally speaking, they include the following: a 'corporatized' model that relies on market mechanisms and competition, a 'services style of government' model that emphasizes customer-relations management, a 'common participation' model that emphasizes group participation, a 'civic groups model' that emphasizes the role of special interests, a 'growth support' model that emphasizes long-term sustainable development, and a 'social welfare' model. Each of these has its advantages and disadvantages.

The service-style of government model, for example, recognizes the importance of development concepts in how it serves the 'customers' of a city or those who hold a stake in building up the city, but it fails to break away from a delivery model that is still 'top-down'. It focuses on the behaviour of just one side of the equation, namely changing government functions, rather than creating a two-way interaction with the stakeholders.

Given China's current state of public services, the degree to which the country has become market-oriented, and the country's current stage of urbanization, several approaches might be explored as possible public-service delivery modes. The first is a 'direct government-delivery model'. In this model, the government directly supplies those things that are hard to price, for which contracts are difficult to enforce, and for which competition is not possible. Such things include the handling of such crises as floods and epidemic diseases.

The second is a 'licensed-delivery model'. This would be used for those services that can easily be priced and that meet the definition of 'serving the public interest' in terms of urban public-service projects. Agreements would be signed with private operators to deliver such services, using one of a variety of business models including contracting, leasing, trusteeship, long-term licensing, joint shareholding with government bodies, and internal competition. This model should serve as the primary mode of delivering public services in an economy that operates under a market-oriented system.

The third model involves having the market deliver public services. In principle, all urban public services that can realize a form of 'exclusivity' can be supplied through market forces. The role of the government is to exercise supervisory control, according to laws and contracts. One aspect of market-supplied services must be avoided, however, namely a potential bias away from the public interest. This damages social equity and the interests of society at large.

Set up a basic pension system for urban areas

As soon as possible, a pension system should be set up that extends coverage in both urban and rural areas. It should be a 'basic' system with the individual paying in premiums and the government contributing a portion of the total. Participation should be open to urban residents who are a full 18 years of age or older and who are not yet participating in any other pension plan. The percentage that the individual must pay in should be between 5 per cent and 30 per cent of the urban citizen's average salaries in the previous year, with the specific amount to be decided upon freely by the individual. The period for paying in premiums must be over 15 years when people are between the ages of 18 and 44; for those between 45 and 59, it should be calculated by subtracting the age of the person, when the system was initiated, from 60. People over 60 can participate and not have to pay premiums. The funding for pension benefits should come from two sources: the individual's own premiums and subsidies from public finance (from the basic pension fund).

Set up a 'secure' housing system [i.e., one that provides a secure fallback for people in need]

For the next 10 years, an imbalance in supply and demand of urban housing is going to remain a major problem in the country. Because of this, we should increase construction of 'secure' housing [low-income housing] in order to ensure adequate supply. We recommend that the total quantity of new low-income housing construction should be no less than 50 percent of the total amount of 'housing construction' overall. This should apply to the incremental amount of new construction being done every year over the next 10 years. At the same time, we recommend using a variety of methods and channels in order to accomplish this low-income housing construction. In particular, both Central and local governments should increase their direct investment into low-rent housing. Cities that have an extreme scarcity of such housing should build more but should also buy in existing housing and convert it to low-income use. Those units who are qualified and licensed may be allowed to build collective dormitories, in order to resolve the housing issues of a portion of rural migrant workers. In cities that are even more highly populated than others, great effort should be put into public housing in order to alleviate housing shortages for middle- to low-income families and newly employed workers, as well as labourers who 'come in from the outside' to work. The building of these can be done with private investment, and it can, moreover, be done on land that is provided by the local government at a favorable price. Pilot sites can be set up in some cities to experiment with using public housing funds for building such housing.

Ensure that vulnerable groups are provided with public services

Given China's overall level of economic development, the country cannot afford to set up a highly advanced social security system at this time, but it is fully capable of setting up a 'relief-oriented' social welfare system that is fair to all. China must focus on ensuring that the country's most vulnerable groups enjoy the 'right to exist' and the 'right to develop'. We must adhere to the principle of relative fairness, which takes as its starting point the concept that vulnerable groups have an equal right to exist. This equal right to exist must be the foundation of our security system. In keeping with the special needs of the most vulnerable groups, including rural migrant workers, the elderly, the youth, and the disabled, we must provide targeted assistance that meets their needs. They should be receiving more humanitarian concern. We should do our utmost to ensure that every single person in the country has the basic prerequisites for existence. Vulnerable groups [as well as everyone else in society] should be able to participate in and enjoy the results of the country's development.

Notes

1 In real life, the supplies of products and services are often mixed together and are difficult to be strictly divided. The division can only be made in the relative sense. Although housing security is often supplied in kind, people still habitually regard various types of social security as services. Therefore, this report includes housing security in the scope of 'services'. In addition, the fact that public services are mainly provided by government does not necessarily mean they are solely provided by government. Individuals, families, enterprises and civic and social organizations can all participate in the provision of public services.

2 As Chapter 2 has been devoted to the issue of turning rural migrant workers into urban residents, this chapter mainly discusses the public services for migrant population in the wider sense instead of the public services specifically for rural migrant workers.

7   Creating sustainable processes for building and financing urban infrastructure

Not only is urbanization a process that draws together people and industries, but it is a process that actually builds up a city in physical terms. To a certain extent, a city's 'public goods' and its basic infrastructure determine how livable in that city is, how well it serves urban functions, how well it delivers public services.

Moreover, the process of urbanization is a long-term undertaking. Once the initial input into infrastructure is made, services need to be operated and maintained. Sustainability is therefore something that needs to be built into the ongoing funding and building of cities.

As the basis for all urban activities and operations, basic infrastructure must come foremost in the process of building a city and also in the process of addressing deficits in China's urban landscape, deficits that are the result of China's recent history. It is time for the country to undertake more investment in construction that is 'future-oriented'. Funding and building, to the appropriate degree, should be done in line with principles that adhere to necessary urban functions. Given the reality of financial constraints, any concepts and methods that are not sustainable must be modified. Models for funding, operating, and managing urban infrastructure should be innovative and aligned with principles of sustainability.

China's current situation with respect to urban infrastructure, and challenges that need to be faced

Demand for basic infrastructure in China's cities is constantly increasing given the dramatic rise in the number of cities and their populations as well as the rapid rise in the amount of space being occupied by cities. In this report, the term 'urban infrastructure' is taken to mean the necessary 'engineered' framework for operating a city. It includes things like water supply, sewage disposal, transportation systems, environmental protection, disaster prevention, and public safety.[1]

Given that China's urbanization is still in full stride, the need for investment in infrastructure continues to grow. Momentous changes have occurred in the fabric of urban life in China over the past 30 years, as manifested in such things as transportation, water supply, natural gas supply, sewage treatment and solid-waste treatment, the 'greening' of cities, and so on. At the same time, urban infrastructure still faces intense challenges. These include the relative under-supply of certain things, imbalances in regional development and in the development of different industries, constantly increasing per-unit costs, and the constant upgrading of urban standards. They include the fact that pricing of municipal facilities is not yet 'rational', which compromises the profitability of suppliers.

A further increase in funding for China's urban infrastructure is going to be necessary in light of these things, and in light of the future increase in the country's urban population. In addition to mere funding, however, we must press forward with reform of industries and corporate structures, in order to increase efficiencies and ensure that the use of invested funds is proper and generates better results.

Building up basic infrastructure in China's cities: the current situation

Investment in urban infrastructure has been intensifying in China under the impetus of local governments [i.e., provincial and municipal governments]. As measured in Five-Year-Plan increments, each five-year period has seen multiple increases in the total size of investment. During the 8th Five-Year Plan (FYP), for example, investment was 5.2 times what it was during the 7th FYP. Investment in the 9th FYP was 2.7 times what it had been under the 8th FYP. Investment in the 10th FYP period was nearly 3 times what it had been under the 9th FYP. RMB 260 billion was invested in urban infrastructure in the 8th FYP period, RMB 700 billion in the 9th FYP period, and RMB 2 trillion in the 10th FYP period.

Investment during the 11th FYP period is expected to reach between RMB 4 trillion and RMB 4.5 trillion, doubling what it was in the 10th FTP period. The percentage of GDP that is being invested in urban infrastructure is also increasing. It was 1.3 per cent in the 8th FYP period, 1.7 per cent in the 9th, and 2.9 per cent in the 10th, and was expected to be 3.3 per cent in 2009.

Corresponding to this increase in investment, China has seen a tremendous increase in the intensity of investment per population and per unit of space. In 1980, the investment per square kilometer of built-up area in China's cities was only RMB 260,000. By 2008, that had risen to RMB 20.3 million, 78 times as much or an average annual growth rate of 17 per cent. The investment per 'new urban resident' also rose dramatically, by 217 times between 1980 and 2007, from RMB 294 in 1980 to RMB 64,000 in 2007.

Given this ongoing increase in investment in basic infrastructure, the ability of China's cities to supply both goods and services has constantly improved. Passenger flow has increased substantially with improvements in transportation. By the end of 2008, China had 412,000 'standard vehicles' in operation in public-transport systems. Among these, 9858 were 'rail transport' vehicles. Per unit of 10,000 people, this came to 11.13 'standard vehicles'. In addition, China had 968,800 taxis in urban areas and 848 passenger ferries. By the end of 2008, there was a total of 259,700 kilometers of urban roads and there were 3.15 billion square meters of 'road surface' or 12.21 square meters of 'urban road surface' per person. As compared with 1990, these figures were, respectively, 1.7 times higher, 3.5 times higher, and 2.9 times higher.

As the capacity of cities to supply water to residents has improved, the issue of water supply to urban populations has basically been addressed. The 'access rate' to running water in cities went from 35 per cent in 1980 to 94.7 per cent in 2008. Per capita urban water use went from 120 to 180 liters during this period. By the end of 2005, the ratio between urban water supply capacity and the highest daily demand for water had gone from 0.88 to 1.33. Water stoppages became 'history' for the majority of China's cities.

General household access to natural gas also rose dramatically, from 17 per cent in 1980 to 89.6 per cent in 2008. The great majority of households in the northern part of the country no longer use coal burners to heat their homes. The percentage of households using natural gas went from 5 per cent in 1980 to 36.7 per cent in 2007.

With regard to sewage treatment, in the early years after reform and opening-up policies began, each province had only one sewage treatment facility. By now, each city has, on average, at least two. Sewage treatment has gone from an 'access rate' of less than 20 per cent in 1980 to 70 per cent in 2008, with corresponding improvements in the public hygiene of residential districts. The capacity to deal with solid-waste disposal has gone up by 140 times since the early years of reform and opening up. More than 66 per cent of garbage is now 'detoxified'. The amount space devoted to parks in cities has gone up by 15 times over the past 30 years; the extent to which the built-up area of cities have been 'greenified' [or landscaped] has gone from 10 per cent to 37 per cent.

Challenges that the 'building up' of urban infrastructure is facing

China's population is continuing to grow rapidly at present, and the dynamics of the situation dictate that intense pressures will continue to be placed on urban infrastructure. The challenges include the following considerations.

First, the metric by which we currently measure the 'urban population' is too low and under-represents the real population. This therefore means that we over-estimate the 'coverage' [or availability] of urban infrastructure per capita.

Right now, the urban population as measured by our statistics counts population according to 'household residency' plus a 'temporary' population. That temporary population is defined as one that has a proper residency permit to live in a city on a temporary basis. However, it does not include the great majority of rural migrant workers and their families. The actual urban population is dramatically under-estimated as a result.

In 2008, the official figure for the 'temporary population' in urban areas in China was 35.17 million. In fact, the National Bureau of Statistics estimated that the number of rural migrant workers actually working in cities exceeded 130 million. The official figure was not even one-third the actual figure. When we are formulating urban policies and plans, we generally overlook and do not incorporate a large number of people. They are not yet accounted for even though they are essentially living permanently in cities. Once our plans and policies are realized and turned into public resources, the fact that public-infrastructure supply is grossly inadequate to demand may become extremely apparent.

Second, some forms of infrastructure are more inadequate than others due to the way demand for them is growing faster. Urban roads are one example. The amount of road surface in China grew 20-fold between 1978 and 2008, from 220 million square meters to 4250 million square metres, but ownership of cars grew even faster, by 37 times in the same period. The amount of road surface per car fell by 45 per cent. The density of roads in urban areas is also low – in 2008, the road-surface area as a percentage of built-up area of cities in general was 12.4 per cent. Major cities in China, such as Beijing and Shanghai, have a far lower area of road surface relative to built-up area than comparable cities overseas (see Figure 7.1). All of these factors create a host of problems, including urban congestion, and are indicative of inadequate supply for the amount of demand.

Third, imbalances in regional development and uneven development of industries have also created 'weak links' in the supply of basic infrastructure. Compared with the fairly high rates at which people have access to water and natural gas, for example, the provision of sewage treatment and garbage detoxification facilities is distinctly low.

In 2008, only 70 per cent of urban residents in China were provided with adequate sewage treatment facilities, and only 67 per cent had 'garbage detoxification' services. Right now, the amount of garbage in cities is increasing at a rate

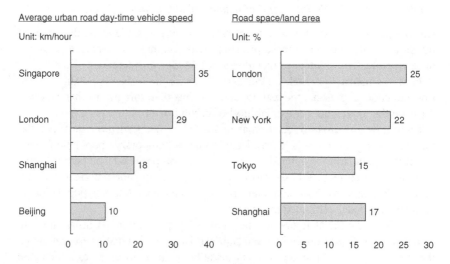

Figure 7.1 Road efficiency disparity of the world's main cities.

Source: McKinsey & Company: *Shanghai's Third Traffic Survey in 2005*.

of 8 per cent to 10 per cent per year, while garbage disposal capacities are increasing at a rate of only 5 per cent per year. Only one-third of China's cities currently have garbage treatment plants.

Sewage facilities are not only grossly inadequate, but, where facilities do exist, they often do not function properly due to a lack of standardized pipe sizes, among other reasons. Around one-third of China's sewage treatment plants are not operating normally.

Public transport in cities has been slow to develop. Nationwide, public transport carries only 10 per cent of total traffic. In super-large cities, the figure is still only around 20 per cent. This is markedly lower than the 40–60 per cent figure for major cities in Europe, Japan, and Latin America. What is more, the rate in China's major cities has declined by around six percentage points over the last few years. Public transport systems that can move large numbers of people have yet to be developed. By the end of 2008, there was a total of 776 kilometers of rail transport in China's dozen or so largest cities, which was roughly the amount contained by London alone.

In addition, there are massive disparities in infrastructure between different sizes of cities and among different regions in China. The contrast between the eastern part of the country and the central and western regions is particularly acute. This is reflected most notably in the supply rates for fuel gas, sewage facilities, and garbage treatment. The supply of infrastructure is worse in smaller cities, where access to fuel gas comes to only 78.1 per cent, which is 13 percentage points less than the figure in large cities. The sewage treatment rate is only 63.3 per cent, which is eight percentage points less than the rate in large cities.

Considering that small cities hold a population of 120 million people, or one-third of all urban residents in China, this basic shortage of infrastructure has broad ramifications. It lowers the capacity of smaller cities to draw in rural people and shift the demographic structure, thereby putting even more pressure on China's larger cities.

In addition, China's cities share a pronounced problem of focusing on initial construction but then neglecting maintenance. Over the past decade, funds allocated for maintenance come to only around 10 per cent of funds for new construction of infrastructure, which is not enough. In 2005, incidents arising from rusted-out pipes accounted for 86 per cent of all 'dangerous incidents' having to do with public infrastructure.

As standards for 'urbanization' become more stringent, the physical build-up of cities will be moving more in a vertical direction and less in horizontal expansion. Low-rise buildings will increasingly give way to high-rise buildings and also to greater use of underground space. Not only does this increase the difficulty of building, which puts higher demands on quality control, but it also quickly increases the density of urban populations.

Despite this trend, at present the 'technological component' of China's urban development is far from being adequate. Cities are not meeting the constantly increasing demands of urban residents for higher quality of services. Water quality is one example. The national government has mandated that 106 indicators of drinking-water quality be tested in all cities, but equipment for such testing is in short supply. A survey of over 126 water-supply entities has revealed that, at most, 92 indicators were being tested in any one place, and some places were only testing for 17 indicators. In addition to the quality of the end-result, therefore, low technology is impacting the efficiency of operations.

The supply of heating in urban areas is another example. The average efficiency of heating systems is currently only around 30 per cent. This is 10 per cent higher than it was in the 1980s, and has been achieved by improving furnace efficiencies and reducing the heat loss from pipes exposed to the outside. Nevertheless, the heat loss from temperature imbalances in the overall system means that as much as 20–30 per cent of potential heat is being lost. Flow-measuring equipment needs to be improved, and temperature imbalances between water intakes and outtakes need to be moderated. Planning for additional investment needs for these things is inadequate, which influences the returns on investment and overall efficiency. It enables ongoing waste of the resource.

The funding needs for building up urban infrastructure

The demand for urban infrastructure in China is not going to slacken, even if we do not keep up the pace of urbanization that we have seen over the past 10, 20, even 30 years. Given that the foundation of our existing basic infrastructure is still quite weak, given imbalances among regions and industries in the country, and given the 'urbanization' of people who are already long-term residents in cities but will now be entitled to urban services, demand for infrastructure can only grow.

In fact, municipal governments are already planning for this. They not only have a very proactive attitude toward massive demand in the future, they are using the building up of their cities as a 'growth point' in their future plans. The huge size of investments that cities are discussing is shocking. The funding contradictions and the potential investment risk are quite apparent from these figures.

Funding needs over the next ten years

We have estimated a 'minimum scenario' for infrastructure needs over the next 10 years, based on demand as well as infrastructure projects that are currently under way. Based on that, we have come up with a forecast for the least amount of funding that will be necessary for building out infrastructure by the year 2020. This scenario takes into account future population growth. It assumes that average levels of infrastructure nationwide will be at the current existing level in China's most advanced cities, in terms of both quality and quantity. It takes into account inflation, and increased costs per unit due to rising labor costs.

The scenario comes up with estimated figures for the funding of various kinds of infrastructure, and it then adds them all together. The composite figure shows

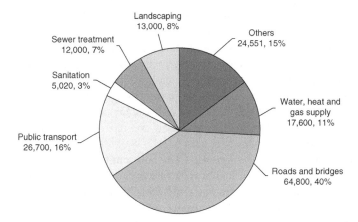

Figure 7.2 Minimum funding demand of future urban infrastructure construction (unit: 100 million yuan).

Source: Liu Jingsheng: *Background Report, 2009.*

that China will need around RMB 16 trillion in funding for the building of basic urban infrastructure by the year 2020.

Figure 7.2 shows the funding needs of various components of basic infrastructure, and their relative percentages of the total. Funding of road and bridge construction is a notably weighty component. It comes to RMB 6.5 trillion in total and constitutes 40 per cent of total investment demands. Public transport is another major category, requiring RMB 2.7 trillion before 2020, and constituting 16 per cent of the total.

By August of 2009, around 27 cities in China were formulating plans for a subway system. Among these, 22 had received Central approval to move forward. By around the year 2015, such cities as Beijing and Shanghai will have completed 79 new rail transport lines, a total of 2260 kilometers, with total investment of RMB 882 billion. By the end of 2008, however, only 10 cities in China had rail transport. These encompassed a total of 29 lines, including an 'operational mileage' network of 835 kilometers. This means that both the number of cities with rail transport systems and their total operational mileage will have to double in the next few years.

The figures may look large, but in fact the above funding estimates are quite conservative. By charting the relationship between level of economic development and the building of urban infrastructure, we can estimate a figure that is more in line with actual needs for future funding. This second scenario looks at the level of economic development and the level of urban construction.

International experience indicates that the cost of basic infrastructure tends to be a standard percentage of GDP. A fairly early World Bank study estimated that this figure was an average 4 per cent for developing countries, which is in line with the recommendation of the United Nations that developing countries should put 3–5 per cent of GDP into basic infrastructure. When other countries have been in a rapid phase of urbanization, this indicator has stood at between 3 per cent and 5 per cent. China has been undergoing rapid urbanization for the past 20 years, however, and has been spending a far lower percentage of its GDP on basic infrastructure. The country's spending on infrastructure remains modest.

According to the results of the Second National Economic Census, China's GDP was over RMB 31 trillion in 2008, and grew at a rate of 8.7 per cent in constant-price terms over the next year to reach a total GDP of over RMB 33 trillion in 2009.

Using conservative assumptions, from now until 2020, China's GDP will maintain an 8 per cent nominal growth rate every year, at which time the real GDP of the country will reach some RMB 79 trillion. If the country were to start spending 4 per cent of GDP on basic infrastructure every year from 2010, between 2010 and 2020 it will have spent in excess of a cumulative figure of RMB 24 trillion (see Figure 7.3).

The limitations of having local governments use 'land transfer fees' as the primary source of their funding

It will be very hard to satisfy this enormous demand for funding simply by using the model currently employed in China. That model allows local governments to

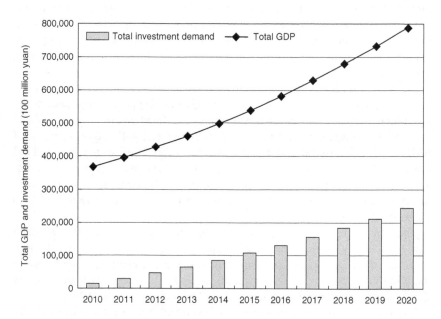

Figure 7.3 GDP and urban infrastructure investment, 2010–2020.

Source: National Bureau of Statistics; Liu Jingsheng: *Background Report, 2009.*

rely on the land under their control for funding their budgets. The three primary sources of local-government funding are ostensibly loans, public revenues, and self-generated funding by enterprises. The reality, however, is that governments are intensely reliant on land for their income.

In 2008, funding for basic infrastructure came from the following trio of sources: local governments invested 32.2 per cent, bank loans constituted 29.6 per cent, and the self-funding of enterprises constituted 28.7 per cent. Other sources came to 9.5 per cent. These figures need closer analysis, however. First, the 32.2 per cent invested by local governments came mainly from land operations. In the early 1980s, the Central government contributed 26 per cent of basic infrastructure funding to local governments, through allocations from fiscal revenues. By the early 1990s, that figure had declined to 5 per cent, and by 2008, it was a mere 1.1 per cent. Local governments are therefore the primary investors when it comes to 'government funding', not the Central government.

Under the current framework by which China's tax system operates [the system that dictates the tax split between local and Central], income from taxes and fees that goes into local budgets is not robust. The situation in 2007 can serve as an example: fiscal budgetary income of all urban areas came to RMB 2.4 trillion, while fiscal budgetary expenditures came to RMB 3.8 trillion. Even when transfer payments from the Central government are figured in, cities are still operating at a loss in terms of straight revenues and expenditures. Many places around the country are therefore facing the problem of not having enough cash to meet daily expenses. Basically, if any investment is to go into building up public infrastructure, the funding has to come from what is called 'operating land' [this refers to land that is put to for-profit uses other than farming].

Second, the 'self-funding of enterprises', which constituted 28.7 per cent of all local funding in 2008, comes from what are called local urban investment funds or 'financing platform companies'. Ultimately, however, the source of money for repaying these loans comes mostly from selling off operating rights to land. Meanwhile, banks make loans to municipalities mainly on the basis of using land for collateral. That is, they base the loans on the land-use rights that are held by a given locality. The future yield off the land is what repays the bank loan.

In 1991, domestic loans constituted a mere 15 per cent of the sources of all urban funding in China. By 2008, the figure was approaching 30 per cent in terms of the amount of bank credit, and this was directly related to the ability of local governments to use land as collateral. We can look at the example of Chongqing, where we conducted a research project into the sources of investment funds. The total amount of money raised between 2002 and 2008 in Chongqing came to RMB 850 trillion. Bank loans constituted 40 per cent of this amount. Of all bank loans, 63 per cent were backed by land as collateral and funded by the yield off that land. In addition, income from 'reorganizing land' contributed another 13 per cent to funding.

Self-generated funding is similarly closely related to income off land and to public finance. This category includes two main types: operating income generated from the operations of corporations and income derived from issuing stocks and bonds. Income from corporations is minimal and such corporations even have to depend on government subsidies.

We evaluated data from 50 urban investment companies that were chosen as a representative group. Their net cash intake from operations was RMB 11.5 billion, while net cash outflows went up to RMB 132.8 billion. Their operating cash was only some 9 per cent of what they needed: they derived a considerable part of the difference from government subsidies. Of the 50 urban investment companies, 25 were *de facto* operating in the red, yet only 2 of the companies had pre-tax earnings that were negative. The difference in the figures was made up for by government subsidies, again mostly in the form of taking advantage of appreciating land values.

Since 2009, the 'hot' way to finance investment is through issuing bonds. A number of urban investment companies and regional financing platforms have been relying heavily on this source of funding, which, in turn, relies on the combination of land and public finance. By August 2009, a cumulative sum of RMB 163.4 billion worth of all kinds of local enterprise bonds had been issued in China. The total amount for 2008 had been only RMB 68.4 billion. The great majority of bonds issued in 2009 had debt repayment guarantees in the form of local government 'support' or 'commitments' and most of these related to land. For example, in the case of Changzhou, the 'reserve funds for urban construction' served as guarantor (2008 Changzhou urban bond issue). In the case of bonds issued in 2009 by Huaihua city, the municipal government and the urban investment company signed a 'repurchasing agreement'.

Furthermore, local municipal governments generally use various methods to increase the net asset value of their local investment companies in order to improve sale of their bonds. The methods include accounting for land as one of the company's assets. Of the total assets of the 50 urban investment companies that we studied, an average 30 per cent were classified as 'intangible assets', composed mainly of land-use rights. Ten had intangible assets that were between 20 and 30 per cent of their total assets. One company had 51 per cent of assets listed as 'intangible', meaning land-use rights.

The gap in funding for urban infrastructure

China currently funds its urban infrastructure development by relying on income from land. Given increasing demands for funding in the future, it is going to be difficult for this model to suffice. According to estimates by the Ministry of Housing and Urban–Rural Development, in 2009, 48 per cent of all funding of urban infrastructure came from 'licensing out' land. The total sum of urban-infrastructure funding from land revenues came to RMB 334.1 billion in 2009. This represented revenue from direct investments of [municipal] governments in land development, and from investments of 'municipal investment companies' that were 'subsidized' by those governments and that were investing 'in the name of' corporations.

China's total sum of funds derived from 'land licensing' in 2009 came to RMB 1.59 trillion. Therefore, 21 per cent of that total was used on urban infrastructure development.

An estimated RMB 16–24 trillion will be needed for infrastructure development over the next 10 years. Extrapolating from the above figures, if 50 per cent continues to be derived from licensing out land, then, over 10 years, land-licensing fees will have to total between RMB 8 and 16 trillion. And if the same 21 per cent of total land revenues continues to be the amount put into urban infrastructure development, then total land revenues will have to amount to some RMB 3.81–5.71 trillion over the next decade.

The figure of RMB 3.81–5.71 trillion is between 2.4 and 3.6 times the amount of revenue generated from land licensing in 2009, even though 2009 represented the highest level of such revenue in recent years. Given the vast increases in the funding that will have to come from land revenues, the sustainability of the financing model is clearly in question.

First, the amount of land for which land-use rights can be granted is limited. This constitutes a fundamental 'hard' constraint. According to the Ministry of Housing and Urban–Rural Development, there is currently around 1.83 billion mu of arable land in China. China has set a hard bottom line, what it calls a 'red line', of 1.8 billion mu of land that must be maintained as farmland. Over the next decade, the country therefore has a strict quota on land that can be 'transferred to non-farming purposes'. That total quota is 1.9 million mu per year [1.8 billion mu = 296.46 million acres].

There is already an intense scarcity of land. If we cannot make radical changes now in how we conserve arable land, and instead rely solely on such things as rehabilitating already degraded or 'used' land, we will be seeing a multiple price increase in the cost of land.

[The following calculation explains the predicament.] If we were to grant land-use rights to 2.2 million mu of land every year in the decade between 2010 and 2020, in order to raise more than RMB 3 trillion of land-use revenues each year, we would soon find land prices going as high as RMB 1.36 million per mu. This is 2.7 times the average price of land in 2009, which was RMB 370,000 per mu.

Such excessive increases in land prices must not and cannot become the normal expectation of the market. The reason is that expensive land increases the costs of urban infrastructure and makes it impossible for municipal governments to supply such things as guaranteed low-cost housing. With higher land prices, cities face the risk of lower returns on their investment in basic infrastructure. The result therefore constrains the whole process of [our stated policy goal of] 'urbanization that takes the human being as the core value'.

Furthermore, as cities continue to pay people more for their land, that is, the people who were previously farming that land, cities have less remaining funds with which to invest in infrastructure development.

Data from various surveys indicates that the percentage of land-use income paid to farmers since the 1990s remained low for quite some time. Farmers generally received between 5 per cent and 10 per cent of land-use revenues [from their former land]. Recognition of the severe problems that resulted from such inequitable distribution of revenue led to a very high degree of concern [on the part of the Central government]. In 2003, the [Central] government introduced changes to the land-requisition system. It improved the procedures for requisitioning land, which now include timely and reasonable compensation to farmers.

The current situation is that a portion of provinces and municipalities have indeed led the way in raising the percentage of land-use revenue that goes to farmers. The Chinese Academy of Sciences carried out a survey in Kunshan in Jiangsu Province, Tongcheng in Anhui Province, and Xindu District of Chengdu City in Sichuan Province. The average figures for sample districts in these places showed that the percentage of land-use revenues from requisitioned land that went back to the original farmers came to 15.9 per cent in Kunshan, 15.6 per cent in Tongcheng, and 28.5 per cent in Xindu (Wang Xiaoying et al., 2007).

Over the next decade, it is going to be hard for the Chinese [Central] government to extend greater support to municipalities from within its own budgetary income. First, the speed with which fiscal revenues have been increasing is going to slow down. The major reform of China's fiscal system took place in 1994, and since that time fiscal revenues nationwide have increased at an average rate of around 20 per cent. As compared with the last decade of the twentieth century, however, future GDP growth rate is going to be dropping somewhat.

Second, fiscal revenues as a percentage of GDP have grown quickly, from 10.5 per cent in 1997 to 19.5 per cent in 2007. At the same time, however, compensation to labourers as a percentage of GDP has declined, from 52.8 per cent of GDP in 2007 to 39.7 per cent in 2007. The [Central] government has determined that this must change: the share of citizens' income should increase as a percentage of total GDP, in order to stimulate an economic growth model that is led by consumer demand. Given this line of thinking, there is little likelihood that fiscal revenues as a percentage of GDP are going to continue to rise to any major extent.

Finally, the share of the Central-government budget that is allocated to investment on urban infrastructure may well decline. The structure of China's economic growth needs to change. Government functions must be modified to accommodate this and public spending on such things as education, medical treatment, social security and so on needs to continue to increase.

In our *China Annual Report of 2008–2009*, we forecast that the percentage of fiscal income being spent on social welfare expenditures would need to be increased from 27 per cent in 2007 to 35 per cent in 2008. Even that increase would only be able to ensure the most basic coverage of low-level welfare benefits to the entire body of people in the country. Ongoing increases in this percentage of government spending, to be spent on social welfare, are going to limit the possibility of ongoing increases in spending on capital construction.

The risks of the financing model that we currently employ

Our current model of funding [for urban infrastructure development] is incubating fairly high levels of risk. There are 50 'urban investment companies' in China. We calculate that they have 1.19 times as much operating net cash inflow as they have outflow in terms of interest costs and dividends, on average. That is to say, paying out interest and dividends already basically uses up any net inflows of operating cash. They have little room to maneuver when it comes to paying back any loan principal.

Among the total number of 50 companies, 22 have a ratio as described above that is less than 1. That is, operating cash flow does not cover interest costs. Another 20 of the companies have performance that is even worse. Their average ratio is a mere 0.63. In point of fact, the way these 'local investment platforms' make ends meet, in order to 'package themselves' as meeting licensing requirements, is through issuance of shares and the granting of land-use rights. The investment companies, however, in fact lack control over the subsidiary companies that are represented on their consolidated statements. It is hard to say whether or not the companies actually have the ability to pay back their loans.

Secondly, some of these urban investment companies have a liabilities-to-assets ratio that is on the high side. Given poor cash flow, local governments are constantly injecting more 'land' and 'shares' into urban investment companies, thereby increasing the net assets of the companies in order to improve their balance sheets. Even so, the ratios of liabilities to assets of some companies are alarmingly high. By our calculations, the mean figure for all 50 urban investment companies in our survey is 54 per cent, that is, liabilities are 54 per cent of assets. Compared with the figure for industrial companies of a considerable scale nationwide, which is 57 per cent, this does not seem to be too bad, but there are great disparities among the urban investment companies. Eight of them have liabilities that are 70 per cent of total assets. The worst single case has liabilities that are 87 per cent of assets.

Third, the pricing of assets held by municipalities is not standardized. A certain controversy exists with respect to the pricing of assets and particularly the pricing of land. One urban investment company, for example, issued bonds on the basis of land as collateral that it valued at RMB 1.5 million per mu. Media reports soon revealed, however, that two neighboring patches of land had recently been sold at auction for prices of RMB 600,000 per mu and RMB 810,000 per mu. One state-owned investment company has even issued bonds recently using land as collateral that it valued at RMB 1 million per mu. Some 2500 mu of this land, however, was salinized and yet to be reclaimed [or restored to any value].

Finally, interlocking mutual guarantees are increasing risk. In theory, third-party guarantees are meant to reduce the risk of breach of contract. At present, however, we are seeing an increase in risk from the 'financing chain', as different urban investment companies in a given locality in the same province guarantee one another. Complex guarantees in such forms of urban financing can easily trigger chain reactions in credit risk.

Looked at on a deeper level, there is a possibility that risk will begin to concentrate in China's banking system as local governments increasingly leverage their public finances. Urban investment companies/financing platform companies are of a very special nature in China. At the end of the day, their debt is the responsibility of local governments. The debt levels of local governments are already in themselves quite high. According to estimates by the Fiscal Research Institute of the Ministry of Finance, the balance of liabilities of local governments nation-wide in 2007 came to around RMB 4.1 trillion. This was roughly 15.9 per cent of GDP in that year, and it was 174 per cent of local fiscal revenues in that year. Of total liabilities of local governments, 61 per cent or around RMB 2.4 trillion was the responsibility of 'prefecture-level municipalities and their districts', and the county level of government.

In 2010, the Central government issued RMB 200 billion in bonds on behalf of local governments, in the process of implementing a general stimulus program in the country. The effort was far from slaking the 'thirst for funding' of local governments, however. Borrowing from banks increased even further. According to data from the China Banking Regulatory Commission, at the end of June 2010, loans on the books to local-government financing platforms came to RMB 7.66 trillion.

In contrast, liabilities of these platforms at the beginning of 2008 totaled just RMB 1.7 trillion. Right now, 23 per cent of loans are at 'high risk' in terms of debt servicing. That means that the risk exposure of local-government financing platforms comes to some RMB 1.5 trillion.

History has taught us that local governments are far more inclined to interfere in banking systems when their fiscal deficits increase. ('Interference' includes such indirect forms of interference as using fictitious increases in land values in order to use it as higher-priced collateral when raising funds.) As a result, the non-performing loan rates of such local governments increase.

Right now, the gap between fiscal revenues and expenditures of local govern-ments is increasing. In addition, camouflaged forms of highly leveraged funding are concentrating risk. 'Local-government financing platform companies' are, in themselves, a tool for increasing leverage. Under their protection and conceal-ment, borrowed funds also are transformed into funding for subsidiary compa-nies, which then seek further debt, multiplying the final amount of leverage. Disclosure of relevant information is not transparent, meaning that neither inves-tors nor banks are privy to the details of the transactions. They cannot uncover risk in a timely fashion and adopt measures to reduce their exposure. Right now, direct intervention [by local governments in banking systems and funding mech-anisms] is still limited, but indirect methods exist, such as using land as collateral for funding. The risks involved should not be ignored.

We must look for methods of financing [urban development] that are sustainable

Most likely, demand for investment in urban infrastructure development will continue to increase tremendously over the next decade. Not only are our current models for financing inadequate in terms of the amount of funding they can deliver, but they also subject us to considerable risk, as well as other problems. We now face an urgent need to transform our funding models. We need to undertake systemic innovations that are in line with the principles of sustainability and diversification and to find multiple channels for funding urban infrastructure development.

New lessons are being learned in other countries, as a result of looking at various ways of resolving funding problems in the public sector. China too has undertaken a number of significant experiments in this arena, integrating both international experience and our own national circumstances to come up with several models. This chapter introduces several models that are already fairly well established, as described below.

Government bonds for urban construction

Government bonds for urban development

Local governments are still the primary entities that invest in municipal infrastructure development. This holds especially for such non-operating-type projects as building municipal roads, landscaping cities ['greenifying'], and some public transport projects. International experience has shown that municipal bonds are a workable innovative method for financing such things. The practice of issuing municipal bonds involves having either a city itself or an institution it has authorized to act on its behalf issue priced securities in the market. The funds raised from the issue are used in building municipal infrastructure or put towards public-service-type projects.

Municipal bonds are the primary method by which municipalities in major countries around the world raise funds for infrastructure building. The method not only helps raise money but avoids an over-concentration of risk in the banking system. Right now, among 53 major countries in the world, 37 allow their local governments to float bond issues. Some 70 per cent of the world's developing countries issue municipal bonds in support of municipal development.

At the end of 2008, the amount of outstanding municipal bonds in the USA totaled US$ 2.6 trillion, which was 18.2 per cent of GDP in that year. Municipal bonds constituted 9 per cent of the total sum of bonds of all kinds in the country, and were the primary form of financial support for municipal governments.

Even in Japan, where banks are the primary source of financing, municipal bonds in 2008 came to 12.5 per cent of GDP. The practice of issuing municipal bonds is something China too should adopt, after precautions are taken to limit risk.

China has indeed undertaken some experiments in what could be called 'semi-municipal bonds', given the nature of bonds issued by the country's urban investment/local financing platforms. Results are extremely varied, however, since each place has its own *modus operandi*. This makes the practice hard to regulate. Problems have erupted, including the difficulty in understanding the true [ownership] nature of the resulting capital and the nature of mutual guarantees.

In one sense, the practice of issuing 'consolidated statements' of municipal bonds is helpful in the process of evaluating and controlling risk. In 2009, the Central government issued RMB 200 billion worth of bonds on behalf of local governments. It stated that it was serving as agent in 'issuing' the bonds, but not in 'repaying' them. The idea behind the action was that local governments would assume the burden of repaying principle and interest in return for the right to use the funds. The bonds resembled municipal bonds in many ways, including the tax-free interest income to individual investors, but there were restrictions on what the funds could be used for and how long they could be used.

Local governments should be allowed to issue bonds in China only if they first address a host of issues, including the following:

- the whole issue of government accounting and information disclosure (see Box 7.1);
- the contradictions that are embodied in China's Budget Law;
- the problem that local governments do not have the authority to levy taxes;
- the fact that local governments lack a stable source of tax revenue and a guaranteed way to repay both interest and principal on borrowed funds (overseas, the primary source of local tax revenue is the property tax).

In addition, market-oriented mechanisms must be cultivated that allow an environment in which the market can set the prices of bonds, in which the investors also carry some risk, and in which municipal governments also bear risk when a bond issue fails. Once this foundation is established, through designing different bond-issue structures, various forms of municipal bonds can be issued in order to meet different financing needs.

First, China should address the unbalanced nature of funding for different sizes of cities and particularly the inadequate funding for infrastructure in small- and medium-sized cities. The country can set up 'collective funds' and 'dedicated accounts' for several cities that join in a kind of collective municipal funding effort. These would be supplemented by professional institutional guarantors, which would accelerate the process of financing infrastructure development in small and medium-sized cities. It would ameliorate the huge funding disparity that now exists between large and smaller cities. Collective mechanisms and state-supported institutional guarantors would add several layers of credit. The use of funds and repayment of funds could be managed by professional management companies. All of this would also mitigate risk concerns on the part of investors with regard to small and medium-sized cities. It would lower financing costs and increase the term of any given cycle of funding.

Second, China should address the problems of low operating efficiencies of municipal investments, 'blind' investments, and investments made purely for the sake of image. The country can draw on the experience of what is called 'financing through tax income off the increased value of a particular property'. This involves demarcating a specific area that is to be rebuilt in a city and investing in basic infrastructure to improve that area. The financing can be through loans or issuing bonds; repayment of the debt is then sourced from tax income off the improved property. This ties together the financing, investment, and income of a given place, whether it is a development area, commercial center, or industrial park. It forces the local government to focus on the end-results of the investment,

(Continued)

Box 7.1 China's problems with respect to disclosure requirements, statistical measures, and local government accounting standards, as seen by international municipal bond-rating standards

We have assembled the main criteria used to rate municipal bonds as done by CRISIL, which is India's leading ratings agency [with the majority shareholder being Standard & Poor's]. China's greatest defects lie in the areas of disclosing debt and disclosing financial conditions in general. At the very least, therefore, before issuing municipal bonds, local governments in China should draw up budgets and make then public. The budgets should include detailed outlines of balance sheets, as well as cash receipts and expenditures. Only then can comparable indicators be drawn up a serve as reference. CRISIL also focuses on the CAPEX ratio ['capital expenditure ratio']. If this is too high, the municipality is overly reliant on credit for financing and has insufficient amounts of internally generated funding.

Municipal bond rating method	Whether feasible now	Major parameters	Whether computed or not	Whether disclosed or not
Legal and administrative factors		**Economic basis**		
Effective administrative division	✓	Population and population growth	✓	✓
Tax power	✓	Intra-regional deposits and loans	✓	✓
Tax collection and management ability and tax-arrears handling experience	✗	Industrial power consumption	✓	✓
Central government's subsidy transfer	✓	Industrial water consumption	✓	✓
Borrowing ability	✗	Collection of sales tax	Inapplicable	Inapplicable
Ability to undertake debt service with government revenue	✓	Collection of property-transfer stamp tax	Inapplicable	Inapplicable
		Per capita income	✓	✓

Box 7.1 (Continued)

Municipal bond rating method	Whether feasible now
Economic basis	
Population factor and land scope	✓
Level of industrial activity	✓
Level of commercial activity	✓
Tax-base diversity and elasticity	✓
Possibility of expanding tax coverage	✗
Level of per capita income	✓
Fiscal conditions	
Rating of government accounting report quality	✗
Analysis of government surplus/deficit	✓
Growth factors of tax revenue and non-tax revenue	*
Analysis of taxation efficiency and debtors	✗
Degree of dependency on subsidy and transfer payment from central government	*
Main public service expenditure	✓

Major parameters	Whether computed or not	Whether disclosed or not
Number of motor vehicles	✓	✓
Telephone network demand	✓	✓
Bank deposit growth	✓	✓
Current fiscal conditions		
Tax revenue/total revenue	✓	*
Non-tax revenue/total revenue	✓	*
Same-level tax revenue/total revenue	✓	*
Same-level revenue/total revenue	✓	*
Non-tax revenue/total revenue	✓	*
Central government subsidy/total revenue	✓	✗
Fiscal surplus/deficit	✓	*
Surplus/total revenue	✓	*
Non-debt capital revenue/capital expenditure	✗	✗
Capital expenditure/total expenditure	✗	✗

Indicator	Rating	
Demand for past/anticipated debt service	Grossly inadequate	
Collateral multiplier for past/anticipated debt service	Grossly inadequate	
Current assets	×	
Projected revenue/expenditure growth	Grossly inadequate	
Management rating		
Organizational structure and responsibility division	✓	
Systems and procedures: level of informatization	✓	
Project management ability	×	
Political environmental management	×	
Measures for strengthening resource management	×	
Intensity of expenditure control measures	×	
Total surplus/deficit	×	×
Tax collection ratio	✓	×
Debt service ratio	Grossly inadequate	×
Detail debt ledger (sources, terms, interest rates, debt service arrangements)	Grossly inadequate	×
Interest guarantee multiplier	Grossly inadequate	×
Operations of municipal institutions		
Main public service expenditure/total expenditure	✓	×
Wage expenditure/total expenditure	✓	×
Per capita water supply	✓	✓
Per capita expenditure on elementary education	✓	✓
Per capita expenditure on medical and health services	✓	✓

Note: ✓, China qualified; *, partially qualified; ×, unqualified.
Source: Liu Jingsheng: *Background Report, 2009.*

at the planning and investment stage. It creates an organic link between investment and results, and helps in preventing the waste of resources.

Market-oriented operations and 'pay-by-user' operations

A considerable amount of urban infrastructure is not in fact of the classic 'public products' kind, but instead is of a kind that can be put to use with market-oriented mechanisms and operations. Such kinds of infrastructure include transport facilities, water supply, gas and heating supply, and even garbage disposal services. All of these can be supplied by corporations who may earn profits through the sale or supply of the service. Any utility that can earn a profit can, like any industry, grow and develop, use financing channels, raise funds for building up the business and so on. This is contingent upon three other key spheres of reform, however.

First, the enterprises involved need to undergo ongoing reform, in order to improve the efficiency of their investments and operations. The key to enabling market mechanisms to play their proper role in the sphere of municipal facilities is to push forward enterprise reform that has, as its primary goal, the improvement of operating efficiencies. Low returns on urban infrastructure-type businesses are directly related to low operating efficiencies.

Right now, despite years of reform, a considerable number of basic infrastructure enterprises are directly controlled by government and even by 'grassroots-level units'. Since there is no differentiation between 'government' and 'enterprise', there is no competition. This leads to low operating efficiencies. Losses that are defined as 'policy-type losses' [in that they are ostensibly made for the public good] conceal the reality of 'business-type losses'. Little scientific management is applied to operations, there is no incentive to improve the efficiency with which investment is used, and talented people are not attracted to the business. Recognizing these things, the public being served by the enterprise is distrustful and opposed to even necessary and rational increases in prices. As a result, the enterprise sinks into a vicious cycle of ever lower operating efficiencies.

Second, competitive mechanisms must be adopted, which means reforming the systems in China that govern who is allowed to enter into any given public utility. At the end of the day, the success of reforms in the sphere of public utilities depends upon introducing competitive mechanisms. Since the start of the twenty-first century, the Central government has indicated its explicit intent to accelerate reform of public utilities, as well as the state-owned enterprises that are involved in them. Relevant departments in the State Council have issued policy documents that support and regulate [or standardize] reform of public utilities.

Since starting these reforms, and especially since beginning licensed operations, a considerable amount of private investment and investment from overseas has come into the market for municipal facilities. Currently, 'people-operated' [i.e., private, or non-government] enterprises still constitute only around 10 per cent of public utilities nationwide, however, whether that is in terms of numbers of companies or of their operating revenues.

Private capital brings with it much more than funding. More importantly, its competitive nature stimulates reform, puts more focus on results and on service, and forces policies to be more transparent and more sustainable. In the end, private capital improves efficiencies and lowers the cost of operations.

Third, more rational price mechanisms should be realized as pay-by-user systems are adopted. As we are undertaking the above reforms to do with enterprises and operating efficiencies, we should be aware that consumers of public utilities in China are increasingly able to pay for their services. There is a reasonable margin to be made off the consumer, and this should help relieve the pressure to find funds for building up municipal infrastructure.

Water supply is one example. Right now, the average cost of water to the consumer is not high enough to earn a reasonable rate of return on the costs involved. The World Bank has made a study of the subject. It estimates that the charges on water should be no lower than RMB 2 per cubic meter in order to recover costs. The actual average charge in 36 large cities in the country is RMB 1.76 per cubic meter. This does not cover even the basic costs of water treatment, which average RMB 1–1.5 per cubic meter.

Raising the user-pay component of utilities should not be something that is limited to increasing prices. It should be applied to a broader range of municipal services, in order to reduce pressures on excessive increase in demand for certain kinds of infrastructure (see Box 7.2).

Box 7.2 China's water price of 0.26 dollars per cubic meter is unduly low when compared with international water prices

Water price	Developing countries	Industrial countries
<0.2 dollar/m^3	Inadequate to recover basic operational and maintenance costs	Inadequate to recover basic operational and maintenance costs
0.2–0.4 dollar/m^3	Adequate to recover operational and some maintenance costs	Inadequate to recover basic operational and maintenance costs
0.4–1.0 dollar/m^3	Adequate to recover operational and maintenance costs and most investment costs	Adequate to recover basic operational and maintenance costs
>1.0 dollar/m^3	Adequate to recover operational, maintenance and investment costs, but few countries reach this level	Adequate to recover all costs of modern water supply systems in most high-income cities

Source: World Bank: *Water, Electricity and the Poor*; Komives et al. (2005).

Adopt innovative financing measures for basic infrastructure

In order to break through bottlenecks that are preventing funding of infrastructure, and to promote further development of China's urban infrastructure, we should adopt certain financing models that have been used successfully in other countries. China too has experimented with some of these methods, which apply market-oriented funding tools to public goods and services.

In addition to the usual funding methods, a number of innovative approaches have been tried internationally that have specific applications. They are helpful in diversifying potential sources of funding and enabling all different kinds of capital to enter the sphere of urban infrastructure.

The PPP model of financing

In the 'public–private partnership' (PPP) model, the public sector and the private sector set up a partnership to provide public goods or services. The partnership enables the ongoing development of public endeavors. This model has been proven to work and can be one approach to resolving the issue of how to finance municipal infrastructure. The standard operating mode is as follows: the government signs a licensing contract with a supplier after having been through a bidding procedure, and the successful bidder takes on the responsibility of funding, building, and operating the utility or service. The government comes to a direct agreement with the funding institution that is supplying the loan. It commits to paying relevant fees [or expenses] to the successful bidder as per the contract that has been signed. This agreement enables the successful bidder, the supplier of services, to get funding more easily.

Generally speaking, there are three main forms of PPP arrangements, namely outsourcing, licensed operations, and privatization. The essence of the PPP model is that the government grants long-term operating rights to the private sector, together with the right to earn a profit. This facilitates the funding of basic infrastructure and ensures that operations are effective.

One example of an attempt to use the PPP model in Beijing is the No. 4 Subway line. Hong Kong's subway is profitable, indeed Hong Kong's Mass Transit Railway [MTR] is the only profitable subway in the world, and as a result Beijing would like to build on this example. The city hopes to combine the successful experience of 30 years of MTR operations in Hong Kong with the specifics of Beijing's situation, and to explore a new mode of financing, building, and operating for public transport.

The 'Beijing MTR Corporation' is the result of joint investment from three bodies, the Beijing Infrastructure Investment Co., Ltd, the Beijing Capital Group, and the MTR Corporation. The Beijing Municipal People's Government has signed a licensing agreement with this entity, to build and operate the No. 4 Subway line. The company is in charge of building and operating the subway system, as well as developing other types of business associated with the rail line, as in accord with relevant laws and regulations. The No. 4 Subway line in Beijing is a 'licensing-type' form of PPP model. The government itself is responsible for setting ticket prices, and also has regulatory authority over the business.

Creating an 'investment fund' for building infrastructure

Two different kinds of such investment funds have appeared in recent years. In one, the government puts up the funding, and takes in private participation and allows private management. In the other, the private sector puts up the funding, and also operates the business. Both forms have two roles with respect to investing in basic infrastructure. First, they serve a 'balancing function' in funding. The private sector supplements investment by the government, and is thereby able to create a greater net asset value with which to leverage the amount of debt. Second, the professional nature and profit-oriented nature of the model help 'rate' the amount of risk in a given project. This frequently enables such projects to engage directly in the capital markets.

China has institutional investors with funds that are appropriate for investing in 'basic infrastructure funds'. Such funds are in line with the needs of things like insurance companies and social security pools, since they are long-term investments with fairly stable returns. This kind of institutional investor in China has considerable 'real strength' and is indeed quite interested in such infrastructure projects.

In April 2009, the China Insurance Regulatory Commission relaxed previous restrictions on insurance companies by allowing them to invest in basic infrastructure projects. By June 2009, insurance companies had invested some RMB 75 billion in basic infrastructure projects. Another positive aspect of such 'infrastructure funds' is that they help disperse risk through professional portfolio management, which increases the security of the invested funds.

Project financing

In this model, the sponsor of a project sets up a company for both the financing and operation of the project. The cash flow and earnings of the project company are what pay off the source of funding. The collateral used for the loan, or other form of funding, comes from the assets of the project itself or from the authority invested in the project to undertake a given business. The method involves a loan that is either 'without recourse' or 'with limited right of recourse'. In the international arena, such project financing is mainly used for engineering projects that require massive amounts of funding or are highly risky. At the outset, they are therefore unsuited to conventional types of financing, yet on completion their revenue stream is quite stable. Such endeavors include large-scale development of natural gas, coal, oil, and other natural resources. They include major construction projects in the fields of transport, electricity, agriculture, forestry, electronics, and some public utilities.

Asset securitization

Although the various forms of financing as described above can help relieve the pressure on banks in a given city or region to finance all basic infrastructure, at present banks are already faced with a considerable amount of existing risk in their loan portfolios. Such risk still needs to be dispersed and asset securitization can help in this regard.

This mode of financing basic infrastructure can take the following two forms in actual application.

The first involves asset securitization of for-profit projects. This method is already being applied in China, and involves using the cash flow of the project for repayment of principal and interest. An example is the Nanjing Urban Construction project for sewage treatment. The company has been licensed to treat sewage for the next four years, and fees to be earned from that business serve as the pricing mechanism for setting the 'basic asset'. RMB 721 million worth of 'earnings vouchers' have been issued on the basis of this underlying asset. The earnings vouchers come in four different term limits, from one year to four years. The predicted yield on the vouchers ranges between 2.9 per cent and 3.9 per cent. Essentially, this model of financing enables an enterprise to have up-front access to a stream of future earnings. It allows fees that will be earned from sewage treatment to substitute for interest on bank loans. In effect, the funds are reinvested in the Nanjing Urban Construction company so that it can provide the service.

International experience shows that the benefits of private infrastructure funds can be combined with rational use of asset securitization. This speeds up the 'asset cycle', or the rate at which the same asset can be put to use again. It increases the potential size of investment and raises the return on infrastructure funds. It thereby stimulates their sound development. In a certain sense, the two practices – infrastructure funds and asset securitization – complement and enhance each other.

The second form of asset securitization involves securitizing loans made for developing infrastructure. The principal and interest on the loan are what give rise to the securitization. When used appropriately, this can be effective in dispersing the massive amount of risk that banks have built up in the course of financing infrastructure.

Since the onset of the recent financial crisis, people have been leery about such 'derivative projects' as asset securitization. Nevertheless, looked at objectively, what the financial crisis has taught us is the need to strengthen regulation and self-discipline. It does not indicate that we should throw out all financial innovations. This is particularly true of China, where financial innovation is in its infancy, and not excessive. In the USA, the rate of securitizing housing mortgages has gone as high as 68 per cent. In China, the rate is a mere 0.3 per cent. In the future, there is still considerable margin left in this country to employ securitization methods.

Note

1 Due to the lack of statistical data, the data about urban infrastructures in this chapter cover cities at the county, prefecture, and higher levels, but exclude small county cities and administrative towns.

8 A 'green path' toward urbanization

Urban functions started to undergo a fundamental shift once industrialization began. On the one hand, cities now became the major locale of production that was concentrated in one place. On the other, they retained their former role of concentrating the lives and consumption of people in one place. Diversifying city functions brought not only a rapid expansion of urban clusters and a dramatic increase in the size of cities themselves but also a change in social patterns. Modern cities became the most important source of and a major generator of wealth.

In the course of urbanization in general, the use of energy and resources increases, together with a consequent increase in the emission of pollutants. This can lead to environmental degradation and harm to ecosystems. At the same time, the process of urbanization also involves a more intensive use of resources. These are used more efficiently, clean production technologies develop, and cities themselves provide the opportunity to find new solutions to resource shortages and environmental problems.

[Cities therefore are both the cause of pollution and one solution for dealing with pollution. This chapter discusses how dealing with urban pollution should be approached in China.]

The environmental challenges faced by China in the course of its urbanization

A variety of factors can cause environmental pollution as economic activities and people increasingly concentrate in cities. Polluted water comes from industry and the daily lives of people; solid waste and polluting emissions increase tremendously from both industrial and residential uses. The intensity of physical pollutants generally exceeds the ability of nature to decompose and disperse them. In addition to these, however, are the noise pollution from cars and other vehicles, the visual pollution of the masses of glass and metal used in urban buildings, and the light pollution from illumination.

Polluting effects are not limited to what is above ground, however. The earth's surface ecology itself changes with the intensive use of water and resources. Ecological systems in and around cities are made more vulnerable.

Environmental pollution and a deteriorating ecology negatively affect people's sense of their quality of life, impacting not only on the health and lives of urban residents but also on the well-being of the neighboring countryside and indeed the entire country.

Water pollution

Per capita water resources are already quite limited in China, but the situation is made worse as water pollution of China's various bodies of water intensifies. By now, and for the past decade or so, per capita water resources have equaled a mere 2100 cubic meters or so. The southern and central parts of the country have fairly abundant rainfall, but many cities in these areas have now been declared to be 'water-deficient' – the reason being that environmental pollution has polluted most of the surface water.

China has seven large water systems that contain 203 rivers with their drainage basins. The seven are the Yangtze River, the Yellow River, the Pearl River, the Songhua River, the Huaihe River, the Haihe River, and the Liaohe River. In 2009, 408 surface monitoring stations measured the water quality of these river systems and found that 25.7 per cent had to be rated 'Grade V' or 'Grade V-minus'. Water pollution problems were most pronounced in the Haihe, Liaohe, and Huaihe river systems.

In the Haihe River basin, the emission of chemical oxygen demand (COD) was found to exceed 150 million tons in the year 2005. Eleven cities accounted for 65 per cent of this problem in the Haihe River basin, cities that included Beijing, Tianjin, and Shijiazhuang. Of the COD emissions of 'key industrial enterprises', 70 per cent could be traced to five specific industries, namely paper and paper products, industrial chemicals and chemical products, food processing, pharmaceuticals, and textiles (according to the 11th Five-Year Plan for Water Pollution Control in the Haihe River Basin).

Meanwhile, in the middle and upper reaches of the Yellow River, 10 cities have been found to be responsible for 72 per cent of all COD emissions in the overall Yellow River drainage system. These are Xining, Lanzhou, Baotou, Yinchuan, Taiyuan, Baoji, Xianyang, Xi'an, Luoyang, and Hohhot. Five industries emit 90 per cent of all COD and 80 per cent of all ammonia and nitrogen: the industrial chemicals and chemical products industry, oil processing and coking, paper and paper products, food processing and food manufacturing (according to the 11th Five-Year Plan for Water Pollution Control in the Middle and Upper Reaches of the Yellow River).

Compared with the above two drainage systems, the water quality of the Pearl River and Yangtze River basins is better, although some river sections close to cities also have water-quality ratings of less than Grade V in the dry season.

Waste-water discharge has been constantly increasing in recent years in China (Table 8.2). The main cause of this has been increasing waste-water discharge of households in cities. In 2000, the discharged quantity came to 41.5 billion tons, but by 2008 the figure had risen to 57.1 billion tons, an increase over eight years of 38 per cent. In the past 10 years, more than 50 per cent of all discharged waste water can be attributed to urban households, and this percentage is on the rise. It was 53.3 per cent in 2000, and had reached 57.7 per cent in 2008.

Fairly good results have come from attempts to control the amount of waste water discharged by industry. Between 2005 and 2008, the total quantity remained steady at around 24 billion tons, and it even saw slight declines in 2006 and 2008. Discharges from urban households continue to increase at a fast pace, however, with annual increases since 2003 averaging in excess of 6 per cent. One point of particular concern is that there is a declining trend in the efficiency of water use among urban residents in recent years. In 2000, there was 38.4 tons of waste water for every 100 tons of water used by urban households. By 2008, this figure had gone up to 45.2 tons.

If we cannot improve the efficiency with which water is used, and improve sewage treatment levels, China's water shortage problem is going to become even more severe as China's urban population increases.

Air pollution

Urban air pollution in China is severe. China uses coal as its primary source of energy. This means that air pollution mainly comes from the particulates and sulfur dioxide resulting from the burning of coal in both industrial production

Table 8.1 China's waste-water discharge

	2000	2002	2004	2006	2008
Per capita water resource possession (m³)	2193.9	2207.2	1856.3	1932.1	2071.1
Waste water discharge (100 million tons)	415.0	439.0	482.0	536.9	571.6
Industrial sewer (100 million tons)	194.0	207.0	221.0	240.2	241.6
Household sewer (100 million tons)	221.0	232.0	261.0	296.6	330.0
Waste water growth rate (%)	3.5	1.4	5.0	2.4	2.7
Industrial sewer growth rate (%)	−1.5	2.0	4.2	−1.2	−2.0
Household sewer growth rate (%)	8.3	0.9	5.7	5.4	6.4
Household sewer/waste water discharge (%)	53.3	52.8	54.1	55.2	57.7
Household sewer/household water-use (%)	38.4	37.5	40.1	42.8	45.2

Source: The 2000–2006 data originate from the *China Chemical Industry Yearbook 2008* (Volume 24, 2); the 2008 data originate from the *China Statistical Yearbook 2009*.

Note: China's statistics on household sewer discharge include urban household sewer only.

and the daily lives of citizens (the monitoring indicator of particulates is the density of inhalable PM_{10}, that is, particulate matter smaller than 10 micrometres) (Kan Haidong, 2008). Starting in the 1990s, the Chinese government began to put major effort into controlling the air pollution caused by both industry and daily life. Since 2001, smoke emissions have been reduced by 21 per cent and dust emissions have been reduced by 40 per cent.

In recent years, good progress has been made in lowering sulfur dioxide emissions on a nationwide basis. Sulfur dioxide emissions began to decline in total quantity after the year 2006: emissions in 2006 were 223.762 million tons, and by 2008 had declined to 199.137 million tons (Table 8.2). In overall terms, however, China still ranks among the top emitters of sulfur dioxide in the world.

Ownership of cars began to rise rapidly in China's cities after the 1990s, which meant that motor vehicle exhaust became a major new source of air pollution. By 2007, vehicle emissions were accounting for 60–70 per cent of total emissions of carbon monoxide and 20–40 per cent of total emissions of nitrogen oxides in China's larger cities, such as Beijing, Guangzhou, and Shanghai (Ma Tao, 2007).

Production and sale of motor vehicles in China broke through the historic '10-million' mark in 2009, and forecasts indicate that this trend will continue for a fairly long time to come. The International Energy Agency [IEA] and the World Business Council for Sustainable Development have developed plans for the control of nitrogen oxides arising from 'automobile-ification'. These indicate that, by the more conservative estimates, the number of vehicles on the road in China will increase by 72 per cent in the decade between 2005 and 2015, and that the nitrogen oxide emissions from light vehicles alone will increase by 35 per cent.

The industrial discharge of waste gases and motor vehicle exhaust emissions are having a severe impacting on air quality in China's cities. In 2008, air quality in 18 out of China's 31 provincial capitals reached Grade II for only 90 per cent of days in the year. Air quality in Beijing, Hefei, Lanzhou, and Urumqi reached that level for only 80 per cent of days in the year. Fourteen cities did not come up to standards for acceptable inhalation of particulates (which in China is 'National Grade 2 standard', with average annual PM_{10} density being below 0.10 mg/m³). Not a single city came up to National Grade 1 standard, with average annual PM_{10} density being below 0.04 mg/m³. Only 72 per cent of China's cities attained density levels of Grade 2 standard or above, according to the 2007 report entitled *The State of China's Environment*, put out by the Ministry of Environmental Protection. That means that 28 per cent of China's cities are below standard in terms of particulate density. Some twenty provinces, municipalities, and autonomous regions are polluted to a 'fairly heavy degree', including Sichuan, Beijing, and Shanxi.

Solid-waste pollution

Solid waste pollution of cities and their surrounding areas is also increasing rapidly with the ongoing process of urbanization and industrialization. The problem has

Table 8.2 China's emission of main air pollutants in recent years (in units of 10,000 tons)

Year	Sulfur dioxide			Smoke and dust			Industry	Nitrogen oxides		
	Total	Industry	Household	Total	Industry	Household	Smoke and dust	Total	Industry	Household
2001	1947.8	1566.6	381.2	1069.8	851.9	217.9	990.6	—	—	—
2002	1926.6	1562	364.6	1012.7	804.2	208.5	941	—	—	—
2003	2158.7	1791.4	367.3	1048.7	846.2	202.5	1021	—	—	—
2004	2254.9	1891.4	363.5	1094.9	886.5	208.4	904.8	—	—	—
2005	2549.3	2168.4	380.9	1182.5	948.9	233.6	911.2	—	—	—
2006	2588.8	2237.6	351.2	1088.8	864.5	224.3	808.4	1523.8	1136	387.8
2007	2468.1	2140	328.1	986.6	771.1	215.5	698.7	1643.4	1261.3	382
2008	2321.2	1991.3	329.9	901.6	670.7	230.9	584.9	1624.5	1250.5	374
Growth rate	−6%	−6.9%	0.5%	−8.6%	−13%	7.1%	−16.3%	−1.2%	−0.9%	−2.1%

Source: *China Environmental Statistical Yearbooks 2004, 2006, and 2008.*

Note: China began to include nitrogen oxides emission in statistics and the household emission includes the nitrogen oxides from transportation.

now become a direct threat to urban environments and ecosystems. Not only do the large numbers of massive garbage heaps use up land, but they are polluting the underground water of cities as well as their air.

China currently produces 150 million tons of urban garbage every year and that amount is growing at an annual rate of 10 per cent, according to the *Report on the Investment Analysis and Forecast for China's Garbage Treatment Industry 2009–2012*. As this report reveals, China now contains 7 billion tons of household-waste garbage.

Beijing serves as a good example. By 2008, the city was producing 18,400 tons of household-related garbage per day. It was producing 6.72 million tons per year, and the amount continues to increase at a ferocious pace. This is causing an acute problem given that garbage treatment locations in the city are inadequate. Beijing currently has 23 garbage treatment plants, which can process 10,400 tons per day. Over a period ending in 2010, the city had to close down 10 plants due to outdated equipment. At the current rate at which garbage is increasing in Beijing, the city will be facing the problem of having no place at all to dump garbage within the next five years.

It is worth noting that Beijing is not the only city facing this dire situation. The same conditions prevail in other cities.

The World Bank carried out a study on China's future population growth that contained a forecast for solid waste production in cities by the year 2030 (Table 8.3). According to this forecast, if the urban population in China is 880 million in the year 2030, and if each person produces an average of 1.2 kilograms of waste matter per day, as a conservative estimate, then 390 million tons of solid waste will be produced in China's cities every year.

If each person in fact uses around 1.8 kilograms of waste matter per day, on average, then a total of 580 million tons will be produced in one year. The two scenarios differ by a total annual amount of around 200 million tons of garbage. When considering that China may well urbanize faster than World Bank predictions in the next twenty years, if the higher scenario becomes reality and if urban garbage treatment capacity remains weak, China's cities will be ringed with piles of garbage. This does not exaggerate the situation.

Greenhouse-gas emissions

Greenhouse gases, such as carbon dioxide, methane, and others, produce a special kind of environmental pollution. Such gases are seen as a primary cause of the global warming that has been occurring since the start of the industrial era. Global attention is now focusing on the impact that such pollution has on the human environment and on sustainable development. The subject, moreover, is becoming a new point of contention in international politics and economics.

In the decade between 1992 and 2001, the increase in China's carbon dioxide emissions slowed down in relative terms, but in 2002 they began to increase at a faster rate, which was highly noticeable. In the five years between 2002 and 2006, China's annual emissions went from 3.4 billion tons to 6 billion tons. By now,

Table 8.3 World Bank forecast of China's production of urban solid wastes

Year	Projected urban population (1,000s)	Low waste production		Projected waste growth		High waste production	
		Production rate (kg/person/day)	Urban solid-waste production (tons)	Growth rate (kg/person/day)	Urban solid-waste production (tons)	Production rate (kg/person/day)	Urban solid-waste production (tons)
2000	456,340	0.90	149,907,690	0.90	149,907,690	0.90	149,907,690
2005	535,958	0.95	185,843,437	1.00	195,624,670	1.10	215,187,137
2010	617,348	1.00	225,332,020	1.10	247,865,222	1.30	292,931,626
2015	698,077	1.05	267,538,101	1.20	305,757,726	1.50	382,197,158
2020	771,861	1.10	309,902,192	1.30	366,248,045	1.60	450,766,824
2025	834,295	1.15	350,195,326	1.40	426,324,745	1.70	517,680,048
2030	883,421	1.20	386,938,398	1.50	483,672,998	1.80	580,407,597

Source: World Bank: *China's Solid Wastes Management: Problems and Options*, 2005.

the country may well have surpassed the USA in becoming the world's largest emitter of greenhouse gases.

It must be said that even though China's emissions of greenhouse gases are massive in total terms, in per capita terms, the country's emissions are just beginning to approach average levels in the world. They are far below those of developed countries (UNDP, 2010). Data from the World Bank indicate that in 2006 China's per capita emissions of carbon dioxide were 4.65 tons. This was just 24.5 per cent of what they were in the USA and less than one-half of those in the UK, Germany, and Japan.

It is also worth pointing out that part of the reason China's emissions have risen so rapidly is that its factories are producing cheap manufactured goods for export to the West. Among all goods exported in 2008, 70 per cent were labour-intensive and resource-intensive products, and more than 50 per cent were processed goods for export. A research report prepared by the Tyndall Centre for Climate Change Research and the Sussex Energy Group indicates that 23 per cent of China's total carbon dioxide emissions stemmed from net exports (Wang and Watson, 2007).[1] As China's net exports have increased rapidly since 2004, the percentage of its greenhouse-gas emissions from net exports has also increased.

Cities hold the main concentrations of non-agricultural industry in China. The industrial sector accounts for as much as 84 per cent of China's emissions of carbon dioxide. Per unit of GDP, industry is also a much greater emitter than are agriculture or the service industries. According to sector analysis undertaken by the International Energy Agency, emissions from electric power generation and heat generation account for nearly one-half of China's total carbon dioxide emissions. Manufacturing and construction adds another 31.2 per cent, while transport accounts for 6.8 per cent of carbon dioxide emissions and the emissions from residential consumption in general account for 4.2 per cent (Figure 8.1).

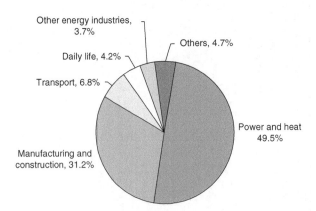

Figure 8.1 Comparison of carbon dioxide emission between China's industrial sectors.
Source: IEA (2009).

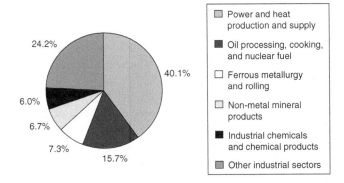

Figure 8.2 Carbon dioxide emissions of China's main industrial sectors.
Source: *China Energy Statistical Yearbook 2008.*

According to China's own industrial classification, the top five emitters of carbon dioxide in China are the electric power and heat generation and supply industry, the oil refining, steel refining, and nuclear fuel production industry, the ferrous metals industry, and the industrial chemicals and chemical products industry (Figure 8.3). These five major industries account for more than 75 per cent of all industrial carbon dioxide emissions in China (UNDP, 2010).

The amount of 'consumption' by people who live in cities is far higher in general than it is in rural areas in China. The very fact of urban lifestyles is going to become a severe challenge to energy conservation and the reduction of green-house-gas emissions in the future.

In 2008, per capita consumer expenditures in cities in China reached RMB 11,243, while in the countryside the figure was RMB 3661. Urbanites consumed three times as much as rural residents. In terms of certain key consumption items, the differential is even greater. In 2008, each hundred urban residents owned on average 8.83 cars, 100.28 air conditioners, and 93.63 refrigerators. In this same year, each hundred rural residents owned an average of 1 car, 9.82 air conditioners, and 30.19 refrigerators. Even though the percentage of greenhouse-gas emissions currently derived from household consumption is relatively low, only 4.2 per cent, in the end, all industrial products are transformed into consumption, and consumption drives production.

The tremendous gap in consumption levels between urban and rural residents in China means that a fairly large percentage of greenhouse gases are in fact emitted in the end by urban residents. 'Urbanization' means that both production and consumption increasingly concentrate in cities. Whether or not China will be able to control greenhouse-gas emissions effectively in the course of its urbanization is one of the questions the country urgently needs to address.

The effect of environmental pollution on economic development

The primary causes of urban environmental pollution and the degradation of ecosystems include such things as unconstrained use of resources, irrational urban planning, inadequate treatment facilities for pollutants, and the lack of adequate environmental controls.

Environmental pollution and deteriorating ecosystems not only constrain the human development of people living in the cities themselves, but also people at a distance from the cities. Environmental pollution has a 'public service nature' to it, in that it affects the well-being of everyone, including regions surrounding the city, the entire country, and indeed all of humankind.

The negative impact of environmental pollution is multi-faceted, when it comes to affecting human development (Liu Minquan and Yu Jiantuo, 2010). First, environmental pollution causes an increase in the incidence of such diseases as cancer, cardiovascular disease, and respiratory disease. It damages the health of the human organism. Second, mitigating the problems caused by environmental pollution often must be done at extremely high cost. Third, environmental pollution and deteriorating ecosystems reduce the rate at which resources necessary to economic development can be accessed. Fourth, the inequality with which environmental pollution affects different groups of people severely damages the equity of a country's economic development, since poor people generally do not contribute as much to creating pollution, yet are the ones most directly and severely affected by it.

Figure 8.3 shows the cost of mitigating environmental pollution in China, using data from the *China Statistical Yearbook* for 2009. Between 2004 and 2008, the annual cost of mitigating or 'dealing with' environmental pollution went from RMB 190 billion to close to RMB 450 billion. This investment in

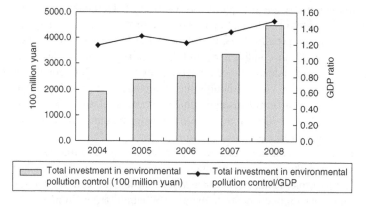

Figure 8.3 China's growing environmental control investment.
Source: *China Statistical Yearbook 2009.*

mitigation went from 1.19 per cent of China's GDP in 2004 to 1.49 per cent in 2008 (Figure 8.3).

The economic and social price that must be paid for environmental pollution is extremely heavy. According to estimates made by China's Ministry of Environmental Protection, total economic losses to the country as a result of environmental pollution in 2004 came to RMB 511.8 billion, which was 3.05 per cent of GDP in that year. The imputed abatement costs, that is, the costs to be expended for abatement of all the pollutants discharged into the environment in the light of current pollution control technologies, came to RMB 287.4 billion, which was 1.8 per cent of GDP in that year. Among these costs, those incurred by damage from water pollution came to RMB 286.3 billion, or over one-half of all costs associated with environmental damage.

Costs incurred by air pollution reached RMB 220 billion. Seventy percent of this was attributed to health costs to urban residents. All of these figures show that the very real costs of environmental pollution are at a stage that can no longer be ignored.

Climate change is also an extremely pressing challenge. China's industrialization and urbanization is primarily based along the east coast. Rising sea levels brought on by the greenhouse effect may well impact upon China's choices when it comes to the site selection of urban areas. It may well also impact upon urban planning, disaster prevention and mitigation, and the setting up of emergency relief systems (Pan Jiahua: *Background Report, 2009*).

The costs of environmental pollution and deteriorating ecosystems are generally distributed unevenly over different demographic groups. To take greenhouse gases as an example, impoverished people and other more vulnerable groups who are situated in places where ecosystems are fragile are more easily affected by the natural disasters that are caused by climate change, climate change that is itself induced by greenhouse-gas emissions. Impoverished groups of people generally have access to fewer of such public services as education and healthcare. Their living conditions are poor, their basic facilities are primitive, and as a result they are less able to deal with the risks brought on by climate change.

The environmental and resource challenges facing China's process of urbanization

In contrast to the way more developed countries were able to urbanize, China's process of urbanization is being done at a time of far more intense environmental and resource challenges. This is due to the combined effects of a host of factors, including the speed and scale at which China is urbanizing, its level of technology as it does so, and the structure and underlying system of its economy.

First, as this Report has already described, China is currently engaged in very rapid urbanization and industrialization. Industrial production, the building of urban infrastructure, and consumption by both urban and rural citizens are all increasing at a fast pace. In objective terms, this creates steep increases in natural-resource use and also in greenhouse-gas emissions. In addition, however, the scale at which China is urbanizing is so massive that it is unique in the history of the world. These combined elements – speed and scale of urbanization – mean that the country is facing a number of 'rigid constraints' in terms of natural resource and energy consumption.

China constructs more buildings every year than any other country on earth. It adds more than two billion square meters of building area to existing construction every year. This takes up roughly 43 per cent of the world's entire annual use of cement, and 35 per cent of the world's annual use of steel (Qiu Baoxing, 2009). What's more, China's consumption of these materials is growing at a pace that is faster than the world average. For the next 20–30 years, the accelerating pace at which China is using resources is expected to continue.

Second, China's energy consumption and its discharge of pollutants are excessive due to its mode of production. This is 'extensive', as opposed to intensive, and uses outdated technology on a widespread basis. In 2006, China used up more than 9 'tce' (tons of coal equivalent) per every 10,000-dollar unit of GDP, at current exchange rates. This was 2.7 times the world's average level. It was 3.7 times the level of tce required in the USA, 5.4 times that of Japan, 1.4 times that of India, and 3.3 times that of Brazil.

The power industry can serve as an example. At the end of 2009, one-third of China's thermal power generators were still operating at low capacity, that is, below 300,000 kilowatt-hours. China's thermal power generators currently consume coal at the rate of 370 grams for each kilowatt-hour of energy produced. This is 40 grams higher than the world average, and 90–100 grams higher than the most advanced generators in the world.

In 2005, China was using 40 per cent more energy on average to produce primary industrial products than the average required by advanced countries. Such products included those in the power, iron and steel, ferrous metals, petrochemical, building materials, chemical, and textile industries and in light industry. In terms of specific industries, the amount of coal that China required for thermal power generation was 22.5 per cent higher, the country's 'comparable energy consumption' for steel production by large and medium-sized steel enterprises was 21.4 per cent higher, its 'comprehensive energy consumption' for copper smelting 65 per cent higher, that for cement production 45.3 per cent higher, that for large ammonia synthesis 31.2 per cent higher, and that for paper and paperboard 120 per cent higher.

In addition, the fuel efficiency of China's motorized vehicles [in 2005] was, on average, 25 per cent lower than that in Europe, 20 per cent lower than that in Japan, and 10 per cent lower than that in the USA. Fuel consumption by trucks was more than twice what was being used by more advanced countries – per 100 kilometers, China's trucks consumed an average of 7.6 liters of fuel (Ni Weidou, 2007).

Third, China's environmental problems are intimately related to the structure of its economy at this specific stage of the country's development. In 2008, secondary industries still constituted 48.6 per cent of China's total GDP. The industrial sector still accounted for nearly 43 per cent of total output. Industry and construction are, by nature, energy-intensive. This means that these sectors contribute to particularly high levels of carbon dioxide emissions.

Fourth, the structure of energy use in China is such that the country still relies heavily on coal. This is another reason greenhouse gas and pollutant levels are high. Compared with coal, natural gas and petroleum generate far less carbon dioxide per unit of thermal energy. Natural gas puts out only around 60 per cent of the carbon dioxide emitted by burning coal, per unit of the resulting thermal energy.

In 2008, the structure of primary energy use in China was as follows: 68.7 per cent coal, 18.7 per cent oil, 3.8 per cent natural gas, and 8.9 per cent 'other', including hydropower, nuclear power, and wind power. In that same year, the structure of energy use in the world at large was: 25.5 per cent coal, 37.4 per cent oil, 24.3 per cent natural gas, and 12.8 per cent 'other', including hydropower, nuclear power, and wind power.

Nearly 70 per cent of the coal that China burns every year is unprocessed and is burned directly as raw coal. The resulting carbon dioxide emissions and discharge of smoke particles contribute between 70 per cent and 80 per cent to China's total emissions. The acid rain caused by carbon dioxide emissions in China is already falling on roughly one-third of the country's land mass. The structure of energy use in China therefore creates an extremely grave problem when it comes to the ability to control greenhouse-gas emissions and other pollutants.

Fifth, China needs to go further in improving its pricing mechanisms for energy and resources. The country's economy has been shifting from a planned-economy system towards a market-economy system since the late 1970s, and the market has supplanted state planning as the main mode by which resources are allocated. This has enabled the economy to achieve monumental success in terms of overall development.

Nevertheless, the process of market-oriented reform has not sufficiently penetrated the realm of resources and the environment. For example, the supply of heating, water, and electricity in China's cities still bears the profound stamp of the 'welfare society' that prevailed during the country's planned-economy period. Prices for these services are set at an artificially low level, which means that provision of these goods and services does not adequately reflect their costs. This is detrimental to conserving resources through more conscious use of them.

Meanwhile, the environment, with its attributes of being a 'public good', lacks any clear demarcation of 'ownership' in that nobody 'owns' it. As a result, nobody is responsible for taking care of it. The absence of management in this regard – what is called the 'vacant position' with respect to management and accountability – has led to an inability to internalize the very real social costs of the way in which environmental services are used.

Not only has the above led to waste in the process of producing and consuming resources, but in addition China maintains 'administrative-type' monopolies in the spheres of resource and energy production. This has also contributed to waste.

A sixth problem, which increasingly constitutes a 'rigid constraint' on China's plans to urbanize, is the overall vulnerability of the globe's environment as well as China's own highly vulnerable ecosystem. China currently ranks first in the world in carbon dioxide emissions, sulfur dioxide emissions, and solid-waste emissions. The ecosystem of the globe has a limited ability to absorb and decompose these pollutants, while China's own ecosystem is by now highly fragile. This intensifies the problem of the country's lack of resources and creates a rigid constraint on its future urbanization.

Water resources are a prime example. Right now, more than 400 of China's 600-plus cities are experiencing water shortages to one degree or another, while 108 of these cities are experiencing severe water shortages. Excessive extraction of underground water in some places is causing the problem of land subsidence. On the plains of Henan province, for example, the rate at which water is being 'overly extracted' exceeds 40 per cent, which is leading to funnel-shaped sinking areas under 11 cities. These include [the major cities] of Zhengzhou, Kaifeng, Jiaozuo, and Pingdingshan. The total area affected comes to 1247.18 square kilometers.

Inadequate water resources, and the fact that the topography of existing cities is already being changed, is going to impact upon the functioning of these cities ever more seriously in the future.

In addition to the six factors listed above, other objective considerations prevent adequate environmental protection and resource conservation. These include low investment in environmental protection, weak basic infrastructure in cities to begin with, in terms of the environment, and limited capacity to administer any kind of environmental protection.

Right now, China spends less than 1.5 per cent of its GDP on environmental protection. This is far below the average level of OECD countries. Garbage-treatment and sewage-treatment capacities are extremely limited in China's cities. By 2008, the rate of centralized sewage treatment in China's cities, nationwide, came to only around 55 per cent. The rate of detoxification of garbage came to only 70 per cent.

In addition, however, many of China's environmental standards are low compared with international standards. Air pollution is one example. World Health Organization standards recommend that particulate densities (PM_{10} density in the air) not exceed 20 micrograms per cubic meter. China's national standard for 'Grade 1 air quality', however, allows for 'no more than 40 micrograms per cubic meter'. Moreover, supervisory regulation over environmental issues, and capacity to enforce regulations, is poor. This enables the rampant practice of excessive and illegal emissions by both enterprises and individuals.

Faced with the above challenges, the Chinese government is right now in the process of taking action and formulating a series of proactive policy measures. The 11th Five-Year Plan of the People's Republic of China for Economic and Social Development (2006–2010), for example, includes a series of environmental measures and energy-saving standards as part of what it calls a 'major strategic mission' to 'create an environmentally friendly and conservation-oriented society'. This Plan sets forth the goal of lowering energy consumption in 2010 to 80 per cent of what it was in 2005. Total carbon demand (COD) and sulfur dioxide emissions in 2010 are to be 10 per cent less than what they were in 2005. Moreover, it is noteworthy that standards set forth in the 11th Five-Year Plan are no longer put forth as 'guiding standards' but are now considered to be 'binding'.

On the eve of the 2009 Copenhagen Climate Summit, China went further in announcing that carbon dioxide emissions per unit of GDP would be reduced by the year 2020 by between 40 and 45 per cent from what they were in 2005.

China has intensified its development efforts with respect to clean-energy technologies in recent years. It has been proactive in mothballing outdated production methods. By the end of 2007, the country's hydroelectric power-generating capacity came to 145 million kilowatts and its annual power generation reached 482.9 billion kilowatt-hours. Both of these capacities ranked first in the world. New generating capacity in both 2006 and 2007 rose by an average 26 million kilowatts, for an annual growth rate of 12 per cent.

In the meantime, however, in 2007, the country closed down small thermal power-generating plants totaling 14.38 million kilowatts in capacity, and got rid of outdated iron smelters totaling 46.59 million tons in capacity. It closed outdated steel-smelting mills totaling 37.47 million tons in capacity, and outdated cement plants totaling 52.99 million tons in capacity. In all, it closed down more than 2000 paper mills that did not conform to policies regulating that industry and that were causing serious pollution. It also closed a number of chemical, printing, and dyeing enterprises that were causing severe pollution. In addition, the country closed down 11,200 small coal mines.

In addition to the above efforts, China has introduced a profusion of laws and regulations concerned with environmental protection and resource conservation. These put major investment into reforestation and the building up of basic environmental infrastructure. It can be said that policies and measures have garnered positive results in many different ways and have laid an initial foundation for proceeding along a 'green path' toward urbanization.

Striving for 'green' urbanization

The process of urbanization enables possibilities for more intensive and efficient use of resources. A mode of development that calls for concentrating people and industry in cities has the potential for greater resource efficiency than one in which people and industries are dispersed, even at the same standard of living. Going from 'potential' to 'realized' efficiencies is not something that happens all on its own, however. Success depends upon a whole series of factors, including the market, policies, and technology.

Faced with environmental constraints and increasingly tight resources, China has no alternative but to do all it can to achieve a 'green path' to urbanization. This involves learning the lessons derived from other developing countries and developed countries as they themselves urbanized. It includes accelerating the transformation of the country's mode of development and economic structure. It means making the process of urbanization more 'compact' and 'intensive', through striving for 'an environmentally friendly, human-habitable, resource-conserving' kind of urbanization.

'Green urbanization' is a concept that integrates a whole suite of factors. These include such multi-layered considerations as low carbon usage, a recycling-style economy, preserving necessary open space, balancing human-oriented and ecosystem-oriented needs, and making cities habitable. The underlying core concept involves a 'new style' of urbanization that uses 'scientific development in an all-round way' to serve 'human development'. In recent years, broadly based experiments, plans, and measures have been undertaken that try to realize this 'green path to urbanization'. A variety of things are being explored that conform to the needs for urbanization as described above (see Box 8.1).

Box 8.1 Green urban design

The concept of 'green urban design' began to develop rapidly after the 1970s on a global basis. China began to promote the concept extensively after moving into the twenty-first century, as both the Central government and local governments advocated for 'green' development. At present, more than 100 cities in the country are creating 'green cities' on various levels, from 'green cities' (urban districts) to 'ecological cities' (urban districts), to 'low-carbon cities' (urban districts).

Tianjin's New Coastal District ['Binhai District'] is one of these. It will incorporate the concept of green design into its regional development plans as it builds nine industrial zones in the form of a 'model green city'.

This will be an ecological-type industrial zone with the highest environmental standards in the country, and it will be the largest such zone in the country. Emphasis will be placed on new-energy development and new materials production. The 'airport industrial zone' will focus on the development of environmentally friendly aerospace products, and will become a 'model zone' for developing applications for and then producing green aerospace technologies.

The Nangang Industrial Zone ['Southern Harbor Zone'] will focus on the 'industrial chain' involved in developing recycling systems for waste materials. It will be setting up a world-class petrochemical base. The Lingang Industrial Zone ['Near the Harbor'], and the Haigang Logistical Zone ['Harbor Zone'] will focus on manufacturing energy-saving and environmentally friendly equipment. This will become a key concentration of environmental equipment manufacturing in the country. Three areas, the Central Tianjin Ecological City, the Central Business District, and the Binhai Tourist Zone, will be flagship areas for the country in terms of how they combine high-end industrial development with an environment that has 'virtuous ecological cycles' and is human-habitable.

Meanwhile, the entire area will be setting up an information platform for 'green cities'. This will be issuing information on a regular basis that provides alerts on such things as industrial policy, development plans, investment priorities, economic performance, and market demand. The service is intended to encourage small and medium-sized enterprises that are leaders in their field to become a part of a strong and vigorous 'low-carbon economy'. The aim is to improve industrial links and consolidate low-carbon-economy industries.

Source: *'10+3 Media' enter Tianjin's Binhai New District to feel green city*, People's Net: www.022net.com/2010/4-26/524622362589536.html.

[Based on the above considerations, this Report makes the following recommendations.]

1 Promote a model for urban development that is sustainable. Support processes that conserve resources and save energy

China's per capita availability of many important resources is quite low and its distribution of resources is highly uneven. In addition, the country's ecosystem is already fragile, which means that each region's urbanization plans must be aligned with the specifics of that region and with the carrying capacity of its ecosystem. The 'positioning' of urban development should be explicitly defined. It should have targeted goals, in order to control the way in which urban concentrations develop. It is imperative that we avoid the environmental problems that arise when individual cities sprawl outwards in linked 'belts'.

In addressing the 'energy flows' and the logistics of cities, priority should be given to daily lives of people as well as industrial and agricultural production. We should plan transport systems and the construction of buildings accordingly. We should re-examine our policies to do with automobile consumption and housing. We cannot afford to copy models for urban development being practiced in developed countries. We must limit irrational consumption of energy and resources – in cities that have already grown to a certain size, we must do our utmost to lessen the impact of urbanization on the local environment.

2 Make the environment an explicit responsibility of all levels of government. Governments at all levels must be the primary entities responsible for environmental protection. We should therefore strengthen the administrative capacities of municipal governments vis-à-vis environmental affairs

China should set up a performance-evaluation system for rating the performance of government officials that incorporates environmental considerations.

Criteria would include meeting standards for pollution control, emissions reduction, for improvement of environmental quality, and for meeting indicators that measure 'green GDP'. The environmental protection standards by which performance is judged should be binding. Moreover, in cities with severe environmental degradation, a system should be set up for very stringent environmental protection that includes 'one-vote veto power' and 'elimination' processes.

Environmental impact assessments should be conducted both in the course of urban planning and in implementation. All levels of government should ensure that their public finance spending gives priority to environmental infrastructure. Responsibilities of the primary entities that provide government funding should be clearly defined. The government must first guarantee that spending on environmental protection will not be lower than specific amounts. Based on that, any gap in funding should be made up by fundraising through various channels. Experimental pilot programs should be started to issue urban environmental bonds, for example. All kinds of environmental subsidy programs should be pursued and improved.

Financing methods that are appropriate to the building of public infrastructure should be employed that enable public funds to be used on the environment in a rational manner. Public funds that are earmarked as priority [for environmental use] should attempt to draw in partner funding from the public at large, so that commercial funds will participate in the building and growth of greener cities.

3 Improve the control mechanisms that apply to environmental protection

Environmental impact assessments should be the basis for development and they should be open and scientific. Prior to undertaking any development, as well as during and after the process, every link in the development chain should have stronger regulatory control. Controls should apply to government procurement, the building of public utilities, and the implementation of policy.

Cities should have much better information systems to handle transmittal of environmental information and reports of environmental pollution.

There should be 'virtuous' interactive feedback between government and the media, which operates by virtue of having public participation. Channels by which the public at large can participate in environmental protection should be expanded. The people's 'right to know' about environmental issues should be safeguarded, as well as the public's right to play a supervisory role.

The appropriateness of environmental policies and the effectiveness with which policies are being implemented should be improved via taking in feedback from the public. Systems should be strengthened to ensure compliance, including 'demonstrations' and 'warnings'. Coordinated action between and among governmental departments and regional governments should be encouraged.

While comprehensive environmental controls should be strengthened across all cities on a nationwide basis, specific pilot case 'models' should be continued. The work of 'testing cities' and 'creating new models' should carry on, in order to set up resource-conserving and environmentally sound urban systems that can serve as models for others.

At the same time, there should be much greater exposure of the problems occurring in cities where environmental protection is backwards. Local environmental responsibility systems should be put into place, as well as methods for ensuring there is accountability. Research should be undertaken on how to regulate the potential sources of risk. Emergency-relief technologies should be developed to deal with urgent environmental pollution problems; technical support capacities should be improved in this regard.

Urban clusters should set up information-sharing channels among themselves, as well as cooperative mechanisms for environmental protection. These should include information notifications, joint inspection procedures, and early-warning systems. Management and monitoring systems should be established that are dynamic in nature. Procedures for dealing with environmental risk should be coordinated so that major environmental disasters can be prevented and dealt with in a coordinated fashion.

4 Improve municipal planning systems such that the environment becomes a leading element in the process

Irrational urban planning is frequently the cause of traffic congestion and deteriorating air quality. It prevents sewage and solid-waste material from being treated effectively. In the course of urbanization in China, everything should stem from the concept of considering 'human development' in all its many facets. Planning should be scientific, forward-thinking, participatory, and authoritative. It should be carried out in line with the specific conditions in each area.

There should be a division of labor and adequate coordination both between cities and between urban and rural areas, so as to create urban environments that are 'habitable' and can be enjoyed by all.

In principle, classic high-polluting industries should not be allowed within urban districts, in order to improve urban spatial configurations. Great effort should be made to ensure that industry is located in industrial parks. All new construction projects should gradually be located within these parks, where infrastructure for pollution control is prepared in advance.

The surrounding countryside should be incorporated in urban planning processes. The urban advantages of funds, technology, and human resources should be applied to overall prevention of pollution in both urban and rural settings. Areas surrounding cities, but particularly the interface zones between cities and rural areas, should be subject to environmental protection efforts.

At the same time, the pernicious expansion of urban areas ['sprawl'] must be prevented. Irrational use of land must be avoided, so as to avoid polluting neighbouring environs. Supervisory controls and regulatory oversight should be applied to every step of the formulation and implementation of urban planning. The legal standing of each part of the process must be confirmed and ensured.

Mandatory requirements of the environmental assessment process should be incorporated in laws and regulations. Pilot-site programs should be set up to start the process, but the formulating and enacting of laws should then gradually become an ongoing part of medium-range and long-range environmental planning for cities.

5 Continue to improve price-determination mechanisms for energy and resource supply. Take full advantage of the fundamental role of the market in allocating resources and all inputs

The prices of resources should be increased to the ultimate consumer, in order to reflect costs and reduce waste. This should be done by reducing the current price distortions in the markets for resources and factors. What are currently 'external costs' [paid for by society at large] should be 'internalized' in the process of adhering to such principles as 'the user pays for use of the resource' and 'the polluter pays the cost of polluting'. In order to do this, property rights have to be explicitly defined.

Differential prices should be applied to water, depending on different kinds of water usage in cities. A system of additional charges should be applied to any water used in excess of determined amounts. The standard charges for sewage treatment, as currently defined, should be adjusted.

With the goal of 'turning sewage into a resource', we should accelerate the pace of building sewage-treatment facilities. We should improve the development and application of water reclamation and reuse technologies. In addition, with a key focus on reforming the existing way heat supply is billed in cities, we should be proactive in undertaking reform of urban heat-supply systems.

Under the planned-economy system in China, housing was distributed as a benefit to urban residents, together with a supply of heat. This can no longer meet the needs of the new market-economy system and the way in which housing is being monetized. The old way of accounting for heating is one of the primary economic causes of China's waste of heat resources. We must gradually turn hidden subsidies for urban heating into explicit subsidies, and then be proactive in beginning to charge for the amount of heat actually used. The old way of charging on the basis of 'space' should be turned into charging on the basis of metered usage.

As we reform the pricing mechanisms for energy and resources, we should make sure that price subsidies are available as appropriate to vulnerable groups in cities.

6 Build 'green' production and consumption systems

We must speed up the process of transforming old technologies and using new, high-technology methods in every aspect of production. This includes new processes, facilities, and so on, but also new ways to incentivize people to adopt new systems. Corporations should be guided in the direction of using clean technologies and zero-emission technologies.

Greater effort should be put into developing and then applying technologies for the energy industries and for such fields as 'new-energy automobiles'. Energy-saving methods should be adopted extensively in all transportation and construction industries. We should accelerate the development of wind energy, solar energy, geothermal energy, and other forms of 'clean energy', in order to change the existing structure of the country's energy consumption.

We must reduce the per-unit emission of greenhouse gases and other pollutants. We must put massive effort into developing public transport, particularly rail lines within cities and among cities, so as to enable urban clusters to become 'single units' and take advantage of 'concentration effects' and 'intensification effects'. In the process of building cities, we must at all times promote energy conservation and the use of environmentally sound materials and technologies. The goal is to reduce energy consumption and pollutant emissions at the source, so that standards of living can be maintained at a lower level of energy use.

China burns coal as its primary source of energy. Aimed at this structural problem, we must intensify research into clean coal technologies, including the IGCC ('integrated gasification combined cycle'). We must improve the efficiency with which we use coal, while lowering the discharge of pollutants at the same time.

Farming methods employed on the outskirts of cities should be improved in ways that enable resources to be consumed more efficiently in the agricultural industry.

The amounts of sewage and garbage produced in cities should be reduced, but they should also be turned into resources and their treatment should be industrialized. Pipelines should be installed that capture grey water and reuse it; a consumer market for grey water should be developed. Garbage collection should be done by different categories of garbage and treated accordingly, with the installation of the proper systems.

We must begin to educate people about 'green consumption' concepts. We should establish environmental logos and certification methods for green products so as to encourage and support the production of green products. Government spending should be used to create incentives in this regard, including tax reduction (and abatement) and direct subsidies to consumers. In all ways, we should promote the production and consumption of energy saving products and lower-emission products. We should adopt comprehensive fiscal measures that promote green energy, green technologies, green products, green transport, and green buildings.

7 Set up systems within cities that enable nature to self-regulate and restore itself. Create 'natural' and 'ecosystem' elements that are integral to municipalities

It is imperative that we construct the 'ecological and environmental framework' within which we protect urban water sources, ecological corridors, and other highly sensitive parts of urban ecosystems. To do this, we need to strengthen controls over urban hydrological systems, both rivers and lakes. We must preserve the ability of ecosystems to maintain their own natural functions, particularly in how they use water. We should build open spaces, green belts around cities, green zones in residential districts, and woodlands and parks in enterprise districts. We should ensure that the main transportation routes around cities, and water systems within cities, have green corridors alongside them.

We must strengthen the ability of natural ecosystems within cities to restore themselves, and to withstand interference in their functioning. We should implement policies that increase biodiversity, and that use the adjustment mechanisms of ecosystems themselves to increase their own carrying capacity and environmental 'containment'.

Through setting up green urban structures, we should allow natural systems to connect with one another and enhance network functions through the interplay of ecological information, energies, and substances. This should improve the survivability and environmental carrying capacity of biodiversity, which in turn should enable ecosystems to process urban waste more effectively.

Note

1   Wang, T. and Watson, J.: *Who Owns China's carbon emissions*, Tyndall Center Briefing Note 23, 2007.

9 Innovative approaches to managing 'urbanization' and 'city governance'

Innovative reform is going to be critical in moving China's 'quasi-urbanization' to 'full urbanization' status. Two key aspects of innovative reform relate to how the process of urbanization itself is 'managed', and how cities are 'governed'.

Within the next 10 years, more than 200 million people among China's rural population will likely be moving into cities and becoming legitimate urban residents. China's myriad cities are currently undergoing frantic development. If the process is not effectively 'managed' and 'governed', it is not unlikely that a very considerable amount of land will be 'hardened' or put under asphalt. The resulting problems will include such things as over-consumption of energy, increase in polluting emissions, erosion of sound ecosystems, heavy traffic congestion, decline in urban competitiveness, increase in urban poverty, environmental deterioration, and social conflict.

We now, therefore, need to re-evaluate the models by which we have managed and governed cities in the past. We need to take aim at the most pronounced problems and contradictions currently appearing in urban development, for they have become a monumental challenge facing all levels of government in the country. We need to develop more innovative ways to manage our urbanization and govern our cities, in line with 'scientific' and 'coordinated' development concepts. This involves managing the process of urbanization from an overall perspective, and coordinating the internal dynamics of cities in terms of their politics, economies, and social and environmental issues.

The current situation with respect to managing urbanization and governing cities in China

The difference between 'managing the process of urbanization' and 'city governance'

The purpose of both of these things is to prevent the negative side-effects or externalities that occur in the process of urbanization. Both involve mitigating conflicts between different interest groups, coordinating various interests, and enhancing the sustainable and equitable development of cities. The two concepts of managing urbanization and governing cities have similarities but also distinct differences.

'Managing urbanization' refers primarily to managing a process. 'Governing cities' refers to managing the internal considerations of cities, including economic, social, and environmental issues. Managing urbanization is a form of macro-management, while urban governance is, in relative terms, a form of micro-management.

The primary entity involved in managing urbanization is 'government' at its various levels, including Central, local [provincial], and urban governments. The primary entities involved in urban governance are more diverse and include not merely urban governments but also enterprises, urban residents themselves, and all kinds of non-governmental organizations.[1]

Both of these refer to processes that are not simply 'control-oriented' and 'restraining', but also incorporate voluntary and positive guidance and support.

The necessary nature of 'managing urbanization' and 'governing cities'

Both urbanization and urban development contain what could be called 'externalities' or external consequences. Urbanization is mainly the result of market forces and the fact that enterprises seek expansion and growth. At a certain point, however, the sheer scale of cities can also increase costs to society, including the cost of time spent in congested traffic, constantly rising land costs, astronomically housing costs, the relatively higher cost of maintaining good health, and higher costs associated with carbon emissions and environmental deterioration. As externalities, these things are not 'internalized' by corporations or households in the sense that they do not pay for them or deal with them. As a result, the 'concentrating' effect of cities may benefit certain individual groups at the expense of society at large (OECD, Regional Affairs, 2009).

City governments, residents, enterprises, non-governmental social organizations, and so on can all be characterized as interested parties or stakeholders. In the course of urbanization, each of these may seek specific results in their own interests. Corporate interests, partial interests, or local interests may prevail, while the interests of the city at large are sacrificed. Specific behaviour then sacrifices not only the interests of members of the entire society but also the interests of future generations.

For this reason, such things as decisions about urban development should not be given over to the control of developers. Developers may well disregard urban planning requirements, regarding building densities, among other considerations, which may well lead to untrammeled development of land.

Or, to take another example, any urban development necessarily involves the occupation of spatial resources, including arable land, woodlands, grasslands, areas of the ocean, and underground water. The value of these things to our current generation may be high, but it is much higher to those generations of people yet to come. Under a situation regulated solely by the market, there is basically no way in which the current market price can reflect the higher prices of the future. In order to ensure sustainable development, there must be other control mechanisms that regulate excessive development of these spatial resources.

The management of urbanization has a very specific practical meaning in China. This is not just because the country is facing the most monumental urbanization ever to occur in history, but because it is also in the process of an important turning point in its development. If we are not able to be innovative in time, with respect to transforming our development model, our economic system, and also our very concepts of what development means, then it is very likely we will simply be multiplying all negative externalities as we urbanize.

In terms of our conceptual approach to development, for example, some cities are still striving to maximize GDP while neglecting any kind of sustainable coordinated approach to growth. To them, the whole process of increasing urbanization will simply become a tool for increasing GDP. Our national goal of 'furthering human development in an all-round way' will not be given any consideration.

The development model that has arisen to date is investment-driven. Governments at the provincial level and below are the ones who control the primary asset involved in urbanization, namely land. They are both 'owners' of the land and the beneficiaries of licensing out rights to use it. The amount of public finance revenue that a city can muster depends specifically on how much land that city possesses. Government spending is therefore intimately related to land. The development model that naturally arises from this situation is that cities attempt to maximize incomes derived from land and real estate prices. They attempt to draw in investors and investors' funds, in order to increase urban building and real estate development. This contributes to an investment-led model of economic development.

The current situation with respect to managing urbanization and governing cities

China's level of urbanization has risen markedly over the more than 30 years of reform and opening up, and urban systems are now basically formed. The framework of a socialist market-economy system has been set up that features public ownership as the primary force in cities while entities owned by other forms of ownership develop in tandem. Cities have become the supporting pillars of the market-economy system in China, while urban economies have become the main players in China's market economy (Zhang Junkuo, Liu Feng, and Gao Shiji, 2008).

As urbanization has proceeded, municipal governments have come to play an ever-stronger role in China. Under the planned-economy system, China's cities did not in fact have independent decision-making power. Instead, they played a subsidiary role to the Central government, serving as intermediaries in a top-down structure. Although they had the advantage of being able to maintain direct contact with lower social structures, and thereby understand the needs of people at large, they lacked any fundamental authority with respect to the local population. They were both incapable and unwilling to assume any independent responsibility for the results of their own administrative actions.

Once reform and opening up began, the Central government had to break out of the mould of operating in a centrally planned fashion. It began to change the old model by which it managed urbanization. Adjustments were made in the previous relationships between government and enterprises, government and the public [or 'society'], and Central and local governments. Local governments now obtained a measure of authority over administrative decisions, and over economic management. They became relatively independent entities with their own interests and their own decision-making power.

As urbanization proceeded, the constituency of any given city became its primary responsibility. Cities now aimed at providing public services for the needs of the local populace, stimulating the socioeconomic development of the local economy, and improving the welfare of the local people.

The internal structure of both urbanization management and city governance improved as this occurred. To an initial degree, a framework with functions distributed among 'planning', 'construction', and 'governance' became more clearly defined. A start was made on addressing the very prevalent phenomenon in China's cities of 'going light on planning, heavy on construction, and light on governance'. The functions of government began to change, and cities exercised less and less interference in market forces. Instead, cities began to make greater use of legal and economic measures to adjust macroeconomic performance and to manage their publics.

Meanwhile, the scope and level of public services saw an ongoing improvement. The functions of municipal governments with respect to providing public services continued to expand once reform and opening up began. Levels of basic infrastructure for urban residents, education, medical services and healthcare, social security, public transport, housing, and public security all improved (see Chapters 6 and 7 for details). The quality of life in many cities has improved in recent years, with the adoption of urban measures aimed at making cities habitable, green, unique in one way or another, more humane, and better coordinated.

Meanwhile, China has established a better legal framework for city governance. It has promulgated a series of laws and regulations concerned with urbanization management and city governance. To an initial degree, these things are now on a path to 'having laws on which to rely'. Laws and regulations now in place, for example, include the *Law of the People's Republic of China on Administrative Punishments*, the *Law on Urban Planning*, the *Law on Environmental Protection*, the *Regulations on the Administration of Urban Appearances and Environmental Hygiene*, and the *Regulations on the Administration of Urban Roads*.

China has also strengthened the establishment of communities and encouraged the public to participate in these communities. Some cities have carried out pilot-site reforms related to public-participatory budgeting reform, democratic forums, public hearings, and so on. These enable urban citizens to have an effective voice in the distribution of urban resources. They enable citizens to determine the priority ranking of urban social policies, and to carry out supervisory regulation over policies concerned with people's livelihood. These public-participation experiments have dramatically improved the extent to which the public participates in and is knowledgeable about urban policies. They have improved the standards by which policy is formulated, and have contributed to social equity.

Box 9.1 Participatory public budgeting experiments in Wuxi and Harbin

Participatory budgeting represents an innovative way of formulating policy. The process involves holding regular periodic discussion forums in order to expand the channels through which the public at large can voice recommendations on public spending. It allows the public to participate in the process of formulating policies that relate to how resources are distributed, and to decide on spending priorities. It also allows them to have supervisory oversight over the budgetary process.

In the short run, participatory budgeting allows government to select policy options that best reflect the needs of the public. It therefore enhances social equity. In the long run, participatory budgeting contributes to public knowledge of and participation in social endeavors. In order to realize social equity, it promotes better policy formulation and resource distribution, it increases the transparency with which spending policies are made, and it aids in transforming the functions of public finance.

With active support from the China Development Research Foundation, in 2006, the cities of Wuxi and Harbin undertook experiments in participatory budgeting reform in certain communities. In 2007, the cities expanded the experiments to include more pilot-site communities. By the end of 2007, there were a total of 28 neighbourhoods (or 'towns') in the two cities that had instituted participatory budgeting procedures. From a large number of project proposals concerned with public needs [people's livelihood], the cities chose 63 on which to focus. Funding amounts for these came to more than RMB 75 million. In certain districts, the amounts of money under discussion were as much as 1 per cent of the total government budget at a given level of government.

This experiment in conducting participatory budgeting in Wuxi and Harbin garnered fairly good results. It not only furthered good relations between government and the public, but also raised the efficiency with which government funds were being used.

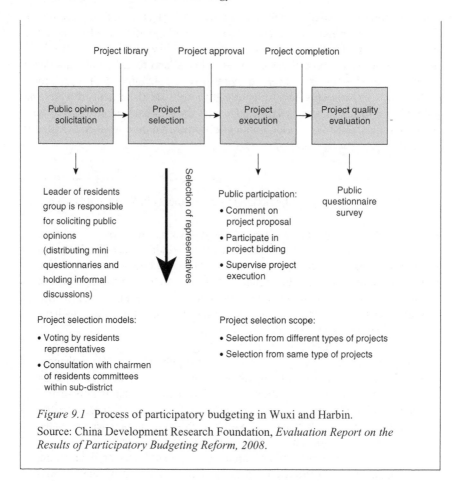

Figure 9.1 Process of participatory budgeting in Wuxi and Harbin.

Source: China Development Research Foundation, *Evaluation Report on the Results of Participatory Budgeting Reform, 2008.*

Main problems concerning urbanization management and city governance

Some of the problems that are arising in the course of rapid urbanization in China have to do with incomplete urbanization management structures and the irrational ways in which city governance is structured. The Central government set forth policies that called for a general strategy of urbanizing 'promptly' way back in the year 2000. Since that time, however, there has been no specific operational plan. No consensus has formed about long-term, unified, policies and *modus operandi*. Every year, the Central government convenes a 'Convention on Rural Affairs'. In a centralized and unified way, this researches issues to do with agriculture and rural development in China. It has been extremely important in ensuring that agriculture continues to develop, that the countryside is stable, and farmers' incomes increase. China's urban population will soon be greater than its rural population, however. A similar 'work conference' should be convened at high levels that addresses urban issues on a national basis.

In fact, many members of the public have begun to express their views on a variety of issues that affect the 'people's livelihood'. These include the problem of finding jobs for college graduates, the excessive cost of housing, irrational distribution of income, unequal educational opportunities, the high cost of medical care, traffic congestion, poor environmental quality, and so on. All of these, together with their attendant social problems, need to be considered in a centralized and overall fashion. They need to be evaluated within the context of the monumental and epoch-making strategic process of urbanization in China. Policies that address the issues in fundamental ways will only be possible if we take this kind of comprehensive approach to the subject.

Functions that are wrongly assumed by government, and functions that government mistakenly does not undertake to fulfill at all

'Strengthening management of urbanization' and 'strengthening city governance' is not the same as saying that the government should be involved in everything. On the contrary, government should focus exclusively on affairs that are within its purview. Each level of government, moreover, should only undertake affairs that are appropriate to that level.

The problem right now is that government has been interfering in many matters with which it should not be involved, and at the same time has not been concentrating its efforts on things that it should indeed handle.

The processes of economic growth and urbanization are mutually complementary. Many policies that spur economic growth also have the effect of spurring urbanization and urban development. When the state determines the spatial configuration of urbanization in certain areas, and implements policies that favour specially designated zones, when it funds super-large infrastructure projects, and so on, this generates urbanization around these zones. It influences the development of specific cities and it changes the spatial configuration of urbanization in general. Policies that set up development zones stimulate consumption of housing and cars in cities, they generate the building of roads and rail lines, lead to different distribution of revenues off land, and so on. All of these promote the growth of urbanization either directly or indirectly, and particularly the growth of large cities.

Other policies, in contrast, restrain the growth of urban populations, and constrain urbanization. These include the household registration system that separates urban-resident from rural-resident status. They include the basic systems that govern land, including 'farmland protection' and 'land management through issuing land quotas'.

Right now, it is hard to figure out who in the various Chinese governmental departments is responsible for what aspects of urbanization management. No specific department has been given the explicit responsibility for handling this. The only thing that comes close to it is one line in the mandate of the

National Development and Reform Commission, which says that the Commission is to 'research and suggest major policies and development strategies for urbanization'. All other tasks relating to urban development not only have merely a tangential effect on urbanization but are also scattered among a number of departments. For example, the National Development and Reform Commission is responsible for plans to do with the national economy and social development. It is responsible for the annual plans of the country, for arranging for government spending, for reviewing and authorizing major projects, and so on.

The *Ministry of Land and Resources* is responsible for land-use planning. It is tasked with managing both planning for and the use of land for building purposes. The *Ministry of Housing and Urban and Rural Development* is responsible for drafting all plans for the national urban system, as well as for urban plans. It is in charge of the building of urban infrastructure and management of real estate development in cities. The *Ministry of Transportation* is responsible for managing the building of urban and inter-urban rail lines and transport. The *Ministry of the Environment* is responsible for managing all urban environmental protection. The *Ministry of Public Security* is responsible for managing the whole household-registration system. The *Ministry of Civil Affairs* is responsible for demarcating administrative divisions and managing the systems that administer cities. All of these different responsibilities affect the course of urbanization, but from different angles.

Meanwhile, the role that municipal governments play in the process of urbanization is actually much greater than that of the Central government. The ways and means by which urban governments 'manage' urbanization include the following.

First, they draft and revise urban plans. Urban departments directly in charge of plans then authorize specific 'research and design organizations' to present master draft plans. After these have been approved by the municipal government, they are reported on up to the next level of government, i.e., that immediately above the municipality. Once that level of government has approved the plans, they are implemented. These urban plans are the starting point for controlling the size of the urban population and the amount of land being occupied by a given city. Nevertheless, there is not a single city in China that does not expand outwards, using up ever more land. Even if all cities in the country were rigorous in abiding by their 'urban plans', every few years, those plans are revised. Every revision provides for another 'ring' of expansion.

Second, municipal governments expand the area under municipal control by setting up what are called 'development zones'. Out of their need to attract investment and develop their economies, municipalities carve out neighbouring patches of land and begin to incorporate them into plans for such development zones or for 'new urban districts', gradually absorbing them into the 'built up area' of the city itself. Development zones are frequently designed specifically for economic and industrial development and serve as 'special function zones' within cities.

Third, municipal governments expand their cities through reconfiguring and redefining the jurisdictions that govern areas around them. This method relates to the process of 'turning prefectures [*di*] into cities', 'turning counties [*xian*] into cities', 'turning counties into districts [*qu*]', and 'turning townships [*xiang*] into towns [*zhen*]'. It also includes merging parts of what had been separately constituted suburbs into the city itself.

Fourth, municipal government has the power to liberalize or loosen control over the restrictions that prevent people from becoming legitimate 'urban residents'. In recent years, a number of cities have issued policies that relax the restrictions on receiving urban residency status. Those people who satisfy certain conditions are allowed to become legitimate urbanites. [The reason they can do this is that] urban governments are the primary entities with responsibility for providing public services, social security, public housing, family-planning services, population management, social relief, social safety measures [or 'law and order'], public security, disaster mitigation and prevention, and other such social endeavours.

Carrying out 'management' according to administrative divisions

The process of urbanization in China is currently being done according to the administrative organization of a particular area rather than to the economic rationale of an area. At times, therefore, urbanizing an area is simply a matter of changing the administrative definition of that area. Some districts that grow very quickly in economic terms often erode what had been distinct boundaries around their perimeters. As a result, good farmland is absorbed into the process of urbanization. Arable land and 'ecosystem land' are taken over, resulting in population densities that often exceed the carrying capacity of the local environment. Problems of severe over-extraction of groundwater are one consequence in some cities. Traffic congestion and environmental deterioration become prevalent problems.

Other districts that are not economically advanced are incorporated into neighbouring cities anyway, through artificial means. Towns and townships are merged simply for the purpose of expanding the boundaries of a given city, even though true 'urbanization' is not occurring. The size of the population within a given administrative area is intentionally raised in order to elevate the 'urbanization level' of a given place. In reality, this does not advance levels of urbanization.

Inadequate planning systems

The main problem with China's urban planning system is that there is inadequate coordinated planning at the national level, in determining urban spatial configurations. Plans are made according to administrative demarcations, but there is little explicit guidance on what happens when urbanization occurs across administrative lines.

The numerous regional plans that have already been released are confusingly vague and unhelpful. They do not define the functions of the major cities from the perspective of their economic rational. They lack any unified plans for deploying basic infrastructure. They lack binding regulations with respect to controlling the amount of physical space used by urban areas and particularly industrial areas. Municipal and county plans do not include provisions for how they intend to grow in a planned manner. They do not define areas under their jurisdiction that are to be used for specific purposes, such as woodlands, fields, roads, waterways, and so on. There is no sort of 'red line' that differentiates between urban and rural, or the specific functions that apply to each. There are no principles to regulate how urban growth occurs or how it is managed.

Urban planning is currently done within the system of administrative jurisdictions in China. These include provinces (together with autonomous regions and cities directly administered by the Central government) and counties. The system tends to strengthen the bias towards promoting urbanization according to administrative jurisdictions. Urban planning does not therefore differentiate among the circumstances of different regions and cities. Everything is determined by two metrics: population and amount of territory or space. Urban plans do not place sufficient weight on a number of vital factors, such as the direction in which the city is expanding, the way in which territory under urban planning districts is expanding, the internal configuration and character of urban areas, deployment of urban infrastructure, and so on.

Meanwhile, the review and approval process for urban planning is chaotic. Entities that are authorized to approve plans are not consistent across administrations. The State Council reviews and approves urban plans of larger cities, but in local [including provincial] areas, the local 'People's Congress' reviews and approves matters relating to socioeconomic development plans.

When plans are being formulated, they generally provide inadequate mechanisms for resolving any issues. When differences of opinion arise, the issues are 'flattened' out without real resolution and the plans are passed as is. This guts the plans of their substance and their essential purpose.

In some places, when the administration in a particular city changes, the plans change as well. Each new leader brings with him his own way of thinking. In large script, he calligraphs a great expansion of the urban population, taking over ever more of the city's surrounding land. At the same time, the mechanisms that link the costs of plans to the size of plans are less than perfect, which affects the scientific nature of urban planning (Lu Dadao, 2006).

The capacities of public finance are not matched up with the functions of government

Income generated by urban construction is an important part of any city's public revenues. Such income includes a variety of taxes, fees, and government allocations: the city maintenance and construction tax, the city public utility surcharge, appropriations from the Central government and local [provincial] governments,

Table 9.1 Source and composition of China's city maintenance and construction
         fund in 2008

Item	Amount (100 million yuan)	Ratio (%)
Total city maintenance and construction fund	5616.422	
Central fiscal appropriation	75.6011	1.35
Provincial fiscal appropriation	89.0386	1.59
Municipal fiscal fund	5190.636	92.42
Municipal fiscal appropriation	1335.693	23.78
City maintenance and construction tax	744.2775	13.25
Urban public utility surcharge	89.6248	1.60
Municipal public facility counterpart fund	331.8355	5.91
Municipal public facility user fee	263.2865	4.69
Land-sale revenue	2105.447	37.49
Water resource fee	25.4199	0.45
Asset replacement revenue	16.299	0.29
Other revenue	284.0119	5.06
Other fiscal funds	255.7795	4.55

Source: Based on data from the *China Urban Construction Statistical Yearbook 2008.*

municipal public facility 'counterpart funds', municipal public facility 'user's fees', revenue from licensing out land-use rights, and revenue from 'replacing assets'.

As Table 9.1 indicates, however, funds primarily come from public-revenue-type income derived from the same level of government. Some 92 per cent of all 'urban construction and maintenance funds' come from local-level sources. Funding assistance from both the Central government and provincial governments is, essentially, symbolic. It accounts for less than 3 per cent.

Revenues from land transactions are the primary source of local funding for 'urban maintenance and construction', that is, funding that comes from the municipal level of government itself. Such revenues constitute 37 per cent of all municipal income. In second place come 'public-finance allocations', which constitute 24 per cent of all municipal funds for urban maintenance and construction. Only 15 per cent of all local funding of urban budgets is derived from what could be considered classic 'tax revenues', as institutionally mustered through 'urban maintenance taxes' and 'urban facilities-use supplementary fees'.

Looking at these figures, it is easy to see why municipal governments are so enthusiastic about land development. They are using the vehicles of 'urbanization' and 'city management' to earn revenue.

Right now, the system by which China divides up tax revenues between Central and local governments has a profound impact on urban municipal-finance capabilities. This system also affects the whole process of urbanization and municipal development.

The system [was set up in 1994], and at that time it reclassified taxes according to how much went into Central coffers and how much stayed in local coffers.

The new corporate value-added tax and the personal income tax were classified as 'shared taxes', while the consumption tax was classified as a Central-government tax. This caused a drop in the percentage of same-level tax revenue to total local revenue. Before [the system was put in place in 1994], local governments took in roughly 70 per cent of their public-finance revenues in the form of such taxes. After 1994, this dropped to less than 50 per cent (it has stayed around 47 per cent). At the same time, however, local-government expenditures have risen dramatically. The result has been a massive disparity between fiscal revenues and fiscal expenditures at the local level (Figure 9.2) (Wang Youqiang, Lu Dapeng, and ZhouShaojie, 2009).

The system by which 'municipalities govern counties' must be reformed

Since 1983, a system has gradually formed in China by which municipalities have jurisdiction over counties. Over the course of nearly 30 years, this model was moderately successful in integrating the governing of 'urban' and 'rural' in China, which had been quite separate. It helped further the country's stated policy aim of 'having cities bring along counties'.

As county-level economies developed, however, the system also began to constrain further county-level economic development. First, as the market-economy system improved throughout China, the system began to block a natural and rational flow of resources between municipalities and counties. This included both social and economic resources. Second, contradictions between urban and

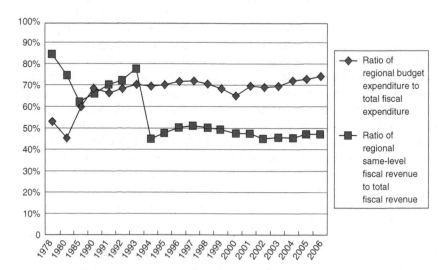

Figure 9.2   Change of ratios of regional fiscal revenue and expenditure 1978–2006.
Source: *China Statistical Yearbook 2007.*

rural development became more intense as this concept of 'cities should stimulate county development' lost effect. Third, municipalities increasingly used administrative clout to carry out 'urban construction' with the use of county-level public-finance funds. This weakened the ability of counties to develop themselves. Fourth, the system added a layer of management and thereby lowered administrative efficiencies.

County-level economies in China have achieved rapid growth since the 1990s. As one example, Zhejiang province has led a national ranking of having 'the top 100 counties' for many years. More than 60 per cent of Zhejiang's provincial GDP is derived from county economies. As counties have grown in strength, however, they have also begun to exhibit a number of problems caused by the system whereby 'cities govern counties'. Public services are distinctly inadequate, together with the ability to manage social issues. This has affected the overall conduct of governmental functions. Regulatory mechanisms that are necessary to the proper functioning of a market are also inadequate. Regulatory provisions are limited, constraining further development and prevent further upgrading of Zhejiang's county economies. Right now, the legal and regulatory framework in which Zhejiang's top counties operate is inconsistent with the provincially mandated goal of expanding their governing authority. This means that the decentralization of certain authorities in Zhejiang, as planned, is in fact not possible.

In addition to having some highly developed counties, Zhejiang also has many other counties that are growing rapidly. Their *de facto* level of social and economic development is not in line with their limited authority over social and economic concerns. This severely impedes their further development.

Meanwhile, counties in the vast reaches of China's central and western regions have severely mismatched levels of 'fiscal authority' and 'governing authority'. It is impossible for these areas to meet their fiscal responsibilities, so public services are severely underfunded. In the course of 'marketizing' the economy, the system whereby 'municipalities govern counties' has undercut the original support systems that prevailed in these places, and eroded institutional capacities. The performance of institutions is now markedly diminished, which is also exposing problems in the national policy of further integrating various regions of China.

The great majority of countries around the world adopt a two-tiered system or at most a three-tiered system of government. Cities and counties are autonomous actual entities that operate as independent structures – one does not report to another. While taking China's own national circumstances into account and thinking about development in the immediate future, the country might consider creating a similar structure in which cities and counties are administered separately. This would mean reforming the existing system. It would mean having provinces administer counties directly, rather than through the intermediate level of municipalities. The reform would benefit the economic vitality of counties. It would strengthen their capacity to meet fiscal responsibilities. It would improve the level of public services. It would help in establishing horizontal ties and better socioeconomic cohesion within urban clusters and between county-level governments.

Box 9.2 Regional experiments on reforming the 'city-governing-county' system

Zhejiang province was the earliest to start experimenting with the expansion of county-level authority. In 1992, the province began implementing expanded authorities within 13 of its more advanced counties. Starting in 2002, several other provinces have also begun to implement similar reforms that 'expand authority to the strongest counties'. These provinces include Hubei, Henan, Guangdong, Jiangxi, Hebei, and Liaoning.

The reforms involve handing authority over economic management down to key counties, and therefore taking it away from local-level municipalities. In terms of economic management, this then creates a pattern that resembles what could be called 'direct provincial jurisdiction over counties'.

Hainan province has already completed a separation of governing authority between cities and counties, due to its relatively small size and lower population. Cities in Hainan are responsible solely for managing themselves, while counties are administered directly by the provincial government. As for Chongqing, once it became a city under the direct administration of the Central government, it too transitioned to having direct administration of counties and districts. These examples have helped the country build up a certain amount of experience.

The model by which 'provinces administer counties' has received tremendous attention in recent years, and is a key focus of administrative reforms in China. By now, pilot-site reforms are being instituted nationwide. Data from the Ministry of Finance indicate that around two-thirds of all provincial cities are now implementing reforms, including 18 provinces and the four major cities under direct administration of the Central government. The 18 provinces include Hebei, Shanxi, Hainan, Liaoning, Jilin, Heilongjiang, Jiangsu, Zhejiang, Anhui, Fujian, Shandong, and Henan. The cities are Beijing, Shanghai, Tianjin, and Chongqing. This model whereby 'provinces govern counties' is one of the objectives of the 11th Five-Year Plan. As the year 2010 approached, this systemic reform picked up speed.

Source: Wang Hongru, Zhang Juncai and Zhang Yibiao: *Province-governing-county reform: redistribution of regional powers*, People's Net, 15 June 2007, http://politics.people.com.cn/GB/30178/5845418.html.

China's unsound performance evaluation system

'Government performance', which involves the evaluation of certain criteria applied to governments, is a very important tool in China. It affects the speed of economic development as well as its quality and efficiency. To a considerable degree, it also influences China's urbanization, by affecting how fast this is accomplished, the paths it takes, the resulting spatial configuration, and the quality of the results.

Right now, each level of government in China generally evaluates the performance of the level of government or municipality directly below it. It measures whether or not and how well this level of government meets certain criteria. The criteria include such things as how well a place is establishing a 'moderately prosperous society', whether it meets standards for being a 'garden city on a national level', a 'sound ecosystem city on a national level', a 'hygienic city on a national level', a 'civilized city on a national level', and so on.

In Jiangsu province, for example, there are specific sub-category indicators that are rated in order to meet the requirements of the general category of being a 'moderately prosperous society in an all-round way'. There are a total of 18 components within the four general categories of 'economic development, standard of living, social development, and ecosystem and the environment'. Within these 18 sub-categories, there are 27 specific indicators. For example, 'economic development' includes indicators that measure per capita GDP, the percentage of non-agricultural industry within the GDP, the level of urbanization, and the recorded unemployment rate in cities.

Box 9.3 lists the ways in which each of various ministries [or departments] in China measures the performance of cities. Each rates and manages cities depending on its own perspective and in accordance with 'titled programmes' that fall under its jurisdiction. Since this is the way municipal-government performance is rated in China, the system unavoidably has a strong influence on urban development.

Absence of civil-society entities in city governance

In recent years, urban governance in China has begun to focus on strengthening communities. The effort aims at enabling communities to serve as self-managing grassroots-level organizations for residents. An effort has also begun to enable urban residents to play a role in urban governance. Citizens are being encouraged to participate in certain spheres of decision making, such as the pricing of water and electricity, ticket prices for admission to local scenic spots, and so on. Public hearings are being instituted to involve local people. Overall, however, urban governance still faces the problem of a lack of participating entities.

First, self-governing organizations run by urban residents, such as social organizations and community institutions, are inadequate. As housing became commercialized in China, that is, sold through a market rather than being supplied as a public benefit, and as job markets developed, services became 'socialized'

Box 9.3 Titled programmes by which cities are evaluated, and their
sponsoring ministries

	Title	Sponsor
1	National Garden City	Ministry of Urban–Rural Construction
2	National Ecological City	State Environmental Protection Administration
3	National Sanitary City	Patriotic Public Health Campaign Committee
4	National Civilized City	Central Steering Commission on Spiritual Civilization Development
5	China's Best Tourist City	State Tourism Administration
6	National Model City in Landscaping	National Afforestation Committee
7	National Model City in Environmental Protection	State Environmental Protection Administration
8	National Model City in Integrated Environment Improvement	Ministry of Construction
9	National Model City in Integrated Social Security Improvement	Central Commission on Integrated Management of Public Order
10	China Living Environmental Award	Ministry of Urban–Rural Construction
11	Charming City in China	China Central Television
12	International Garden City	National Park Association

Source: Lu Dadao et al.: *China Regional Development Report: Urbanization Process and Spatial Expansion*, Commercial Press, 2006.

---

rather than being supplied by the 'unit' that once employed a person. Residents began to be public citizens as opposed to people who belonged to any given 'unit'. The managerial 'layer' of the unit now Commercial Press, 2006 disintegrated. That layer ceased to exist in between the municipal government and the now-fragmented and dispersed 'members of society'.

In the meantime, a new 'management network' failed to materialize that could provide public services and satisfy the diversified needs of a different kind of public. Social organizations were inadequately cultivated. The government was suddenly faced with a myriad of social problems. It had to deal directly with thousands of disparate individuals whose needs were not being met by grassroots-level entities or residents' self-governing bodies.

Second, entities that do in fact involve urban residents do not have recognized 'standing' in the process of urban governance. Constant progress has been made, and 'democratic procedures' are now being incorporated into all kinds of social endeavours. Nevertheless, the standing or official status of entities that represent urban residents has never been fully established.

For example, authority to undertake construction projects is basically shared only between the government and enterprises (this includes the local government). Local urban residents have no influence whatsoever on deciding where construction will take place. They are not allowed to participate in decision making and, in the end, can only passively accept whatever is decided. This has led to the many so-called 'social incidents' [or 'mass incidents'] in recent years, brought on by problems associated with construction projects. Issues include environmental impact, forced occupation of land, and the demolition of homes and removal of populations.[2]

Box 9.4 Allow non-governmental organizations to participate in city governance

The Stuttgart Regional Association in Germany closely cooperates with many civil-society groups on various social and economic measures. For example, the Association joined the Stuttgart Cultural Zone in 2001. This is an association established in 1991 to publicize the cultural features of the Stuttgart region. It joined the Stuttgart Sport Zone in 2001, a city association that incorporates a professional sports association and a sports club. The Association has also conducted joint research with the Stuttgart Women's Forum, a network established by women professionals and politicians to advocate gender equality and safeguard women's interests in regional transportation planning. The research results have been incorporated into the Association's own regional transport plan. Bringing city authorities and the private sector together, and allowing their respective institutions to be mutually involved, can help develop wider and closer coordination between public and non-public participants.

For example, in Germany, the Hanover City Authority is a member of several international chambers of commerce (for example the Germany–Italy Bilateral Chamber of Commerce). In Hungary, the Law on Regional Development and Planning mandates that associations and enterprises have the right to participate in decision making, on a voluntary and consultative basis, before any planning process commences. Business-sector representatives also participate in the Greater Budapest Development Commission through the local chambers of commerce.

In Korea, the executive leadership of Seoul has, in recent years, encouraged urban residents to play a greater role in city management. For example, it has encouraged the public to participate directly in controlling corruption. If people suspect that illegal activity is occurring, or activity that is in any way detrimental to the public interest, they may ask government departments to verify the state of affairs. The city has also taken advantage of the high-speed Internet in the country to establish an online system to handle civil affairs. This is called '*Open*', which stands for 'Online Civic Application Enhancing Programme'. By logging onto the city's Internet websites, residents can monitor the progress of their anti-corruption notifications, as well as other affairs of the city. The Seoul Management Authority is also giving monetary incentives to residents to encourage them to report suspected corruption. Finally, the city encourages residents to report directly to regulatory agencies of various kinds when they suspect corruption. More than 30 per cent of the committee members of these agencies must be female so as to increase the rate of female participation in social affairs.

In France, a law passed in 1999 set up urban communities and communities in urban clusters. This Regional Planning Law provides that 'development councils' (*conseil de développement*) must be established. Council representatives include participants from metropolitan-level governments who are meant to coordinate various interests as they formulate detailed strategic plans and measures for urban governments. However, the law as passed does not provide for any regulations with respect to how they are to operate. There is therefore a tremendous disparity among the different councils in terms of their standing and the qualifications of members (Lefevre, 2006). In general, it is the chambers of commerce, corporate associations, and higher-educational institutions that participate in these meetings, although residents can also attend. In some places, these meetings are jointly chaired by government agencies. On the whole, these meetings are under-staffed and under-budgeted, but still help to improve the often-imperfect relationship between the private and public sectors.

Source: OECD: *Background Report, 2010.*

The direction of innovative developments in the management of 'urbanization' and city governance in China

Given the overall context of extremely fast urbanization in China, the country needs to strengthen its innovative approaches to urbanization management and city governance.

First, in order to minimize the negative consequences to society at large that arise in the process of urbanization, a coordinated approach needs to be developed between the Central government and local governments. This includes an overall approach and coordinated mechanisms with respect to allocation of resources, formulation of plans, taxation, and criteria for evaluating performance.

Second, since monumental changes have taken place within the social structures of cities, urban politics, economics, and social issues need to be coordinated to promote equitable development. Urban residents have become actively involved in unprecedented ways in the decision-making and construction activities of cities, in all ways that have to do with urban economics, society, and environmental issues. The overall goal, then, is to set up mutually supportive mechanisms that enable joint participation of government, enterprises, and public organizations. Both efficiency and fairness have to be taken into account. The results must be beneficial to healthy urbanization and sustainable development. A 'new form of urbanization management' has to be set up, together with a 'new form of city governance'.

Principles underlying the overall goal

Take the human being as the core consideration

A key component of the whole process of urbanization must be turning rural migrant workers into legitimate urban citizens. This has to be done via what could be called 'urbanizing the entire population within a city'. The process of urbanization must truly promote overall development of human beings. It cannot be aimed solely at economic growth. It cannot be aimed solely at such material things as bringing more land under municipal control and building ever more high-rise buildings.

Focus on 'intensive' and 'balanced'

China's limited land and large population mean that its environment is vulnerable and its ecosystem already fragile. This is the reality from which all policies must proceed. The country must take the path of 'intensive' as opposed to 'extensive' development in its urbanization. Each city and all cities must strive to be compact. Economic concentrations and human populations must be balanced overall across the entire country.

Coordinate policies from an overall perspective

In the course of urbanization, the policy aim of 'building up a new countryside' must be coordinated with the policy aim of 'urbanization'. Agriculture, rural economies, and farmers' interests must not be sacrificed as the cost we are willing to pay for urbanization. Within cities, the interests of all must be coordinated, including rural migrant workers, existing holders of urban household registration, and also other migrant populations. Different uses of national territory must also be coordinated, including areas that serve the ecosystem, areas that produce agricultural products, and areas that are designated for urban development. In addition to coordinating these structural uses, geographic regions must be coordinated as well. Eastern, central, and western parts of the country should be viewed within a comprehensive whole. The functions of urban clusters should be defined in terms of the integrated roles of their large, medium-sized, and smaller cities and towns. Systems must be designed that govern the closely related issues of household registration, housing, social security, and education.

Focus on reform and innovation

We must further the transformation of the functions of government, and, to do that, we are going to have to build up the capacities of municipal governments. Those governments are going to have to guide urban development by improving a number of capacities: ability to achieve social balance, guide the public, innovate and learn new things, regulate through macro- as opposed to micro-management, attract resources, and govern by the rule of law. We must also promote the advance of democratization. We must create conditions that enable more urban residents to participate in city governance.

Use 'openness' as the main driving force

Economic development is increasingly a matter of regionalization and globalization. This means that managing urbanization transcends the simple matter of managing a single city. The new 'urbanization management' is going to have to be adept in reorganizing resources and innovating in the context of globalization. Regional cooperation and coordination are going to be necessary against the backdrop of regionalization.

Transform the functions of municipal governments

The main problem with the way in which municipal governments currently define their functions is that they put too much emphasis on economic growth while neglecting social issues. They should strengthen functions that have to do with providing public services and managing 'society'. Municipal governments should be providing excellent public services to city residents. As appropriate, they should be investing in public infrastructure in those areas in which investment from the private sector is inadequate. City governments should put their emphasis on improving public facilities, improving the living environment of inhabitants, and improving public services. Through various means, such as authorizations, licensing, contracting and subcontracting, they should shift certain functions over to not-for-profit social organizations. Governments themselves should serve primarily as organizers and regulators.

Establish a performance evaluation system that allows for scientific urban development

China must set up a system that conforms to the requirements of a 'scientific approach to development'. The general principle in this regard is to strengthen evaluations that relate to the provision of public services, improved social management, and increased capacities for sustainable development. Based on this commonality, different regions can then institute separate evaluation systems that have different emphases.

For example, for cities in regions that are regarded as 'optimum for pursuing urbanization', we should set up performance-evaluation criteria that put the priority on transforming the mode of economic development. We should aim for strengthening things that focus on economic structure, resource conservation, environmental protection, self-generated innovation, the percentage of service industries, turning rural migrant workers into urban residents, 'localizing' people who have come into the city from elsewhere (who are other than rural migrant workers), and so on. We should weaken evaluations that focus purely on the rate of economic growth, on pulling in investment, on urbanization that is being done solely by looking at the statistics for the long-standing population, and so on.

For cities that are located in regions that are 'key areas for developing the urbanization programme', we should implement performance evaluations that do in fact put the priority on economic development but that have comprehensive considerations. These would include quality and efficiency of growth, industrial structure, resource conservation, environmental protection, industrialization, turning rural migrant workers into urban residents, and so on. We should downplay criteria that have to do with the rate at which investment is growing, attracting investment from outside, pegging urbanization rates solely to the number of long-standing urban residents, and so on.

For areas that are primary agricultural producers, and areas regarded as important ecosystems, as well as cities located in such places, performance evaluations should be conducted that place priority on agricultural development and on environmental protection. Such economic indicators as industrialization, urbanization, and economic growth should not be emphasized as performance criteria.

Set up planning systems that are advantageous to the healthy development of urbanization

From the perspective of furthering urbanization, we should emphasize the integration of plans that deal with municipal and county-level spatial configurations. Depending on the size of the 'spatial unit', the current profusion of planning efforts should be reduced and simplified to the following: plans that deal with 'main-function zones' on a nationwide basis, regional plans, plans that look at the spatial development of both cities and counties, urban plans, town and township plans, and village plans.

The state should strengthen its planning efforts with respect to 'nationwide main-function zones'. It should draft and implement plans for main-function areas that cross provincial administrative boundaries. The objective should be to conduct planning that relates to national territory on a nationwide basis and that involves main-function zones.

Regional planning should work within the national plans and should focus on urbanized areas (urban clusters) that are specified as being 'main-function zones' by the national plan.

At the level of cities and counties, development plans should focus on zones that are under the jurisdiction of cities and counties. Plans should be drawn up that 'unify three planning aspects', namely socioeconomic, urban–rural, and land. They should integrate all relevant plans that exist at the city and county level into master plans so that each city and each county has a plan to follow.

The formulation of plans for cities, towns and townships, and villages should be based on the spatial configuration laid out by the city–county development plans. These are the internal plans for each of the 'dots' on the overall plan. They should focus on zoning for various functions, the distribution of basic infrastructure, and the overall pattern and character of the city.

These should not be plans for 'tracts of land', in the sense that they should not focus simply on how to expand the amount of area under an urban jurisdiction. All plans should incorporate all types of urban districts, including development zones, industrial parks, universities, 'villages within cities', and so on. All of these should come under the unified control of the urban planning process. The basic principle should be that plans for smaller areas are to comply with the plans for larger areas.

Simplify the number of administrative layers in government and reform the model that governs how cities position themselves

We should consider reducing the number of 'layers' in the Chinese administrative hierarchy from the current five down to three. Right now, the five levels of government consist of the Central government, provincial governments (which include the categories of autonomous regions and centrally administered municipalities), prefectural governments (which include some cities), county governments (which also include some cities), and towns (which include some townships). These would thereby be reduced to Central, provincial, and city–county levels of government.

Cities at the prefectural level would no longer have direct administrative responsibility for counties and county-level cities. These would come under the direct jurisdiction of provincial governments. Towns and townships would no longer constitute a 'level of government'. Instead, they would be represented by institutions in the city–county level of government.

China should now eliminate the practice whereby a place can upgrade its status or 'level of government' once it complies with certain criteria. In principle, we would no longer be allowing 'prefectures to turn themselves into cities', 'counties to turn themselves into cities', 'counties to turn themselves into districts', and 'townships to turn themselves into towns'. It will no longer be possible for an administrative district to change its 'title' and thereby increase the scope of its jurisdiction.

The country should also reform the system whereby 'larger cities' govern 'smaller cities'. Once the population in the 'built-up area' of a county-level city or 'administered town' reaches a certain level, that place should go through a specific legal process in order to be turned into an officially designated 'administered town'. The minimum population requirement right now is 200,000. Many administered towns already far exceed that figure, however. Indeed, they exceed the population of large cities. Their administrative designation should be modified at the earliest possible time so that instead of 'towns' they are now recognized as 'cities'.

Accelerate reform of the fiscal system

The fiscal authority vested in municipal governments is not currently aligned with the tasks required of municipal governments, particularly the task of providing public services. Municipalities lack stable sources of funding. They lack channels for funding that increase as their populations increase. This is one of the reasons they are unwilling to receive rural migrant workers into their midst as residents with access to all urban services.

From the perspective of our intent to promote 'urbanization', we should design fiscal systems and tax systems that are in alignment with governing responsibilities. As urban populations increase, we need mechanisms that will ensure a commensurate increase in tax revenues. We also need a scientific approach to dividing up authorities and responsibilities between the Central government and local governments.

In line with the principle that these two things should be symmetrical, governing responsibility and the ability to pay for such responsibility, we should allocate a portion of stable tax revenue to local governments and/or to municipal governments.

The percentage of fiscal revenue that is retained by the city–county level of government should be increased. The principle should be that the benefits of tax revenues go back to the people who have paid the taxes. A larger percentage of the source of funds for 'building up the city' should therefore be coming from taxes paid out by urban residents.

The personal income tax system and the way in which it is currently split up should accordingly be reformed. After an employer has deducted personal income tax from an employee's wages or salary, a percentage of the retained portion should be designated as going to the grassroots-level government in which that person resides.

Taxes on real estate and an 'environmental tax' should now be levied. A portion of those taxes should, similarly, be allocated to the municipal government in which the taxed entity is located.

The subsidizing mechanisms by which Central finances support the basic infrastructure of municipalities should be improved. In principle, Central finance should not be subsidizing the basic infrastructure of municipalities. In cases where subsidies are necessary, specific amounts should be tied to the willingness of a municipality to absorb a certain number of rural migrant workers into the city as proper urban residents.

Strengthen the building up of communities, and create more innovative systems

Communities occupy a key position in the structure of city governance, and are a key link in the process of governing. They are the 'common entities' in which residents live their lives and the entities through which they govern themselves. They also serve as a bridge between the legitimate administration of government and the legitimate self-governance of residents, the term 'legitimate' in this sense meaning 'according to established law'. Communities serve as the bonding force between government and their own self-management.

China should adhere to the process of combining social participation with the guidance of government. The country should set up systems and procedures whereby communities can manage themselves, in accordance with the country's socialist market-economy system. Community organizations and 'team building' should be supported in order to raise the level of professionalism in the work being undertaken by communities. All levels of government should increase their inputs into the basic infrastructure of communities. They should cultivate mechanisms that enable greater public participation, through nurturing policies, diverse channels of funding, mutual use of resources, and mutual support.

The country should improve the basic conditions and public-service facilities of communities. Communities should be managed by the community residential committees, supported by public efforts, and participated in by the public at large.

While the primary concern of communities should be the provision of services, communities should also focus on the 'substantive aspects' of communities themselves. These include improving the general hygiene of a given area, enriching its culture, beautifying its environs, improving its public security, and improving all of its functions in general.

The aim is to create a 'new style' of modern community, one that is well managed, has excellent services, beautiful surroundings, is convenient and safe to live in, and allows for congenial relations with neighbours.

Enable residents and social organizations to play a role in city governance

If we are to set up a 'modern model for city governance', it is imperative that we encourage the residents of cities and all kinds of social organizations to participate in that governance.

First, the participation of residents will greatly reduce conflict between urban governments and urban residents. It will increase the sense of 'ownership' and 'stewardship' that residents have towards the place in which they live. Second, it will lower the costs of governance.

All kinds of organizations can serve as effective routes to participating in governance. These include social groups, industrial associations, specialized organizations, intermediary institutions, and other non-profit social organizations. These are not well developed in China at present, since there are still many obstacles put in their way. Problems range from registering organizations, charitable donations, the legal status of such groups, and their standardized behaviour. Nevertheless, we should be fully aware of the useful role these social organizations can play. In creating innovative models for city governance, it is extremely important that we create a role for such organizations. We should establish ways for information to be passed up and down among such organizations and governmental departments as well as citizens themselves. We should promote openness in government affairs and encourage public participation in the entire process of governance, from making decisions to implementation of policies to supervision of the resulting actions.

Notes

1 Social organizations were introduced in the Decisions of the Central Committee of the Communist Party of China on Major Issues Concerning the Building of a Socialist Harmonious Society made at the 6th Plenary Session of the Party's 16th Central Committee. In general, social organizations have basically the same contents of 'non-governmental organizations', and include social groups, foundations, private non-corporate institutions, and intermediary service organizations.
2 In recent years, a few projects, such as the petrochemical project in Xiamen, have been stopped or relocated due to opposition from local residents.

10 Policy recommendations

This Report puts forth a strategy for a 'new kind of urbanization that is designed to promote human development'. In order to implement the strategy, we hereby present summaries of 14 policy recommendations.

1 Strengthen the leadership role of the Central government in carrying out urbanization

We recommend that the Central Committee of the Communist Party of China convene a plenary session to discuss the overall thinking behind 'urbanization' in China. The Central Committee should come to a conclusive decision about several major issues that this strategy involves. The Central Committee should seek to unify thinking on these major issues, come to a consensus, and agree on the steps forward.

Major issues to be addressed include the conversion of rural migrant workers into legitimate urban residents, the spatial configuration of urbanization in China, the main forms that urbanization will take, the creation of urban infrastructure and public service systems, issues of real estate development and the housing system, funding sources for urban development, and, finally, how to handle the contracted land and former housing of rural migrant workers once they have become urban residents.

Following on this first plenary session, we recommend that a conference then be convened annually on this subject. It should be held in the name of the Central Committee, that is, it should be a 'Central Committee working meeting'. It should consider new issues to do with urbanization every year from a centrally coordinated perspective. It should formulate major governmental principles and policies to do with urbanization. It should allocate the work to be done on all the various issues, including turning rural migrant workers into legitimate urban residents, developing urban clusters, and addressing issues of urban industries, urban housing, urban basic infrastructure, and the setting up of public services.

2 Regard one essential task as being primary in China's urbanization, namely, the conversion of rural migrant workers into legitimate urban residents

Starting from the beginning of the 12th Five-Year Plan period and ending no later than 2020, the first group of rural migrant workers and members of their families should be converted into legitimate urban residents. This first group should include people who have stable employment and pay taxes, who already enjoy social security, and who have a fixed place of residence. It should also include those rural migrant workers who are already in cities and will have been there for five years [by the time the 10-year period is up]. In all, this should include nearly 200 million rural migrant workers and their families.

People who are converted to urban residency status should be willing to take up fully entitled residence in cities on a voluntary basis. The process should address their household-registration status and the public services they are able to receive as a consequence of their new status.

Before 2030, another 200 million rural migrant workers and their families should be converted to urban residents, with fully entitled urban-resident status. Over a period of roughly 20 years, therefore, we should realize a transition that enables rural migrant workers to enter cities, establish legitimate residency, and enjoy the same public services as those people who were originally living in the cities.

We should not adopt a blanket method for all places at the same time in this process. Instead, we should institute controls over the total number of conversions through a method that gradually relaxes the criteria by which people can change their status. In other words, we should adopt an incremental approach that still retains the household-registration system. At all times, we should ensure that conversions are being done on a voluntary basis.

Small and medium-sized cities and towns in the western and central parts of the country may move more quickly in fully relaxing restrictions on household-registration status than cities in the east. Rural migrant workers may be able to enjoy full urban residency in those places earlier than in other parts of the country. In the eastern part of China, small and medium-sized cities and towns can also, in principle, fully relax restrictions. Large and ultra-large cities should gradually change as their individual circumstances allow. They should stay within the comprehensive carrying capacity of their situations.

For rural migrant workers who do not want to adopt residency in the place of their employment, we should continue to implement policies that allow for a two-way movement of people between urban and rural areas. At the same time, we must respect and protect the rights and interests of rural migrant workers [even though they are not legitimate urban residents]. We must ensure that they have fair compensation, workers' protection, education for their children, medical services, and adequate housing.

We recommend that the country revise the Land-Contracting Law [i.e., the law on '*chengbao*' contracts that governs the land-use rights of farmers]. When rural migrant workers opt to take up urban residency together with their families, the provisions in the law that ensure their contractual rights to land that they previously farmed should be eliminated. Consideration might be given to maintaining a grace period of three to five years in which contracted land-use rights still apply.

We recommend setting up a mechanism that links the number of people a city can absorb to the amount of land that the city has under its jurisdiction. This mechanism would therefore create a direct correlation between 'land' and 'people'. Every year, an additional amount of 'land quota' would be allocated to cities depending on the number of rural migrant workers being converted to urban residency in that year. Cities absorbing more people would be allocated more quota; those absorbing fewer people would get less, and those not taking in any people would get no quota at all.

Consideration might also be given to a system that links the amount of space used by cities to the amount of space used by 'rural' areas. As urban land use increased in the 'building up' of the city, rural land use would decrease, while the increase in people absorbed into cities would reflect a decrease in those remaining in the countryside – the ratios between the two places would be linked to one another. Similarly, different regions in the country would apply similar correlations: cities in certain regions would be allocated more land quota only when they absorbed certain numbers of people into their urban residency systems. In doing this, we would institute a balancing mechanism that allowed for reduction in the urban use of arable land in one place when land was taken by urban development in another.

We recommend setting up a mechanism that correlates the number of people to the amount of public funding. Depending on the number of rural migrant workers that a given city absorbs into its systems, Central finance and provincial finance would set up transfer payments to cities depending on the number of rural migrant workers they absorbed into their systems. Central finance would subsidize the finances of the cities every year with specifically targeted funds.

The funds would be used primarily for enabling municipal governments to provide greater social security, medical facilities, compulsory education, job training, and low-rent housing for rural migrant workers and their family members. They would be aimed at building up and revamping the urban facilities provided by municipal governments.

In raising the funds for these subsidies, we might consider issuing special-issue national bonds. We might also consider allocating a percentage of the profits that are 'handed up' to the state every year by the country's state-owned enterprises.

We recommend that a state-level organization be tasked with formulating a comprehensive plan for the conversion of rural migrant workers into legitimate urban residents. This would then be approved and implemented under the auspices of the State Council. At regular intervals, it would be re-evaluated and revised as necessary.

3 Make 'urban clusters' the primary form by which China urbanizes

First, the wording of the strategy should be changed in official documents of the Party and the state to reflect the new orientation of our urbanization. We should restore use of the term 'urbanization' [*cheng-shi-hua*, which focuses on cities as opposed to towns]. We should no longer use a previous term that allowed for the expansion of towns [*cheng-zhen-hua*].

China must follow a path of 'urbanization' [*cheng-shi-hua*] that is 'compact', 'intensive', and 'dense', given the country's fundamental situation of having a large population on a small amount of land. The 'guiding thinking' and the 'work principles' behind our process of urbanization must therefore explicitly support the formation of 'urban clusters'. The aim is to prevent the kinds of urban syndromes that arise from excessive concentration of urban functions, while also enabling an intensive use of land.

We should therefore develop existing small-sized cities, county seats, and those towns with the right potential, in the proper manner, and after taking into consideration their carrying capacity in terms of resources and the environment. We should promote urbanization in a 'dot' pattern as opposed to a pattern that allows for extended 'tracts' of developed land. In following this kind of urbanization, we should strengthen the unique qualities of different places, as opposed to trying to create 'comprehensive cities' that have no key features at all.

Our primary form of urbanization in the future should not allow small towns to expand until they become cities. We should therefore discard the policy principle whereby we emphasized the development of small towns [*cheng-zhen*], since it runs counter to the laws of urbanization.

4 Establish a spatial configuration for urbanization that includes 'two horizontal axes and three vertical axes'

The spatial configuration of China's 'urbanization' will rely mainly on 20 'urbanized regions' as described in the main text of the Report above.

These will be arrayed across the country in a pattern that can be described as 'two horizontal axes and three vertical axes'. The two horizontal axes follow the Yangtze River corridor and the land-bridge corridor [to the north of it.] The three vertical axes follow the coastal corridor, the Jing-Ha-Jing-Guang corridor and the Bao-Kun corridor [that is, the Beijing–Harbin–Nanjing–Guangzhou corridor, and the Baotou–Kunming corridor]. This configuration takes into account resource and environmental carrying capacities, the existing level of development and potential for future development, and such factors as history, ethnicity, and national defense.

China's 20 'primary urbanized areas' will then include three mega-cities, eight large urban clusters, and nine urbanized districts.

The three mega-cities will be in the Bohai Rim area, the Yangtze River Delta area, and the Pearl River Delta area. The eight large urban clusters will be located in the Harbin–Changchun region, the southeast Fujian region, the Jianghuai region, the Central Plains, the middle reaches of the Yangtze River, the Guanzhong Plains, the Chengdu–Chongqing region, and the Baibu Bay region. The nine urbanized areas will be in the central and southern parts of Hebei Province, the central part of Shanxi Province, the Hohhot–Baotou–Erdos–Yulin region, the central part of Guizhou Province, the central part of Yunnan Province, the central and southern parts of Tibet, the Lanzhou–Xining region, the area of Ningxia along the Yellow River, and the region north of the Tianshan Mountains.

Smaller cities and towns should be classified into different categories with policy guidance that applies to each category. Urban development should be enhanced in the 'port cities' that are situated along China's inland border areas.

5 Undertake projects that enable the cities within each urban cluster to be an integral whole

The functions of different cities within each urban cluster should be differentiated so that the cluster as a whole works as one organism. The 'positioning' of industries in each one should complement the others. Basic infrastructure should be linked up in network fashion. Convenient and easy passage of personnel should enable the entire urban 'body' to be one network.

Super-large cities that lie within urban clusters should disperse their urban functions so as to strengthen the urban functions of small and medium-sized cities in the cluster. The comprehensive carrying capacity of the whole should be strengthened as a result.

Urban planning should be done on a unified basis. Planning for the functions of each city and the positioning of its industries should be carried out from an overall perspective. Planning for provision of public services, residential districts, and ecosystem patterns should be coordinated so as to preserve open space and green belts between cities.

Systems that interconnect cities within urban clusters should be set up in unified patterns that enable all residents to partake of them. They should be evenly balanced in terms of quality standards, and should be set up as an integrated network. Such systems include the infrastructure for transportation, energy, communications, environmental protection, and disaster prevention.

6 Increase population density in the built-up area of cities to a very substantial degree

One key task of China's urbanization process must be to increase population densities considerably. This applies to urban development in cities and county seats as well as to administered towns. There must be a reasonable balance in the rate at which people are 'urbanizing' and the rate at which land is being 'urbanized', that is, taken over by cities and no longer serving a rural use.

The appropriate ministries [or departments] at the state-government level should formulate binding regulations that define the population 'standards' applicable to different sizes of cities, depending on specific circumstances. These should have the effect of radically increasing the density of urban populations nationwide. County seats and administered towns should also put major effort into increasing the population densities of their 'built-up areas'. At the very least, they should no longer allow population densities to continue to decline.

Cities that contain more than two million people should raise the density of their population until it is around 15,000 people per square kilometer. Those with between 500,000 and two million people should raise the density to around 12,000 per square kilometers. Those with fewer than 500,000 people should raise the density until it is around 10,000 per square kilometer.

China should establish standards that regulate the intensity of development and that define the boundaries of urban development. Controls should be in line with the carrying capacity of a given environment and its resources, and should regulate the amount of economic activity, the size of the population, the structure of the local economy, the number of cars, and so on. Binding restrictions in the form of mandated quotas should apply to each major urbanized district within a given area, and these too should be matched to the carrying capacity of the land. China must control the rampant expansion of cities. The country must prevent cities from encroaching any further on neighboring farmland and 'ecosystem land'. Restrictions must apply to any land development, industrial development, and real estate development that falls outside the boundaries of cities.

7 Simplify the existing levels of government administration, and reform the ways in which 'administered cities' can be set up

Consideration should be given to reducing the number of levels of government from the existing five levels down to three. Currently, China's governmental operations are divided into five distinct levels: Central, provincial (including autonomous regions and cities directly under the jurisdiction of the Central government), prefectures (including some cities), counties (including some cities), and towns (including townships). The country should consider going to a system that includes three levels: Central government, provincial government, and municipal-county government.

Cities at the prefectural level would no longer govern counties directly, nor would they govern cities at the county level. Towns and townships below the county or municipal level could set up representative entities within municipal-county governments. They would no longer constitute a 'level' of government in themselves.

Moreover, China should now eliminate the practice whereby a place can upgrade its status or 'level of government' once it complies with certain criteria. In principle, we should no longer be allowing 'prefectures to turn themselves into cities', 'counties to turn themselves into cities', 'counties to turn themselves into districts', and 'townships to turn themselves into towns'. It should no longer be possible for an administrative district to change its 'title' and thereby increase the scope of its jurisdiction.

China should also reform the system whereby 'larger cities' govern 'smaller cities'. Once the population in the 'built-up area' of a county-level city or 'administered town' reaches a certain level, that place should go through a specific legal process in order to be turned into an officially designated 'administered town'. The minimum population requirement right now is 200,000. Many administered towns already far exceed that figure, however. Indeed, they exceed the population of large cities. Their administrative designation should be modified at the earliest possible time so that they are recognized as 'cities' now, instead of 'towns'.

8   Redefine the standards by which 'city size' is defined, and change the way that cities are classified

The newly adopted Law on Urban and Rural Planning did not specify standards by which the sizes of cities are to be measured. As a result, many policies have no basis for accurate definition as they are being formulated. We should now redefine 'city size' in explicit terms and at specific levels.

Given the reality that China has a very large population, we recommend that cities be defined in the following six ways: mega-cities, extra-large cities, large cities, medium-sized cities, small cities, and small towns.

Based on these definitions, we can classify 'urbanized areas' into different categories, but these should be used only for planning and statistical purposes, not for purposes of administration. They should not be regarded as constituting a 'layer' of government. 'Urbanized areas' can be defined by the density of the population that lives within a certain measurement of space. ['Urbanized areas' refers to areas that contain more than one city, nor areas within a city that are urbanized.]

Municipal governments of the cities within any given 'urbanized area' should draft unified plans for basic infrastructure, as per their own situations and the needs of their own departments. At the same time, they should establish area-wide planning commissions, which should be composed of democratically elected representatives and representatives from the each of the individual municipal-government entities in the area. These planning commissions would primarily be responsible for formulating, examining, and evaluating plans that cut across administrative jurisdictions. Among other things, they would be responsible for reviewing and evaluating the environmental impact assessments associated with any major projects that involve more than one jurisdiction.

9   Improve the systems that provide public services in cities

China should define the public service responsibilities of governments at each different level in a way that is clear and rational. In this determination, the Central government should be responsible for defining the scope of public services, what things are to be included, standards, regulations, laws, and certain regional plans. Based on this determination, the Central government should also be responsible for providing the most basic public services for all members of society, without discrimination, including those things that cannot be 'urbanized' and those things that achieve social equity.

If the Central government continues to receive its current percentage of total public-finance revenues, then it should become fully responsible for paying for compulsory education, social security, basic medical treatment, and other such fundamental public services. Existing responsibilities would therefore need to be adjusted.

Provincial governments should be responsible for funding public services that have relatively less of a 'public nature' to them, including the government-funded portion of high-school and higher-education costs, social relief, job creation, disaster prevention and mitigation at the regional level, public order, and public culture.

Municipal governments should be responsible for providing the public utilities necessary to maintain and safeguard urban functions and operations, and for which the beneficiaries are extremely clear-cut. Such things would include roads, bridges, public transport, municipal sewage and garbage treatment, city parks and green space, protection of urban water sources, provision of low-rent housing, publicly owned rental housing, and so on.

China should reform the model by which is delivers urban public services by diversifying how services are supplied. Diversified methods can still include direct government provision of services, but should also include provision through licensing and through market forces. The country should encourage non-governmental sources of capital to invest in the provision of urban public services, including capital from abroad. Methods should include joint ventures, cooperative arrangements, and licensed or authorized operations. Constant and ever-increasing efforts should be made to improve the provision of public services to vulnerable groups in China. This should include both specific action and the budgeting of more funds, and it should be made a primary task of municipal governments [i.e., subject to performance evaluations].

10 Incorporate rural migrant workers who are now living in cities into the housing security system

China should lower the prices at which commercial property is currently being sold by undertaking a variety of measures. These would include increasing the supply of land that is available for residential housing purposes. They would include beginning to levy a real estate tax, and they would also include lowering the price of land. The country must vastly expand the amount of low-rent housing and publicly owned rental housing that is available, in order to incorporate those rural migrant workers who wish to take up legitimate residency in cities and enable them to participate in housing security and relief systems. Those rural migrant workers who qualify should be granted low-rent housing and relief coverage.

The country should explore methods whereby collective economic organizations use 'rural construction land' [land designated for building use in rural areas] to construct apartment blocks for rural migrant workers. These would be specifically for rental by rural migrant workers who have taken up permanent urban residency and other people who have migrated into cities and taken up residency.

Policies should be adopted that extend preferential terms to rural migrant workers in order to assist them in purchasing low-cost housing in cities. Rural migrant workers who have taken up urban residency would be entitled to subsidies that government provides through commercial banks. These would lower the percentage of full price required for a down-payment, they would extend the repayment period, lower the deed tax, and lower interest rates on the mortgage.

11 Adopt proactive employment policies

Job creation should become a priority goal of China's socio-economic development policies. Proactive employment policies should not only be implemented in general but also be extended to groups of rural migrant workers through intensifying the provision of employment services.

Meanwhile, the country should learn from international experience in redefining 'employment' and 'unemployment', and should improve the statistical measures by which it conducts employment surveys. Criteria relating to employment and unemployment should be included in the performance evaluations of local governments and should be given a fairly high weighting in those evaluations.

Proactive employment policies should seek to improve the 'employable capacity' of people laid-off from state-owned enterprises in cities who are not highly qualified in terms of their 'human-resource capital'. Public employment services should be provided to the group of college students who need jobs, including an appropriate level of social security, job training, and job-finding intermediary services.

China should improve the capacity of the central and western parts of the country to absorb a greater percentage of the rural population that is migrating into cities and looking for jobs. As the economic structure in the east changes [moving from manufacturing to more service-oriented industries], labor-intensive and low-end service industries will move in sequential fashion first to the central and then the western regions. In the future, the central and western regions will therefore play a greater role in absorbing the rural population into cities.

Right now, there is still a tendency to invest in heavy industry in these places, which deviates from the relative advantage they hold with respect to labor-intensive industry. Policies should be adjusted in time to enable the shift of industries from the east. At the same time, as this industrial shift occurs, adequate provision should be made for environmental protection and resource conservation through more intensive use of resources. Workers' rights and interests must also be safeguarded.

In around 2015, China's labor supply will reach a peak figure, after which it will gradually decline at a modest rate. The period in which China has been enjoying a 'population bonus' will then turn into a period in which the country suffers from a 'population liability', in the sense that the burden of paying for an aging population will greatly increase. We urgently need to 'fix the roof before it starts to rain'. We need to set up pension systems on a nationwide basis that provide coverage for the country's entire body of people. We need to improve the old-age security system in both urban and rural areas. In parts of the country that meet certain conditions, we can go further in relaxing family-planning policies in order to defer the start of the 'population liability' period.

12 Follow a sustainable and green path toward urbanization

In the face of ever more stringent resource and environmental constraints, we must take advantage of lessons learned by other countries in the course of their own urbanization. We should accelerate the process of changing our economic structure and our mode of economic development. We must follow a path of urbanization that is more 'compact' and 'concentrated', that conserves resources, is environmentally friendly, and is more suited to human habitation.

Urbanization must abide strictly by plans that govern the needs of 'main-function zones'. Development should occur only in line with the carrying capacity of the resources and environment of each different area. It should be highly targeted and carried out through the use of different methods. Zoning for industrial and other functional areas should be done in a rational way. Cities should strengthen a cooperative division of labor between cities and between urban and rural areas. They should create urban environments that are 'habitable' and that are enjoyed by all residents.

Mechanisms should be instituted that enable pricing and taxation to play a leveraging role in achieving greater conservation of resources and greater environmental protection. Costs that are currently external to both business and living should be internalized, so that the 'user pays the cost [of actual usage]' and 'the polluter pays the cost [of polluting]'. In order to abide by this principle, property rights must be clarified.

Energy conservation must be promoted in all transportation and construction projects through prioritizing the use of scientific methods. Massive effort should be put into developing public transport, especially urban rail lines and inter-urban rail lines. Environmental impact assessments should be strengthened together with public regulatory oversight of those assessments.

Mechanisms that provide for public participation and non-governmental participation in the process should constantly be improved. Regulatory oversight by society at large should be enhanced at all the links in the process of undertaking a public endeavor. This includes the stages at which enterprises make investments, production proceeds, public utilities are built, and also the stage at which policy is enforced.

13 Diversify funding sources for the building of urban infrastructure, as well as for the provision of public services

China's investment in public services and urban infrastructure is going to be increasing tremendously over the next decade. Not only will it be hard for the country's current funding models to meet demand in terms of total quantity, but the current model carries with it high financial risk and various other problems. We are in urgent need of transforming our financing model.

First, we can adopt a progressive fee-pricing system for users of services. People who use less of a given service would pay less per unit than people who used more, which would lessen the burden on impoverished segments of the population.

Second, we can allow the issuing of municipal bonds for urban construction, in order to mitigate the financing pressures on 'local-government [provincial and municipal] funding platforms'. Small and medium-sized cities may undertake to issue bonds on a collective basis.

Third, partnerships between the public and private sectors may be set up to provide public services on a joint basis. Through the use of different procurement methods, the relevant government entity may sign contracts with successful bidders for raising funds, construction, and operations. The government can accelerate the process of developing infrastructure by giving long-term licensing rights and revenue rights to successful bidders in the private sector.

Fourth, China should make greater use of project financing, which means that the revenue stream and cash flow that go back to the company managing the project would serve as the source of funds for repaying project loans. The assets and authorized rights of the projects would serve as collateral for loans. The loans would be made either on a no-recourse or a limited right of recourse basis.

Fifth, on a very stable and secure basis, China should promote the securitization of assets. This mode of financing is useful in expanding funding sources for building infrastructure when the infrastructure results in a stable cash flow. In China, the method has considerable room for growth in the future.

Sixth, China should speed up the pace of reforming its tax system. Specifically, at the earliest possible time it should begin to levy a tax on real estate as well as an environmental tax. Based on these initial actions, it should proceed to set up a sound municipal tax system in order to keep municipalities from relying excessively on 'land as the source of public finance' as they develop.

14 Promote the democratization of city governance

Relevant laws and regulations should be improved so that citizens' rights are effectively guaranteed with respect to city governance. These include, specifically, the right to know, the right to participate, and the right to exercise supervisory oversight.

Representatives to the 'Municipal People's Congresses' should be elected by direct vote [of the people]. Participatory public budgeting should be promoted. Mechanisms should be established that enable a kind of democratic consultation and dialogue between government organizations, community organizations, economic organizations, and social intermediary organizations, and urban residents. All social and public endeavors should be published on the Internet to the maximum extent possible. Mechanisms for public inquiries, public hearings, and public supervisory oversight should be established.

In order to achieve an integration of 'government guidance' and 'social [or public] participation', operating mechanisms and community management systems should be set up that are appropriate to the way a socialist market-economy system functions. This will involve the strengthening of community organizations and their staff. In order to raise the professionalism of community work and expand community capacities, working mechanisms should be established that are sponsored by community committees, supported by social forces, and participated in by the public at large.

China should explore having rural migrant workers participate in democratic governance in cities. It should have actual mechanisms whereby rural migrant workers are able to express their own interests and it should gradually institutionalize these mechanisms. This includes enabling rural migrant workers to participate in grassroots-level democratic elections, democratic forums, and democratic supervisory oversight, as well as participating in direct elections to the Municipal People's Congresses. In communities that have particular concentrations of rural migrant workers, the country should institute public opinion polls and residents' discussion forums. Rural migrant workers should be actively encouraged to participate in city governance through such things as public hearings.

China should relax controls over the 'entry provisions' or rules that currently apply to setting up social [civic] organizations. The country should in fact put great effort into developing such organizations, so as to improve their ability to reflect social demands, regulate behavior, harmonize interests, and serve society.

Appendices*

	Human development index in 2008	Life-expectancy index in 2008	Educational index in 2008	GDP index in 2008	Standing in terms of human development index in 2008	Standing in terms of human development index in 2006	Standing in terms of change of human development index 2006–2008
National	0.808	0.816	0.857	0.749			
Beijing	0.938	0.960	0.934	0.920	1	2	1
Tianjin	0.901	0.880	0.924	0.898	3	3	0
Hebei	0.820	0.842	0.864	0.753	13	9	−4
Shanxi	0.803	0.809	0.869	0.731	18	14	−4
Inner Mongolia	0.832	0.770	0.919	0.808	10	15	5
Liaoning	0.861	0.870	0.911	0.803	6	7	1
Jilin	0.834	0.817	0.931	0.755	9	11	2
Heilongjiang	0.807	0.796	0.883	0.742	17	12	−5
Shanghai	0.935	0.939	0.922	0.944	2	1	−1
Jiangsu	0.862	0.853	0.890	0.842	5	5	0
Zhejiang	0.863	0.863	0.873	0.853	4	4	0
Anhui	0.767	0.812	0.815	0.674	26	26	0
Fujian	0.826	0.815	0.866	0.796	12	10	−2
Jiangxi	0.794	0.822	0.882	0.678	23	23	0
Shandong	0.845	0.845	0.877	0.812	8	8	0
Henan	0.798	0.810	0.861	0.725	20	20	0
Hubei	0.815	0.833	0.887	0.727	15	17	2
Hunan	0.812	0.840	0.890	0.706	16	18	2
Guangdong	0.854	0.854	0.874	0.833	7	6	−1
Guangxi	0.797	0.825	0.886	0.680	21	22	1
Hainan	0.802	0.870	0.833	0.703	19	16	−3
Chongqing	0.829	0.875	0.900	0.711	11	13	2
Sichuan	0.791	0.849	0.841	0.684	24	24	0
Guizhou	0.698	0.743	0.760	0.592	30	30	0
Yunnan	0.727	0.751	0.779	0.651	28	29	1
Tibet	0.651	0.715	0.571	0.667	31	31	0
Shaanxi	0.816	0.833	0.901	0.713	14	19	5
Gansu	0.727	0.778	0.758	0.644	29	28	−1
Qinghai	0.759	0.779	0.792	0.705	27	27	0
Ningxia	0.791	0.841	0.823	0.709	25	25	0
Xinjiang	0.796	0.807	0.853	0.727	22	21	−1

Appendix 2: GDP figures and the GDP index for China and its provinces in 2008

	Per capita GDP (yuan)	Per capita GDP (PPP US$)	GDP index
National	22,698	8,901	0.749
Beijing	63,029	24,717	0.920
Tianjin	55,473	21,754	0.898
Hebei	23,239	9,113	0.753
Shanxi	20,398	7,999	0.731
Inner Mongolia	32,214	12,633	0.808
Liaoning	31,259	12,258	0.803
Jilin	23,514	9,221	0.755
Heilongjiang	21,727	8,520	0.742
Shanghai	73,124	28,676	0.944
Jiangsu	39,622	15,538	0.842
Zhejiang	42,214	16,555	0.853
Anhui	14,485	5,680	0.674
Fujian	30,123	11,813	0.796
Jiangxi	14,781	5,796	0.678
Shandong	33,083	12,974	0.812
Henan	19,593	7,684	0.725
Hubei	19,860	7,788	0.727
Hunan	17,521	6,871	0.706
Guangdong	37,589	14,741	0.833
Guangxi	14,966	5,869	0.680
Hainan	17,175	6,735	0.703
Chongqing	18,025	7,069	0.711
Sichuan	15,378	6,031	0.684
Guizhou	8,824	3,460	0.592
Yunnan	12,587	4,936	0.651
Tibet	13,861	5,436	0.667
Shaanxi	18,246	7,155	0.713
Gansu	12,110	4,749	0.644
Qinghai	17,389	6,819	0.705
Ningxia	17,892	7,016	0.709
Xinjiang	19,893	7,801	0.727

Note: The data on nominal per capita GDP originates from the *China Statistical Yearbook 2009*; the per capita GDP (PPP US$) in 2008 as calculated at purchasing power parity is based on the PPP index estimated by the World Bank.

Appendix 3: School enrollment rates at the national and provincial levels, and the education index in China in 2008

	Enrollment rate of school-age children in primary school (%)	Enrollment rate in junior high school (%)	Enrollment rate in senior high school (%)	Enrollment rate in higher education, as measured by average enrollment rate of children aged 18–20 (%)	Integrated enrollment index	Adult literacy rate (%)	Education index
National	99.9	100.6	72.5	23.0	0.740	91.6	0.857
Beijing	99.0	100.0	100.6	57.3	0.892	95.5	0.934
Tianjin	106.0	100.2	86.3	49.4	0.855	95.8	0.924
Hebei	100.0	98.6	64.0	17.5	0.700	94.6	0.864
Shanxi	98.6	100.0	63.8	21.0	0.709	94.9	0.869
Inner Mongolia	105.9	106.6	85.6	20.6	0.797	98.1	0.919
Liaoning	100.8	100.8	77.3	31.2	0.775	97.9	0.911
Jilin	101.4	105.0	74.4	25.4	0.765	101.4	0.931
Heilongjiang	98.2	97.6	55.8	26.5	0.695	97.7	0.883
Shanghai	99.2	101.0	101.6	46.6	0.871	94.8	0.922
Jiangsu	102.0	102.9	83.7	30.2	0.797	93.6	0.890
Zhejiang	101.1	102.3	90.4	27.9	0.804	90.8	0.873
Anhui	99.7	100.6	65.6	17.4	0.708	86.8	0.815
Fujian	101.8	101.5	78.7	19.7	0.754	92.2	0.866
Jiangxi	99.1	99.2	78.0	29.2	0.764	94.1	0.882
Shandong	102.0	101.6	77.3	22.0	0.757	93.7	0.877
Henan	101.5	101.0	62.3	14.3	0.698	94.2	0.861
Hubei	99.9	103.7	78.6	28.7	0.777	94.1	0.887
Hunan	98.9	102.7	70.8	18.9	0.728	97.0	0.890
Guangdong	101.5	98.7	65.5	15.4	0.703	95.9	0.874
Guangxi	100.1	103.0	65.3	13.8	0.706	97.6	0.886
Hainan	99.5	96.6	55.0	18.2	0.674	91.2	0.833
Chongqing	99.3	104.2	87.6	28.6	0.799	95.1	0.900
Sichuan	100.0	104.4	82.4	19.8	0.767	87.9	0.841
Guizhou	97.4	98.2	48.9	10.2	0.637	82.2	0.760
Yunnan	95.7	95.5	51.3	10.8	0.633	85.2	0.779
Tibet	97.0	93.8	42.0	12.4	0.613	54.9	0.571
Shaanxi	99.4	103.7	79.3	25.7	0.770	96.6	0.901
Gansu	97.6	98.6	69.9	14.8	0.702	78.6	0.758
Qinghai	96.5	96.4	77.9	10.5	0.703	83.7	0.792
Ningxia	99.2	98.8	75.9	15.5	0.723	87.3	0.823
Xinjiang	97.4	100.4	52.0	12.7	0.656	95.2	0.853

Notes: 1. School-age children's primary school enrolment rates originate from the *China Statistical Yearbook 2009* and the *China Education Statistical Yearbook*.

2. Gross junior-high enrolment rate (normal and vocational junior high schools):

$$\text{Gross junior-high enrolment rate} = \frac{\text{Total junior-high enrolment (excluding adults)}}{\text{Population of 12–14 age group}} \times 100\%$$

3. Gross senior-high enrolment rate (normal senior high schools, adult senior high schools, normal secondary vocational schools, adult secondary schools, vocational senior schools, and polytechnic schools):

$$\text{Gross senior-high enrolment rate} = \frac{\text{Total senior-high enrolment}}{\text{Population of 15–17 age group}} \times 100\%$$

4. Gross higher-education enrolment rate:

$$\text{Gross higher-education enrolment rate} = \frac{\text{Total higher-education enrolment}}{\text{Population of 18–22 age group}} \times 100\%$$

Appendix 4: Life expectancy and the life-expectancy index in China and its provinces in 2000, 2005, and 2008

Region	Life expectancy in 2000	Life expectancy in 2005	Life expectancy in 2008	Life-expectancy index in 2008
National	71.4	73.0	73.98	0.816
Beijing	76.1	80.09	82.58	0.960
Tianjin	74.91	76.71	77.81	0.880
Hebei	72.54	74.38	75.51	0.842
Shanxi	71.65	72.83	73.55	0.809
Inner Mongolia	69.87	70.70	71.2	0.770
Liaoning	73.34	75.71	77.17	0.870
Jilin	73.1	73.67	74.01	0.817
Heilongjiang	72.37	72.60	72.74	0.796
Shanghai	78.14	80.13	81.35	0.939
Jiangsu	73.91	75.32	76.18	0.853
Zhejiang	74.7	76.00	76.79	0.863
Anhui	71.85	73.00	73.7	0.812
Fujian	72.55	73.37	73.87	0.815
Jiangxi	68.95	72.25	74.31	0.822
Shandong	73.92	75.02	75.69	0.845
Henan	71.54	72.82	73.6	0.810
Hubei	71.08	73.48	74.96	0.833
Hunan	70.66	73.60	75.42	0.840
Guangdong	73.27	75.10	76.22	0.854
Guangxi	71.29	73.29	74.52	0.825
Hainan	72.92	75.55	77.17	0.870
Chongqing	71.73	75.27	77.48	0.875
Sichuan	71.2	74.11	75.91	0.849
Guizhou	65.96	68.20	69.58	0.743
Yunnan	65.49	68.29	70.03	0.751
Tibet	64.37	66.56	67.91	0.715
Shaanxi	70.07	73.11	75	0.833
Gansu	67.47	70.06	71.66	0.778
Qinghai	66.03	69.55	71.75	0.779
Ningxia	70.17	73.44	75.47	0.841
Xinjiang	67.41	71.12	73.44	0.807

Note: The life expectancy in 2008 was calculated by figuring the annual average growth rate between 2000 and 2005.

Appendix 5: National and provincial populations, urban population percentages, and birth rates in China and its provinces between 1995 and 2008

Region	Total population (year-end) (10,000 persons)				Urban population (year-end) (10,000 persons)				Urban population percentage (year-end) (%)			Birth rate (per 1,000)			
	1995	2006	2007	2008	1995	2006	2007	2008	2006	2007	2008	1995	2006	2007	2008
National	121,121	131,448	132,129	132,802	35,174	57,706	59,379	60,667	0.44	44.94	45.68	17.12	12.09	12.10	12.14
Beijing	1,251	1,581	1,633	1,695	946.2	1,333	1,380	1,439	0.84	84.50	84.90	8	6.26	8.32	8.17
Tianjin	942	1,075	1,115	1,176	545.57	814	851	908	0.76	76.31	77.23	10.23	7.67	7.91	8.13
Hebei	6,437	6,898	6,943	6,989		2,652	2,795	2,928	0.38	40.25	41.90	13.9	12.82	13.33	13.04
Shanxi	3,077	3,375	3,393	3,411		1,452	1,494	1,539	0.43	44.03	45.11	16.6	11.48	11.30	11.32
Inner Mongolia	2,284	2,397	2,405	2,414	873.1	1,166	1,206	1,248	0.49	50.15	51.71	17.2	9.87	10.21	9.81
Liaoning	4,092	4,271	4,298	4,315	1,780.9	2,519	2,544	2,591	0.59	59.20	60.05	9.9	6.4	6.89	6.32
Jilin	2,592	2,723	2,730	2,734	1,157.46	1,442	1,451	1,455	0.53	53.16	53.21	12.07	7.67	7.55	6.65
Heilongjiang	3,701	3,823	3,824	3,825		2,045	2,061	2,119	0.54	53.90	55.40	13.23	7.57	7.88	7.91
Shanghai	1,415	1,815	1,858	1,888	1,022.73	1,610	1,648	1,673	0.89	88.70	88.60	5.5	7.47	9.07	8.89
Jiangsu	7,066	7,550	7,625	7,677		3,918	4,057	4,169	0.52	53.20	54.30	12.32	9.36	9.37	9.34
Zhejiang	4,319	4,980	5,060	5,120	730.8	2,814	2,894	2,949	0.57	57.20	57.60	12.66	10.29	10.38	10.20
Anhui	5,923	6,110	6,118	6,135		2,267	2,368	2,485	0.37	38.70	40.50	16.07	12.6	12.75	13.05
Fujian	3,237	3,558	3,581	3,604	609.6	1,708	1,744	1,798	0.48	48.70	49.90	15.2	12	11.90	12.20
Jiangxi	4,063	4,339	4,368	4,400	968.92	1,678	1,738	1,820	0.39	39.80	41.36	18.94	13.8	13.86	13.92

Shandong	8,705	9,309	9,367	9,417	1,589.1	4,291	4,379	4,483	0.46	46.75	47.60	0	11.6	11.11	11.25
Henan	9,100	9,392	9,360	9,429		3,050	3,214	3,397	0.32	34.34	36.03	14.41	11.59	11.26	11.42
Hubei	5,772	5,693	5,699	5,711	1,730.4	2,494	2,525	2,581	0.44	44.30	45.20	16.18	9.08	9.19	9.21
Hunan	6,392	6,342	6,355	6,380		2,455	2,571	2,689	0.39	40.45	42.15	13.02	11.92	11.96	12.68
Guangdong	6,868	9,304	9,449	9,544	1,245.7	5,862	5,966	6,048	0.63	63.14	63.37	18.1	11.78	11.96	11.80
Guangxi	4,543	4,719	4,768	4,816		1,635	1,728	1,838	0.35	36.24	38.16	17.54	14.44	14.19	14.40
Hainan	724	836	845	854	248.1	385	399	410	0.46	47.20	48.00	20.12	14.59	14.62	14.71
Chongqing		2,808	2,816	2,839		1,311	1,361	1,419	0.47	48.34	49.99	13.16	9.9	10.10	10.10
Sichuan	11,325	8,169	8,127	8,138	1,938.7	2,802	2,893	3,044	0.34	35.60	37.40	17.1	9.14	9.21	9.54
Guizhou	3,508	3,757	3,762	3,793	552.58	1,032	1,062	1,104	0.27	28.24	29.11	21.86	13.97	13.28	13.49
Yunnan	3,990	4,483	4,514	4,543		1,367	1,426	1,499	0.31	31.60	33.00	20.75	13.2	13.08	12.63
Tibet	240	281	284	287	34.24	79	80	65	0.28	28.30	22.61	24.9	17.4	16.40	15.50
Shaanxi	3,513	3,735	3,748	3,762		1,461	1,522	1,584	0.39	40.62	42.10	15.93	10.19	10.21	10.29
Gansu	2,438	2,606	2,617	2,628		810	827	845	0.31	31.59	32.15	20.65	12.86	13.14	13.22
Qinghai	481	548	552	554		215	221	227	0.39	40.07	40.86	22.01	15.24	14.93	14.49
Ningxia	513	604	610	618	149	260	269	278	0.43	44.02	44.98	19.28	15.53	14.80	14.31
Xinjiang	1,661	2,050	2,095	2,131		778	820	845	0.38	39.15	39.64	18.9	15.79	16.79	16.05

Source: *China Statistical Yearbook 2009.*

Appendix 6: Industry-specific employment in China and its provinces at the end of 2008

Region	Total employment (10,000 persons)	Composition of employment						Employment in informal sectors as a percentage of the non-agricultural population (%)
		Employment in primary industries (10,000 persons)	(%)	Employment in secondary industries (10,000 persons)	(%)	Employment in tertiary industries (10,000 persons)	(%)	
National	77,480.0	30,654.0	39.6	21,109.0	27.2	25,717.0	33.2	29.2
Beijing	1,173.8	66.0	5.6	256.5	21.8	851.3	72.5	39.9
Tianjin	503.1	78.1	15.5	203.9	40.5	221.2	44.0	30.4
Hebei	3,651.7	1,488.4	40.8	1,195.5	32.7	967.8	26.5	25.8
Shanxi	1,583.5	642.8	40.6	417.4	26.4	523.3	33.0	27.6
Inner Mongolia	1,103.3	556.7	50.5	186.2	16.9	360.4	32.7	38.1
Liaoning	2,098.2	698.2	33.3	534.7	25.5	865.3	41.2	43.1
Jilin	1,143.5	511.0	44.7	227.8	19.9	404.8	35.4	34.1
Heilongjiang	1,670.2	775.6	46.4	343.0	20.5	551.6	33.0	35.0
Shanghai	896.0	49.4	5.5	352.1	39.3	494.5	55.2	65.0
Jiangsu	4,384.1	917.1	20.9	1,945.4	44.4	1,521.6	34.7	47.1
Zhejiang	3,691.9	671.6	18.2	1,715.5	46.5	1,304.8	35.3	38.2
Anhui	3,594.6	1,605.3	44.7	971.7	27.0	1,017.5	28.3	22.3
Fujian	2,079.8	647.8	31.1	739.7	35.6	692.2	33.3	25.2
Jiangxi	2,223.3	903.9	40.7	609.6	27.4	709.8	31.9	30.3
Shandong	5,352.5	2,001.2	37.4	1,691.5	31.6	1,659.8	31.0	27.2
Henan	5,835.5	2,847.3	48.8	1,563.9	26.8	1,424.2	24.4	17.1

Hubei	2,875.6	1,016.7	35.4	706.7	24.6	1,152.1	40.1	26.0
Hunan	3,811.0	1,889.9	49.6	762.2	20.0	1,158.8	30.4	22.9
Guangdong	5,478.0	1,552.6	28.3	1,831.5	33.4	2,094.0	38.2	37.2
Guangxi	2,807.2	1,549.4	55.2	561.9	20.0	695.8	24.8	27.1
Hainan	412.1	221.5	53.8	46.6	11.3	144.0	34.9	36.3
Chongqing	1,837.1	681.2	37.1	488.6	26.6	667.3	36.3	23.5
Sichuan	4,874.5	2,192.7	45.0	1,068.3	21.9	1,613.5	33.1	24.9
Guizhou	2,301.6	1,206.0	52.4	261.2	11.3	834.4	36.3	13.2
Yunnan	2,679.5	1,678.6	62.6	328.2	12.2	672.7	25.1	35.6
Tibet	160.4	89.3	55.7	16.8	10.4	54.4	33.9	41.5
Shaanxi	1,946.6	910.4	46.8	403.5	20.7	632.6	32.5	30.5
Gansu	1,388.7	734.4	52.9	198.6	14.3	455.7	32.8	20.8
Qinghai	276.8	123.3	44.5	59.0	21.3	94.5	34.2	35.6
Ningxia	303.9	136.4	44.9	76.2	25.1	91.4	30.1	34.3
Xinjiang	813.7	419.9	51.6	111.5	13.7	282.3	34.7	40.8

Source: *China Statistical Yearbook 2009*.

Note: 'Employment in informal sectors' includes self-employment and employment in the private and sector, and 'non-agricultural employment' means total employment minus agricultural employment.

Appendix 7: The number of registered unemployed in China's provinces, and the registered or official rate of unemployment in those provinces

Region	Unemployment (10,000 persons)						Unemployment rate (%)					
	1990	2004	2005	2006	2007	2008	1990	2004	2005	2006	2007	2008
Beijing	1.7	6.5	10.56	10	10.6	10.3	0.4	1.3	2.11	2	1.8	1.8
Tianjin	8.1	11.8	11.71	12	15.0	13.0	2.7	3.8	3.7	3.6	3.6	3.6
Hebei	7.7	28	27.82	29	29.3	32.2	1.1	4	3.93	3.8	3.8	4.0
Shanxi	5.5	13.7	14.27	16	16.1	17.5	1.2	3.1	3.01	3.2	3.2	3.3
Inner Mongolia	15.2	18.5	17.74	18	18.5	19.9	3.8	4.6	4.26	4.1	4.0	4.1
Liaoning	23.7	70.1	60.4	54	44.5	41.7	2.2	6.5	5.62	5.1	4.3	3.9
Jilin	10.5	28.2	27.64	26	23.9	24.3	1.9	4.2	4.2	4.2	3.9	4.0
Heilongjiang	20.4	32.9	31.3	31	31.5	32.1	2.2	4.5	4.42	4.3	4.3	4.2
Shanghai	7.7	27.4	27.5	28	26.7	26.6	1.5	4.5		4.4	4.2	4.2
Jiangsu	22.5	42.9	41.62	40	39.3	41.1	2.4	3.8	3.56	3.4	3.2	3.3
Zhejiang	11.2	30.1	28.97	29	28.6	30.7	2.2	4.1	3.72	3.5	3.3	3.5
Anhui	15.2	26.1	27.77	28	27.2	29.3	2.8	4.2	4.4	4.2	4.1	3.9
Fujian	9	14.5	14.86	15	14.9	15.0	2.6	4	3.95	3.9	3.9	3.9
Jiangxi	10.3	22.4	22.83	25	24.3	26.0	2.4	3.6	3.48	3.6	3.4	3.4
Shandong	26.2	42.3	42.9	44	43.5	60.7	3.2	3.4	3.33	3.3	3.2	3.7
Henan	25.1	31.2	33.02	35	33.1	36.5	3.3	3.4	3.45	3.5	3.4	3.4
Hubei	12.7	49.4	52.64	53	54.1	55.1	1.7	4.2	4.33	4.2	4.2	4.2
Hunan	15.9	43	41.86	43	44.4	47.0	2.7	4.4	4.27	4.3	4.3	4.2
Guangdong	19.2	35.9	34.49	36	36.2	38.1	2.2	2.7	2.58	2.6	2.5	2.6
Guangxi	13.9	17.8	18.5	20	18.5	18.8	3.9	4.1	4.15	4.1	3.8	3.8
Hainan	3.5	4.7	5.08	5	5.4	5.6	3	3.4	3.55	3.6	3.5	3.7
Chongqing		16.8	16.88	15	14.1	13.0		4.1	4.12	4	4.0	4.0
Sichuan	38	33.3	34.3	36	34.5	37.9	3.7	4.4	4.61	4.5	4.2	4.6
Guizhou	10.7	11.6	12.13	12	12.1	12.5	4.1	4.1	4.2	4.1	4.0	4.0
Yunnan	7.8	11.9	12.97	14	14.0	14.8	2.5	4.3	4.17	4.3	4.2	4.2
Tibet		1.2						4				
Shaanxi	11.2	18.5	21.54	21	21.0	20.8	2.8	3.8	4.18	4	4.0	3.9
Gansu	12.5	9.5	9.25	10	9.5	9.4	4.9	3.4	3.26	3.6	3.3	3.2
Qinghai	4.2	3.5	3.63	4	3.7	3.9	5.6	3.9	3.93	3.9	3.8	3.8
Ningxia	4	4.1	4.35	4	4.4	4.8	5.4	4.5	4.52	4.3	4.3	4.4
Xinjiang	9.6	13.3	11.13	12	11.7	11.8	3	3.5	3.92	3.9	3.9	3.7

Source: *China Statistical Yearbook 2009.*

Appendix 8: Fiscal revenues and expenditures of China's provinces (2008)

Region	Total revenues (10,000 yuan)	Total expenditures (10,000 yuan)	Per capita fiscal revenues (yuan)	Per capita fiscal expenditures (yuan)
Beijing	18,373,238	19,592,857	10,840	11,559
Tianjin	6,756,186	8,677,245	5,745	7,379
Hebei	9,475,858	18,816,696	1,356	2,692
Shanxi	7,480,047	13,150,175	2,193	3,856
Inner Mongolia	6,506,764	14,545,732	2,696	6,026
Liaoning	13,560,812	21,534,348	3,143	4,991
Jilin	4,227,961	11,801,223	1,546	4,316
Heilongjiang	5,782,773	15,423,004	1,512	4,032
Shanghai	23,587,464	25,939,161	12,490	13,736
Jiangsu	27,314,074	32,474,927	3,558	4,230
Zhejiang	19,333,890	22,085,756	3,776	4,314
Anhui	7,246,197	16,471,253	1,181	2,685
Fujian	8,334,032	11,377,159	2,312	3,157
Jiangxi	4,886,476	12,100,730	1,111	2,750
Shandong	19,570,541	27,046,613	2,078	2,872
Henan	10,089,009	22,816,093	1,070	2,420
Hubei	7,108,492	16,502,763	1,245	2,890
Hunan	7,227,122	17,652,249	1,133	2,767
Guangdong	33,103,235	37,785,681	3,468	3,959
Guangxi	5,184,245	12,971,100	1,076	2,693
Hainan	1,448,584	3,579,708	1,696	4,192
Chongqing	5,775,738	10,160,112	2,034	3,579
Sichuan	10,416,603	29,488,269	1,280	3,624
Guizhou	3,478,416	10,537,922	917	2,778
Yunnan	6,140,518	14,702,388	1,352	3,236
Tibet	248,823	3,806,589	867	13,263
Shaanxi	5,914,750	14,285,208	1,572	3,797
Gansu	2,649,650	9,684,336	1,008	3,685
Qinghai	715,692	3,635,950	1,291	6,560
Ningxia	950,090	3,246,064	1,538	5,255
Xinjiang	3,610,616	10,593,638	1,694	4,972

Source: *China Statistical Yearbook 2009.*

Appendix 9: Average income and income sources of urban families in China and its
provinces, per capita, in 2008 (in yuan)

Region	Disposable income	Income from wages	Net operational income	Income off assets	Income from transfer payments
National	15,780.76	11,298.96	1,453.57	387.02	3,928.23
Beijing	24,724.89	18,738.96	778.36	452.75	7,707.87
Tianjin	19,422.53	12,849.73	863.52	256.87	7,203.93
Hebei	13,441.09	8,891.50	1,078.67	224.86	3,946.39
Shanxi	13,119.05	9,019.35	983.21	202.31	3,654.11
Inner Mongolia	14,432.55	10,284.43	1,555.31	324.64	3,031.05
Liaoning	14,392.69	9,494.59	1,483.30	248.04	4,610.32
Jilin	12,829.45	8,677.27	1,154.14	97.74	3,676.88
Heilongjiang	11,581.28	7,393.39	1,241.37	122.83	3,506.48
Shanghai	26,674.90	21,791.11	1,399.14	369.12	6,199.77
Jiangsu	18,679.52	12,319.86	1,999.61	307.31	5,548.78
Zhejiang	22,726.66	15,538.83	3,161.87	1,324.94	4,955.14
Anhui	12,990.35	9,302.38	959.43	293.92	3,603.72
Fujian	17,961.45	12,668.82	2,185.13	952.91	3,879.29
Jiangxi	12,866.44	9,105.96	1,106.31	265.35	2,985.96
Shandong	16,305.41	12,940.62	1,194.40	346.90	3,067.05
Henan	13,231.11	9,043.52	1,161.96	156.46	3,545.86
Hubei	13,152.86	9,474.81	1,114.68	244.13	3,340.65
Hunan	13,821.16	9,070.97	1,575.08	316.48	3,614.74
Guangdong	19,732.86	15,188.39	2,405.92	701.25	3,382.95
Guangxi	14,146.04	10,321.20	1,314.40	441.15	3,316.44
Hainan	12,607.84	8,999.75	1,311.38	396.89	2,890.59
Chongqing	14,367.55	10,957.62	788.26	205.94	3,265.92
Sichuan	12,633.38	9,117.00	1,040.14	262.90	3,265.06
Guizhou	11,758.76	7,811.16	770.86	110.90	3,492.70
Yunnan	13,250.22	8,596.88	1,165.96	849.45	3,505.74
Tibet	12,481.51	12,314.69	303.34	138.08	891.42
Shaanxi	12,857.89	9,794.82	544.00	151.46	3,356.85
Gansu	10,969.41	8,354.63	638.76	65.33	2,610.61
Qinghai	11,640.43	8,595.48	763.07	50.17	3,458.63
Ningxia	12,931.53	8,793.54	1,856.94	182.67	3,285.49
Xinjiang	11,432.10	9,422.22	938.15	141.75	1,976.49

Source: *China Statistical Yearbook 2009.*

Appendix 10:   Average income and income sources of rural families in China and its
provinces, per capita, in 2008 (in yuan)

Region	Net income	Income from wages	Net family operational income	Income from assets	Income from transfer payments
National	4,760.62	1,853.73	2,435.56	148.08	323.24
Beijing	10,661.92	6,389.31	2,058.57	1,142.80	1,071.25
Tianjin	7,910.78	4,064.95	3,097.14	463.39	285.30
Hebei	4,795.46	1,979.52	2,416.22	118.63	281.09
Shanxi	4,097.24	1,713.55	1,986.38	153.05	244.26
Inner Mongolia	4,656.18	806.48	3,218.01	114.90	516.79
Liaoning	5,576.48	2,035.53	2,931.26	201.29	408.40
Jilin	4,932.74	810.17	3,344.72	183.20	594.66
Heilongjiang	4,855.59	916.76	3,163.70	243.57	531.57
Shanghai	11,440.26	8,108.32	711.26	849.83	1,770.85
Jiangsu	7,356.47	3,895.50	2,812.00	253.47	395.50
Zhejiang	9,257.93	4,587.44	3,762.93	437.52	470.04
Anhui	4,202.49	1,737.84	2,114.24	119.04	231.37
Fujian	6,196.07	2,421.46	3,146.09	179.03	449.49
Jiangxi	4,697.19	1,842.36	2,552.59	66.55	235.69
Shandong	5,641.43	2,263.46	2,962.96	163.93	251.07
Henan	4,454.24	1,499.93	2,699.30	53.00	202.02
Hubei	4,656.38	1,742.33	2,690.83	40.82	182.40
Hunan	4,512.46	1,990.52	2,196.61	57.06	268.26
Guangdong	6,399.79	3,684.47	2,001.50	339.47	374.35
Guangxi	3,690.34	1,283.39	2,190.62	41.76	174.58
Hainan	4,389.97	808.63	3,235.09	53.58	292.68
Chongqing	4,126.21	1,764.64	2,016.64	50.90	294.03
Sichuan	4,121.21	1,620.40	2,061.70	71.37	367.74
Guizhou	2,796.93	1,002.68	1,512.47	63.92	217.86
Yunnan	3,102.60	617.47	2,156.80	109.83	218.50
Tibet	3,175.82	759.72	1,845.04	185.46	385.60
Shaanxi	3,136.46	1,243.57	1,475.01	86.01	331.87
Gansu	2,723.79	867.98	1,543.24	19.49	293.08
Qinghai	3,061.24	983.16	1,602.74	148.55	326.80
Ningxia	3,681.42	1,260.04	2,032.01	65.73	323.64
Xinjiang	3,502.90	422.82	2,779.71	121.15	179.23

Source: *China Statistical Yearbook 2009.*

Appendix 11: Annual spending on consumption of urban families in China's provinces in 2008 (yuan)

Region	Consumer spending	Itemized spending								
		Food	Clothing	Home equipment, articles, and services	Medical care	Transportation and communications	Educational, cultural and entertainment services	Housing	Miscellaneous goods and services
National	11,242.85	4,259.81	1,165.91	691.83	786.20	1,417.12	1,358.26	1,145.41	418.31
Beijing	16,460.26	5,561.54	1,571.74	1,096.57	1,563.10	2,293.23	2,383.52	1,286.32	704.24
Tianjin	13,422.47	5,005.09	1,153.66	817.18	1,220.92	1,567.87	1,608.97	1,528.28	520.49
Hebei	9,086.73	3,155.40	1,137.22	574.84	808.88	1,062.31	946.38	1,097.41	304.28
Shanxi	8,806.55	2,974.76	1,137.71	471.65	769.79	931.33	1,041.91	1,250.87	228.53
Inner Mongolia	10,828.62	3,553.48	1,616.56	672.64	869.71	1,191.70	1,383.53	1,028.19	512.81
Liaoning	11,231.48	4,378.14	1,187.41	507.40	913.13	1,295.70	1,145.46	1,270.95	533.29
Jilin	9,729.05	3,307.14	1,259.62	510.49	914.47	954.96	1,071.80	1,285.28	425.30
Heilongjiang	8,622.97	3,128.10	1,217.04	494.49	864.89	749.05	906.19	941.25	321.95
Shanghai	19,397.89	7,108.62	1,520.61	1,182.24	755.29	3,373.19	2,874.54	1,646.19	937.21
Jiangsu	11,977.55	4,544.64	1,166.91	813.45	794.63	1,357.96	1,799.75	1,042.10	458.10
Zhejiang	15,158.30	5,522.56	1,546.46	713.31	933.11	2,392.63	2,195.58	1,333.69	520.95
Anhui	9,524.04	3,905.05	1,010.61	579.59	633.93	920.77	1,160.14	988.12	325.82
Fujian	12,501.12	5,078.85	1,105.31	722.17	540.63	1,777.06	1,453.18	1,300.10	523.83

Jiangxi	8,717.37	3,633.05	969.58	623.17	483.96	872.57	945.99	851.15	337.91
Shandong	11,006.61	3,699.42	1,394.11	806.35	799.79	1,410.45	1,277.43	1,247.04	372.01
Henan	8,837.46	3,079.82	1,141.76	633.32	790.87	915.12	988.95	963.59	324.03
Hubei	9,477.51	3,996.27	1,099.16	604.40	675.32	890.12	1,037.24	914.26	260.74
Hunan	9,945.52	3,970.42	1,090.72	674.84	790.95	971.05	1,110.11	960.82	376.62
Guangdong	15,527.97	5,866.91	975.06	947.54	836.39	2,623.08	1,936.38	1,748.16	594.45
Guangxi	9,627.40	4,082.99	772.28	603.84	529.36	1,376.03	1,081.54	891.33	290.04
Hainan	9,408.48	4,226.90	491.84	565.51	536.40	1,303.50	930.87	1,106.39	247.08
Chongqing	11,146.80	4,418.34	1,294.30	842.09	878.25	1,044.36	1,267.03	1,096.82	305.60
Sichuan	9,679.14	4,255.48	1,042.45	590.51	564.93	1,121.45	947.01	819.28	338.03
Guizhou	8,349.21	3,597.94	851.50	525.70	471.39	871.15	934.73	836.54	260.27
Yunnan	9,076.61	4,272.29	1,026.50	331.94	606.86	1,216.46	732.95	739.20	150.42
Tibet	8,323.54	4,262.77	1,011.82	310.22	317.08	966.74	419.59	634.94	400.38
Shaanxi	9,772.07	3,586.13	1,047.61	618.16	862.70	967.52	1,281.58	1,007.68	400.68
Gansu	8,308.62	3,183.79	1,022.62	546.23	654.82	817.17	936.33	846.26	301.40
Qinghai	8,192.56	3,315.94	945.14	538.54	610.02	787.63	880.86	802.73	311.72
Ningxia	9,558.29	3,352.83	1,178.88	596.81	816.87	1,096.32	1,043.72	1,069.15	403.71
Xinjiang	8,669.36	3,235.77	1,245.02	535.31	643.48	1,003.89	812.36	781.90	411.63

Source: *China Statistical Yearbook 2009.*

Appendix 12: Annual spending on consumption of rural families in China's provinces in 2008 (in yuan)

Region	Total consumer spending	Itemized spending								
		Food	Clothing	Housing	Home equipment and services	Transportation and communications	Cultural, educational, and entertainment goods and services	Medical care	Other goods and services
National	3660.68	1598.75	211.80	678.80	173.98	360.18	314.53	245.97	76.67
Beijing	7284.65	2470.72	577.81	1162.96	402.56	950.53	883.35	709.44	127.29
Tianjin	3825.43	1568.95	292.52	699.21	153.61	402.87	324.47	301.06	82.75
Hebei	3125.55	1192.93	203.74	696.14	151.94	346.73	250.07	219.32	64.68
Shanxi	3097.54	1206.69	276.23	486.75	138.26	328.74	380.70	210.32	69.85
Inner Mongolia	3618.11	1483.61	239.96	569.60	128.80	406.74	399.35	320.62	69.43
Liaoning	3814.03	1549.00	298.82	601.71	158.91	426.47	387.97	283.37	107.78
Jilin	3443.24	1362.44	254.05	530.69	124.80	355.58	341.70	380.71	93.27
Heilongjiang	3844.73	1267.68	308.49	871.51	130.00	395.02	437.57	351.05	83.41
Shanghai	9119.67	3731.27	467.33	1806.08	503.96	879.57	855.30	697.11	179.06
Jiangsu	5328.37	2202.58	276.39	860.35	250.11	614.23	713.23	290.93	120.56
Zhejiang	7534.09	2779.10	454.79	1659.88	364.05	851.06	747.00	532.06	146.14
Anhui	3284.11	1454.18	180.04	650.51	165.53	280.63	294.84	199.44	58.94
Fujian	4661.94	2162.30	263.59	777.51	222.86	534.68	390.15	197.85	113.01

Jiangxi	3309.21	157.75	559.39	155.00	301.68	236.01	205.68	60.58
Shandong	4077.05	250.29	804.75	240.91	452.55	417.27	280.49	79.00
Henan	3044.21	209.75	712.61	169.61	290.79	214.38	215.00	66.27
Hubei	3652.57	187.07	651.50	234.92	290.44	267.13	210.36	99.80
Hunan	3804.97	169.06	629.75	171.11	286.01	278.67	244.17	78.67
Guangdong	4872.46	177.67	964.53	189.01	483.66	272.87	259.00	136.82
Guangxi	2985.03	91.19	535.45	124.01	261.85	172.73	154.32	50.81
Hainan	2883.10	89.89	391.04	104.07	261.57	288.49	123.82	86.67
Chongqing	2884.92	160.34	328.97	167.74	238.43	211.83	197.15	42.87
Sichuan	3127.94	174.59	469.73	163.99	256.08	173.26	209.22	53.49
Guizhou	2165.70	112.46	427.40	94.36	159.61	122.10	96.38	33.75
Yunnan	2990.61	119.63	626.12	118.97	248.25	168.55	181.97	43.97
Tibet	2199.59	248.68	324.07	140.06	147.21	62.26	53.84	70.09
Shaanxi	2979.37	175.50	598.59	155.07	270.63	351.99	251.23	60.70
Gansu	2400.95	134.66	387.83	95.58	234.69	219.91	164.72	31.05
Qinghai	2896.62	200.26	568.79	110.35	316.75	148.86	270.06	61.54
Ningxia	3094.86	217.17	582.47	123.91	299.29	192.57	318.77	72.20
Xinjiang	2691.79	218.61	492.77	97.58	276.31	168.99	244.59	46.24

Source: *China Statistical Yearbook 2009*.

Appendix 13: Number of health institutions and health personnel in China and its provinces in 2008

Region	Health institution						Health personnel			
	Total	Hospital	Health center	Clinic	Disease prevention and control center	Maternity and child care center	Total	Health personnel	Certified doctor	Certified nurse
National	278,337	19,712	39,860	180,752	3,534	3,011	6,169,050	5,030,038	2,082,258	1,653,297
Beijing	6,497	529	123	4,355	31	19	194,307	150,411	59,053	55,411
Tianjin	2,784	247	181	1,435	24	23	85,886	65,161	25,890	21,979
Hebei	15,632	1,111	1,958	10,989	190	185	303,232	247,451	109,968	69,038
Shanxi	9,431	1,025	1,569	5,854	131	132	191,152	159,591	72,259	48,765
Inner Mongolia	7,162	471	1,329	4,168	137	115	131,175	109,727	49,542	31,459
Liaoning	14,627	854	1,062	11,277	133	111	274,890	217,904	90,714	80,470
Jilin	9,659	568	802	5,664	68	70	162,303	127,905	57,523	41,066
Heilongjiang	7,928	911	938	5,065	192	136	203,528	161,939	66,771	51,353
Shanghai	2,822	299		1,906	22	24	162,160	127,471	51,047	48,758
Jiangsu	13,357	1,094	1,429	8,290	168	104	360,845	291,125	119,461	100,736
Zhejiang	15,290	635	1,871	6,989	101	87	288,340	242,908	101,893	78,284
Anhui	7,837	720	1,845	3,854	127	119	227,438	187,770	73,826	60,856
Fujian	4,478	332	871	2,705	87	85	124,213	103,341	43,013	37,760

Jiangxi	8,229	491	1,545	5,023	137	111	168,472	139,764	55,187	48,241
Shandong	14,973	1,253	1,755	10,314	177	149	438,009	375,817	159,809	122,866
Henan	11,683	1,174	2,089	7,239	181	167	396,078	309,923	119,316	96,571
Hubei	10,305	593	1,203	6,871	110	99	284,832	233,823	92,037	80,614
Hunan	14,455	767	2,344	10,268	145	135	281,421	232,084	96,305	72,551
Guangdong	15,819	1,028	1,399	10,948	136	126	479,817	384,134	144,467	135,922
Guangxi	10,427	450	1,258	7,985	100	103	190,152	155,620	60,825	55,992
Hainan	2,220	187	311	1,544	27	25	42,682	33,875	12,850	13,212
Chongqing	6,265	355	1,041	4,579	43	40	109,014	88,744	39,415	26,799
Sichuan	20,738	1,144	4,818	13,441	208	201	324,525	267,591	121,851	77,892
Guizhou	5,848	475	1,459	3,263	105	90	106,038	89,313	38,830	28,642
Yunnan	9,249	692	1,396	6,396	152	148	151,859	126,237	57,276	42,011
Tibet	1,326	99	665	412	81	57	11,680	9,435	4,376	1,920
Shaanxi	8,812	816	1,733	5,596	123	117	183,510	148,328	58,264	46,918
Gansu	10,534	377	1,333	8,140	104	100	104,179	87,633	36,176	24,950
Qinghai	1,582	126	406	744	56	22	25,568	21,745	9,414	7,280
Ningxia	1,629	148	239	1,056	25	22	31,571	26,415	11,444	8,897
Xinjiang	6,739	741	888	4,382	213	89	130,174	106,853	43,456	36,084

Source: *China Statistical Yearbook 2009.*

Appendix 14: The situation with respect to basic pension insurance in China and its provinces in 2008

Region	Basic pension insurance participants at year-end	Employees	Retired personnel	Unemployment insurance participants at year-end (10,000 persons)	Unemployment insurance beneficiaries at year-end (10,000 persons)	Urban basic medical insurance participants at year-end (10,000 persons)		
						Total	Employees	Retired personnel
National	21,891.1	16,587.5	5,303.6	12,399.8	261.2	19,995.6	14,987.7	5,007.9
Beijing	757.2	577.0	180.1	614.3	2.6	871.0	688.5	182.4
Tianjin	376.5	247.2	129.3	232.5	3.2	399.1	257.3	141.8
Hebei	862.5	639.8	222.7	481.7	9.8	738.5	539.1	199.5
Shanxi	539.4	411.4	128.0	312.2	7.3	441.8	333.0	108.8
Inner Mongolia	389.5	286.5	102.9	225.5	3.1	373.7	265.1	108.6
Liaoning	1,406.2	976.4	429.9	622.7	15.7	1,209.3	822.8	386.5
Jilin	525.3	369.9	155.4	233.7	16.5	450.9	319.1	131.8
Heilongjiang	857.8	581.8	276.0	467.6	10.3	788.3	572.3	216.0
Shanghai	967.7	609.9	357.8	511.8	14.0	1,171.7	850.8	320.9
Jiangsu	1,751.6	1,373.1	378.6	1,052.2	21.5	1,604.3	1,213.9	390.3
Zhejiang	1,386.9	1,192.1	194.8	731.1	6.3	1,053.9	855.6	198.3
Anhui	578.4	420.3	158.1	373.1	12.8	528.8	380.6	148.1
Fujian	557.2	454.6	102.6	338.7	4.6	435.7	334.3	101.4
Jiangxi	550.3	421.9	128.5	266.3	3.4	503.2	353.8	149.4

Shandong	1,565.9	1,260.8	305.0	864.1	24.9	1,266.2	1,010.1	256.2
Henan	972.0	732.9	239.1	683.4	18.4	840.9	620.1	220.8
Hubei	932.3	680.4	252.0	422.9	7.4	714.9	504.0	210.9
Hunan	829.1	593.7	235.3	390.1	8.3	682.0	475.5	206.5
Guangdong	2,444.3	2,171.2	273.0	1,471.9	13.7	2,370.7	2,130.4	240.3
Guangxi	368.1	273.1	95.0	234.6	8.0	361.4	257.6	103.8
Hainan	156.2	114.2	42.0	84.7	3.3	121.8	87.8	34.0
Chongqing	406.1	275.4	130.7	210.1	4.4	326.2	211.0	115.1
Sichuan	1,017.9	711.1	306.7	436.9	12.2	893.5	596.8	296.7
Guizhou	215.9	156.6	59.3	141.4	1.3	257.4	184.4	73.0
Yunnan	293.7	204.4	89.3	191.9	3.7	356.8	253.2	103.6
Tibet	8.5	5.5	3.1	7.8	0.0	20.1	14.8	5.3
Shaanxi	433.4	309.0	124.4	329.3	9.1	432.7	299.9	132.8
Gansu	221.0	157.0	64.0	162.6	5.6	248.9	180.1	68.8
Qinghai	68.3	49.7	18.6	35.4	2.3	72.1	47.6	24.5
Ningxia	82.6	63.7	18.8	44.4	1.4	83.2	60.5	22.7
Xinjiang	346.3	248.7	97.6	224.8	6.1	376.6	267.6	109.0

Source: *China Statistical Yearbook 2009.*

Appendix 15: Percentages of public-finance expenditures spent on education and health, and percentages of GDP spent on education and health, in 2000, 2005, and 2008

Region	Education expenditures as a percentage of total public-finance expenditures			Education expenditures as a percentage of GDP			Health expenditures as a percentage of total public-finance expenditures			Health expenditures as a percentage of GDP		
	2000	2005	2008	2000	2005	2008	2000	2005	2008	2000	2005	2008
National	15.67	14.83	17.30	1.64	2.03	2.83	4.65	4.04	5.50	0.49	0.55	0.90
Beijing	13.56	13.78	16.14	2.42	2.12	3.02	6.44	6.20	7.40	1.15	0.95	1.38
Tianjin	16.5	15.20	16.33	1.88	1.82	2.23	4.65	4.29	4.83	0.53	0.51	0.66
Hebei	17.72	17.42	20.03	1.45	1.69	2.33	4.20	4.60	6.39	0.34	0.45	0.74
Shanxi	16.96	15.27	17.87	2.32	2.44	3.39	4.64	4.21	5.44	0.64	0.67	1.03
Inner Mongolia	12.03	11.54	14.19	2.12	2.02	2.66	3.68	3.06	4.11	0.65	0.54	0.77
Liaoning	12.72	11.81	14.23	1.41	1.81	2.28	3.31	2.85	3.90	0.37	0.44	0.62
Jilin	13.74	11.75	15.93	1.97	2.05	2.93	3.60	3.28	5.04	0.52	0.57	0.93
Heilongjiang	12.83	13.53	16.64	1.51	1.93	3.09	3.56	3.56	4.65	0.42	0.51	0.86
Shanghai	13.82	11.11	12.57	1.85	2.00	2.38	5.35	3.17	4.71	0.72	0.57	0.89
Jiangsu	19.86	15.43	18.25	1.37	1.41	1.95	5.51	4.49	4.58	0.38	0.41	0.49
Zhejiang	18.13	18.30	20.56	1.30	1.72	2.11	6.32	5.13	6.47	0.45	0.48	0.66
Anhui	16.69	16.47	17.38	1.78	2.18	3.23	3.62	3.51	6.30	0.39	0.47	1.17
Fujian	19.12	18.80	20.51	1.58	1.70	2.16	4.98	4.37	6.53	0.41	0.39	0.69

Jiangxi	17.07	15.59	17.09	1.90	2.17	3.19	4.62	3.87	6.36	0.52	0.54	1.19
Shandong	19.26	16.97	20.37	1.38	1.34	1.77	4.61	3.71	5.19	0.33	0.29	0.45
Henan	17.36	16.78	19.46	1.51	1.77	2.41	3.88	3.75	6.38	0.34	0.39	0.79
Hubei	15.64	15.26	17.22	1.35	1.82	2.51	5.18	4.00	5.76	0.45	0.48	0.84
Hunan	14.63	14.08	17.63	1.38	1.89	2.79	3.42	2.80	4.96	0.32	0.38	0.79
Guangdong	13.4	14.38	18.61	1.50	1.47	1.97	4.42	3.60	5.32	0.49	0.37	0.56
Guangxi	17.3	17.21	19.37	2.18	2.58	3.50	4.50	4.25	6.07	0.57	0.64	1.10
Hainan	15.02	16.01	15.54	1.86	2.71	3.81	4.37	4.31	5.21	0.54	0.73	1.28
Chongqing	13.56	12.45	15.11	1.60	1.98	3.01	4.28	3.11	5.08	0.51	0.49	1.01
Sichuan	14.34	12.99	12.52	1.62	1.90	2.95	4.85	4.58	4.87	0.55	0.67	1.15
Guizhou	15.77	17.93	21.80	3.20	4.72	6.89	5.49	4.96	6.40	1.11	1.30	2.02
Yunnan	15.05	15.96	16.46	3.19	3.52	4.24	5.40	5.85	7.11	1.14	1.29	1.83
Tibet	11.64	10.99	12.37	5.94	8.15	11.89	5.40	3.83	4.30	2.76	2.84	4.13
Shaanxi	14.15	15.54	18.54	2.32	2.63	3.87	3.05	3.40	5.49	0.50	0.58	1.14
Gansu	14.64	15.72	18.89	2.80	3.49	5.76	4.28	4.16	6.02	0.82	0.92	1.84
Qinghai	10.65	11.96	13.42	2.76	3.74	5.08	4.13	5.22	6.78	1.07	1.63	2.56
Ningxia	13.28	12.18	16.65	3.04	3.22	4.92	3.86	3.37	5.27	0.88	0.89	1.56
Xinjiang	16.42	14.00	18.80	2.30	2.79	4.74	5.58	4.99	5.54	0.78	0.99	1.40

Source: *China Statistical Yearbook 2009.*

Appendix 16: National and provincial imports and exports as a percentage of national and provincial GDP

Region	Exports as a percentage of GDP				Imports as a percentage of GDP			
	2000	*2006*	*2007*	*2008*	*2000*	*2006*	*2007*	*2008*
National	20.8	36.4	36.0	33.0	18.8	29.8	28.3	26.2
Beijing	40	38.4	39.8	38.1	125.8	121.6	117.1	141.8
Tianjin	43.6	61.2	57.3	46.0	43.1	56.6	50.3	41.9
Hebei	6	8.8	9.4	10.3	2.5	3.9	4.7	6.2
Shanxi	6.2	6.9	8.7	9.3	2.7	4.2	6.7	5.1
Inner Mongolia	5.7	3.6	3.7	3.2	9.8	6.4	6.0	4.8
Liaoning	19.2	24.4	24.4	21.7	14.5	17.3	16.7	15.7
Jilin	5.7	5.6	5.5	5.2	6.0	9.2	9.3	9.3
Heilongjiang	3.7	10.9	13.2	14.0	3.9	5.7	5.4	5.3
Shanghai	46.1	87.4	89.7	85.8	53.4	87.6	86.7	77.5
Jiangsu	24.9	59.1	60.1	54.5	19.2	45.5	43.1	35.3
Zhejiang	26.7	51.1	51.9	49.9	11.5	19.4	19.7	18.4
Anhui	5.9	8.9	9.1	8.9	3.2	7.0	7.4	6.9
Fujian	27.3	43.2	41.1	36.6	17.6	22.4	20.2	17.9
Jiangxi	4.9	6.4	7.5	8.3	1.8	4.2	5.5	6.3
Shandong	15	21.2	22.0	20.8	9.2	13.2	13.9	14.6
Henan	2.4	4.2	4.2	4.0	1.3	2.0	2.2	2.6
Hubei	3.7	6.6	6.7	7.2	2.5	5.8	5.5	5.5
Hunan	3.7	5.4	5.4	5.2	1.9	2.4	2.6	2.6
Guangdong	78.8	91.9	90.3	78.9	67.0	68.5	64.8	54.3
Guangxi	6	5.9	6.5	7.1	2.2	5.1	5.3	5.7
Hainan	12.8	10.4	8.5	7.6	7.7	11.1	13.4	14.0
Chongqing	5.2	7.7	8.3	7.8	4.1	4.8	5.4	5.2
Sichuan	2.9	6.1	6.2	7.3	2.4	4.1	4.2	5.0
Guizhou	3.5	3.6	4.1	4.0	2.0	2.0	2.2	3.1
Yunnan	5	6.7	7.6	6.1	2.7	5.6	6.5	5.6
Tibet	8	6.1	7.3	12.4	1.2	2.9	1.5	1.0
Shaanxi	6.5	6.4	6.5	5.5	4.1	3.0	3.1	3.0
Gansu	3.5	5.3	4.7	3.5	1.3	8.1	10.9	9.8
Qinghai	3.5	6.6	3.7	3.0	1.5	1.5	2.2	1.9
Ningxia	10.2	10.6	9.3	8.0	3.6	5.5	4.2	3.9
Xinjiang	7.3	18.7	24.8	31.9	6.4	5.1	4.8	4.8

Source: *China Statistical Yearbook 2009.*

Appendix 17: Land holdings and land usage in China by province in 2008

Region	Total land area (10,000 km²)	Per capita land area (m²)	Farmland area (1,000 hectares)	Per capita farmland area (m²)	Forest area (10,000 hectares)	Per capita forest area (m²)	Forest coverage (%)
National	960	72.29	121,715.90	0.92	17,490.92	13.17	18.21
Beijing	1.64	9.68	231.70	0.14	37.88	2.23	21.26
Tianjin	1.18	10.03	441.10	0.38	9.35	0.80	8.14
Hebei	18.77	26.86	6,317.30	0.90	328.83	4.71	17.69
Shanxi	15.63	45.83	4,055.80	1.19	208.19	6.10	13.29
Inner Mongolia	118.3	490.11	7,147.20	2.96	2,050.67	84.96	17.70
Liaoning	14.8	34.30	4,085.30	0.95	480.53	11.14	32.97
Jilin	18.7	68.40	5,534.60	2.02	720.12	26.34	38.13
Heilongjiang	45.4	118.68	11,830.10	3.09	1,797.50	46.99	39.54
Shanghai	0.63	3.34	244.00	0.13	1.89	0.10	3.17
Jiangsu	10.26	13.36	4,763.80	0.62	77.41	1.01	7.54
Zhejiang	10.18	19.88	1,920.90	0.38	553.92	10.82	54.41
Anhui	13.94	22.72	5,730.20	0.93	331.99	5.41	24.03
Fujian	12.14	33.68	1,330.10	0.37	764.94	21.22	62.96
Jiangxi	16.69	37.93	2,827.10	0.64	931.39	21.17	55.86
Shandong	15.71	16.68	7,515.30	0.80	204.64	2.17	13.44
Henan	16.7	17.71	7,926.40	0.84	270.30	2.87	16.19
Hubei	18.59	32.55	4,664.10	0.82	497.55	8.71	26.77
Hunan	21.18	33.20	3,789.40	0.59	860.79	13.49	40.63
Guangdong	17.98	18.84	2,830.70	0.30	827.00	8.67	46.49
Guangxi	23.67	49.15	4,217.50	0.88	983.83	20.43	41.41

(*Continued*)

Appendix 17: (Cont'd)

Region	Total land area (10,000 km²)	Per capita land area (m²)	Farmland area (1,000 hectares)	Per capita farmland area (m²)	Forest area (10,000 hectares)	Per capita forest area (m²)	Forest coverage (%)
Hainan	3.54	41.45	727.50	0.85	166.66	19.52	48.87
Chongqing	8.24	29.02	2,235.90	0.79	183.18	6.45	22.25
Sichuan	48.5	59.60	5,947.40	0.73	1,464.34	17.99	30.27
Guizhou	17.62	46.46	4,485.30	1.18	420.47	11.09	23.83
Yunnan	39.4	86.73	6,072.10	1.34	1,560.03	34.34	40.77
Tibet	120.24	4189.55	361.60	1.26	1,389.61	484.18	11.31
Shaanxi	20.58	54.70	4,050.30	1.08	670.39	17.82	32.55
Gansu	45.44	172.90	4,658.80	1.77	299.63	11.40	6.66
Qinghai	71.75	1294.43	542.70	0.98	317.20	57.23	4.40
Ningxia	6.64	107.50	1,107.10	1.79	40.36	6.53	6.08
Xinjiang	166.49	781.35	4,124.60	1.94	484.07	22.72	2.94

Source: China Statistical Yearbook 2009.

Appendix 18: The evolution of policies of the Central Committee of the Communist Party of China with respect to urbanization [cheng zhen hua] and the handling of small towns, as described in Party documents. [Note: these are excerpts from Party documents that date from between 1979 and 2007.]

1979

1979: Decision of the Central Committee of the Communist Party of China on various issues to do with accelerating agricultural development.

'Build up small towns [*cheng-zhen*] in a planned manner and strengthen urban support for rural areas. This is the path we must take toward realizing the modernization of agriculture and the four modernizations, and toward reducing urban/rural disparities and disparities between industry and agriculture.'

'We must focus on building up the strength of small towns [*cheng zhen*] by arming them with modern industries, modern transport, modern commercial services, modern science, education, culture, and healthcare, so that they can serve as the "advance guard" in the transformation of the whole aspect of rural areas nationwide. There are more than two thousand county seats throughout China right now. We should first strengthen planning with respect to the somewhat more advanced areas among them, including those settlements [*ji zhen*] or the locations of communes [*gong she*] that are under the county level. We should gradually build them up, depending on the needs and potential of their level of economic development. We can also build up some satellite towns [*cheng zhen*] around the perimeters of existing large cities [*cheng shi*] and use the strength of those cities to support agriculture.'

1998

1998: Decision of the Central Committee of the Communist Party of China on various major issues to do with accelerating agricultural development and with the Party's work in rural areas.

'Put major effort into developing town-and-village enterprises [*xiang zhen qi ye*]. Shift surplus labor out of agriculture through a variety of channels. Set rural areas "on their feet" by broadening and deepening the extent of rural production. Develop secondary and tertiary industries, and build up small towns [*xiao cheng zhen*]. Open up a broader path to greater employment in rural areas, while at the same time accommodating the objective needs of towns and developed regions by guiding and enabling the orderly and rational flow of rural labor.'

'Developing small towns [*xiao cheng zhen*] is a strategic way to mobilize the rural economy and social development. It is helpful in preventing rampant [or uncontrollable] migration of people into large and medium-sized cities [*cheng shi*] while still enabling a large-scale shift of surplus labor away from agriculture and towards a relative concentration in town-and-village enterprises. It is beneficial to improving the quality of life and general caliber of farmers, as well as to increasing domestic demand and stimulating faster growth of the economy. We should formulate and improve policies and measures that encourage the healthy development of small towns [*xiao cheng zhen*], while going further in reforming the administrative system of household registration in small towns. Small towns should be configured in a rational way, with scientific planning. Emphasis should be put on basic infrastructure and we must ensure that land is used sparingly and that the environment is protected.'

Appendix 18: (Cont'd)

2000

2000: Recommendation of the Central Committee of the Communist Party of China on formulating China's 10th Five-Year Plan for national economic and social development.

'One of the pronounced problems with our economic development at the present time relates to economic structure. That is, it relates mainly to an irrational industrial structure, uneven development of different regions, and a low level of urbanization [using the term *cheng zhen*, which refers to urbanizing small towns as opposed to urbanizing *cheng shi*, or cities].'

'Raising the level of urbanization [again, *cheng zhen*] and thereby shifting the rural population will provide vast markets and a long-term engine for economic growth. It is a major means by which we can optimize the economic structure of the urban/rural economies, encourage a virtuous cycle in the national economy and more coordinated [or harmonized] social development. As agricultural productivity has improved in China, and as industrialization has accelerated, the conditions are ripe to press forward with the urbanization of towns [*cheng zhen*]. We should not waste the opportunity to implement a strategy of urbanization [*cheng zhen hua*] right away.'

'We need to focus [on building up] economic ties between cities [*cheng shi*], and to drive that process we should enable the growth of small and medium-sized towns [*cheng zhen*]. While emphasizing the development of small towns, we should also actively develop small and medium-sized cities [*cheng shi*]. We should improve the capacities of regional centers, enable large cities to radiate their influence into surrounding areas, and raise the levels of planning, development, and overall administration of cities of all kinds. We should take a path of urbanization [*cheng zhen hua*] that coordinates the development of large, medium, and small-sized cities [*cheng shi*] and small towns [*cheng zhen*], and that conforms to China's specific national conditions.'

2002

2002: 'Build a moderately prosperous society in an all-round way,' and ' Forge a new situation with respect to the specifically Chinese form of socialism'.

'A shift of surplus rural labor from agriculture into cities is an inevitable trend of industrialization and modernization. We therefore must gradually raise levels of urbanization [*chen zhen hua*]. By adhering firmly to the coordinated development of large, medium, and small-sized cities and small towns, we must take a path of urbanization [*chen zhen hua*] that is aligned with China's specific circumstances. Developing small towns must be done on the basis of existing county seats and those "administered towns" that have the requisite conditions. It must be done with scientific planning and rational allocation of space [i.e., zoning]. The development of town-and-village enterprises should be combined with the development of rural service industries. We should eliminate any systemic obstacles and policy obstacles that are detrimental to further urbanization [*cheng zhen hua*], and we should allow an orderly and rational flow [or movement] of rural labor.'

2003: Decision of the Central Committee of the Communist Party of China on various issues relating to improving China's socialist market-economy system.

'[We should] set up a system that is beneficial to gradually changing the existing dual structure of urban and rural economies.'

'Allowing a two-way flow of surplus rural labour between cities and countryside is an important way to increase farmers' incomes and promote the process of urbanization [*chen zhen hua*].'

'In order to unify labor markets in cities and the countryside in a gradual way, [we should] strengthen our guidance and management over a process that forms an equal employment system for laborers in both cities and rural areas. We should deepen reform of the household registration system, improve controls over the migrant population [or transient population], guide surplus rural labor to shift employment in an orderly and stable way. [We should] accelerate the course of urbanization [*chen zhen hua*] by allowing farmers who have a stable job in cities and a place to live to apply for household residency permits, either where they are employed or where they are living. This must comply with regulations of the place in question. [Farmers given urban household residency permits] should, moreover, enjoy the rights and benefits of anyone living in the place, as they should also assume the duties and responsibilities of being a local resident.'

2003

2007: 'Lift the great banner of a specifically Chinese form of socialism', and 'Strive to achieve new victories in the process of setting up a moderately prosperous society in an all-round way'.

'Mechanisms that allow for mutually stimulating growth between urban and rural areas and among regions and China's "main-function zones" have now basically been formed. The process of "building up a new socialist countryside in China" has achieved tremendous progress. The numbers of people living in "towns" [*cheng zhen*] has markedly increased.'

2007

'Take a Chinese-style path of urbanization [*cheng zhen hua*]. This means abiding by the principles of "coordinated development of urban and rural areas", "rational deployment [of resources]", "economizing on land", "improving all functions", and "enabling the large to bring along the small". It also means encouraging the coordinated growth of large, medium-sized, and small cities and small towns [*cheng zhen*]. In order to achieve a stronger overall carrying capacity, it means cultivating new "magnetic poles" of economic growth by forming urban clusters that rely on the radiating capacities of super-large cities.'

Appendix 19: Urbanization experiences and policies in representative countries around the world

The first Industrial Revolution initiated 'modern' urbanization in the world, starting in the 1760s. Prior to that time urbanization had been slow and uncertain, since at no point in human history had the global population exceeded one billion people.

By 1800, there were around 900 million people on the globe, of whom only 3 per cent were 'urban'. By 1900, the percentage of people living in cities had risen, but only to some 14 per cent of the world's total population. By 2000, urban populations were accounting for 47 per cent of all people in the world and more than 6 billion people were urban residents (see Figure A19.1) (UNFPA, 2007).

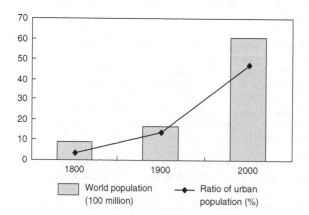

Figure A19.1 World urban population growth since the Industrial Revolution.
Source: UNFPA (2007), UNDP (2004).

In 2008, the world's urban population outnumbered its rural population for the first time in history (UNFPA, 2008).

Urbanization in Britain

Both industrialization and urbanization began in Britain, which had the necessary resources, labour, material, and markets for both, given agricultural and commercial revolutions that had been ongoing since the sixteenth century, and given the existence of Britain's overseas colonies. These considerations led to certain industries being developed prior to others, including textiles, mining, and metallurgy (He Hongtao, 2006; Ji Xiaolan, 2004).

The first Industrial Revolution transformed what had been handicraft operations into mechanized industries. Workshops now became factories, and farmers began to disengage from their traditional farming to become 'workers' and urban dwellers. Industrial urbanization began its forward march.

In 1750, around 25 per cent of Britain's entire population was urban. By the end of the eighteenth century, this figure had risen to 30 per cent and urbanization began to accelerate in the nineteenth century. In 1851, England's urban population constituted 50 per cent of the total; by the end of the nineteenth century, the urban population was over 70 per cent of the total.

The Industrial Revolution remoulded the spatial configuration of Britain's cities. Some cities that were not suited to industrial purposes quickly declined and some were even abandoned. At the beginning of the seventeenth century, for example, Norwich was second in terms of population in the country, but by 1801 it was down to eighth. York was third in population, but by 1801 had become seventeenth, while Exeter was sixth but fell to fifteenth. In contrast, towns located in resource-rich areas, or towns close to transport, suddenly emerged and grew to be large cities – Manchester, Glasgow, and Birmingham are three examples.

Urbanization in Britain in the early years was unrestricted and, allowed to take its own course, generated a number of 'urban syndromes'. Huge numbers of people surged into cities from the countryside, even though these cities were unable to provide them with sufficient jobs. Unemployment became an outstanding problem and urban poverty was rampant. According to some statistics, 44 per cent of residents in the core city area of London's East End were living under the poverty line in 1887; 43 per cent were living under the poverty line in North London, and 47 per cent in South London (Du Hengbo, 2004).

The scarcity of housing and the extreme inadequacy of public services led to the formation of large numbers of slums. By the end of the eighteenth century, London's slums were holding more than 200,000 people (Engels, 1975) London's air and water were severely polluted while public health facilities were essentially non-existent, leading to the incubation and spread of disease. Throughout the nineteenth century, the life expectancy of farmers in Britain was higher than the life expectancy of people living in urban areas.

Crime rose dramatically in London during the Industrial Revolution. Educational facilities were insufficient and child labour was prevalent. Development of the human intellect, of the spirit, and of any sense of ethics was neglected. In addition to these problems, however, the utter lack of urban planning meant that the city developed in a random and chaotic fashion.

As standards of living rose and as modern transport gradually enabled people to distance themselves from the negative aspects of urbanization, more and more chose to live in suburbs, leading to what is known as suburbanization. Between 1801 and 1851, the population of London's commercial center was extremely stable, staying at around 130,000 residents, but in the second half of the nineteenth century, this core commercial district began a dramatic decline as transport enabled the move of commerce out to the city's perimeter. The population of the core area came to less than 51,000 in 1881 and it was a mere 27,000 in 1901.

Between 1901 and 1911, the populations of the eight largest cities in England and Wales declined by 90,000. Between 1891 and 1901, the population of 22 textile cities in the north of England declined by 41,000, while that of 14 industrial cities declined by 146,000 between 1871 and 1901. In the south, the population of 11 industrial cities declined by 48,000 between 1841 and 1891. This decline in the populations of city centers was accompanied by an increase in the numbers of people living in suburbs. This changed the form of many cities. Instead of being 'large cities with a centralized focal point', they became low-density suburbs without a true center.

In 1861, London's suburbs held a population of 414,000 people. In 1891, they held 1.405 million people, and by 1901 the suburban population had gone up to 2.045 million people (Su En, 1978).

Faced with the problems generated by urbanization, the government began to assume more responsibility. Its increasing involvement in and regulation of the process of urbanization played an important role in beginning to turn urbanization into something positive. First, in terms of social welfare, Britain passed an amendment to the Poor Law in 1824 that provided greater guarantees for the urban poor. Then, between the end of the nineteenth and the beginning of the twentieth centuries, Britain implemented unprecedented social reforms by passing a series of legislative provisions that gradually set up the modern social security system. This system was composed of a fairly complete set of benefits that dealt with old-age pensions, unemployment, medical treatment, and children. Reforms included the Workmen's Compensation Act (1897), the Old Age Pensions Act (1908), the National Unemployment Insurance Act (1911), the National Health Insurance Act (1911), the Education Act (1906), and the Children's Act (1908).

The enactment and implementation of these laws gradually enabled Britain to set up a modern social security system, which served as the basis for taking the path of a welfare state after the Second World War.

To build up basic infrastructure and provide social services, Britain passed public health acts in 1848 and 1875. In 1866, it passed an environmental sanitation act, which ruled that the government had an obligation to provide public health facilities and services. In 1868 and 1875, the country passed laws on workers' housing. These actions gradually led to slums being demolished and replaced with a variety of urban facilities and infrastructure, including shops, parks, transport stations, parking garages, cinemas, and so on.

To begin to plan for urban and rural development, in 1909, Britain passed the world's first law on urban planning. From this time onward, urban planning became one of the functions of government. Another law on urban and rural planning was passed in 1947. In addition, laws were passed to cover various specific aspects of urban planning, including an industrial zoning act in 1945, a new cities act in 1946, a state public parks and inter-urban rail system act in 1949, and a town development act in 1952. The passing of these laws, and their implementation, brought Britain's urbanization into a more organized stage of development.

Britain's efforts in creating 'garden cities', and parks within cities, were inspirational to the process of urbanization in the rest of the world. In 1932, while the country was still in the midst of the Great Depression, Britain began to build 100 'new towns' throughout the country. In 1935, the London County Council appropriated two million pounds for specific use in requisitioning land for a system of green belts. Sir Montague Barlow established a royal commission to survey the 'industrial population' of the country. In 1940, the *Barlow Report* came out, recommending that London's growth be controlled and that the city carry out redevelopment in order to address unbearable congestion. Industry and populations were to be dispersed from the most congested areas. The Report called for more 'balanced' regional growth. It recommended that the last two garden cities or garden suburban areas be completed, that satellite towns and trade zones be developed, as well as existing small towns and regional centers more remote from London.

A plan for post-war reconstruction was already started in 1941. Patrick Abercrombie completed the County of London Plan (1943) and the Greater

London Plan (1944). This plan employed concentric circles around the core city, with population and industry being dispersed away from the central ring. The surrounding suburbs were to encircle the city with a green belt, rather than allowing development to continue. The aim was to prevent further urban expansion.

Outside this circle of 'countryside', the plan allowed for development of existing towns as well as the building of eight wholly new towns, in order to accommodate the population and industry spillover from London. Among the 525,000 people who would be living in these expanded towns, 350,000 were to be situated in the new towns. Between 1946 and 1949, eight new towns were in fact designated for construction within the Greater London area (Gu Chaolin, 2009).

After various policy adjustments, Britain's process of urbanization settled into a fairly stable period after the Second World War. Development went ahead on a sound basis. 'Urban syndromes' were basically dealt with, and the urban population of the country grew at a stable rate. By the end of the twentieth century, Britain's urban population amounted to 90 per cent of its total population, making the country one of the most 'urbanized' in the world.

Urbanization in France

France started urbanizing half a century after Britain began the process, and France also urbanized more slowly. In 1850, at a time when UK had already basically 'urbanized' (in the sense that its 'urbanization rate' exceeded 50 per cent), France was still only 25 per cent urbanized. Only in 1930 did the urban population in France exceed 30 per cent of the total population. The expansion of cities also occurred at a gentler and more even pace (Yang Lan et al., 2008).

By the end of the Second World War, urban social structures in France were showing distinct differences from cities in various countries on the European continent. For example, since working-class people in the 16th arrondissement in Paris were not very mobile or 'transient', they were able to set up small social units in this area. The social fabric of the area was different in that it had closely knit neighbourhoods and strong social networks. Many areas also retained the social stratification that had characterized an earlier age. In some 'shanty towns', unregulated separate houses had been built, primitive dwellings that contained large numbers of poor people. These places were distinctly different from suburban areas that exhibited a far greater degree of individualism.

Urban construction in France went through a period of several decades when virtually no new housing was built, due to the Depression and the Second World War. Faced with a housing shortage as its population increased, France began to implement a rent-control policy. Population shifts and an ever-increasing birth rate created a housing crisis after the war, and the government then began a large-scale program of building mass-produced standardized apartment blocks. Inadequate attention was paid to a number of critical factors, however, including the location of these units, facilities to service them, and their overall quality as housing. By 1964, France had built 200 such housing districts, each containing over 1000 households.

Meanwhile, the extent of urbanization among various regions in France remained highly uneven up until the 1950s. The amount of land occupied by Paris was only 2 per cent of the country's total, yet Paris held 20 per cent of the country's population. Paris accounted for 50 per cent of the nation's total commerce as well. It held 50 per cent of France's electronics industry, 56 per cent of its aircraft-manufacturing industry, 64 per cent of its automotive industry, and 76 per cent of its pharmaceuticals industry. Only three other urban centers held more than 500,000 people in the entire country, namely Marseille, Lyon, and the Lille–Roubaix–Tourcoing complex.

Starting in 1954, France began to apply public control measures to its national territory. It restricted further development of large cities and promoted the development of small and medium-sized cities as well as more balanced development among different regions. Primary measures included the following (Yang Lan et al., 2008). First, France reconfigured the placement of industry in the country. By providing subsidies and incentives, the country encouraged industrial enterprises that were based in Paris and the northern part of the country to transfer their operations and factories to less-developed parts of the country. At the same time, the state forbade the construction of any factory within Paris or other large cities that took up more than 500 square meters of space. Second, France put major effort into developing industries that were already located in less-developed regions. It built basic infrastructure, improved transport lines, contributed to education, and provided training in agricultural technologies in order to promote the modernization of local agriculture. Third, France adjusted the configuration of cities in the country. It built 'new-style cities' on the outskirts of Paris and other large cities, with the aim of encouraging people to move out from the city center. The increase in population was guided toward 'priority development axes', in line with their natural, economic, and human geography requirements (Gu Chaolin, 2009).

Between 1954 and 1962, some 3 million people moved out from Paris and other large cities into other districts. Another 4.5 million people moved out of large cities between 1968 and 1975. The population of Paris declined by 11 per cent between 1968 and 1975; the population of Lyons declined by 14 per cent, and other large cities saw similar declines (Yang Lan et al., 2008). Such measures very clearly ameliorated the problem of unbalanced regional development in France.

The amount of 'urban space' in France, that is, space used for urban development, started growing rapidly in the 1960s. Between 1968 and 1999, it increased by five times and commuting times quadrupled, even though populations grew only by 50 per cent. This led to a decline in the density of urban populations. Population density in cities went from 705 people per square kilometer in 1968 down to 256 people per square kilometer in 1999. Population density in greater metropolitan areas went from 506 people per square kilometer in 1968 to 442 people per square kilometer in 1999 (Zhang Zhenlong et al., 2008). Reasons behind the sprawl of cities included technological improvements in both transport

Table A19.1 Urban population change in France (1968–1999)

Urban area	Population growth rate (%)			
	1968–1975	*1975–1982*	*1982–1990*	*1990–1999*
Central area	0.29	−0.44	−0.1	−0.12
Suburban area	2.13	0.94	0.87	0.43
City rim	1.40	2.24	1.66	0.97
Total	1.19	0.58	0.64	0.42

Source: INSEE – Censuses of Population; Paulus (2002).

and telecommunications, the improvement and broader coverage of urban infrastructure and facilities, and the implementation of policies with respect to public housing.

Urban centers in France have shown a negative growth rate since the 1970s due to the centrifugal effect of having economic activity and housing increasingly situated outside core areas (Table A19.1). Urban centers have continued to play a primary role in urban development, however, serving as cultural centers and places with highly developed services and facilities. The population of areas around urban centers has grown at a fast pace – indeed it grew twice as fast as urban core areas during the 1990s. One notable trend is the pattern in which traditional suburban areas have deteriorated. Suburbs closer to urban centers were affected by the encroachment of industry and populations in the 1950s, but development was stymied by the lack of infrastructure and by worsening environmental conditions. Both people and industry gradually moved further out, causing an even faster decline in these areas, sometimes to the point of economic collapse. Since investment was inadequate, environmental conditions became even worse, thereby forming a vicious cycle. Eventually, the immediate suburban areas of cities became 'low-lying belts' in between urban centers and their more distant perimeters, in terms of their lack of appeal to people and business. The French government has made various attempts to stop this worsening trend, such as increasing investment and improving the look of residential districts. Nevertheless, the results have been modest (Zhang Zhenlong et al., 2008).

Even though the centers of many large cities in France have declined in terms of population and employment, the greater urban area of these cities has continued to expand. Paris is a good example. The population of Paris declined by 25 per cent between 1962 and 1999, but the population in surrounding areas grew by two and a half times. The population in the outer periphery of Paris grew by nine times. By now, given the way the countryside around Paris is being urbanized, the 'urban peripheral belt' has already expanded outside the administrative jurisdiction of Greater Paris itself.

Urbanization in the USA

Urbanization occurred at a notably faster pace in the USA than it did in either Britain or France. In 1890, 30 per cent of the US population was urbanized; within just three decades, by 1920, that figure had gone up to over 50 per cent. Urbanization in the USA occurred under the impetus of the second Industrial Revolution, at a time when electrification was improving productivity tremendously. Cars were becoming widespread among the middle class due to the invention of the internal combustion engine and the use of factory-line production methods. Urbanization and mechanization developed in tandem.

After the 1920s, the percentage of people living in cities continued to rise in the USA, but the centripetal drawing force of urban centers had already reached its peak. Factors of production now began to flow between cities rather than accumulate in any specific city. As a result, urban clusters began to develop and mature. Urban clusters were an expression of the human geography of different regions, which concentrated factors of production in line with regional development.

Some 60 per cent of Americans were living in the countryside at the start of the twentieth century. After the Great Depression of 1929, and Roosevelt's New Deal, urban populations increased rapidly. Once the Federal Housing Administration was established, it was able to stimulate housing construction and ownership by adjusting the provisions by which people could receive mortgages. The Housing Act of 1937 established the US Housing Authority, which began to implement measures to eliminate slums, create job opportunities, stimulate economic growth, demolish dilapidated old housing, and provide poor people with public housing. At the same time, the Labor Promotion Administration hired planners to do in-depth research on urban development. By 1970, 69 per cent of Americans were living in metropolitan areas.

By the 1970s, 90 per cent of Americans were accessing systems that could be called 'urban systems for daily life'. As these systems developed, they had a profound effect on the spatial configuration of the nation. At the outset, the pattern encircled a specific and clear 'center' while at the same time exhibiting a 'cone' shape. The lower down on the cone, the lower the population density became. Levels of income and education declined while the number of poor people increased.

Forces that had pulled resources in to the center and formed this 'cone-shaped' spatial configuration began to change, however, and more specific forms of spatial configuration began to appear. Indicators measuring the intensities of a variety of factors declined with distance from the center. Between 1910 and 1970, all density gradients dropped gradually, which meant that city-center densities were declining and metropolitan areas were expanding outward at a fast rate. In addition, densities were beginning to balance out throughout the entire urban area. The distinction between 'urban' and 'rural' was beginning to diminish to the point of disappearing altogether. The sudden mobility of people, materials, and information changed both quickly and also over an extended period of time, which brought on a whole new situation in terms of the ambient environment.

From having been a country with distinct but interconnected regions, the USA became integrated. It became a country with a true 'national culture'. Changes in transportation and information technologies were part of the reason. They propelled the country into the post-industrial era. A social system with multiple 'nodes' and interconnecting 'links' began to function and to influence the shape of American cities.

Since the 1970s, the rate at which populations in American metropolitan areas had been growing has slowed down. Between 1960 and 1970, population growth in the 'standard metropolitan statistical areas' (SMSA) of the country declined at an average rate of 0.6 per cent per year. After the 1970s, this began to decline at 0.4 per cent per year (subtracting out the case of merging cities). Most notably, the tendency of populations to move towards suburbs reversed direction: between 1960 and 1970, metropolitan areas took in more than 3 million 'immigrants', although this trend has gradually declined since the 1970s.

Between 1960 and 1970, the number of people moving into non-urban areas surrounding cities declined, but since the 1970s the number has again begun to increase. From a balanced two-way movement, the flow began to go in the other direction. This phenomenon has been called 'counter-urbanization' [or 'de-urbanization']. It represents a process of people moving from a more concentrated to a more dispersed condition.

In addition, populations grew rapidly in America's conurbations, or linked urban clusters. Between 1950 and 2000, cities with populations of over one million grew to contain 117 million people. By 2000, they held 83 per cent of the USA's urban population and represented 90 per cent of the increase in its total population. Due to economies of scale and the concentrating effect of economic activity in general, people began to cluster in the northeastern part of the country, in Boston, New York, Philadelphia, Baltimore, and in the Great Lakes area, in such cities as Pittsburgh, Cleveland, and Detroit. As a result, these two huge 'urban-cluster belts' have developed. They incorporate more than 20 metropolitan districts, each of which contains a minimum of one million people. The two belts hold more than 70 per cent of American manufacturing. They constitute super-large industrialized areas (manufacturing zones). They therefore represent the highest levels of urbanization in the country, with the densest populations as well as the highest degree of industrialization.

Urbanization in Japan

Japan went through a developmental stage of fast, large-scale urbanization and industrial modernization after the Meiji Restoration of 1868, but especially during the Showa period (1925–1989). During this time, the country gradually transitioned from being agrarian to becoming today's post-industrial nation.

After the Second World War, in order to restore the country's economy, Japan's government employed a development model that gave priority to heavy industry. It built up industry along the Pacific coast and, in the process, created tremendous employment opportunities. Since the industrial sector was mainly concentrated in cities, the rural population moved *en masse* into urban areas. This led to urbanization that, after the war, was of a 'restorative' nature.

The Korean War erupted in 1950. Driven by demand created by war, Japan's economy grew quickly, with a corresponding acceleration of urbanization. Starting in 1947, therefore, the urban population rose constantly from its previous platform of 30 per cent, but the increase incorporated extreme discrepancies in people's incomes as well as disparities among different parts of the country.

In 1954, the Planning Department of Japan's Economic Deliberation Agency issued a *Comprehensive Development Strategy (Draft)*, in order to deal with a variety of problems. These included the unbalanced regional development and unbalanced development between urban and rural areas that had been brought on by rapid urbanization and industrialization, the severe inadequacy of basic infrastructure, and the declining efficiencies caused by overly concentrated industries.

In 1962, Japan promulgated its very first National Plan for Integrated Development. This set forth the goal of achieving a basic balance among regions by the year 1970. In addition, to prevent the disparity among regions from widening further, Japan issued a number of laws starting in the mid-1950s. These included the Law on the Promotion of Industrial Development in Underdeveloped Regions (1961), the Law on Promoting the Building Up of New Industrial Cities (1962), and the Law on Promoting Industrial Reorganization in Special Regions (1964).

In the course of implementing these various laws as well as the National Plan, Japan's heavy industry diffused in a more balanced way throughout the country instead of being concentrated along the Pacific coast. To be more specific, the Japanese government recognized a set of 'new industrial cities' and 'special zones for industrial reorganization'. At the same time, the country increased its public spending on basic infrastructure projects in these regions. These efforts gradually reduced the disparities among regions in Japan, as well as the gap between urban and rural economies, with particular focus during the period 1970–1975, but more generally from the early 1960s to the 1970s.

To a certain degree, the actions of the Japanese government as described above were successful in reducing disparities among regions, but large cities continued to attract a disproportionate percentage of the population. This was due to the ongoing disparity between regional urban hubs and the three major metropolitan hubs, given different levels of economic development (Yoshio et al., 2002).

Throughout the 1950s and even up to the 1970s, Japan's population continued to gravitate towards the three largest cities: Tokyo, Osaka, and Nagoya. Between 1956 and 1970, the net increase in people of these three cities came to 8.2 million (Yasumitu, 2008). They therefore formed an 'urban belt of mega-cities along the Pacific'.

Only after the 1970s did the numbers of people migrating into Japan's three major metropolitan hubs begin to show a marked decline. This was after the oil crisis and accompanying economic depression, and it was combined with a gradual reduction in Japan's urban–rural gap (Yasumitu, 2008). At the same time, local governments were pursuing proactive industry-promoting policies that now began to provide substantial job opportunities. Industry began to move towards local areas as they found insufficient amounts of labour in larger cities. For a period, a 'reverse-flow' phenomenon meant that people were moving from large cities back to where they were born. Nevertheless, in overall terms, Japan maintained a fairly high rate of urbanization even during this period. From 43.7 per cent in 1960, the urbanization rate went to 59.7 per cent in 1980, representing an annual average increase of 0.8 percentage points.[1]

With economic recovery, Japan experienced another concentrating of populations in the three metropolitan hubs from the late 1970s to the mid-1980s. This did not last long, however. The population of the three large metropolitan hubs began another swift decline from the mid-1980s to the mid-1990s. Disparities among regions declined. Causes for the net outflow of people included the bursting of the real estate bubble in the early 1990s and the aging of the Japanese population.

Throughout the 1980s and into the mid-1990s, Japan's urbanization entered a stage of slow-paced growth. From 60 per cent in 1981, the urbanization rate rose gently to around 65 per cent in the mid-1990s.

Under the impact of the wave of globalization and 'informatization', Japan has been transitioning to being an 'information society' (or a 'knowledge society') since the latter half of the 1990s. Factories that are carrying on manufacturing have been moving away from the three major metropolitan hubs toward more regional hubs. In order to take advantage of the lower costs and better logistics of 'on-the-spot' manufacturing, many of Japan's enterprises have been shifting their production bases overseas. Tokyo has continued to strengthen its role as the central axis of commerce, however, and the city has continued to draw in a greater population.

Tokyo continues to be pre-eminent in its concentrating effect. At the same time, the 'suburbanization' of the population continues as advanced inter-urban transport systems are established. The distinctions between urban and rural are increasingly hard to define. The radius of Japan's 'urban hubs' is constantly growing, while urban clusters are becoming the primary force guiding Japan's ongoing urbanization. In 2007, the three major metropolitan hubs held 50.7 per cent of Japan's population. They contributed 55.7 per cent of the GDP of the entire country.[2]

Urbanization in certain developing countries

After the Second World War, developing countries began to urbanize rapidly, but the trajectory of their 'urbanization' was unlike the typical curve. This was mainly due to overly rapid urbanization in the face of slower industrialization. Total populations increased rapidly, but were not able to transition properly. Although industrialization was powerfully effective in stimulating economies, in most developing countries the manufacturing sector constituted a small percentage of the total. In 1960, it accounted for around 15.6 per cent of total GDP of developing countries. By the 1980s, it had only risen to 17.5 per cent. More recently, it is approaching 36 per cent.

Statistics generally corroborate the fact that 'urbanization' in developing countries is preceding 'industrialization'. This phenomenon of a discrepancy in the two processes is often described by the terms 'urban inflation' or 'false urbanization' (Bairoch, 1975).

Urbanization in South-Asian countries

The urbanization of countries in South Asia is generally lower than it is in the great majority of African countries. Nevertheless, South Asian countries are facing enormous challenges due to the sheer size of their cities. Calcutta, Delhi, and Bombay in India, Karachi in Pakistan, and Dhaka in Bangladesh are among the largest cities on earth.

At the same time, these countries are characterized by a 'rural' appearance. Most towns have certain commercial functions as a result of being alongside a road or a railroad, but few have much in the way of administrative functions. The driving factor behind urbanization in most South Asian countries is not economic. Rather, it is due to human migration. Because of high birth rates and impoverished conditions in the countryside, people are migrating to cities. Premature urbanization is therefore South Asia's fundamental condition.

Urbanization in the Saharan countries of Africa

Urbanization in the Saharan countries of Africa is independent of the process of economic globalization. Even now, most African countries have a single predominating city, a structure that does not allow for any kind of 'urban network'. In international terms, these cities are rather small. Nevertheless, they hold a high percentage of the national wealth despite the fact that many of them are unbearably impoverished. Since the 1970s, little foreign investment has come in and governments have ruled ineffectively, while populations have continued to increase dramatically. Little investment has been made in basic infrastructure. Piped water, electricity, sewage pipes, roads, and other such facilities constantly wear out, forcing people to move toward the periphery of cities, where prices are cheaper.

In Libya, people are moving into cities at a rate that exceeds 7 per cent increase per year, in order to escape from political strife in towns and small cities. This means that Libya's urban populations are doubling every 10 years. This population increase in cities, as a result of poor economic growth and political instability, is leading to ever-worsening urban problems.

Urbanization in Latin America

Three-quarters of the population of Latin America lives in cities, so the level of urbanization is high. At the same time, however, the urban landscape resembles that of Southeast-Asian countries, where urbanization is quite low. Intense economic competition has forced much of Latin America's manufacturing industries to distance themselves from cities in order to take advantage of lower wages and lower land costs. In San Paolo, Brazil, industrial enterprises are situated as far as 200 kilometers from the city center.

The geographic distribution of urban populations in Latin America is quite dispersed, which means that it therefore occupies a greater amount of farm land. Urbanization in Argentina is notable in this respect, since the process takes over farmers' land and drives farmers to live in cities. Once dispossessed farmers arrive in cities, however, they find no way to make a living. This has led to the enormous problem of Argentina's impoverished slums.

Appendix 20: Changes in the density of populations in the built-up areas of China's cities between 1981 and 2008

	Urban population (10,000 persons)	*Built-up area (km²)*	*Population density (person/km²)*
1981	14,400.5	7,438	19,360.72
1982	14,281.6	7,862.1	18,165.12
1983	15,940.5	8,156.3	19,543.79
1984	17,969.1	9,249	19,428.15
1985	20,893.4	9,386.2	22,259.70
1986	22,906.2	10,127.3	22,618.27
1987	25,155.7	10,816.5	23,256.78
1988	29,545.2	12,094.6	24,428.42
1989	31,205.4	12,462.2	25,040.04
1990	32,530.2	12,855.7	25,304.11
1991	29,589.3	14,011.1	21,118.47
1992	30,748.2	14,958.7	20,555.40
1993	33,780.9	16,588.3	20,364.29
1994	35,833.9	17,939.5	19,974.86
1995	37,789.9	19,264.2	19,616.65
1996	36,234.5	20,214.2	17,925.27
1997	36,836.9	20,791.3	17,717.46
1998	37,411.8	21,379.6	17,498.83
1999	37,590	21,524.5	17,463.82
2000	38,823.7	22,439.3	17,301.65
2001	35,747.4	24,026.6	14,878.22
2002	35,219.6	25,972.6	13,560.29
2003	33,805	28,308	11,941.85
2004	34,147.4	30,406.2	11,230.41
2005	35,923.7	32,520.7	11,046.41
2006	37,272.8	33,659.8	9,889.75
2007	37,051.3	35,469.7	9,466.39
2008	36,988.3	36,295.3	9,221.88

Source: *China Urban–Rural Construction Statistical Yearbook 2008.* The total urban population after 2006 includes both the 'urban population' and the 'urban temporary population'. As there are no statistics on the urban temporary population before 2006, the total urban population for other years includes simply the 'urban population'.

Appendix 21: Changes in the population densities of certain cities in China between 1981 and 2008

	1981			2008			1981–2008
	Population (10,000)	Built-up area (km²)	Population density (10,000 persons/km²)	Population (10,000)	Built-up area (km²)	Population density (10,000 persons/km²)	population density change
Shanghai	613.0	142	4.3169	1815.08	860.2	2.1100	-2.2069
Beijing	466.4	349	1.3364	1439.10	1310.9	1.0978	-0.2386
Guangzhou	233.8	162	1.4432	886.55	895.0	0.9906	-0.4527
Chongqing	190.0	73	2.6027	879.96	708.4	1.2422	-1.3605
Shenzhen	4.5	100	0.0450	876.83	787.9	1.1129	1.0679
Tianjin	380.9	222	1.7158	639.02	640.9	0.9971	-0.7186
Wuhan	263.0	174	1.5115	596.00	460.0	1.2957	-0.2158
Zhengzhou	85.9	65	1.3215	479.45	328.7	1.4588	0.1373
Nanjing	170.2	116	1.4672	478.16	592.1	0.8076	-0.6596
Shenyang	293.7	164	1.7909	468.00	370.0	1.2649	-0.5260
Harbin	209.4	156	1.3423	415.59	340.3	1.2211	-0.1212
Chengdu	137.6	58	2.3643	405.98	427.7	0.9493	-1.4149
Xi'an	153.6	129	1.1907	336.40	272.7	1.2335	0.0428
Kunming	85.9	73	1.1767	317.30	280.2	1.1324	-0.0443
Taiyuan	123	136	0.9044	294.60	238.0	1.2378	0.3334
Hangzhou	90.5	55	1.6606	293.28	367.3	0.7986	-0.8620
Dalian	120.8	87	1.3885	282.59	258.0	1.0953	-0.2932
Jinan	101.1	88	1.1489	281.00	326.2	0.8614	-0.2874
Qingdao	101.3	73	1.3877	276.25	267.1	1.0342	-0.3535
Urumqi	88.0	48	1.8333	273.00	302.8	0.9016	-0.9317
Changchun	125.2	119	1.0521	268.05	327.7	0.8179	-0.2342
Changsha	83.5	53	1.5755	247.28	242.8	1.0185	-0.5569
Wuxi	61.8	36	1.7167	237.42	208.0	1.1414	-0.5752

Shijiazhuang	80.8	58	1.3931	233.89	190.9	1.2255	-0.1677
Shantou	42.7	8	5.3375	222.39	170.4	1.3052	-4.0323
Hefei	53.9	56	0.9625	220.43	268.0	0.8225	-0.1400
Xiamen	28.3	36	0.7861	219.32	197.0	1.1133	0.3272
Guiyang	82.6	59	1.4000	217.27	132.0	1.6460	0.2460
Nanchang	73.2	65	1.1262	213.00	185.0	1.1514	0.0252
Foshan	20.2	11	1.8364	208.67	150.0	1.3913	-0.4450
Luoyang	56.3	36	1.5639	204.17	164.0	1.2453	-0.3186
Suzhou	55.5	29	1.9138	200.28	317.7	0.6304	-1.2834
Nanning	50.5	68	0.7426	197.21	179.1	1.1014	0.3587
Tangshan	86.5	47	1.8404	197.08	213.0	0.9253	-0.9152
Fuzhou	69.0	44	1.5682	197.00	176.6	1.1156	-0.4526
Baotou	89.0	95	0.9368	170.00	180.0	0.9444	0.0076
Ningbo	32.7	20	1.6769	162.19	241.6	0.6714	-1.0055
Anshan	99.6	70	1.4229	154.93	148.0	1.0465	-0.3763
Liuzhou	45.7	64	0.7141	154.72	126.9	1.2194	0.5054
Weifang	22.4	25	0.8960	154.35	132.0	1.1693	0.2733
Handan	66.0	56	1.1786	146.66	104.1	1.4094	0.2308
Zibo	62.3	65	0.9585	145.53	213.1	0.6830	-0.2754
Hohhot	49.8	53	0.9396	136.11	154.0	0.8838	-0.0558
Xuzhou	64.8	51	1.2706	133.59	186.6	0.7159	-0.5547
Fushun	101.2	91	1.1121	131.93	123.9	1.0648	-0.0473
Yantai	25.0	25	1.0000	131.70	211.2	0.6236	-0.3764
Jilin	81.5	72	1.1319	126.93	165.6	0.7663	-0.3656
Datong	59	80	0.7375	125.40	91.2	1.3750	0.6375
Wenzhou	35.7	12	3.0000	124.65	164.0	0.7601	-2.2399
Huizhou	9.2	7	1.3143	121.39	132.0	0.9194	-0.3949
Changzhou	39.3	29	1.3552	119.68	120.5	0.9931	-0.3621
Nanyang	15.4	17	0.9059	114.57	87.4	1.3110	0.4051
Jiangmen	13.8	8	1.7250	113.45	113.8	0.9974	-0.7276

(Continued)

Appendix 21: (Cont'd)

	1981			2008			1981–2008
	Population (10,000)	Built-up area (km²)	Population density (10,000 persons/ km²)	Population (10,000)	Built-up area (km²)	Population density (10,000 persons/km²)	population density change
Baoding	38.5	45	0.8556	113.02	129.0	0.8761	0.0206
Qiqihar	89.9	97	0.9268	110.48	115.3	0.9584	0.0316
Daqing	42.9	43	0.9977	108.68	175.8	0.6183	-0.3794
Huainan	53.9	38	1.4184	102.74	95.8	1.0728	-0.3456
Haikou	17.0	18	0.9444	100.84	91.4	1.1030	0.1586
Qingjiang	16.3	15	1.0584	100.00	100.0	1.0000	-0.0584
Yinchuan	22.6	30	0.7533	98.84	110.8	0.8923	0.1390
Zhuhai	6.1	4	1.5250	97.28	118.3	0.8220	-0.7030
Wuhu	37.0	25	1.4800	96.87	126.3	0.7669	-0.7131
Jinzhou	44.4	30	1.4800	95.70	68.8	1.3906	-0.0894
Shangqiu	11.6	14	0.8286	94.30	58.5	1.6120	0.7834
Benxi	64.3	43	1.4953	92.38	106.5	0.8674	-0.6279
Hengyang	37.3	31	1.2032	90.85	93.0	0.9769	-0.2263
Pingdingshan	26.6	21	1.2667	90.33	61.7	1.4638	0.1971
Qinhuangdao	25.2	41	0.6146	89.78	87.5	1.0263	0.4117
Yingkou	32.4	27	1.2000	88.32	97.1	0.9094	-0.2906
Xining	45.6	46	0.9913	88.02	64.9	1.3558	0.3645
Bangbu	35.8	29	1.2345	87.26	99.8	0.8748	-0.3597
Zhengjiang	27.3	22	1.2188	86.20	98.2	0.8780	-0.3408
Kaifeng	42.3	37	1.1432	84.80	89.5	0.9476	-0.1957
Zhangjiakou	45.8	67	0.6836	83.20	80.0	1.0400	0.3564

Zhaoahuang	19.1	22	0.8682	83.17	106.4	0.7817	-0.0864
Guilin	29.3	28	1.0464	82.03	59.5	1.3777	0.3313
Huaibei	25.4	19	1.3368	80.93	62.8	1.2881	-0.0488
Mianyang	19.2	18	1.0667	79.12	80.5	0.9831	-0.0836
Quanzhou	13.4	6	2.2333	78.80	81.0	0.9728	-1.2605
Huzhou	17.0	7	2.5000	78.50	72.2	1.0873	-1.4127
Fuxin	51.6	32	1.6125	78.00	66.0	1.1818	-0.4307
Xiangfan	24.5	19	1.2895	76.90	79.3	0.9702	-0.3192
Xiangtan	34.3	36	0.9528	76.51	72.7	1.0531	0.1004
Xianyang	21.7	15	1.4467	76.40	54.6	1.4005	-0.0461
Yichang	28.5	25	1.1400	75.76	81.6	0.9289	-0.2111
Chifeng	21.3	22	0.9682	75.67	77.0	0.9827	0.0145
Liaoyang	32.6	41	0.7951	75.50	92.0	0.8205	0.0254
Jiaozuo	28.6	22	1.3000	75.30	90.0	0.8370	-0.4630
Changzhi	21	39	0.5385	74.63	45.3	1.6475	1.1090
Jixi	60.6	58	1.0448	73.97	79.2	0.9336	-0.1112
Xinxiang	36.1	34	1.0618	73.13	94.6	0.7731	-0.2886
Baoji	25.6	20	1.2800	72.71	71.4	1.0191	-0.2609
Zigong	32.8	20	1.6400	72.18	53.2	1.3568	-0.2832
Fuyang	12.0	14	0.8571	71.82	68.6	1.0469	0.1898
Yangzhou	23.2	16	1.4500	71.73	75.0	0.9564	-0.4936
Zhunyi	22.0	47	0.4681	71.60	51.0	1.4039	0.9358
Zhuzhou	30.0	35	0.8571	70.93	89.6	0.7918	-0.0653
Lianyungang	23.5	22	1.0682	70.30	95.0	0.7400	-0.3282
Huangshi	35.8	21	1.7048	70.30	62.0	1.1339	-0.5709
Nanchong	13.4	7	1.9143	69.30	64.1	1.0820	-0.8323
Modanjiang	45.2	38	1.1895	69.10	65.3	1.0582	-0.1313
Anyang	31.9	29	1.1000	69.00	73.0	0.9452	-0.1548
Nantong	22.1	19	1.1818	68.88	68.7	1.0032	-0.1786
Tianshui	11.7	27	0.4333	68.54	42.2	1.6226	1.1893

(*Continued*)

Appendix 21: (Cont'd)

	1981			2008			1981–2008
	Population (10,000)	Built-up area (km²)	Population density (10,000 persons/km²)	Population (10,000)	Built-up area (km²)	Population density (10,000 persons/km²)	population density change
Shaoxing	21.8	11	1.9123	67.31	90.4	0.7446	-1.1677
Dandong	41.4	27	1.5333	65.35	53.4	1.2238	-0.3096
Zhanjiang	28.0	24	1.1667	64.57	77.2	0.8361	-0.3306
Luzhou	21.0	12	1.7500	64.48	53.1	1.2136	-0.5364
Yueyang	14.3	16	0.8938	63.30	78.6	0.8053	-0.0884
Xingtai	22.4	20	1.1200	63.05	70.0	0.9007	-0.2193
Jining	16.1	13	1.2385	62.79	88.0	0.7135	-0.5249
Jiamusi	38.9	42	0.9262	61.10	62.4	0.9793	0.0531
Hegang	45.4	28	1.6214	61.04	43.0	1.4195	-0.2019
Changde	15.4	12	1.2833	60.65	72.5	0.8361	-0.4472
Jiujiang	22.4	21	1.0667	60.63	89.5	0.6777	-0.3890
Anqing	19.4	15	1.2933	59.78	65.5	0.9127	-0.3807
Beihai	10.9	9	1.2111	59.50	68.8	0.8648	-0.3463
Dezhou	13.4	19	0.7053	59.46	46.5	1.2787	0.5734
Taizhou	12.0	10	1.2371	57.45	58.5	0.9821	-0.2551
Shaoyang	18.9	15	1.2600	57.09	47.0	1.2147	-0.0453
Ganzhou	17.5	14	1.2500	57.00	55.0	1.0364	-0.2136
Siping	25.4	24	1.0583	56.60	39.0	1.4513	0.3929
Jinhua	11.6	11	1.1048	56.44	69.7	0.8101	-0.2947
Shaoguan	25.4	18	1.4111	56.40	78.3	0.7203	-0.6908
Weihai	4.5	9	0.5000	56.39	120.0	0.4699	-0.0301
Jiaxing	15.5	15	1.0197	55.97	83.5	0.6703	-0.3494
Yangquan	26	29	0.8966	54.46	51.2	1.0630	0.1665

Cangzhou	18.5	21	0.8810	53.97	44.3	1.2197	0.3387
Ma'anshan	23.2	24	0.9667	53.60	72.0	0.7444	-0.2222
Chaoyang	13.4	13	1.0308	52.50	35.0	1.5000	0.4692
Shiyan	17.1	11	1.5545	52.25	59.5	0.8782	-0.6764
Zhaoqing	11.2	8	1.4000	51.66	71.0	0.7280	-0.6720
Leshan	27.9	6	4.6500	51.34	49.8	1.0305	-3.6195
Chengde	20.8	17	1.2235	50.05	83.7	0.5980	-0.6256
Maoming	7.9	14	0.5643	49.79	67.4	0.7387	0.1744
Neijiang	16.4	9	1.8222	49.48	37.0	1.3373	-0.4849
Anshun	12.0	6	2.0000	48.98	31.5	1.5549	-0.4451
Yiyang	13.4	12	1.1167	48.36	50.5	0.9576	-0.1590
Luohe	8.9	9	0.9889	47.61	51.3	0.9281	-0.0608
Fuzhou	9.6	8	1.2000	47.10	45.0	1.0471	-0.1529
Xinyang	14.7	16	0.9188	46.58	58.2	0.8003	-0.1184
Tonghua	22.6	21	1.0762	46.36	47.3	0.9793	-0.0969
Shuangyashan	33.3	51	0.6529	46.10	58.8	0.7840	0.1311
Shuzhou	8.6	10	0.8600	45.47	45.7	0.9950	0.1350
Tieling	16.4	17	0.9647	45.31	44.0	1.0307	0.0660
Jingdezheng	26.8	21	1.2762	44.96	72.8	0.6172	-0.6589
Xuchang	13.8	13	1.0615	44.80	65.3	0.6861	-0.3755
Tongliao	15.8	32	0.4938	44.73	50.5	0.8857	0.3920
Liaoyuan	34.5	19	1.8158	44.35	42.0	1.0560	-0.7598
Yanji	13.6	15	0.9067	44.00	34.7	1.2687	0.3621
Linfen	12	17	0.7059	42.90	37.4	1.1471	0.4412
Zangzhou	14.0	9	1.5556	42.38	47.5	0.8918	-0.6637
Zhumadian	8.4	10	0.8400	41.89	49.2	0.8507	0.0107
Tongling	16.0	14	1.1429	41.79	47.0	0.8891	-0.2537
Tongchuan	22.8	17	1.3412	41.25	37.4	1.1041	-0.2371
Hebi	14.7	10	1.4700	40.99	48.0	0.8540	-0.6160
Qitaihe	13.7	23	0.5957	40.98	62.4	0.6570	0.0614

(Continued)

Appendix 21: (Cont'd)

	1981			2008			1981–2008
	Population (10,000)	Built-up area (km²)	Population density (10,000 persons/ km²)	Population (10,000)	Built-up area (km²)	Population density (10,000 persons/km²)	population density change
Liu'an	10.5	15	0.7000	40.51	51.3	0.7898	0.0898
Echeng	6.2	8	0.7750	39.74	47.3	0.8402	0.0652
Wuzhou	17.9	11	1.6273	39.57	36.1	1.0961	-0.5312
Chaozhou	12.9	4	3.2250	38.92	41.7	0.9338	-2.2912
Lhasa	10.9	32	0.3406	37.70	59.0	0.6390	0.2984
Jingmen	6.5	12	0.5417	36.93	48.5	0.7610	0.2193
Shizhuishan	19.2	25	0.7680	36.65	94.2	0.3891	-0.3789
Hanzhong	12.1	10	1.2100	36.60	31.0	1.1806	-0.0294
Chenzhou	12.4	15	0.8267	36.59	41.7	0.8775	0.0508
Yibin	17.8	10	1.7800	36.47	49.0	0.7437	-1.0363
Kelamayi	14.6	9	1.6222	35.80	53.3	0.6718	-0.9504
Luodi	6.3	9	0.7000	35.37	41.0	0.8627	0.1627
Pingxiang	21.1	17	1.2412	35.30	41.5	0.8510	-0.3902
Yan'an	6.3	5	1.2600	35.30	26.0	1.3603	0.1003
Meizhou	7.3	4	1.8250	31.90	33.4	0.9559	-0.8691
Suizhou	4.5	5	0.9000	31.82	43.0	0.7400	-0.1600
Daxian	12.0	7	1.7143	31.04	23.2	1.3379	-0.3764
Huaihua	6.9	9	0.7667	30.83	40.0	0.7708	0.0041
Yining	14.3	17	0.8412	30.57	35.6	0.8585	0.0173
Xichang	9.0	13	0.6923	30.00	29.1	1.0323	0.3400
Kashi	12.9	9	1.4333	28.40	41.6	0.6835	-0.7498
Kuerle	9.4	27	0.3481	28.06	45.5	0.6163	0.2681
Ji'an	12.1	12	1.0083	28.02	29.1	0.9622	-0.0461

Sanmenxia	6.8	7	0.9714	27.51	28.5	0.9653	-0.0062
Yichun	7.9	7	1.1286	27.00	32.2	0.8385	-0.2901
Shihezi	11.7	14	0.8357	27.00	27.1	0.9982	0.1624
Baicheng	16.4	15	1.0933	26.38	38.1	0.6922	-0.4011
Zhoukou	9.4	9	1.0444	25.90	42.0	0.6167	-0.4278
Shaotong	6.8	5	1.3600	25.65	22.5	1.1400	-0.2200
Sanming	12.9	13	0.9923	24.95	24.5	1.0175	0.0252
Ujlan Hot	12.8	11	1.1636	24.81	25.4	0.9775	-0.1861
Hami	8.6	25	0.3440	24.02	34.0	0.7065	0.3625
Shangrao	10.6	8	1.3250	23.56	27.1	0.8700	-0.4550
Duyun	8.1	6	1.3500	21.32	14.7	1.4513	0.1013
Laohekou	5.8	5	1.1600	20.78	27.0	0.7696	-0.3904
Nanping	11.6	15	0.7733	20.35	26.1	0.7797	0.0064
Jiayuguan	5.5	20	0.2750	18.06	42.3	0.4270	0.1520
Gejiu	18.4	10	1.8400	17.92	12.2	1.4749	-0.3651
Houma	6	8	0.7500	16.88	18.5	0.9139	0.1639
Yima	3.8	6	0.6333	16.75	15.1	1.1063	0.4730
Kuitun	4.1	18	0.2278	16.33	24.6	0.6649	0.4371
Erlian Hot	0.7	2	0.3500	15.79	20.2	0.7817	0.4317
Lengshuijiang	8.1	9	0.9000	15.40	19.9	0.7739	-0.1261
Yingtan	5.2	10	0.5200	14.16	23.7	0.5980	0.0780
Heihe	5.3	9	0.5889	14.00	19.0	0.7368	0.1480
Kaiyuan	7.1	12	0.5917	12.27	19.5	0.6292	0.0376
Tumen	7.0	9	0.8074	8.59	8.7	0.9908	0.1834
Suifenhe	1.2	3	0.4000	8.20	14.2	0.5762	0.1762
Yumen	7.3	18	0.4056	6.59	23.2	0.2843	-0.1213
Pinxiang	1.4	5	0.2745	6.30	5.1	1.2353	0.9608

Source: *China Urban–Rural Construction Statistical Yearbook 2008.*

Notes

* The data in all the tables in these appendices have been collected and calculated by Wan Haiyuan and revised by Li Shi.

1 See *Japanese Cities*, revised by the city department of the Ministry of Construction, First Law Publishing. What is noteworthy is that the urban population of Japanese cities is defined according to the population in the densely inhabited district (DID). Specifically, DID must meet two criteria: first, the population density must be more than 4000 persons per square kilometer; second, the total population must be more than 5000 persons. As the Japanese standards for urban population are stricter than those of most developed countries, the country's statistical data about the urbanization rate were underestimated among developed countries. For example, Japan's urbanization rate in 2005 was 66 per cent. But if the rate was converted according to the standards of any other leading developed country, the rate would be more than 90 per cent (Tsuchiya Saiki: *Facts and Review of Our Country's Urbanization Rate – From the Perspective of Geographic Economics*, Bank of Japan Working Paper, July 2009).

2 Ministry of Internal Affairs and Communications: Time-Point Population Flow on 1 October 2008; Cabinet Office: County Economic Statistics in 2007.

Bibliography

Chinese

Ahbulizi Y. and Chen Z.: *The Empirical Research of-Poverty Alleviation for Ecological Migrants in Akzo Keping County*, Guangxi University for Nationalities (Philosophy and Social Sciences), 2007.

All-China Federation of Trade Unions: *Research report on next-generation rural migrant workers*. Workers Daily, 21 June 21 2010.

Cai Fang: *Issues of China's transient population*. Henan People's Publishing House, 2000.

Cai Fang (ed.): *Report No. 6 on China's Population and Labour – Social Security and Employment Issues in Cities Categorized as 'Resource Cities'* [those that focus on developing or extracting natural resources]. Social Sciences Academic Press, 2005.

Cai Fang: *Policy options with respect to transforming China's economic structure and improving its income distribution, given globalization*. Reform, 2006, Issue 11.

Cai Fang and Du Yang: *China's urban development in transition – the 'tier structure' of cities, their financing capacities, and their human- relocation policies*. Economic Research Journal, 2003, Issue 6.

Cai Fang and Wang Dewen: *The contribution of labour to China's economic growth, and the sustainability of China's economic growth*. Economic Research Journal, 1999, Issue 10.

Cai Fang and Wang Meiyan: *'Unofficial employment' and the development of labour markets – interpreting the growth of employment in China's cities*. Economic Perspectives, 2004, Issue 2.

Cai Fang, Du Yang, and Wang Meiyan: *Urban poverty and income disparities in China's cities – the impact of labour markets and the influence of unofficial employment*. China Social Policies, 2006, Issue 1.

Cai Fang, Du Yang, and Wang Meiyan: *The transformation of China's mode of economic development, and the inherent impetus provided by energy conservation and the reduction of emissions*. Economic Research Journal, 2008, Issue 6.

Cha Hongwang, Xiong Dongliang and Wang Maotai: *The Report of Economic Development in Western China 2005*, Social Sciences Academic Press.

Chen Bochong and Hao Shouyi: *The Fast Pace of Urbanization in China*. Human Geography, 2005, 05.

Chen Tao: *Relocating people for ecological reasons: analysis from the perspective of environmental sociology*. In: Bing Zheng (ed.): *Reform, Opening Up, and China's Sociology: A Collection of Award-Winning Papers from the Annual Convention of the Chinese Sociology Association*. Social Sciences Academic Press, 2009.

Chen Yi: '*Urbanization' is not incompatible with 'low carbon'*. Global Times, December 29, 2009.

China Development Research Foundation: *China Development Report 2008/2009: Building a Development-Oriented Social Welfare System for All*, China Development Publishing House, 2009.

Cui Gonghao and Ma Runchao: *The 'bottom-up' [as opposed to top-down] process of China's urbanization: development and mechanisms*. Geographic Journal, 1999, Issue 2.

Deng Zhiwei: *Contemporary 'Urban Syndromes'*. China Youth Publishing House, 2003.

Ding Chengri: *Are China's cities 'densely' populated or not?* Urban Planning, 2004, Issue 8.

Ding Yun: *Research into funding sources for urban infrastructure in China*. China Renmin University Press, 2007.

Dong Xiangrong: *Efforts to reduce urban–rural disparities in Taiwan and in South Korea, and resulting accomplishments*. Taiwan Research Quarterly, 1999, Issue 3.

Du Hengbo: *Lessons from the way in which England transformed its rural labour force*. Rural Economy, 2004, Issue 3.

Du Yu: *2009 Review: New developments in building low-rent housing in China*. PRC government website, 13 January 2010, www.gov.cn/jrzg/2010-01/13/content_1509602. htm.

Engels, Frederick: *The Condition of the Working Class in England in 1844*. Complete Works of Marx and Engels, Volume 2, People's Publishing House, 1975.

Fan Gang: *Urbanization is a form of 'systems engineering'*. The China Development Observer, 2009, Issue 2.

Fang Chuanglin: *Standards by which to distinguish spatial configurations of urban clusters in China: research advances and basic determinations*. Urban Planning Journal, 2009, Issue 4.

Fang Chuanglin and Qi Weifeng: *The concept of 'compact' cities and metrics for measuring compactness: research advances and considerations*. Urban Planning Journal, 2007, Issue 4.

Feng Yufeng: *Is the development of small town the only way of urbanization in China?* Economic Geography, 1983, 04.

Gao Peiyi: *A Comparative Study of Urbanization in China and Other Countries (Supplementary Issue)*. Nankai University Press, 2004.

Gao Ruxi and Luo Mingyi: *The Economics of Urban Hubs*. Yunnan University Press, 1998.

Gu Chaolin: *China's Systems with Respect to 'Cities'*. Commercial Press, 1992.

Gu Chaolin: *International research on issues of urbanization*. Urban Planning, 2003, Issue 6.

Gu Chaolin: *Urbanization in China: The Current Status of Research, the Process, and the Prospects*. Chinese Society for Urban Studies: Report on Academic Development in Urban Studies, China Science and Technology Publishing House, 2008.

Gu Chaolin and Chen Zhengguang: *Spatial growth patterns in China's largest cities*. Urban Planning, 1994, Issue 6.

Gu Chaolin and Hu Xiuhong: *Considerations behind policies dealing with urbanization and urban development in China's 'new age'*. Urban Development Research, 1999, Issue 5.

Gu Chaolin and Wu Liya: *Summary of current research on urbanization in China (I)*. Research on urban planning and regional planning, 2008, Issue 2.

Gu Chaolin and Wu Liya: Summary *of current research on urbanization in China (II)*. Research on urban planning and regional planning, 2008, Issue 3.

Gu Chaolin, Zhang Qin, Cai Jianming, Niu Yafei, Sun Ying. et al.: *Economic Globalization and Urban Development – Strategy as China Moves into the Next Century*. Commercial Press, 1999.

Gu Chaolin, Yu Taofang, and Li Wangming: *The Patterns, Processes, and Mechanisms of Urbanization in China*. Science Publishing House, 2008.

Gu Rong et al.: *Public policy analysis with respect to urbanization*. Urban Planning, 2006, Issue 9.

Gu Shengzu: *Research into the Process of 'De-agriculturalization', as Related to Urbanization*. Zhejiang People's Publishing House, 1991.

Gu Shengzu: *The strategy to develop a bimodal form of urbanization, and policy options*. Population Research, 1991, Issue 5.

Guangzhou Service Centre for Labour Resources: *Analysis of the Survey on Rural Migrant Workers in Guangzhou City with Respect to Social Security and Employment Conditions, 2009*.

Han Wenxiu: *Building Basic Infrastructure*. In: *Three Decades of Reform in China*. China Development Publishing House, 2009.

Han Yinsheng and Qin Bo: *Realize sustainable urban development in China by adhering to the concept of compact cities*. Foreign Urban Planning, 2004, Issue 19.

He Hongtao: *Study of how the agricultural revolution in England incubated and contributed to the Industrial Revolution*. Sichuan University Journal (Philosophy and Social Sciences) 2006, Issue 3.

Hu Jun: *China's Urban Models and their Evolution*, China Construction Industry Publishing House, 1995.

Hu Xuwei, Zhou Yixing, and Gu Chaolin: *Study of the Compact Use of Space as Well as Urban Sprawl in Dense Urban Concentrations along China's Eastern Coast*. Science Publishing House, 2000.

Hu Ying: *Quantitative analysis of economically active populations in China between 2000 and 2008*. Unpublished working paper.

Institute of Population Research of the Chinese Academy of Social Sciences: *Sample Survey of Urban Population Migration in China's 74 Cities and Towns in 1986*. China Population Science Editorial Board, 1988.

Ji Xiaolan: *Lessons drawn from an analysis of England's process of urbanization*. Huadong University of Technology Journal (Social Sciences), 2004, Issue 2.

Jia Kang: *Be alert to and guard against the problem of having provincial governments take on an excessive amount of debt*. Macroeconomic Management 2009, Issue 8.

Jin Chan and Wang Jian: *Further the process of urbanization by using 'urban hubs'*. Economic Reference News, 26 January 2010.

Leman, Edward: *Metropolitan Regions: New Challenges for an Urbanizing China*. Paper presented to World Bank/IPEA Urban Research Symposium, 4 April 2005, Brasilia, Brazil.

Li Gangyuan: *Urban syndromes in England, and efforts to address the problems*. Hangzhou Normal College Journal (Social Sciences), 2003, Issue 11.

Li Jingtai: *Policy options for urbanization*. In: *China 2020: Development Goals and Policy Orientation*. China Development Publishing House, 2008.

Li Qiang et al.: *Major Social Issues in the Course of Urbanization, and Analysis of Policy Measures to Deal with those Issues*. Economic Science Publishing House, 2009.

Liu Chuanjiang: *The institutional and innovative potential of the form of urban development that is 'bottom up' as opposed to 'top down'*. Urban Issues, 1998, Issue 3.

Liu Minquan and Yu Jiantuo: *The environment and human development: documents and commentary*. Peking University Journal (Philosophy and Social Sciences), 2010, Issue 2.

Lu Bo: *Exploration into issues of equity in the provision of equal education opportunities for children of rural migrant workers*. Changshu Institute of Technology Journal, 2006, Issue 3.

Lu Dadao et al.: *China Regional Development Report – The Process of Urbanization in Terms of Expanding Use of Space*. Commercial Press, 2006.

Luo Ganghui: *Urbanization in South Korea and the development of a land market*. China Real Estate News, 8 May 2003.

Ma Chunhui: *On China's Urbanization Issues*. Social Sciences Academic Press, 2008.

Ma Jing: *The 'plan to double national income' creates a golden age in Japan*. The Beijing News, 11 July 2008.

Ma Jiwu and Yu Yunhan: *Urban populations in China's feudal age*. Academic Research, 2004, Issue 1.

Ma Kai: *Tutorial Reader for the Summary of the 11th Five-Year Plan*. Beijing Science and Technology Publishing House, 2006.

Ma Tao: *Auto exhaust emissions and general air pollution*. Environmental Protection in China's Oil and Gas Fields, 2007, Issue 2.

Mao Tengfei: *Research on Investing in and Financing the Building of China's Urban Infrastructure*. China Social Science Publishing House, 2007.

Miao Lining: *Village within cities–on the premise of existence of remodeling*, 2008.

Ministry of Construction, Department of General Finance: *China's Urban Construction Statistical Yearbook*. The website of the People's Republic of China Ministry of Construction. http://www.mohurd.gov.cn/zcfg/jsbwj_0/jsbwjcw/

Mo Jianbei et al. (ed.): *Integration [of Populations of People] and Development: A Survey of Rural Migrant Workers in 16 Cities in the Yangtze River Delta*. Shanghai People's Publishing House, 2007.

National Bureau of Statistics: *China Statistical Yearbook 2009*. China Statistical Publishing House, 2009.

National Development and Reform Commission, Centre for the Reform and Development of Cities and Towns: *Research on Issues Relating to Urbanization*, November 2009.

Yasumitsu, Nawata: *Post-war population migrations in Japan, and economic growth*. Economic Prism (Japanese), 2008, Issue 54.

Ni Weidou: *The current situation with respect to energy consumption in China, and the potential for energy conservation*. Science and Technology Daily, 25 January 2007.

Ning Deng: *China's Urbanization Path Problem–Binary Urbanization Strategy Implementation*. Urban Planning Forum 1997, 01.

Ning Yueming: *New urbanization processes – an exploration of the distinguishing features and forces behind urbanization in China in the 1990s*. Geographic Journal, 1998, Issue 5.

Niu Fengrui, Pan Jiahua, and Liu Zhi (eds): *Thirty Years of Urban Development in China, 1978–2008*. Social Sciences Academic Press, 2009.

Office of the National Working Committee on Aging: *Report Forecasting Trends in China's Aging Population*. 2006.

Pan Jiahua, Niu Fengrui, and Wei Houkai (eds): *China Urban Development Report*. Social Sciences Academic Press, 2009.

Qi Kang and Xia Zonggan: *Urbanization and urban systems*. Architectural Journal, 1985, Issue 2.

Qin Hong: *The current situation and direction of reforms with respect to financing invest-ment in China's municipal public facilities.* Urban–Rural Construction, 2003, Issue 7.

Qin Hong (ed.): *Financing Urban Construction.* China Development Publishing House, 2007.

Qiu Baoxing: *Compactness and diversity – core concepts for ensuring sustainable urban development in China.* Urban Planning, 2006, Issue 11.

Qiu Baoxing: *Meeting Opportunities and Challenges – Main Issues and Policy Options in Researching China's Urbanization Strategy.* China Construction Publishing House, 2009.

Qiu Baoxing: *Policy Measures to Deal with Urbanization in China,* http://green.sohu.com/20091104/n267962027.shtml.

Rao Huilin and Qu Bingquan: *Centralized and intensive: the best choice for China's urbanization road.* Research on Financial and Economic Issues, 1989, 04.

Rao Huilin and Cong Qi: *Re Discussion on the Issues of Effectiveness of Urban Scale.* Research on Financial and Economic Issues, 1999, 10.

Research Team of the State Council: *Investigative Report on Rural Migrant Workers in China.* Yanshi Publishing House, 2006.

Research Team on the Coordination of Urbanization and Industrial Development in China: *Economic analysis of the relationship between urbanization and industrial develop-ment.* Social Sciences in China, 2002, Issue 2.

Ru Xing, Lu Xueyi, and Li Peilin (eds): *An Analysis of China's Social Situation in 2010 and a Forecast for the Future.* Social Sciences Academic Press, 2009.

Sheng Laiyun: *New challenges faced by rural migrant workers in the midst of the financial crisis.* Paper delivered at the Academic Symposium on Integrating Welfare Systems of Urban and Rural Areas into One Consistent System, 2009.

Shi Yulong and Zhou Yixing: *An introduction to Goldman's ideas on metropolitan belts.* Economic Geography, 1996, Issue 3.

Song Ji and Zhao Hanqiang: *Post-war Japan's shift of agricultural labour and lessons for China.* Northeast Asia Forum, 2001, Issue 4.

Spencer 2010. "Managing Resource Revenues in Developing Economies," IMF Staff Papers, *Palgrave Macmillan,* vol. 57(1), pages 84–118.

Su Fengjie: *Addressing problems of 'children who are left behind' and 'children who are transient', by a multi-level approach to education and changes in the household regis-tration system.* People's Net, 5 June 2009, www.ngocn.org/?action-viewnews-itemid-48756.

Sugiyama, Takehiko: *Study of post-war Japan's income disparities among cities, and Japan's creation of a transportation infrastructure.* 2008, Issue 3.

UN-HABITAT (translated by Shen Jianguo et al): *The Urbanizing World in 1998.* China Construction Industry Publishing House, 1999.

UNDP Representative Office in China: *China Human Development Report 2010.*

Wang Fan: *The Rational and Vitality of Small Cities.* City Planning Review, 1990, 01, P25–28.

Wang Guangtao: *On the unique issues China faces in its path of urbanization.* Urban Planning, 2003, Issue 4.

Wang Mei (ed.): *Private–Public Partnerships in Urban Projects: A Study of Policy Formulation with Respect to Financing and Investment.* Economic Science Publishing House, 2008.

Wang Mengkui, Feng Bing, and Xie Fuzhan (eds): *China's Unique Path toward Urbanization.* China Development Publishing House, 2004.

Wang Tiejun (ed.): *Twenty-Two Financing Models for China's Local [Provincial] Governments.* China Finance Publishing House, 2006.

Wang Xiaolu and Xia Xiaolin: *Promote Economic Growth by the Optimization of Urban Size.* Economic Research Journal, 1999, 09, P22–29.

Wang Xiaoting, Lu Qian, and Wu Haixia: *Analysis of how different levels of urbanization ameliorate urban–rural income discrepancies.* Ecological Economy, 2009, Issue 2.

Wang Xiaoying, Huo Mingyu, and Gao Yong: *Empirical research into the distribution of revenues derived from land-use transfers of arable land. Based on a statistical sampling of three locations in Kunshan, Tongcheng, and Xindu.* Chinese Academy of Social Sciences Net, http://rdi.cass.cn/uploadfile/200731680625.pdf.

Wang Yang (ed.): *A Study of Urban-Development Planning during the 10th Five-Year Plan.* Planning Publishing House, 2001.

Wang Youqiang, Lu Dapeng, and Zhou Shaoji: *Public-finance behaviour of local [provincial] governments: the relationship between financial resources and development.* China Administration, 2009, Issue 2.

Wang Jian: Promote Urbanization by Metropolitan Circle, 2010. http://finance.ifeng.com/news/20100120/1729635.shtml

Wei Liqiang: *Environmental problems caused by urbanization.* Changchun University Journal, 2003, Issue 6.

Wu Chuanqing: *An overview of urban clusters around the world.* Ningbo Economy, 2004, Issue 4.

Wu Chuanqing: *The development of urban clusters around the world.* China Regional Development Net, www.china-region.com/News/HTML/20060926164248_3196.htm.

Wu Liya and Gu Chaolin: *Globalization, foreign capital, and urbanization in developing countries – the case of Jiangsu province.* Urban Planning, 2005, Issue 7.

Wu Youren: *China's urbanization path problems seminar held in Nanjing.* Economic Geography, 1983, 01.

Wu Zhiqiang: *An overview of urban planning systems in various developed countries and regions of the world.* Planner, 1998, Issue 3.

Xie Yang: *Exploring China's specific needs as the country urbanizes: considering setting up development goals for specific key 'towns' across the country.* Small Town Construction, March 2005.

Xu Caishan: *The Process of Urbanization in China under the Policy Guidance of a Scientific View of Development that Uses a Human-Centred Approach and that Uses Models that are Practical.* People's Publishing House, 2009.

Xu Xieqoamg and Ye Jia'an: *Differences in degree of urbanization among provinces in China.* Geographic Journal, 1986, Issue 6.

Xu Xueqiang, Liu Qing, and Zeng Xiangzang: *Development and Urbanization in the Pearl River Delta,* Zhongshan University Press, 1988.

Xue Fengxuan and Yang Chun: *Urbanization under the influence of foreign capital, with the Pearl River Delta as a case in point.* Urban Planning, 1995, Issue 6.

Yan Xiaopei: *The thinking behind what is called 'de-urbanization' in western countries.* Urban Planning, 1990, Issue 3.

Yang Kaizhong and Li Qiang: *Urban Sprawl.* Machinery Industry Publishing House, 2007.

Yang Lan et al.: *The process of urbanization in France and lessons for contemporary Chinese urbanization.* Research on France, 2008, Issue 4.

Yang Weimin: *Four key issues concerning China's specific path of urbanization.* Studies in Urban Planning and Regional Planning, 2008, Issue 2.

Yang Xiaoli, Luo Xiandong, Zhou Meichun, and Liu Qing: *How surplus rural labour was shifted [away from agriculture] in the United States and Japan, and lessons for China.* Corporate Economy, 2004, Issue 9.

Yao Hongliang and Kobaye, Sho-ichiro: *Analysis of the structure and movements of Japan's agricultural labour*. Agro-technology Management, 1998, Issue 8.

Yao Shimou: *The Feature, Type and Space Configuration of City Cluster in China*. Urban Problems, 1992, 01.

Yao Xianguo: *The evolution of China's labor market and governmental behavior*. Paper delivered at the 68th Annual Conference of the American Society for Public Administration, 2007. Originally published at Journal of Public Management 2007, 4(3).

Yao Yang: *Impressions of India (IV)*, Southern Weekly, 4 April 2007, www.infzm.com/content/9089.

Yu Chiming: *The investment demands and financing strategies for building urban infrastructure during the 10th Five-Year Plan period*. Urban Development Research. 2001, Issue 4.

Yu Xiaoming: *The Reflection of Urbanization in China. Urban Problems*, 1999, (5) P12–16.

Yuan Xin and Tang Xiaoping: *Urban hubs: a new form of urbanization strategy for China*. China's Population, Resources, and Environment, 2006, Issue 4.

Yuan Xin and Tang Xiaoping: *City Rims: Japan's experience and development of China's three major city clusters*. Qiushi Journal, 2008, Issue 2.

Yun Yingxia and Wu Jingwen: *Volume incentives and the transfer of development rights – an international comparison*. Tianjin University Journal (Social Sciences), 2007, Issue 2.

Zang Quan: *The impact of China's urbanization process on environmental quality*. Teaching and Research, 2009, Issue 3.

Zhang Guanzeng: *Commercial monopolies in western European cities during the Middle Ages*. History, 1993, Issue 1.

Zhang Jifeng: *The transformation of surplus rural labour in post-war Japan and its specific features*. Japan Journal, 2003, Issue 2.

Zhang Junkuo, Liu Feng, and Gao Shiji: *Achievements made in the governance of China's cities, and ways of thinking about how to improve and how to set targets*. China Development Observation, 2008, Issue 6.

Zhang Ming and Gu Chaolin: *Rural urbanization: comparison between the Southern Jiangsu model and the Pearl River model*, Economic Geography, 2002, Issue 4.

Zhang Qizhi and Yan Cunbao: *Options for Financing the Building of Basic Public Infrastructure in Cities*. China Finance Publishing House, 2008.

Zhang Xinzhu: *Green Paper No. 2 on Urban Public Utilities in China – The Country's Experience in Reforming Public Utilities in the Context of Urbanization*. Intellectual Property Publishing Housing, 2008.

Zhang Yan: *Urbanization development and education*, Education Development Research, 2005, Issue 8.

Zhang Yushan: *Lessons with Respect to Imbalances in the Development of the Korean Economy*. Hubei Provincial People's Government Website 2006, www.hbzyw.gov.cn/shownews.asp?id=5496.

Zhang Zengxiang: *Monitoring China's Urban Expansion via Remote Sensing*. Xinqiu Map Publishing House, 2006.

Zhang Zhenlong et al.: *The spatial expansion of cities in France: models and mechanisms*. Urban Development Research, 2008, Issue 4.

Zhao Yanqing: *China's urbanization in the context of the country's pattern of international strategies*. Compilation of Urban Plans, 2000, Issue 1.

Zhong Xiaoming: *China's Urbanization path problems at the Turn of the Century*. Science Economy Society, 2000, 01.

Zhou Ganzhi: *Urbanization and Sustainable Development.* City Planning Review, 1998, 03.

Zhou Mila and Gan Wencheng: *The role of public finance investments in financing urban infrastructure.* Prices and Markets, 2008, Issue 6.

Zhou Muzhi: *Strategies for developing China's major urban clusters in the context of the financial crisis.* City and Regional Planning Research, 2009, Issue 4.

Zhou Yixing: *Reflections on the speed with which China is urbanizing.* Urban Planning, 2006, supplement.

Zhou Yixing: *Urban Geography.* Commercial Press, 1995.

Zhu Xigang and Ding Wenjing: *The international experience with respect to urban development and to transitional policies.* Guangming Daily, 19 September 2006.

Zou Deci: *Becoming aware of several issues to do with China's urbanization.* Compilation of Urban Plans, 2004, Issue 3.

Zuo Guangxia and Feng Bang: *Social discrimination and educational equity for the children of China's migrant population.* Modern Education Science, 2009, Issue 3.

Background reports

Chen Huai and Pu Zhan: *Improving Urban Housing Systems in the Course of Urbanization.*

Du Yang and Wang Meiyan: *People, Industrial Development and Jobs in the Course of Urbanization.*

Du Zhixin: *China's Strategy for a 'New Form' of Urbanization, and a Comparative Analysis of China, Japan and South Korea.*

Gu Chaolin: *Spatial Configuration of Urbanization in China, and Determining Mechanisms,* 2009.

Gu Chaolin: *The International Experience of Urbanization, Including Policies and Trends,* 2009.

Han Jun: *Turning Rural Migrant Workers into Legitimate Urban Residents: Current Status and Future Prospects, Including Policy Options.*

Li Shantong: *The Impact of Urbanization on Economic Growth.*

Liu Jingsheng, Li Ming, and Yang Hao: *Meeting the Challenge of Building Urban Infrastructure That Is Going to Cost Some RMB 18 Trillion.*

Liu Minquan and Ji Xi: *Theories of Urbanization and Human Development.*

Liu Shouying and Liao Bingguang: *The Urbanization of Land: Moving from a 'Sprawl' Mode to More Rational Growth.*

OECD: *Urbanization Trends and Policies in OECD Countries,* 2010.

Pan Jiahua: *Creating a Habitable Urban Environment.*

Wang Yanzhong: *Improving Social Welfare Systems in the Course of Establishing China's 'New Form' of Urbanization.*

Ye Xiafei: *Creating Rail Transport Systems That Enable Urban Development.*

Yu Jiantuo: *The International Experience with Respect to Urbanization.*

Yue Xiuhu: *Urbanization in China as Seen from the Perspective of Human Development: A Review of Events to Date and Discussion of Challenges Ahead.*

Zhang Zengxiang: *Report on Monitoring of China's Cities through Remote Sensing,* 2009.

English references

Abe, Kazuhiko, 2001. The upgrading of Japan's industrial structure as Japan urbanized and its regional economies changed: issues confronting small and medium-sized cities in the process of creating super-large cities. In: Urbanization: The Main Theme of China's Modernization. Hunan People's Publishing House.

Ades, A. and Glaeser, E. 1995. "Trade and Circuses: Explaining Urban Giants." Quarterly Journal of Economics, 110: 195–227.

Alan Gilbert, ed., 1996. The Mega-City in Latin America. Tokyo: United Nations University Press, 1996; and James B. Pick and Edgar Butler, 1997, Mexico Megacity Boulder, CO: Westview Press.

Altshuler, A. A., Gomez-Ibanez, J. A., Howitt, A. M. 1993. Regulation for revenue: The political economy of land use exactions. N.W. Washington, D.C.: Brookings institution.

Amin, S., I. Diamond, R. T. Haved, and M. Newby, 1998. Transition to Adulthood of Female Garment-Factory Workers in Bangladesh. Studies in Family Planning, 29 (2): 185–200.

Andre Sorensen, 2002. The making of urban Japan: cities and planning from Edo to the twenty-first century, Routledge.

Anita A. Summers, Paul C. Cheshire, and Lanfranco Senn, (eds.) 1999. Urban Change in the United States and Western Europe: Comparative Analysis and Policy. Washington, DC: Urban Institute Press.

Annez, P.C. 2006. "Urban Infrastructure Finance from Private Operators: What Have We Learned from Recent Experience?" World Bank Policy Research Working Paper 4045, Washington D.C.: World Bank.

Anthony G. Champion, ed. 1989. Counter urbanization: The Changing Pace and the Nature of Population Deconcentration. London: Edward Arnold.

Arai, Yoshio, Kawaguchi, Taro, and Inoue, Takashi (eds.), 2002. Population Migrations in Japan (in Japanese). Gujing Publishing House.

Bairoch, P. 1975. The Economic Development of the Third World since 1900. London: Methuen.

Bahl, R.W. and and Linn, J. 1992. Urban Public Finance in Developing Countries. New York: Oxford University Press.

Baldwin, R., P. Martin and G. Ottaviano, 2001. Global Income Divergence, Trade and Industrialization: The Geography of Growth Take-Off, Journal of Economic Growth, 6, 5–37.

Berrigan, D., R. Troiano, 2002. The association between urban form and physical activity in U.S. Adults. American Journal of Preventative Medicine, 23: 74–79.

Bird, R. M. and Slack, E. 2008. "Fiscal Aspects of Metropolitan Governance", In Rojas, E., Cuadrado-Roura, J. R., and Fernandez-Guell, J.M., (Eds.), Governing the Metropolis: principles and Cases, Washington D.C.: Inter-American Development Bank.

Boarnet, M. G., Day, K., Anderson, C., McMillan, T. and M. Alfonzo, 2005. California's Safe Routes to School Program: Impacts on walking, bicycling, and pedestrian safety. Journal of the American Planning Association, 71 (3): 301–317.

Breheny, M. J., R. Rookwood, 1993. Planning the sustainable city region. A. Blowers (ed.) Planning for a sustainable environment (pp. 150–189). London: Earthscan.

Breheny. M. 1997. Urban Compaction: Feasible and Acceptable. Cities, 14 (4): 209–217.

Cai Dingchuan, 2008. Japan's economic growth and the plan to double national income. www.caogen.com/blog/Infor_detail.aspx?ID=168&articleId=7509.

Cai, Fang and Dewen Wang. 2003. Migration As Marketization: What Can We Learn from China's 2000 Census Data?, The China Review, Vol. 3, No. 2 (Fall), pp. 73–93.

Cai, Fang and Dewen Wang, 2005. China's Demographic Transition: Implications for Growth, in Garnaut and Song (eds.), The China Boom and Its Discontents, Canberra: Asia Pacific Press.

Cai, Fang and Meiyan Wang, 2008. A Counterfactual Analysis on Unlimited Surplus Labor in Rural China, China & World Economy, Vol.16, No.1, pp. 51–65.

Caldwell, J.C. 1979. Education as a Factor in Mortality Decline: An Examination of Nigerian Data. Population Studies, 33: 395–413.

Carole Rakodi, (ed.) 1997. The Urban Challenge in Africa: Growth and Management of its Large Cities. New York: The United Nations University Press.

Castells, M., 1977. The Urban Question: A Marxist Approach, London: Arnold.

CASTELLS, M. 1989. The Informational City. Information, Technology, Economic Restructuring and the Urban-Regional Process, London: Basil Blackwell.

C.D. Foster, 1992, Privatization Public Ownership and the Regulation of Natural Monopoly, Oxford: Blackwell.

CEC (1990). Green paper on the urban environment – communication from the Commission to the Council and the Parliament, Commission of the European Communities (CEC), Brussels.

Cervero, R. 2001. Efficient Urbanisation: Economic Performance and the Shape of the Metropolis. Urban Studies, 38 (10): 1651–1671.

Chan, Kam Wing and Ying Hu, 2003. Urbanization in China in the 1990s: New Definition, Different Series, and Revised Trends, The China Review, Vol. 3, No. 2, pp. 49–71.

Chase-Dunn, C. 1984. Urbanization in the world system: new directions for research, in M. P. Smith (Ed.) Cities in Transformation, Newburg Park, CA: Sage.

Chen, H., Jia, S. S. Y. LauBeisi, 2008. Sustainable urban form for Chinese compact cities: Challenges of a rapid urbanized economy. Habitat International, 32: 28–40.

Chenery, Hollis, 1998. Patterns of Development: 1950–1970, Economic Science Publishing House.

Chinitz, B. 1990. Growth management: good for the town, bad for the nation? Journal of the American Planning Association, 56, 3–8.

Chris J. B. 2000. Cities in Competition: Equity Issues. Urban Studies, 36: 865–891.

Churchman, A. 1999. 'Disentangling the Concept of Density, Journal of Planning Literature, vol. 13 (4), 389–411.

Clarke, M., A. G. Wilson, 1985. The Dynamics of Urban Spatial Structure: The Progress of a Research Programme. Transactions of the Institute of British Geographers, New Series, 10: 427–445.

Cohen, M. 2002. The Five Cities of Buenos Aires: An Essay on Poverty and Inequality in Urban Argentina, in Encyclopedia of Sustainable Development, S. Sassen (ed.) United Nations Economic, Social and Cultural Organization, Paris.

Crowe, T. 2000. Crime Prevention Through Environmental Design: Applications of Architectural Design and Space Management Concepts, 2nd ed., Butterworth-Heinemann, Oxford.

Dantzig, G., T. Satty, 1973. Compact city: a plan for a liveable urban environment, San Francisco: Freeman and Company.

Davis K. 1965. The Urbanization of the Human Population. Scientific American. In: LeGates R T, Stout F. (eds.) 1996 (pp. 1–11). City Reader. London: Routledge.

Department of Economic and Social Affairs Population Division, United Nations (UNESA) 2008. World Urbanization Prospects: The 2007 Revision, ESA/P/WP205, United Nations, New York.

Dhakal, S. 2009. Urban energy use and carbon emissions from cities in China and policy implications. Energy policy. In press.

Dicken, P. 1992. Europe 1992 and strategic change in the international automobile industry, Environment and, Planning, A 24 (1): 11–31.

Dirie, I. 2005. "Municipal Finance: Innovative Resourcing for Municipal Infrastructure and Service Provision", report prepared for the Commonwealth Local Government Forum in cooperation with ComHabiat.

DoE (Department of the Environment) 1992. The Effects of Major Out of Town Retail Development, London: HMSO.

Douglass, M. 1988. The transnational of urbanization in Japan, International Journal of Urban and Regional Research, 12 (3): 425–454.

Douglass, M. 2000. Mega-urban Regions and World City Dormation, The Economic Crisis and Urban Policy Issues in Pacific Asia. Urban Studies, 37 (12): 2315–2335.

Duranton, G. J., D. Puga, 2001. Nursety Cities: Urbanization Diversity, Process Innovation, and the Life Cycle of Products. American Economic Review, 91 (5): 1454–1477.

Dyson, T. 2003. HIV/AIDS and Urbanization. Population and Development Review, 29 (3): 427–442.

Edward Leman, 2006. Metropolitan Regions: New Challenges for an Urbanizing China, WorldBank.

Edwin s. Mills, 1979. Byung-Nak Song, Urbanization and Urban Problems, Harvard Press.

Ewing. R. 1997. Is Los Angeles-style sprawl desirable? Journal of the American Planning Association. 63 (1): 107.

Faris, R., E., Dunham, H., W. 1939. Mental Disorders in Urban Areas: an Ecological Study of Schizophrenia and Other Psychoses. Chicago: The University of Chicago Press.

Friedman, John, 2001, Intercity networks in a globalizing era, in Scott, A. (ed.), "Global City-Regions: Trends,Theory, Policy", Oxford University Press.

Friedman, J. 2005 China's urban Transition. Minneapolis: University of Minnesota Press.

Friedmann, 2006. Four Theses in the Study of China's Urbanization, International. Journal of Urban and Regional Research, 30 (2): 440–451.

Frumkin, H. 2002. Urban Sprawl and Public Health. Public Health Report. 117: 201–218.

Fu-chen Lo and Yue-man Yeung, 1996. The Emerging World Cities in the Pacific Asia, United Nation University Press.

Fujita, M. and J. Thisse, 2002a. "Does Geographical Agglomeration Foster Economic Growth? And Who Gains and Looses from it?" CEPR DP 3135.

Gabaix and Ioannides, 2004. The evolution of city size distributions, in Henderson (ed.) Handbook of Urban and Regional Economics Vol. III. North-Holland Press.

Galloway, P. R., E. A. Hammel, and R. D. Lee, 1994. Fertility Decline in Prussia, 1875–1910: A Pooled Cross- Section, Time Series Analysis. Population Studies, 48 (1): 135–158.

Galster, G., R. Handson, H. Wolman, S. Coleman, J. Freihage, 2001. Wrestling Sprawl to the Ground: Defining and Measuring an Elusive Concept. Housing Policy Debate, 12 (4): 681–717.

Gene M. Grossman and Alan B. Krueger, 1995. Economic growth and the environment. The Quarterly Journal of Economics, 110 (2): 353–377.

Geurs, K., V. E. Ritsema, 2001. Accessibility Measures: Review and Application. Rijksinstituutvoor Volksgezondheid en Milieu, Bilthoven.

Gilbert, A. G. and Gugler, J. 1992. Cities, Poverty and Development: Urbanization in third world, 2nd edition, Oxford: Oxford University Press.

Glaeser, E. L., H. D. Kallal, J. A. Scheinkman, and A. Shleifer, 1992. Growth in Cities. Journal of Development Economics, 56 (1): 181–206.

Gordon, I., P. McCann, 2000. Industrial Cluster: Complexes, Agglomeration and/or Social Networks?. Urban Studies, 37 (3): 513–532.

Gordon, P. and Richardson, H. W. 1997. The Destiny of Downtowns: Doom or Dazzle? Lusk Review, 3 (2): 63–76.

Gordon, P. and Richardson, H. W. 2000. Defending suburban sprawl. The Public interest. Spring, 65–71.

Gottman, J. 1961. Megalopolis: The urbanized Northeastern seaboard of the United States. New York: Kraus.

H. Averch and L. Johnson L. Johnson, 1962. Behavior of the firm under Regulatory Constraint, American Economic Review, 52: 1052–1069.

Haar, C. M. 1998. Suburbs under siege: race, space, and audacious judges. Princeton: Princeton University Press.

Hall, P., and U. Pfeiffer, 2000. Urban Future 21: A Global Agenda for Twenty-First Century Cities. London: E & FN Spon.

Hall, P., Pain, K. 2006. The Polycentric Metropolis: Learning from Mega-City Regions in Europe. London: Earthscan.

Hall, Peter, 2001. Global city-region in the 21st century, in Scott, A. edited "Global City-Regions: Trends, Theory, Policy", Oxford University Press, pp. 59–77.

Handy, S. 1996. Methodologies for exploring the link between urban form and travel behavior. Transportation Research Part D: Transport and Environment, 1: 151–165.

Hanushek, E., 1986. "The Economics of Schooling: Production and Efficiency in Public Schools," Journal of Economic Literature, 49, 3, 1141–1177.

Hardoy, J. E., D. Mitlin, and D. Satterthwaite, 2001. Environmental Problems in Third World Cities. London: Earthscan Publications.

Harpham, T., T. Lusty, and P. Vaughan, 1988. In the Shadow of the City: Community Health and the Urban Poor. Oxford: Oxford University Press.

Harvey, R. O., W. A. V. Clark, 1965. The nature and economics of urban sprawl. A Quarterly Journal of Planning, Housing & Public Utilities. XII (1): 1–10.

Hayward, Steven, 2005. "The China Syndrome and the Environmental Kuznets Curve", Environmental Policy Outlook, December 21.

Henderson, J. V., T. Lee and J. Y. Lee, 2001. Scale Externalities in Korean. Journal of Urban Economics, 49: 479–504.

Henderson, J. V. 2002. Urbanization in Developing Countries. The World Bank Research Observer, 17 (1): 89–112.

Henderson, J. and Hyoung, Gun Wang, 2004. "Urbanization and City Growth." Working Paper at Brown University.

Hussar, W. and W. Sonnenberg, 2001. "Trends in Disparities in School District Level Expenditures per Pupil," National Center on Education Statistics.

IMF, 2006. Asia rising: patterns of economic development and growth, World Economic Outlook, September.

Jacobs, J. 1961. The Death and Life of Great American Cities. New York: Random House.

Jacobs, J. 1969. The Economy of Cities. New York: Vintage.

Jenks, M., Burton, E., K. Williams, 2000. The compact city: a sustainable city urban form. Oxford: Oxford Brookes University.

Jenks, M., N. Dempsey, 2005. The Language and Meaning of Density. Future forms and design for sustainable cities[C]. Oxford: Linacre House, Jordan Hill.

Johannes F. Linn, 1983. Cities in the Developing World, Oxford University Press.

Johnston, R. J. 1980. City and Society: An Outline for Urban Geography, Harmondsworth: Penguin.

Jonsson, A., and D. Satterthwaite, 2000. Overstating the Provision of Safe Water and Sanitation to Urban, Journal of Urbanization, 40: 13–37.

Knox, P. L., L. McCarthy, 1994. Urbanization: an introduction to urban geography. N. J.: Pearson Prentice Hall.

Kojima, R. 1996. Introduction: Population Migration and Urbanization in Developing Countries [J]. The Developing Economies. XXXIV: 4.

Leon, D. A. 2008. Cities, urbanization and health. International Journal of Epidemiology, 37: 4–8.

Leubg, C. K., Ginsburg, N. 1980. China: Urbanization and National Development, The University of Chicago.

Lewis, Arthur, 1972. Reflections on Unlimited Labour, in Di Marco, L. (ed.) International Economics and Development (pp. 75–96). New York: Academic Press.

Lewis, W. A. 1954. Economic Development with Unlimited Supplies of Labor, The Manchester School of Economic and Social Studies 22, 139–191, Reprinted in A. N. Agarwala and S. P. Singh (eds.), The Economics of Underdevelopment, Bombay: Oxford University Press, 1958.

Linden, E. 1996. The Exploding Cities of the Developing Regions. Foreign Affairs, 75 (1): 52–65.

Li Zhi and Xu Chuanzhong, 2003. Modernization of urban transport systems and urban development in Japan. Urban Planning Overseas, Issue 2.

Lodhi, A. Q., C. Tilly, 1973. Urbanization, Crime, Collective Violence in 19th-Century France. The American Journal of Sociology, 79: 296–318.

Logan, John R. (ed.) 2002. The New Chinese City: Globalization and Market Reform. Oxford: Blackwell.

Marcotullio, P. J. 2003. Globalization, Urban Form and Environmental Conditions in Asia-Pacific Cities. Urban Studies, Vol. 40, No.2, pp. 219–247.

McCann, J. 1995. Rethinking the Economic of Location and Agglomeration. Urban Studies. 32 (3): 563–579.

Meyer, D. 1991. "The Formation of a Global Financial Center: London and its Intermediaries," Cities in the World-System, edited by Resat Kasaba (Westport, CT: Greenwood Press), pp. 97–106.

Mills, E. S. 2003. Book review of Urban sprawl causes, consequences and policy responses. Regional Science and Urban Economics. 33: 251–252.

Mills, Edwin S. 1967. "An aggregative model of resource allocation in a metropolitan area". American Economic Review Papers and Proceedings 57 (2): 197–210.

Montgomery, M. R., R. Stren, B. Cohen, and H. E. Reed. 2003. Cities Transformed: Demographic Change and Its Implication in the Developing World. London: Earthscan.

Mumford, L. 1961. The city in history: its origins, its transformations, and its prospects. New York: Harcourt, Brace & World.

Myung-Goo Kang, 1998. Understanding Urban Problems in Korea, Development and Society, Volume 27 Number 1.

Newman, P. 1992. The compactcity – an Australian perspective. Built Environment, 18 (4): 285–300

Notestein, F. 1953. Economic Problems of Population Change in Proceedings of the Eighth International Conference of Agricultural Economists: 13–33. London: Oxford University Press.

OECD, 2009. Trends in Urbanisation and Urban Policies in OECD Countries, OECD Publishing.

OECD, 2006. Competitive Cities in the Global Economy, OECD Publishing.

Olson, M. 1985. Space, Agriculture and Organization. American Journal of Agricultural Economics, Volume 67 (5).

Pannell C. 2003. China's demographic and urban trends for the 21st century. Eurasian Geography and Economics, 44 (7): 479–496.

Paulus, F. (2002), Evolution of the economic structure of the French Urban System, 1954–1999. University of Paris I, doctorate thesis in preparation.

Perkins, D. 1969. Agriculture Development in China: 1368–1968. Chicago: Aldine Publishing Company.

Philleps, D. 1990. Health and Health Care in the Third World. London: Routledge.

Portes, A., Castells, M. and Benton, L. (eds.), 1991, The Informal Economy: Studies in Advanced and Less Developed Countries. London: Johns Hopkins.

Ravallion, Martin, Shaohua Chen, and Prem Sangraula, 2007. "New Evidence on the Urbanization of Global Poverty," Policy Research Working Paper No. 4199 (Washington: World Bank), http://econ.worldbank.org/docsearch.

Richardson, B. M. 1973. Urbanization and Political Participation: The Case of Japan. The American Political Science Review, 67 (2): 433–452.

Rietveld, P., F. R. Bruisma, 1998. Is Transport Infrastructure Effective? Transport Infrastrure and Accessibility: Impact on the Space Economy., Berlin: Springer Verlag.

Romero. H, O. Fernando, 2004. Emerging Urbanization in the Southern Andes. Mountain Research and Development, 24 (3): 197–201.

Ronghua Ma, Chaolin GU*, Yingxia Pu and Xiaodong Ma, 2008. Mining the Urban Sprawl Pattern: A case Study on Sunan, China, Sensors, 8 (10): 6371–6395.

Roseland, M. 1997. Dimensions of the Future: An Eco-city Overview. New Society Publishers, 1–12.

Rosenthal, S. and Strange, W. 2002. "Evidence on the Natures of Sources Agglomeration Economies." in Henderson (ed.) Handbook of Urban and Regional Economics Vol. III. North-Holland Press.

Rosenthal, Stuart S. and William Strange. 2004. Evidence on the nature and sources of agglomeration economies. In Vernon Henderson and JacquesFrançois Thisse (eds.) Handbook of Regionaland Urban Economics, volume 4. Amsterdam: North Holland.

Santos, M. 1979. The Shared Space: The Two Circuits of the Urban Economy in Underdeveloped Countries. London: Methuen.

Scott, A. 2001. Global City-Regions: Trends, Theory, Policy, Oxford University Press.

Sen, Amartya, 1999. Development as Freedom. Oxford: Oxford University Press.

Shahid Yusuf and Tony Saich, 2008. China Urbanizes: Consequences, Strategies, and Policies, Washington. D.C.: The World Bank.

Simmonds, D., Coombe, D. 2000. The transport implications of alternative urban forms. In Achieving Sustainable Urban Form, ed. by Williams, K., Burton, E., Jenks, M. London: Spon Press.

Sit, V. F. S., Yang, C. 1997. Foreign-Investment-Induced Exo-Urbanisation in the Pearl River Delta, China. Urban Studies, Vol.34, pp. 647–677.

Slack, E. 2005a. "Municipal Financing of Capital Infrastructure in North America," Journal of property TaxAssessment and Administration, 2 (1): 63–77.

Stanislav, V. K., E. Harburg, 1975. Mental Health and the Urban Environment: Some Doubts and Second Thoughts. Journal of Health and Social Behavior, 16 (3): 268–282.

Stephens, C. 1996. Health Cities or Unhealthy Islands? The Health and Social Implications of Urban Inequality. Environment and Urbanization, 8 (2): 9–30.

Stern, N. 2007. "The Economics of Climate Change: The Stern Review", Cambridge: Cambridge University Press.

Suen, M. W. (1978). *British Social and Economic History since 1870*, Macmillan Publishing House, 1978. (See reference).

U.S. Department of Housing and Urban Development (HUD), 1999. The State of the Cities Report 1999. Washington D.C.: HUD.

UNDP, 2004. Human Development Indicators.

UNDP, 2009. Human development report.

UN-Habitat, 2004. The State of the World's Cities 2004/2005: Globalization and Urban Culture. London and Sterling, VA: Earthscan.

UNFPA, State of World Population 2007, http://www.unfpa.org/swp/2007/presskit/docs/en-swop07-report.pdf.

UNFPA, State of World Population 2008, http://www.unfpa.org/swp/2008/presskit/docs/en-swop08-report.pdf.

United Nations Center for Human Settlements (UNCHS), 1996. An Urbanizing World: Global Report on Human Settlements. Oxford, England: Oxford University Press for Habitat.

United Nations, 1986. Population Growth and Policies in Mega-Cities: Calcutta, Population Policy Paper No. 1. New York: United Nations.

United Nations, 2001. World Urbanization Prospects (1999 Revision). New York.

United Nations, 2002. World Urbanization Prospects: The 2001 Revision. Data Tables and Highlights. New York: United Nations, Department of Economics and Social Affairs, Population Division.

Vojnovic, I., C. Jackson-Elmoore, J. Holtrop, S. Bruch, 2006. The renewed interest in urban form and public health: Promoting increased physical activity in Michigan. Cities, 23 (1).

Wachs, M. 1989/90 Regulating traffic by controlling land use: the southern California experience Transportation 16: 241–56.

Williamson, J.G. 1988. "Migration and Urbanization", in H. Chenery and T. N. Srinivasan (eds.), Handbook of Development Economics (pp. 425–465). volume 1, Amsterdam: North Holland.

World Bank, 1997. "China 2020: Development Challenges in the New Century", Washington, D. C.

World Bank, 1997. "Clear Water, Blue Skies: China's Environment in the New Century", Washington, D.C.: World Bank.

World Bank, 2000. Entering the 21st Century: World Development Report 1999/2000. New York: Oxford University Press.

World Bank, 2009. Reshaping Economic Geography: World Development Report 2009. www.worldbank.org.

World Factbook, https://www.cia.gov/library/publications/the-world-factbook/fields/2212. html.

Yiftachel, O. and D. Hedgcock, 1993. Urban social sustainability: the planning of an Australian city. Cities, 5: 139–157.

Yusuf, Shahid and Nabeshinma, K. 2008. "Optimizing Urban Development", in Yusuf and Saich (ed.,) China Urbanizes Consequences, Stratigies, and Policies, The World Bank, Washington, D.C.

Zhu Y. 1999. New Paths to Urbanization in China: Seeking More Balanced Patterns. New York: Nova Science Publisher, Inc.

Index